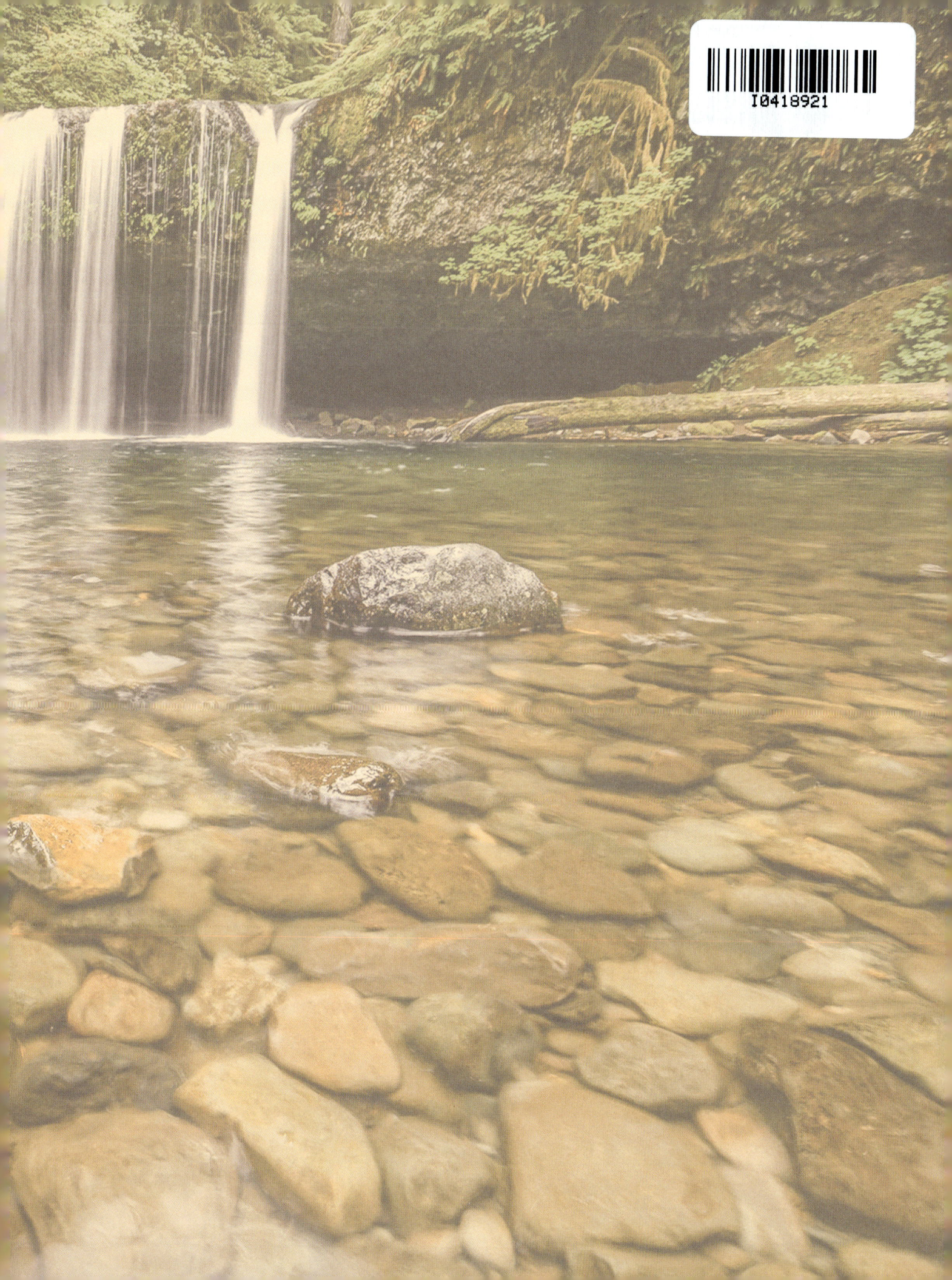

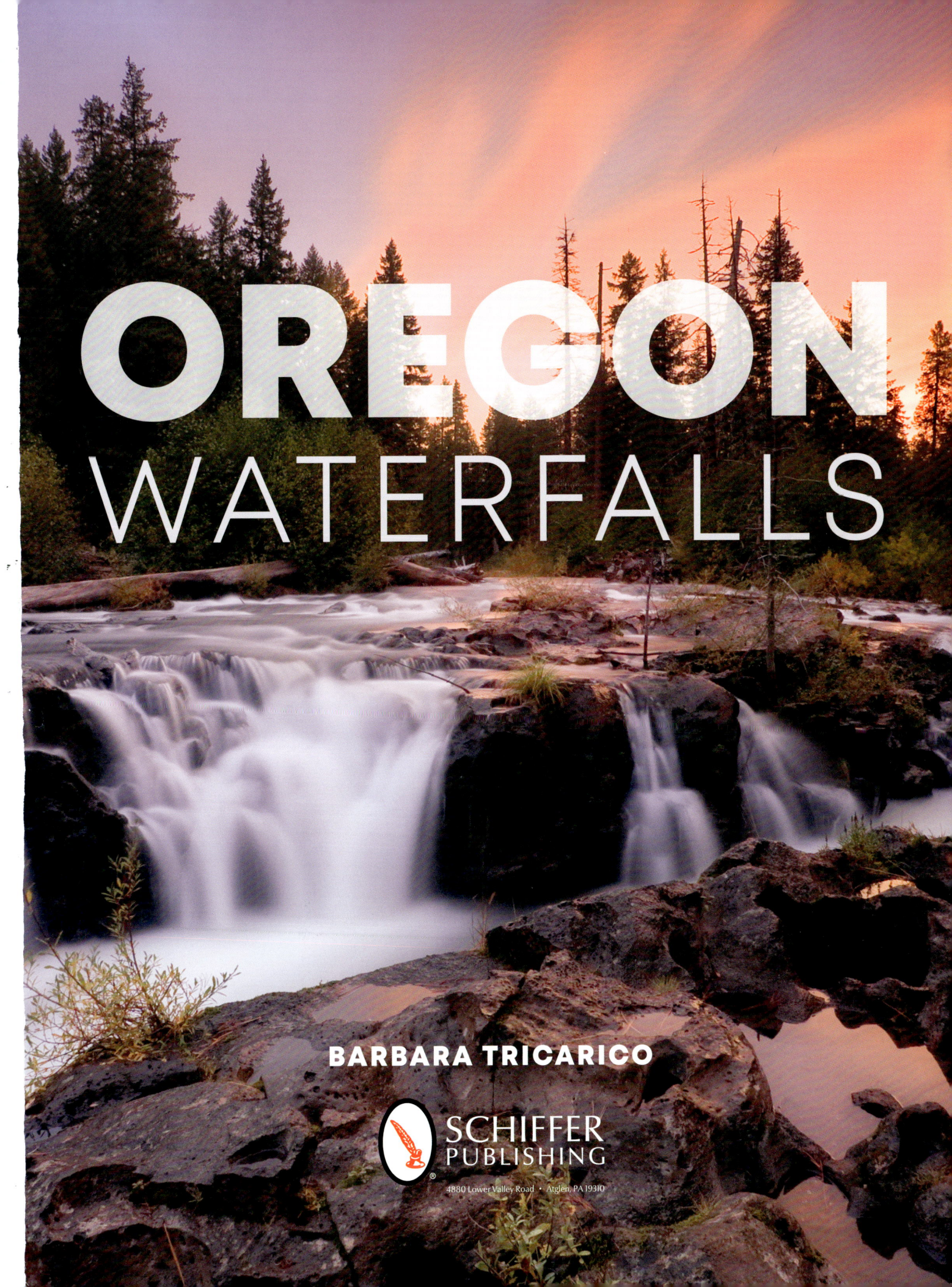

OREGON
WATERFALLS

BARBARA TRICARICO

SCHIFFER PUBLISHING

4880 Lower Valley Road • Atglen, PA 19310

Cover photo by Clemens Gerhard Paslack
Title page photo by Sean Bagshaw
Endsheets photos by Vldn Taylor

Designed by Alexa Harris
Type set in Mont/Sofia Pro/Graveur Variable

ISBN: 978-0-7643-7122-6
ePub: 978-1-5073-0680-2
Printed in China
10 9 8 7 6 5 4 3 2 1

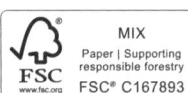

MIX
Paper | Supporting responsible forestry
FSC® C167893

Published by Schiffer Publishing, Ltd.
4880 Lower Valley Road
Atglen, PA 19310
Phone: (610) 593-1777; Fax: (610) 593-2002
Email: info@schifferbooks.com
Web: www.schifferbooks.com

For our complete selection of fine books on this and related subjects, please visit our website at www.schifferbooks.com. You may also write for a free catalog.

Schiffer Publishing's titles are available at special discounts for bulk purchases for sales promotions or premiums. Special editions, including personalized covers, corporate imprints, and excerpts, can be created in large quantities for special needs. For more information, contact the publisher.

CONTENTS

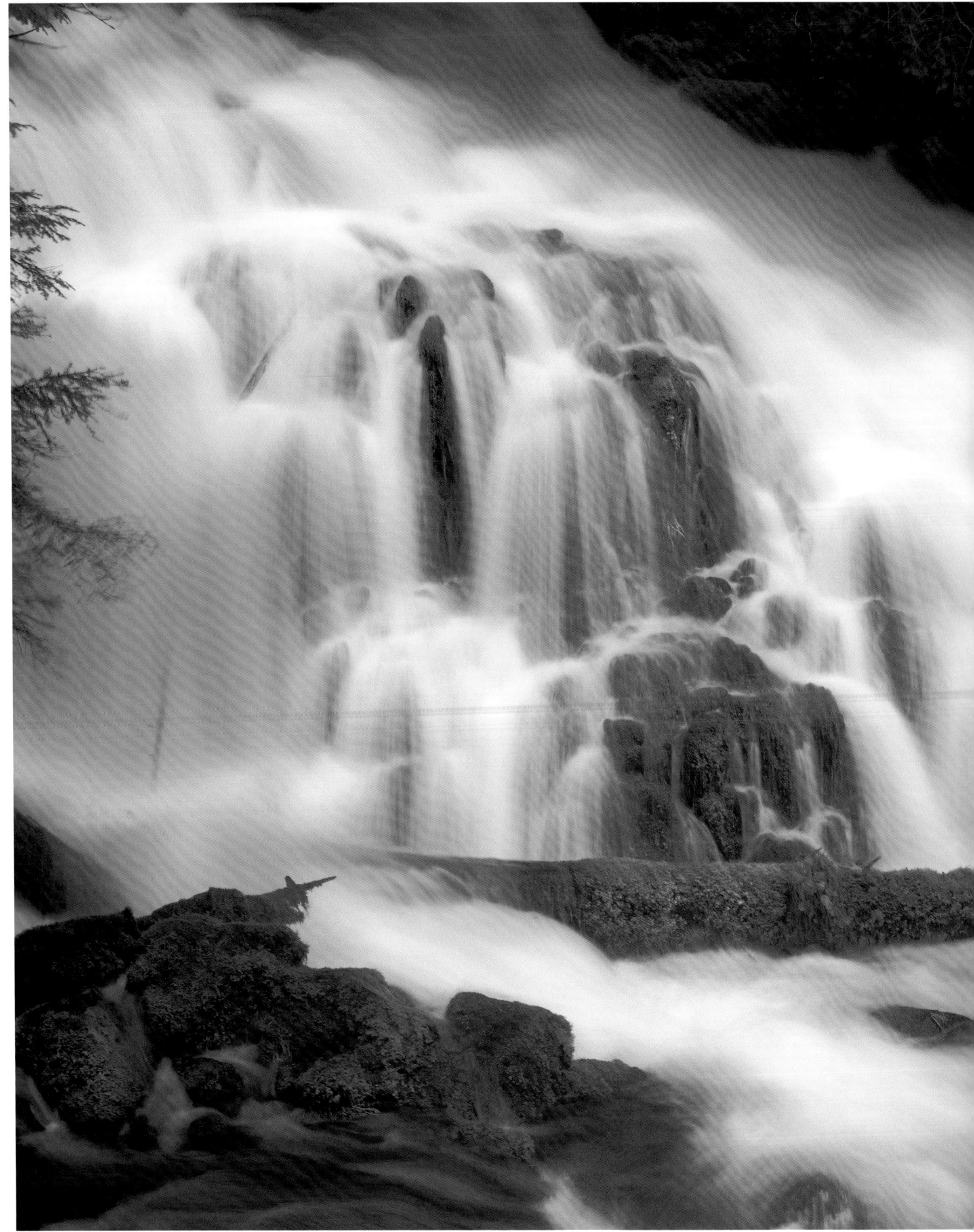

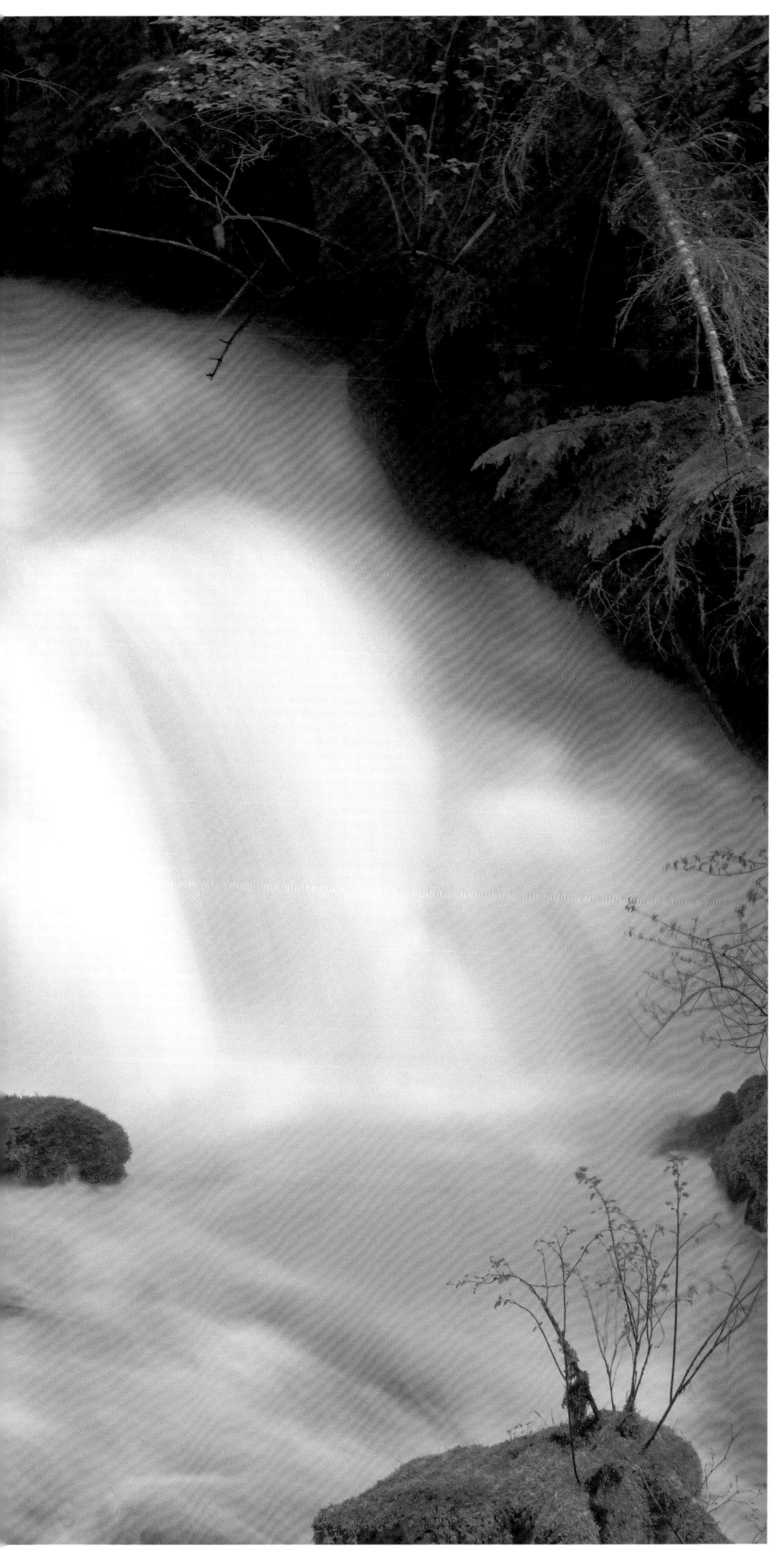

Pearsony Falls. *Photo by Jon Wilbrecht*

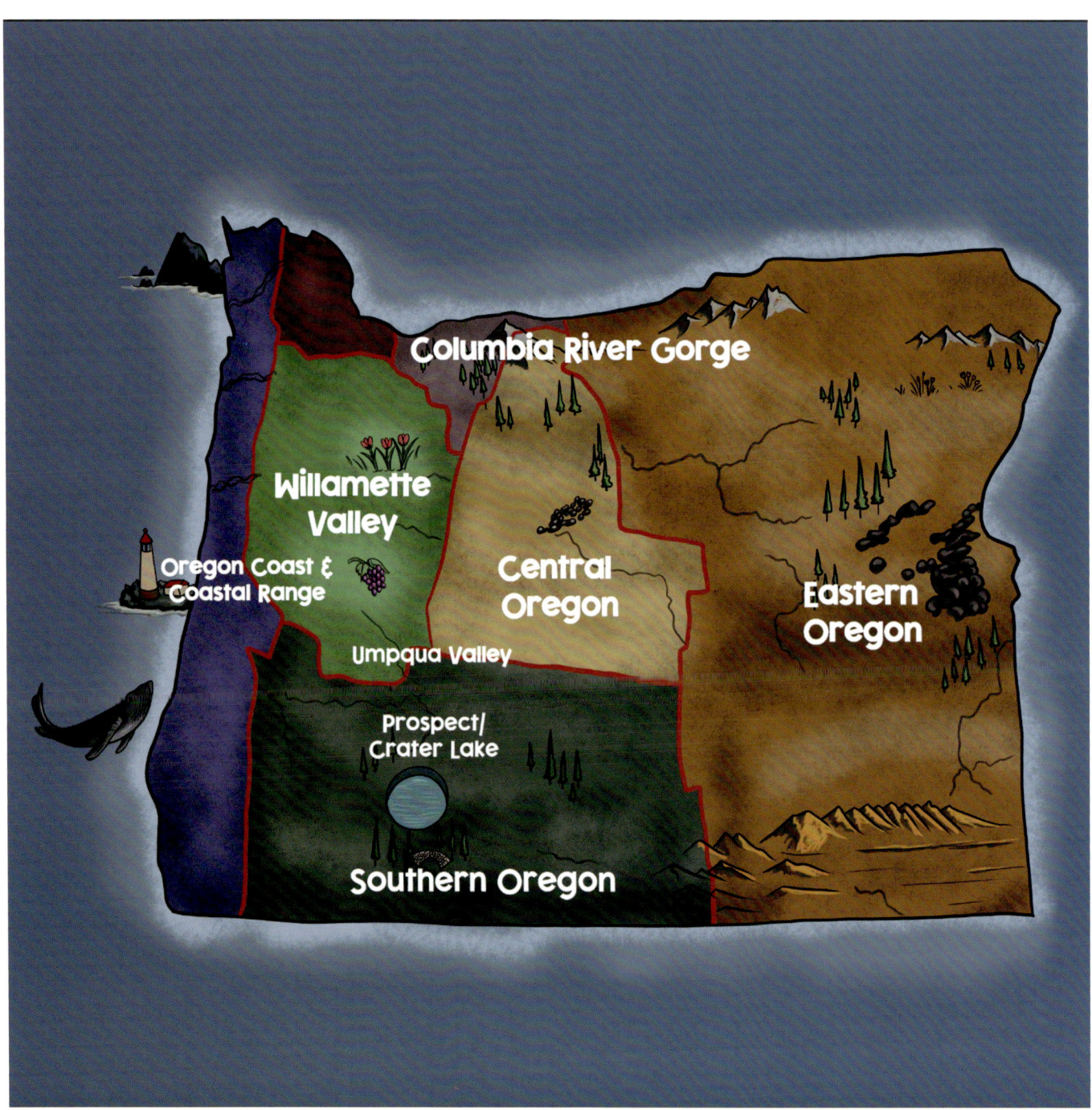

Artistic map of Oregon by Modou S

INTRODUCTION

Oregon Waterfalls

What *is it* about waterfalls? For hikers or photographers, discovering one on a walk in the woods is the dream. Like a charm bracelet, waterfall visits are often "collected" by hikers, local photographers, and visitors to Oregon. The reason? They are abundant, mesmerizing, soothing, tranquil, raging, and often heart–pounding. The treks to get to Oregon waterfalls are often easy, but some are not for the faint of heart.

Oregon is famous for its diverse and breathtaking waterfalls. This book only scratches the surface of the many beautiful Oregon waterfalls that one can see. *The Northwest Waterfalls Survey* has inventoried over 1,641 waterfalls in Oregon, but of those, only about 238 are well known. Some require long, strenuous hikes to reach, while others can be seen from the parking lot. Some are abundantly flowing, but the trails are inaccessible due to fires or landslides.

The majority of waterfalls in Oregon tend to be along the western portion of the state. This is due to frequent rainfall in the Pacific Northwest, winter snow, proximity to rivers, sheer basalt cliffs, dense forests, and mountainous terrain along the foothills of the Cascades. Waterfalls can be classified into eight distinct forms: plunge, horsetail, fan, cascade, punchbowl, block, tier, and segmented. I hope you'll find a sample of each in this book.

While not a comprehensive waterfall guidebook or encyclopedia by any means, this photo book is intended to whet one's appetite to visit Oregon waterfalls. You can almost hear the rushing water on some of the pages. Dozens of Oregon photographers contributed their best images in order to share their experiences with others. It is hoped the photos encourage viewers to explore, to relive previous experiences, or to live vicariously through hikers and photographers who have walked these trails.

The waterfall photos in this book were taken at different times of the year, so vegetation and water flow might look totally different during your own visit. Oregon's rainy season is from October to May, when most waterfalls are gushing. If you explore during the summer, some of the seasonal waterfalls will disappear, while others will have a significantly decreased waterflow. Rain, wildfires, landslides, or drought can change the landscape of a waterfall region immensely and make them dangerous or unattainable to reach. Some areas may be off–limits due to trail work or safety concerns. Some may not be reached if they are on private property. Previously inaccessible areas might suddenly appear after years of being hidden. Yet, often after a fire, beautiful ferns, mosses, grasses, shrubs, and trees can suddenly reappear in the undergrowth.

It pays to be cautious when waterfall hunting. When you decide to explore, talk to other enthusiasts or do your own online research before heading out, to get any cautions. Always check several sources, including the comprehensive AllTrails app and websites such as Oregon State Parks, Oregon

Forest Service, Travel Oregon, or TripAdvisor, to get feedback from those who have recently gone. Remember, conditions often change from day to day. You'll definitely want to bring a detailed map on any hike, since GPS or Google might lead you astray (or not function) in many remote Oregon locations. Take plenty of water, snacks, sunscreen, and insect repellent. Watch out for snakes and insects. For hikes that have swimming or wading possibilities, take some waterproof shoes and remain cautious. You may want to bring trekking poles on some of the more challenging trails, especially if you're unsteady on your feet. Fees are sometimes required to enter parks or trails. In most cases, going early will help you avoid crowds at popular waterfalls, especially on weekends. Also check to see if the trails are ADA accessible or suitable for children, or whether dogs are allowed on the trails. It's been said before, but remember that while visiting any popular natural site, respect the land and leave no trace.

A 2024 study indicates that Multnomah Falls, along the Columbia River Gorge, is the most picturesque waterfall in the country, followed by Yosemite and Niagara Falls. (Researchers studied over 2,700 landmarks and use of hashtags on social media.) With over two million visitors each year, Multnomah Falls, at over 600 feet, is considered the tallest waterfall in Oregon and the most visited natural recreation site in the Pacific Northwest. The falls can be seen from Interstate 84 and the Historic Columbia River Highway. Note that during the popular months of May to September, you'll need to purchase a timed-use parking permit due to high volumes of visitors.

There's a reason you're not seeing any eastern Oregon waterfalls in this book. Most, if not all, are considered "challenging" and remote. Another "fall" you won't see in this book is Klamath Falls. If anything, the "falls" on the Klamath River are small rapids. They were originally called the Link River, and the Klamath and Modoc people referred to the river as a place "where the falling waters rush." Twenty-five years after the town's founding, the river's name was changed to Klamath Falls.

Photographing waterfalls can be tricky for the novice, but even cell phone technology can capture a beautiful waterfall image! The old adage is "the best camera is the one that's with you!" All the photos in this book, however, were taken with professional cameras. You've probably seen those die hard professionals carrying backpacks filled with cameras, lenses, tripods, filters, and protection from the water spray. Determined to get a unique photo, they'll often "shoot" from impossible angles or locations to compose that perfect waterfall. Some "stack" multiple images in camera to make sure everything is sharp and in focus during processing; some combine images by using HDR to increase contrast, detail, shadows, and highlights. The goal is to capture images that are more similar to what the human eye sees. Those creamy water-flow images are the result of a slow shutter speed, while a fast shutter will create a stop-action look to freeze individual water droplets or spray.

A big thank-you to my 45 photographer friends who contributed images for this book. I hope readers will live vicariously through their waterfall quests to imagine the sounds, colors, and shadows of each waterfall and to visit many themselves in the future. Many thanks to my friends Neal R. Thompson and George F. Peterson for their photographic "eagle eyes" when I had too many choices. Special thanks to my husband, Bill, always my sounding board.

I dedicate this book to our four grandchildren: Gemma, Oscar, Benny, and Luca. When they visit Oregon again from the east, I promise to show them some waterfalls!

—Barbara Tricarico

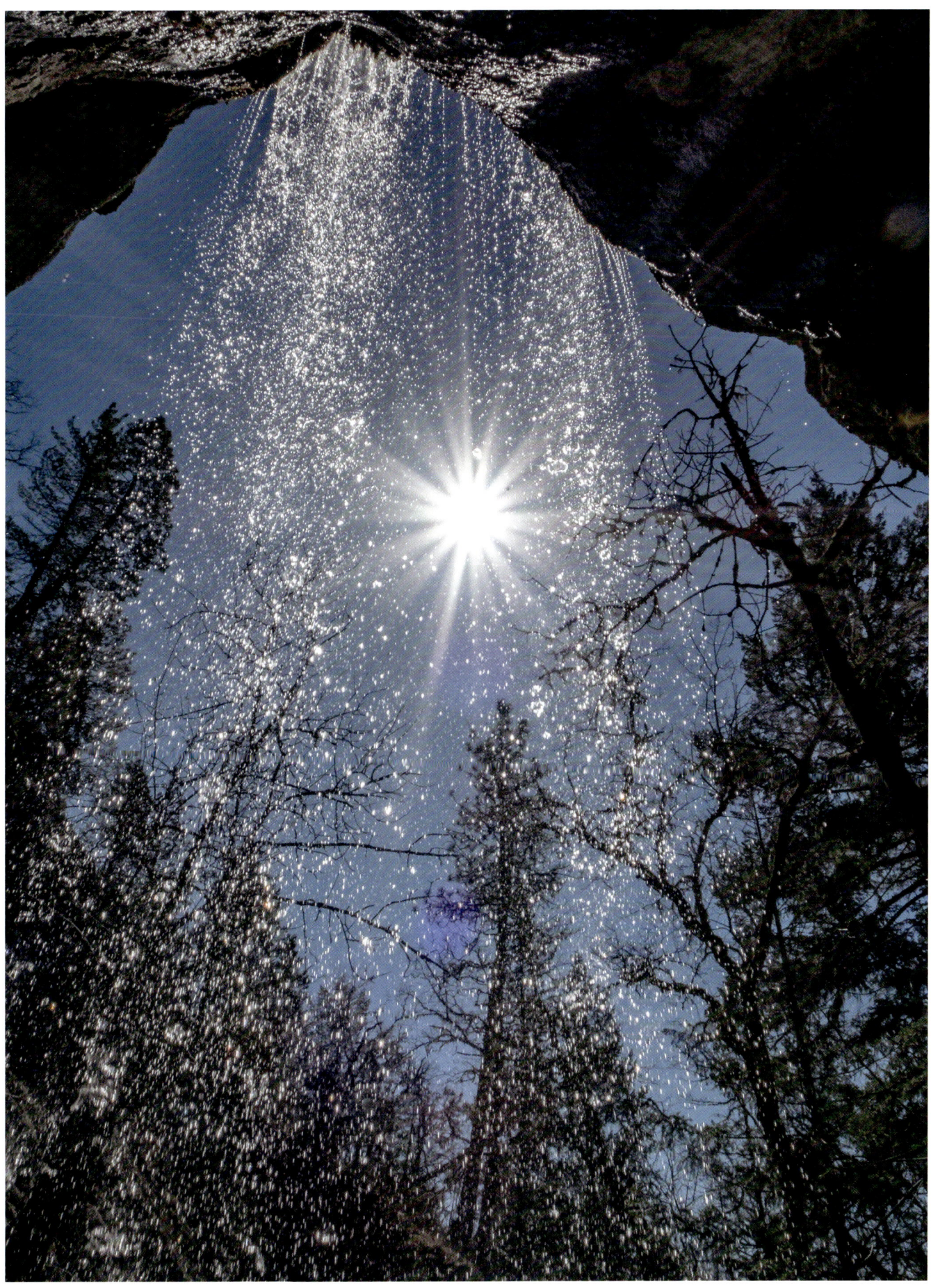

Blue Grotto Falls. *Photo by Bob Palermini*

Celilo Falls (Wy–am)

"The Most Epic Waterfall in Oregon"

Celilo Falls was once a natural, majestic waterfall on the Columbia River, about 12 miles east of the Dalles. For centuries, several tribes of Natives, including the Yakima, Nez Perce, Warm Springs, and Umatilla, perilously fished salmon from large scaffolds. The fishery ran for approximately 9 miles, and the site was considered a spiritual and economic site for many. The once–impressive Celilo Falls was submerged in 1957 by the Army Corps of Engineers for the construction of the Dalles Dam. Native residents were relocated.

The falls stretched approximately 5,800 feet in width, and the rapids dropped into the river for more than 80 feet. During the spring, it is said that many times more water passed over Celilo Falls by volume than passes over Niagara Falls today. The falls, called *Wy–am* in several Native languages, mean "echo of falling water" or "sound of water upon the rocks." The waterfall could be heard from miles away, and the sound still remains in the memory of those who lived nearby.

For centuries, Wy–am was considered the oldest and longest–occupied community on the continent of North America. The site was also home to many ancient rock art drawings. Archeological records show that people had lived and traded in the area around the falls for at least 9,000 years. In 1805–06, the journals of Meriwether Lewis and William Clark estimated that 7,200 to 10,400 Native people were present between the Cascade Rapids and the Dalles. While the falls have been submerged for almost 70 years, sonar technology has shown them to still remain intact, but submerged, beneath the Columbia River.

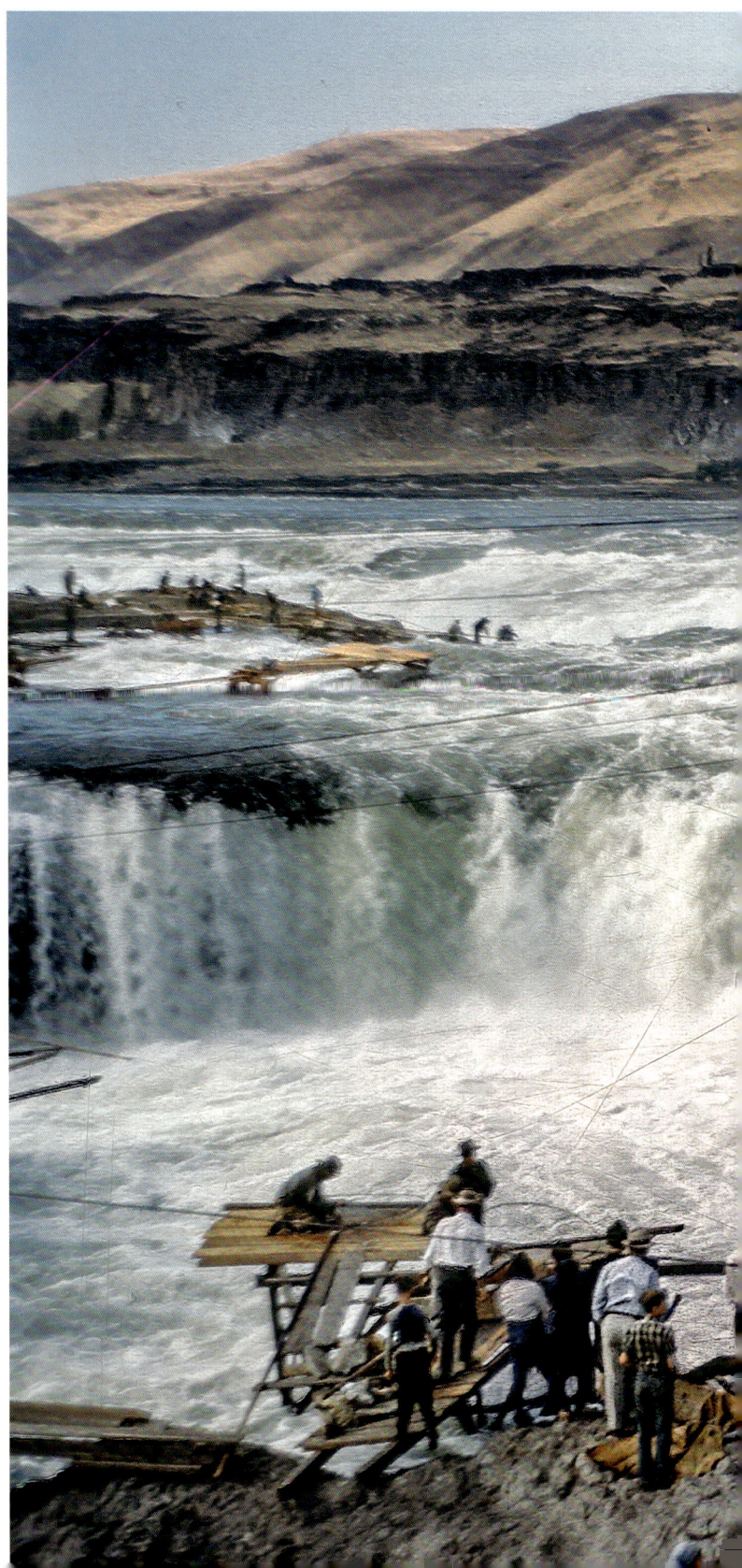

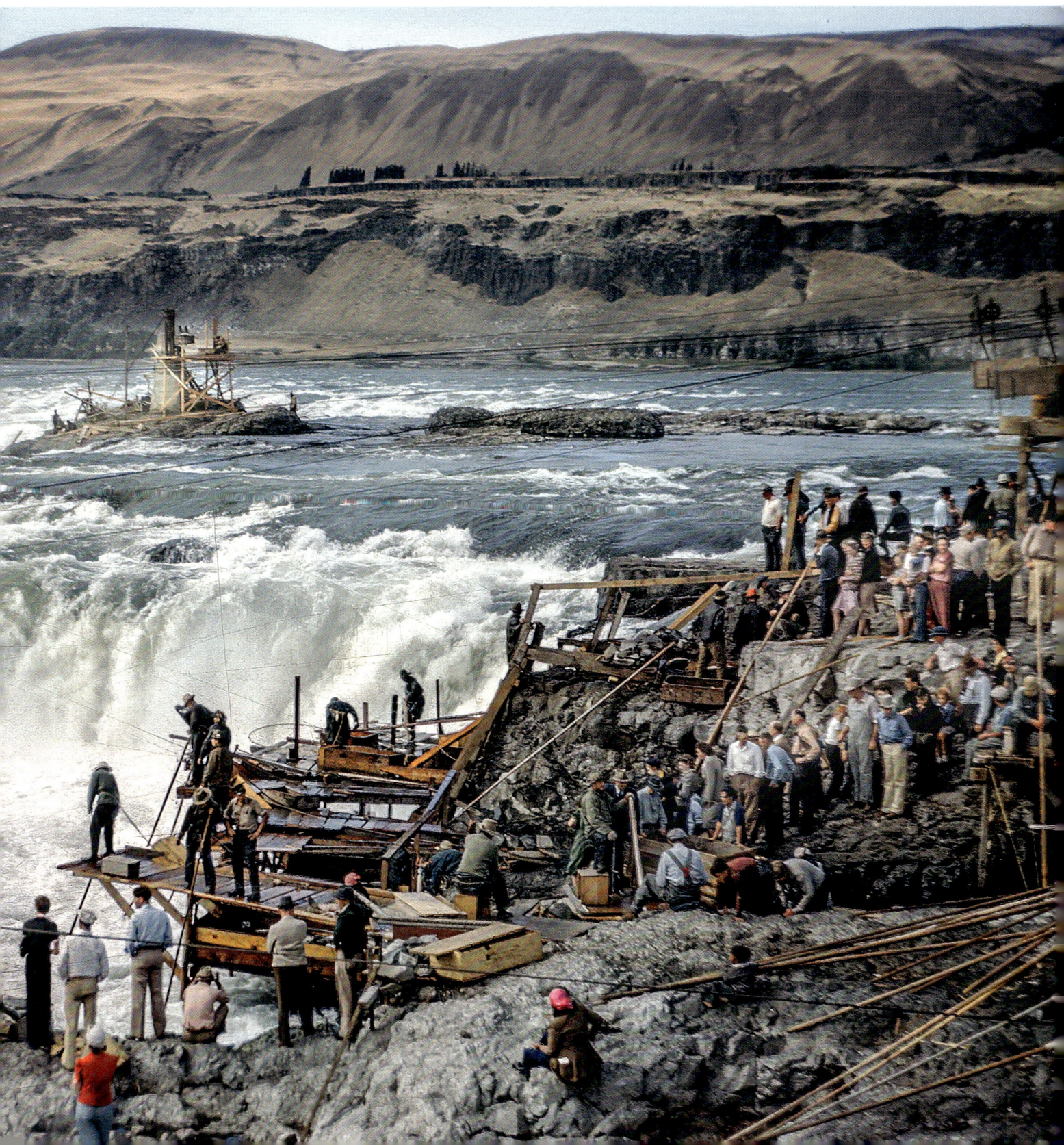

Celilo Falls, ca. 1940. Fishing scaffolding used by Native Americans before the Dalles Dam. *From the collection of Neal R. Thompson, scanned from a Kodachrome photo taken by his father, Clifford Thompson*

2 Columbia River Gorge

Travel Oregon indicates that the Columbia River Gorge is home to more waterfalls than any other region in North America, with the Oregon side of the Columbia River boasting about 90 waterfalls. Several waterfalls in this corridor can be seen in just one day by driving east from Portland along the Historic Columbia River Highway.

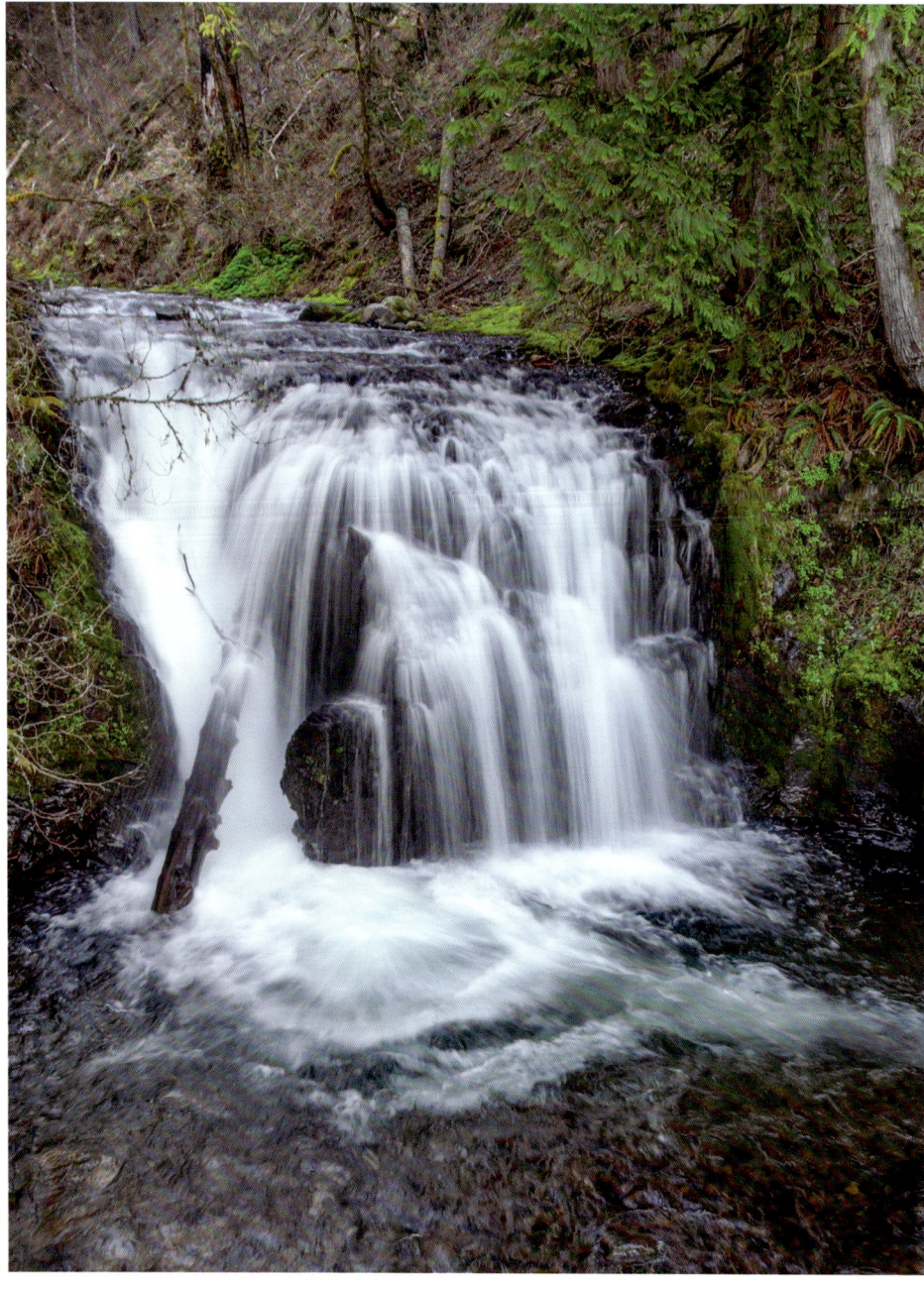

Little Multnomah Falls. Upstream, and high above Multnomah Falls, is a Little Multnomah Falls. It's a 2.4-mile-round-trip hike from the base of the massive Multnomah Falls (and across the 100-year-old Benson Bridge). The water from Little Multnomah Creek cascades 620 feet down to the base of Multnomah Falls. *Photo by Stephanie Ryden*

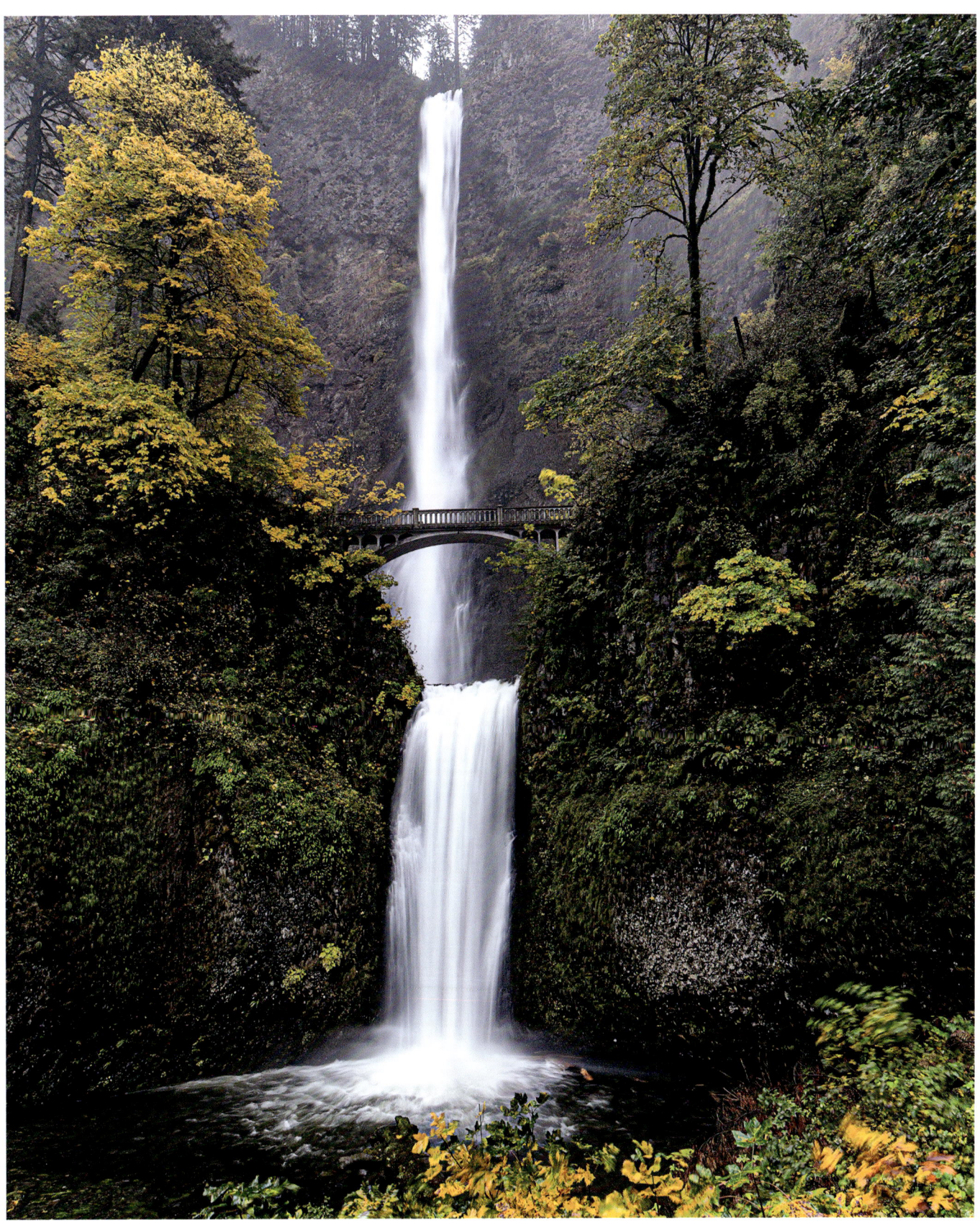

Multnomah Falls. Considered the queen of Oregon waterfalls, this lofty, two-tiered waterfall is the highest waterfall in the Columbia River Gorge at 620 feet. It is viewable while driving along highway I-84. Due to its popularity, especially during the summer, a parking permit will be necessary. (To see even more waterfalls, take the Hop-on-Hop-Off Trolley through the waterfall corridor.) *Photo by Vldn Taylor*

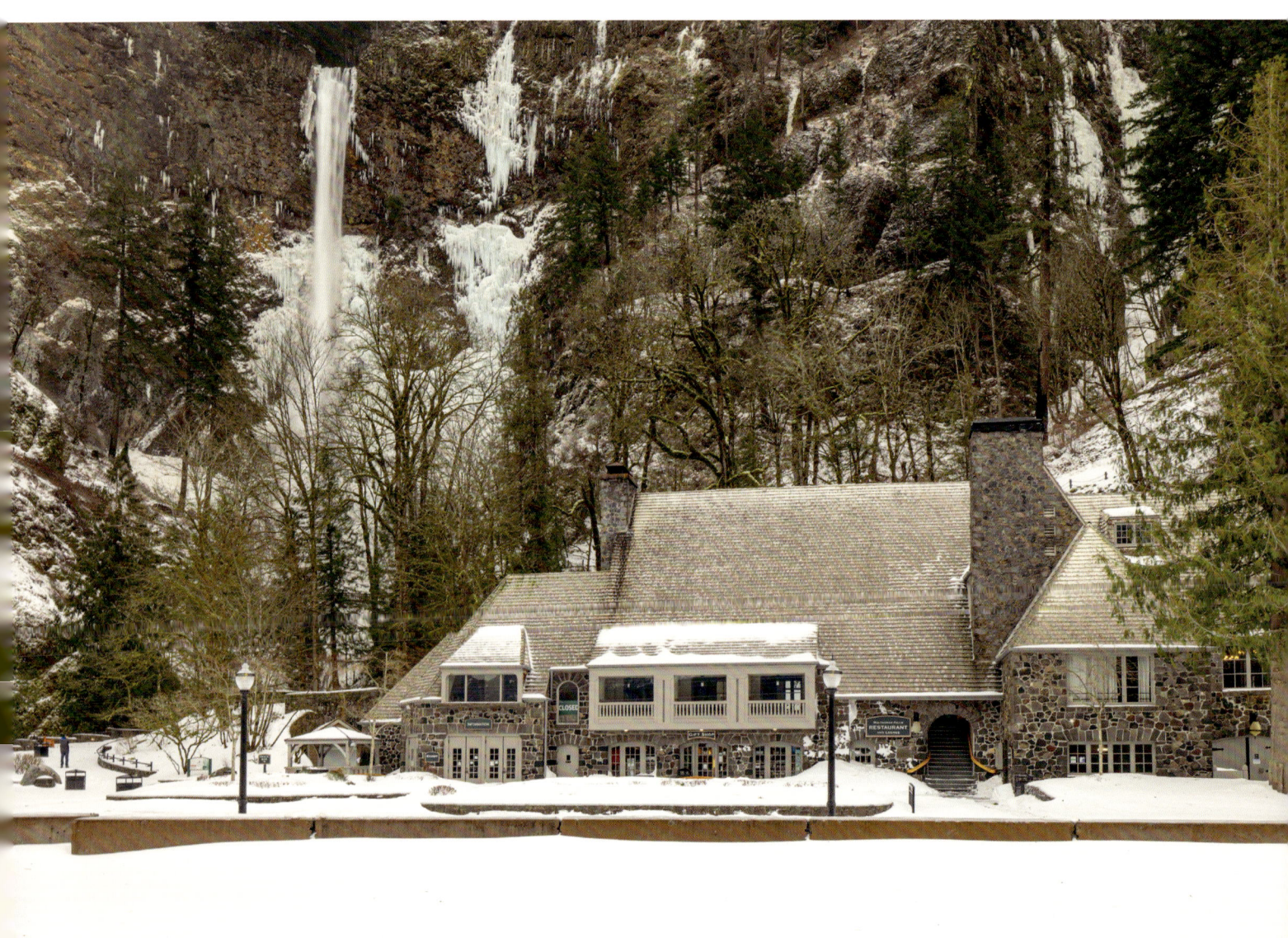

Multnomah Falls Lodge was built in 1925 by the City of Portland and is on the National Register of Historic Places. The stone Tudor-style lodge was built using timber and every type of rock found in the Columbia River Gorge. *Photo by Vldn Taylor*

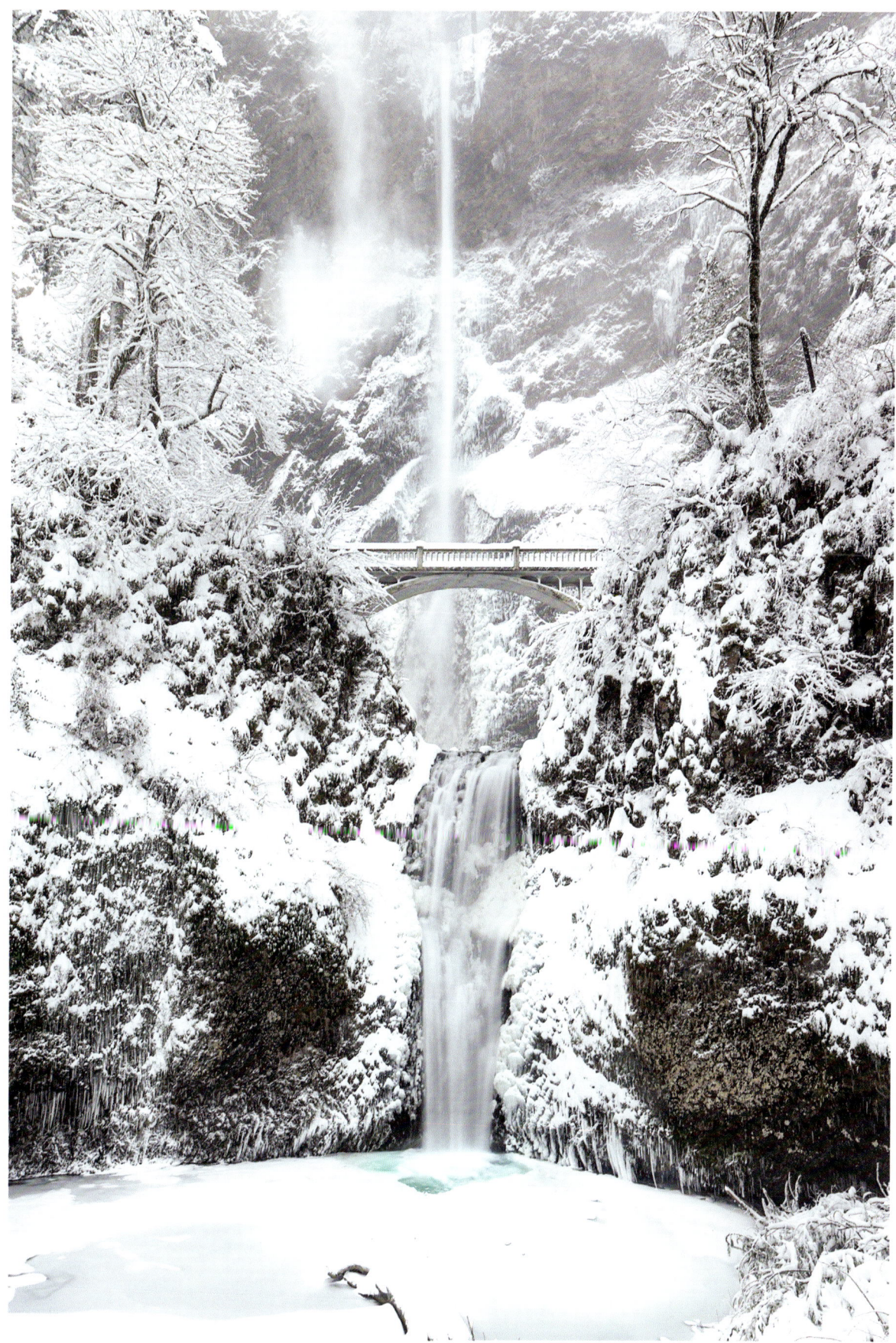

Multnomah Falls in winter. Multnomah Falls is the most visited waterfall in Oregon and is breathtaking in any season. The wooden truss bridge above was originally constructed in 1888 by the Oregon Railway and Navigation Company. It completely decayed by 1899 and was replaced with reinforced concrete in 1916. It still stands, perched 105 feet from the lower Multnomah Falls. *Photo by Vldn Taylor*

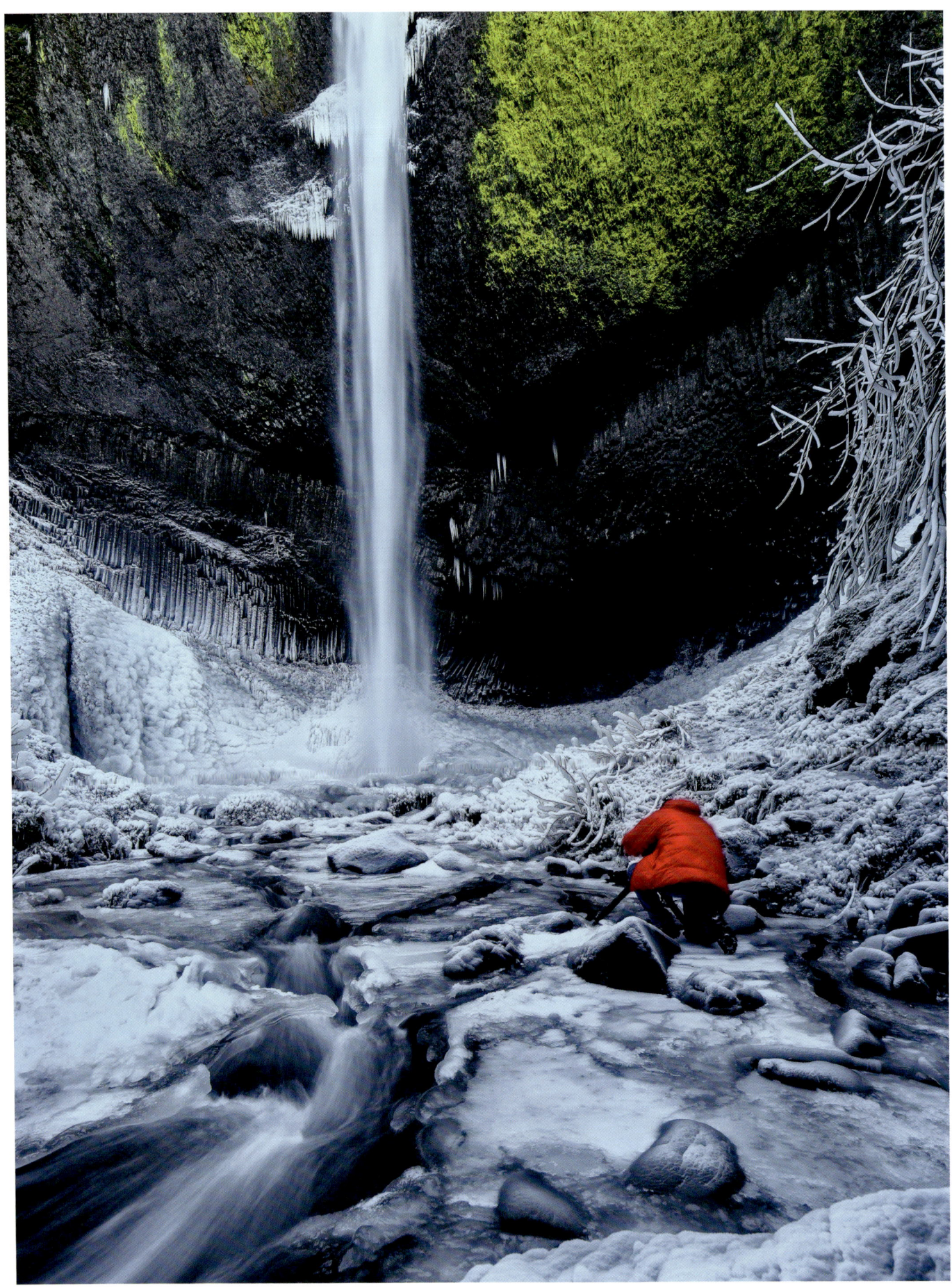

Latourell Falls in winter. A photographer braving the elements to capture this frozen waterfall. *Photo by Clem Paslack*

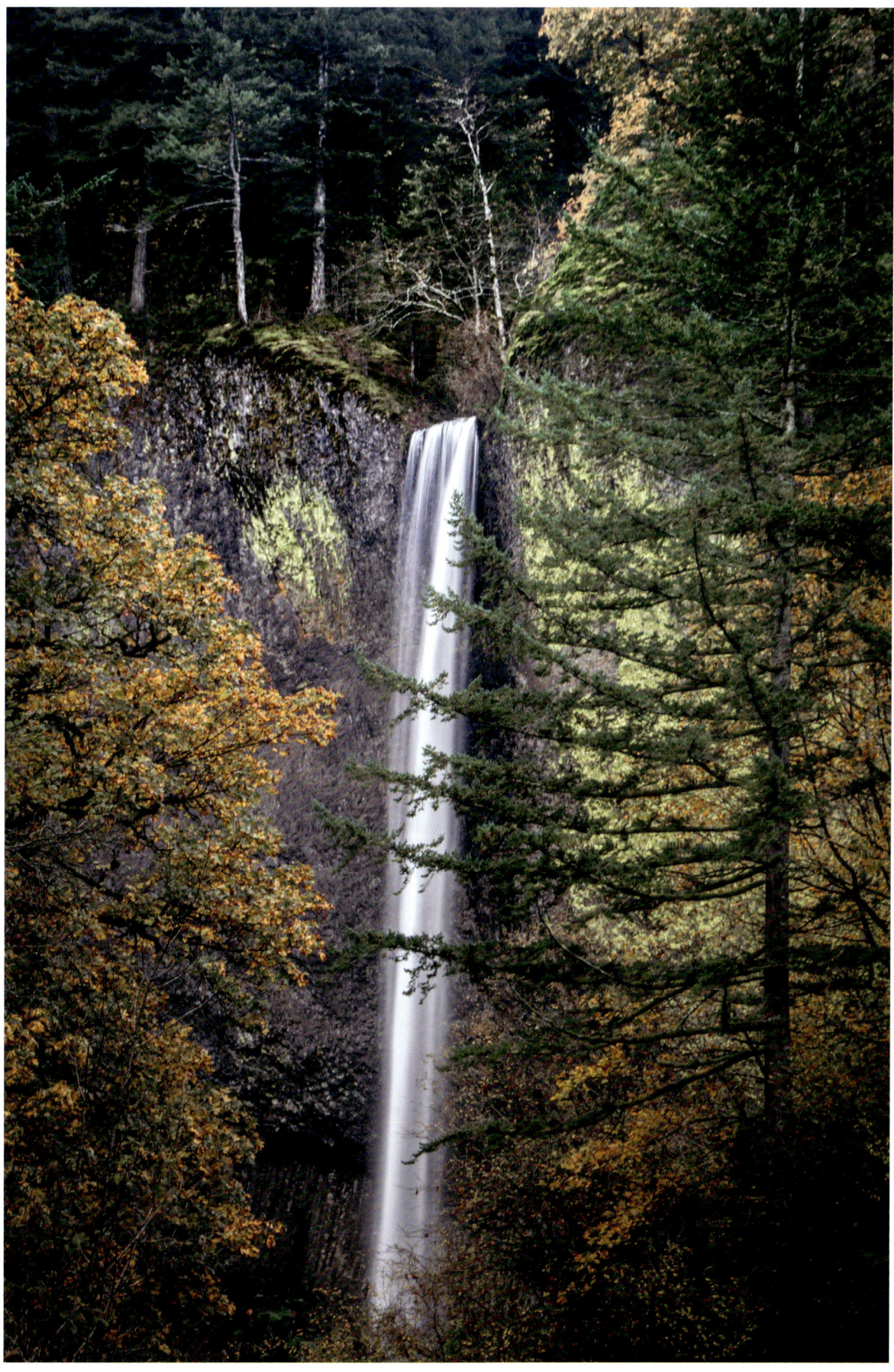

Latourell Falls in autumn. Located in Talbot State Park, this is the third-tallest waterfall in the Columbia Gorge. There is a family-friendly 1-mile hike to the Lower Falls and historic bridge, while the 2-mile loop on the trail leads to the 134-foot Upper Falls. *Photo by Alana Starkweather*

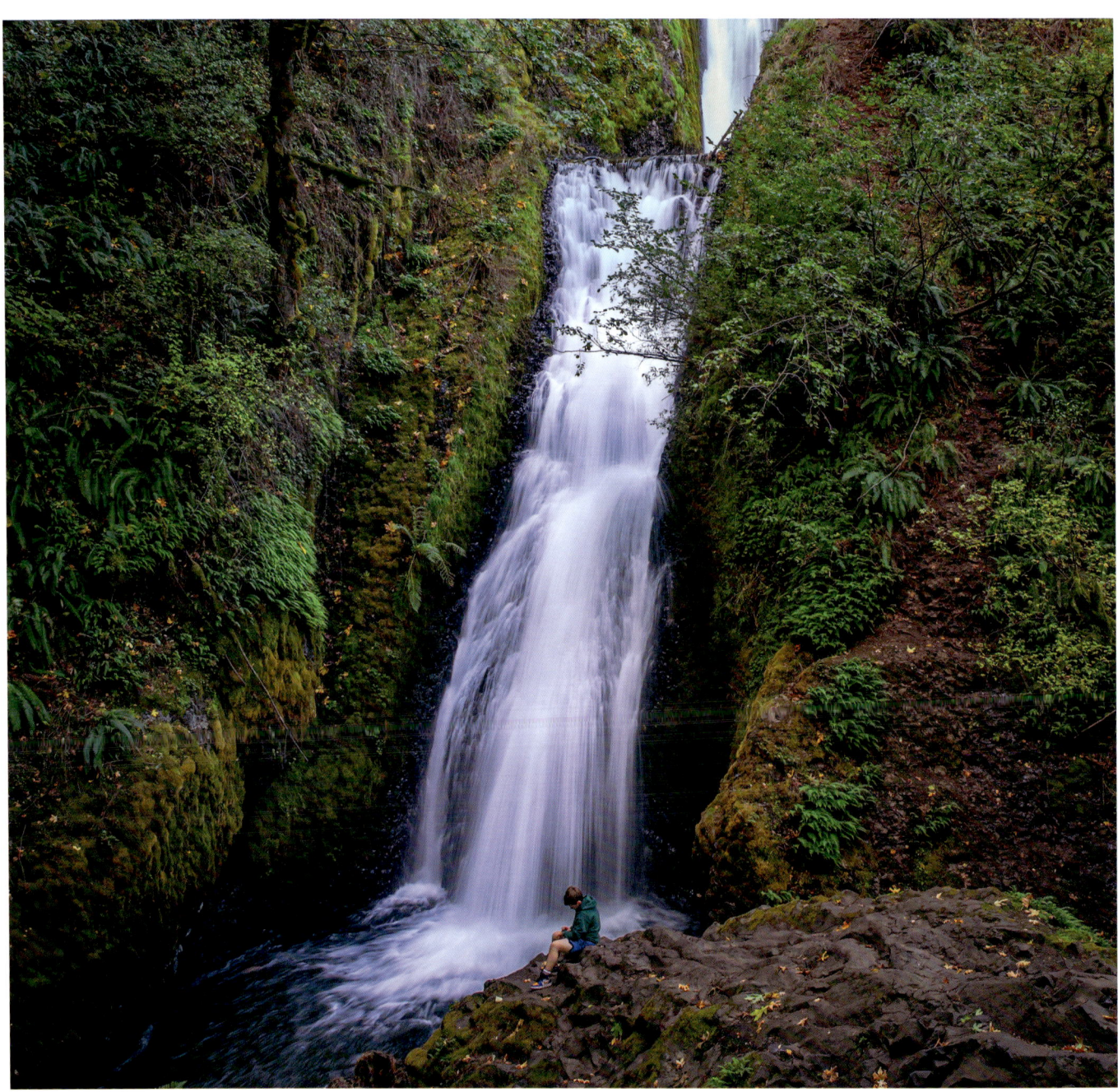

Bridal Veil Falls. This popular and easily accessible waterfall on the Columbia River has two tiers and is accessible from I-84. It is also a short walk to the ghost town of Bridal Veil Falls, once a thriving town with a lumber company that ran for over 100 years. Today only the post office (the third-smallest post office in the US) and a cemetery remain. Brides and grooms have made a tradition of sending their invitations through the post office so they bear the unique "Bridal Veil" postmark. *Photo by George F. Peterson*

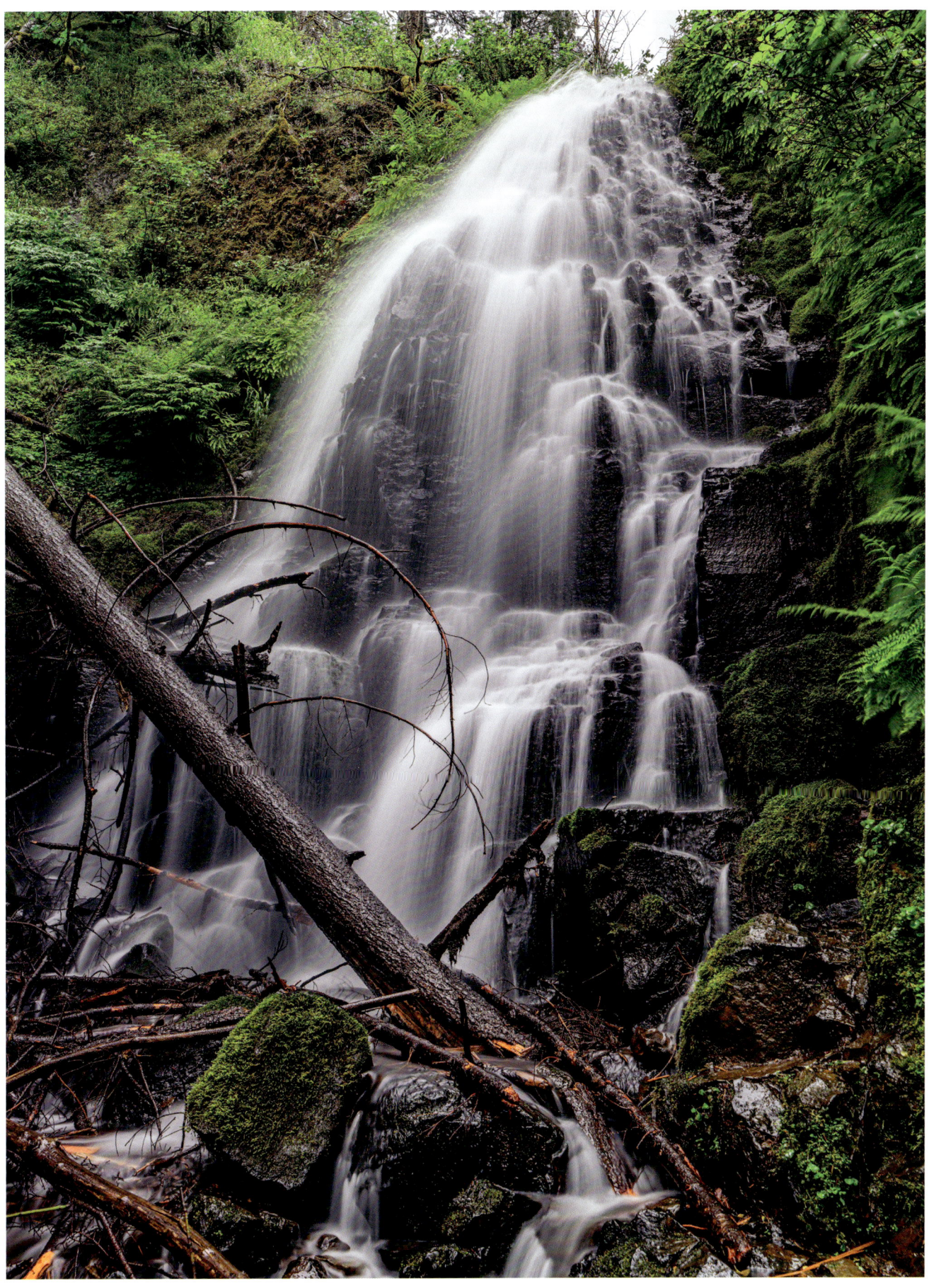

Fairy Falls. The hike to this waterfall is 2.9 miles out and back on the Wahkeena Falls Trail. It's considered a moderately challenging route, and there is a creek crossing and great views. Visitors will be treated to a gentle mist spray at the base. *Photo by David Joarnt*

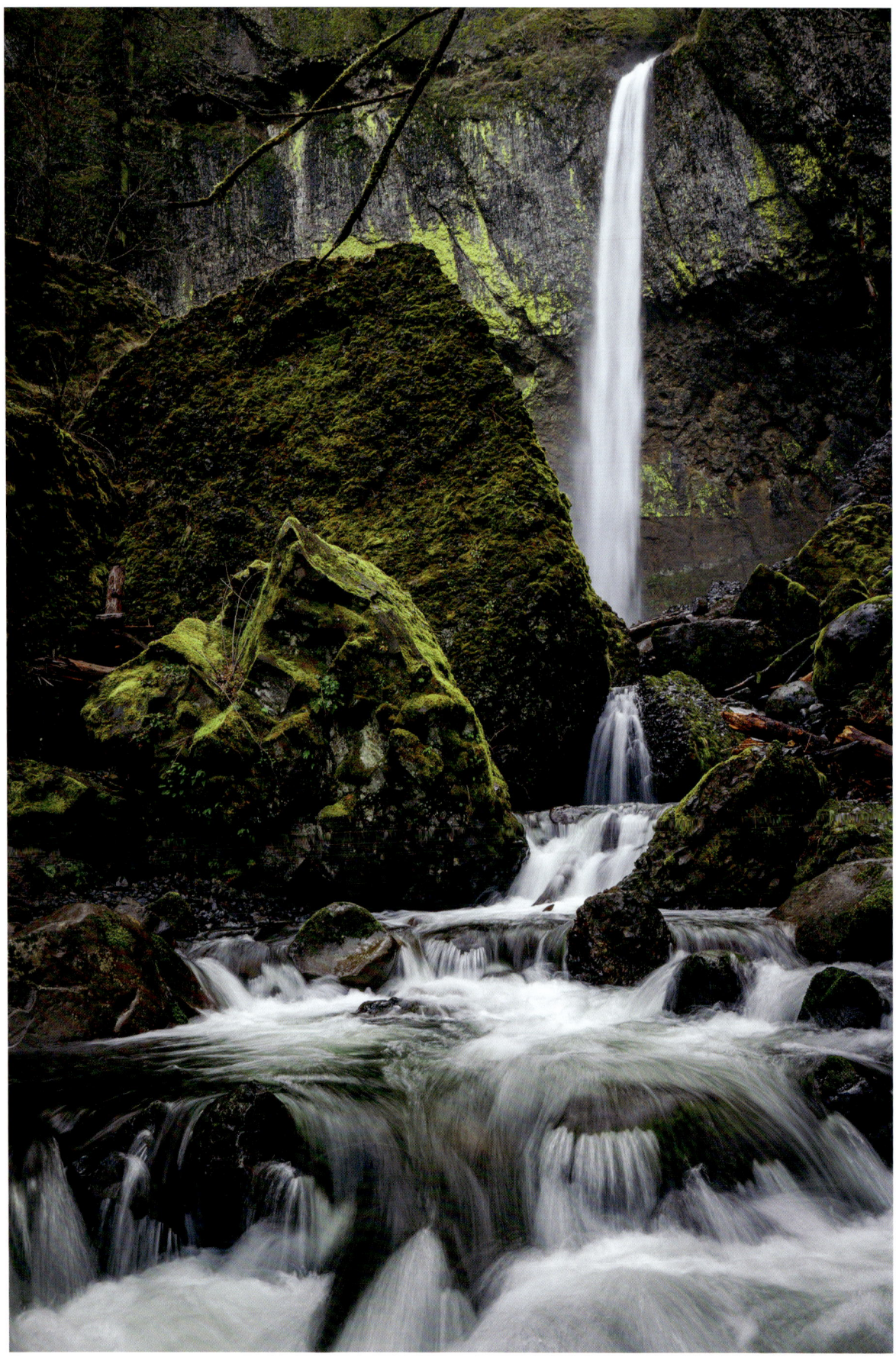

Elowah Falls. Although a seasonal falls, the McCord Creek Falls Trail is open year-round. It's considered a moderately challenging hike. There are two falls to see: Elowah Falls and the Upper McCord Creek Falls. The entire route to see both will take approximately one hour and thirty minutes to complete. Note that there is a short section close to the falls that's a little steep, but most of the trail is well maintained. *Photo by Vldn Taylor*

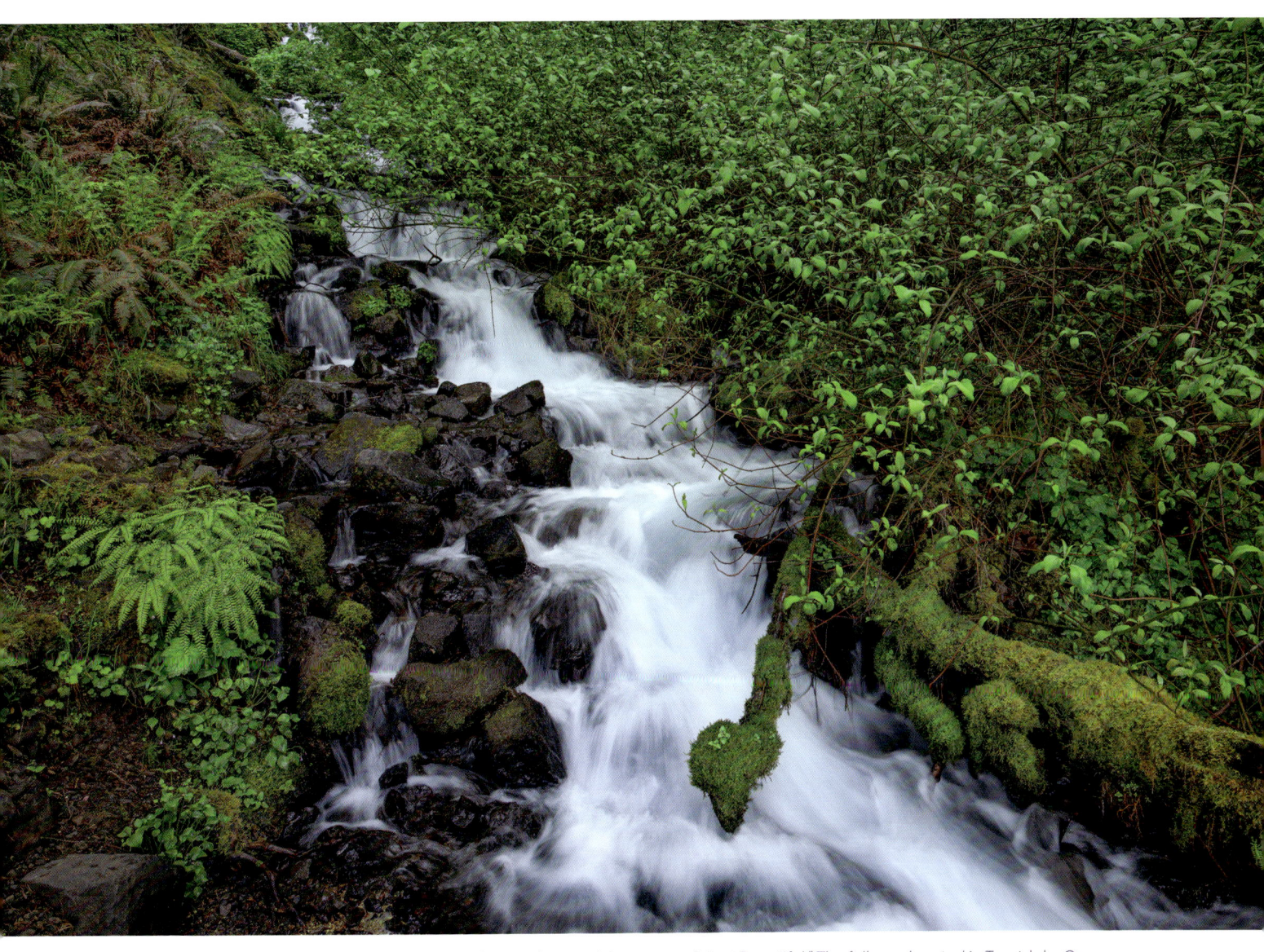

Lower Wahkeena Falls. Wahkeena is a Yakima tribe word that means "Most Beautiful." The falls are located in Troutdale, Oregon, and can be seen from the parking lot or scenic overlook along the highway. Hiking to its base is along a moderate trail and will provide views of a stone bridge and a 242-foot triple cascade. *Photo by John Christer Petersen*

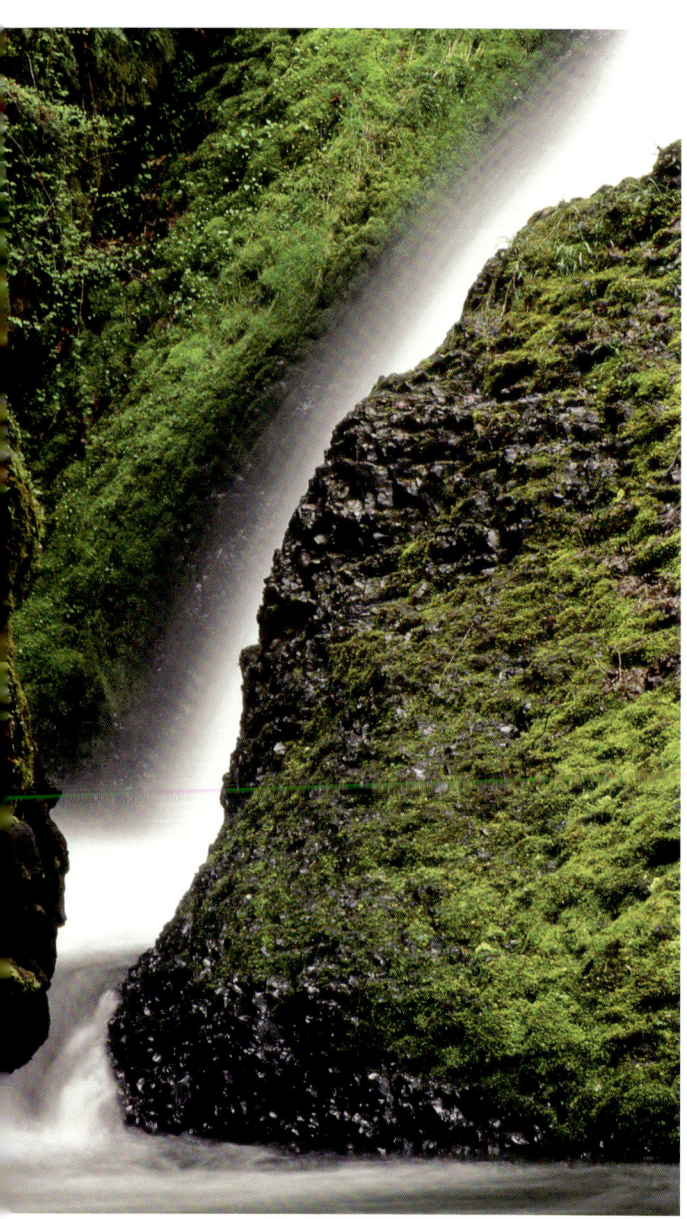

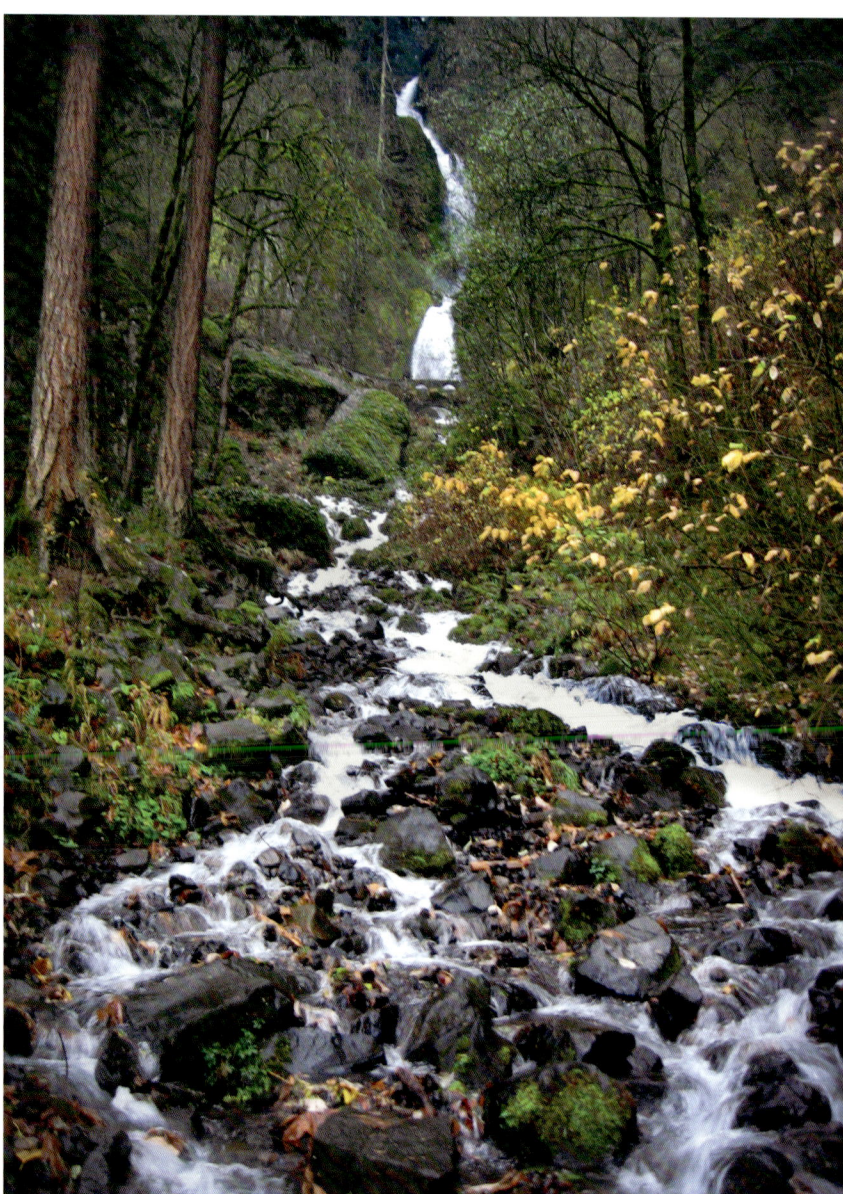

Horsetail Falls. Horsetail Falls is named for its characteristic shape, resembling the tail of a horse as it cascades down. *Photo by Jay Newman*

Horsetail Falls. The falls is located in the Historic Columbia River Highway's "Waterfall Corridor" and plunges 176 feet. *Photo by Patty Albin*

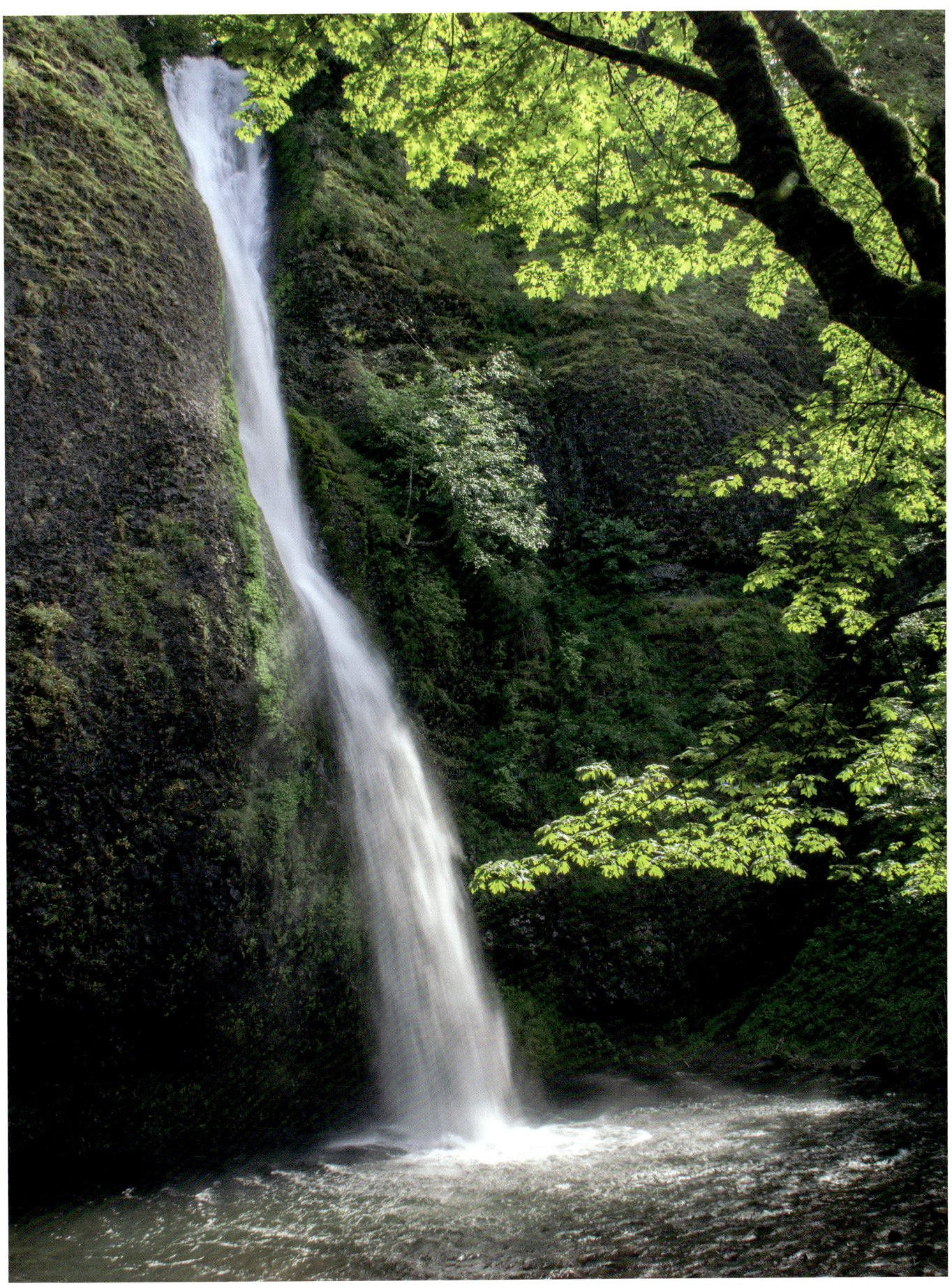

Horsetail Falls. The Horsetail Falls Loop Hike takes in both Horsetail and Ponytail Falls, with views of Oneonta Gorge and the Columbia River Gorge. It is considered a challenging trail. *Photo by Fran Yates*

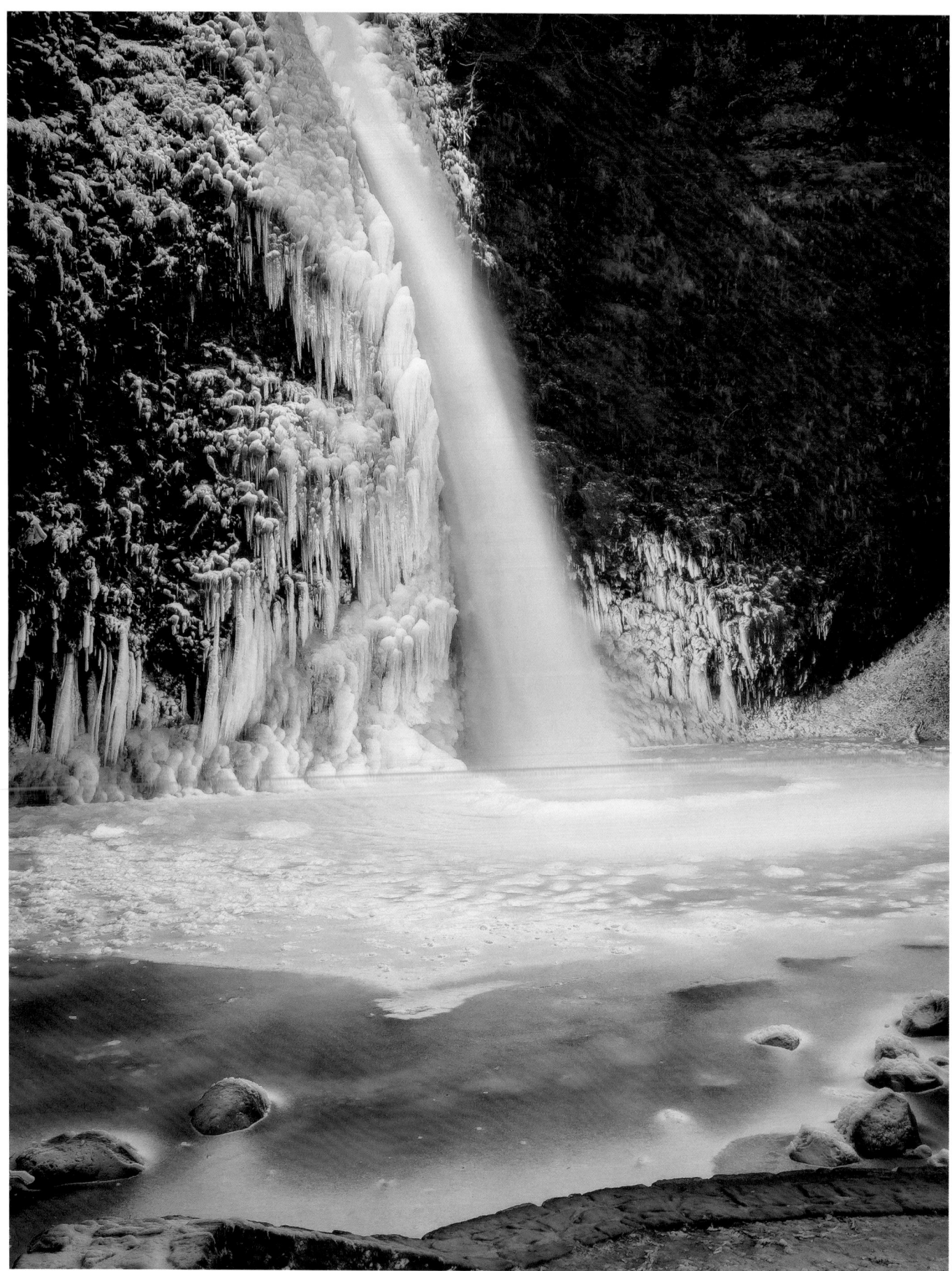

Horsetail Falls. Horsetail Falls is equally beautiful in winter. *Photo by Clem Paslack*

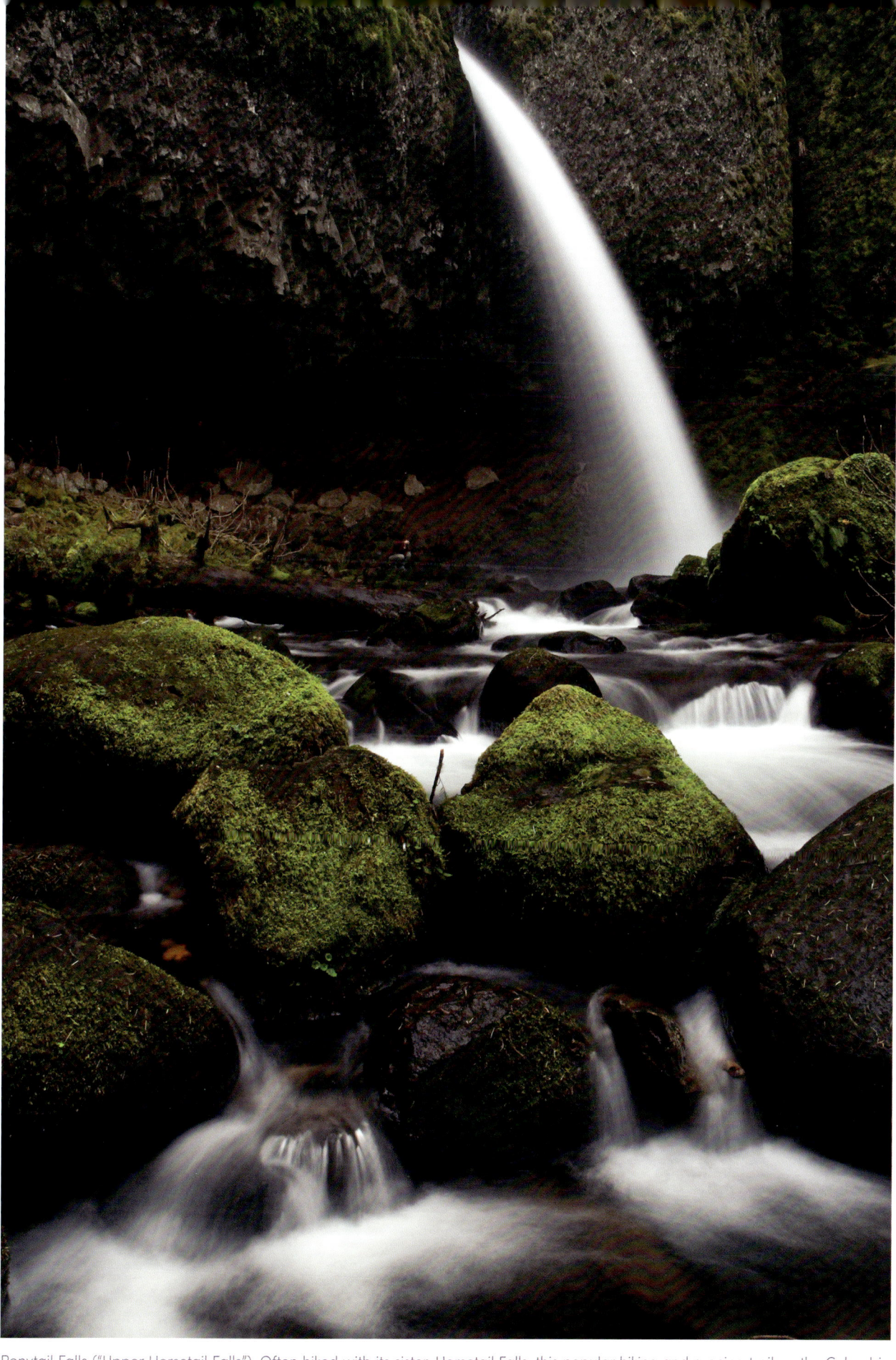

Ponytail Falls ("Upper Horsetail Falls"). Often hiked with its sister, Horsetail Falls, this popular hiking and running trail on the Columbia River Gorge takes only about 30 minutes to see. It is easily accessible from the road but can be busy on weekends. *Photo by Jay Newman*

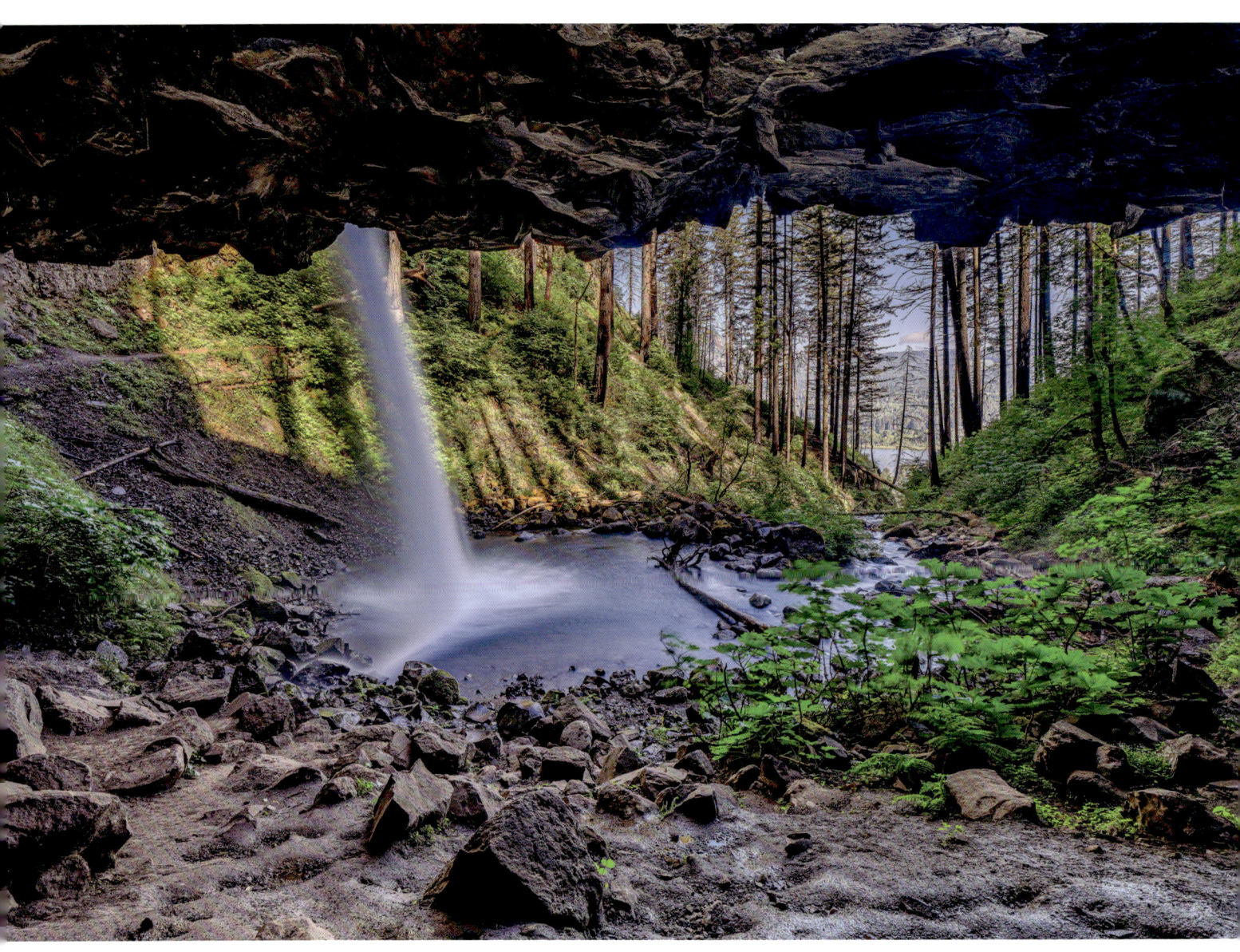

Ponytail Falls. Note that the trail can be rocky, narrow, and slippery. The reward is the walk behind the waterfall. *Photo by David Joarnt*

McCord Creek Falls. This impressive double waterfall can be seen along the McCord Creek Falls Trail. When hiking the moderately challenging trail, be sure to also visit Elowah Falls. There are also great views of the Columbia River Gorge and Mount Adams along the way. *Photo by Vldn Taylor*

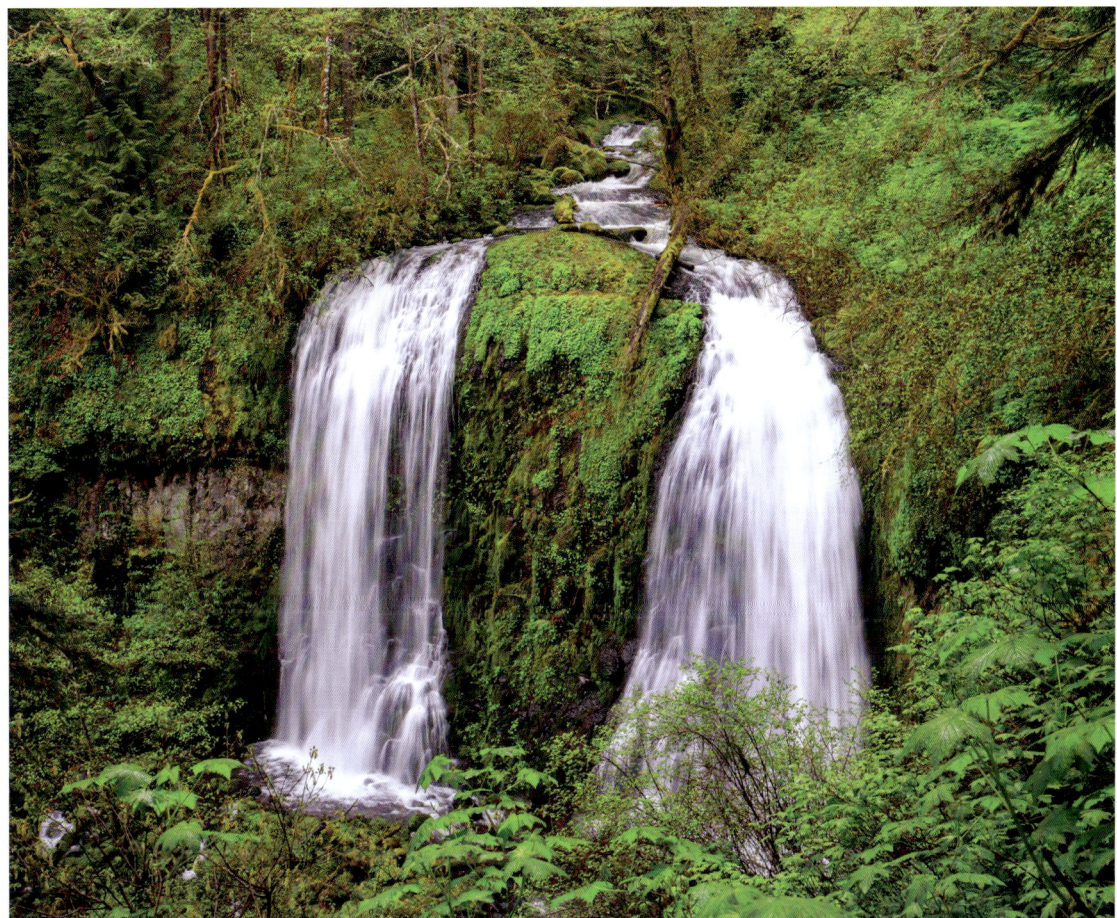

Wahclella Falls. This is a popular area for birding, hiking and running, and swimming. The 1.9-mile-out-and-back trail is near Cascade Locks. After crossing a long wooden bridge, it's only a short hike to the falls. The 2017 Eagle Creek fire closed this area for several years, necessitating a new bridge in 2020. *Photo by Richard Krieger*

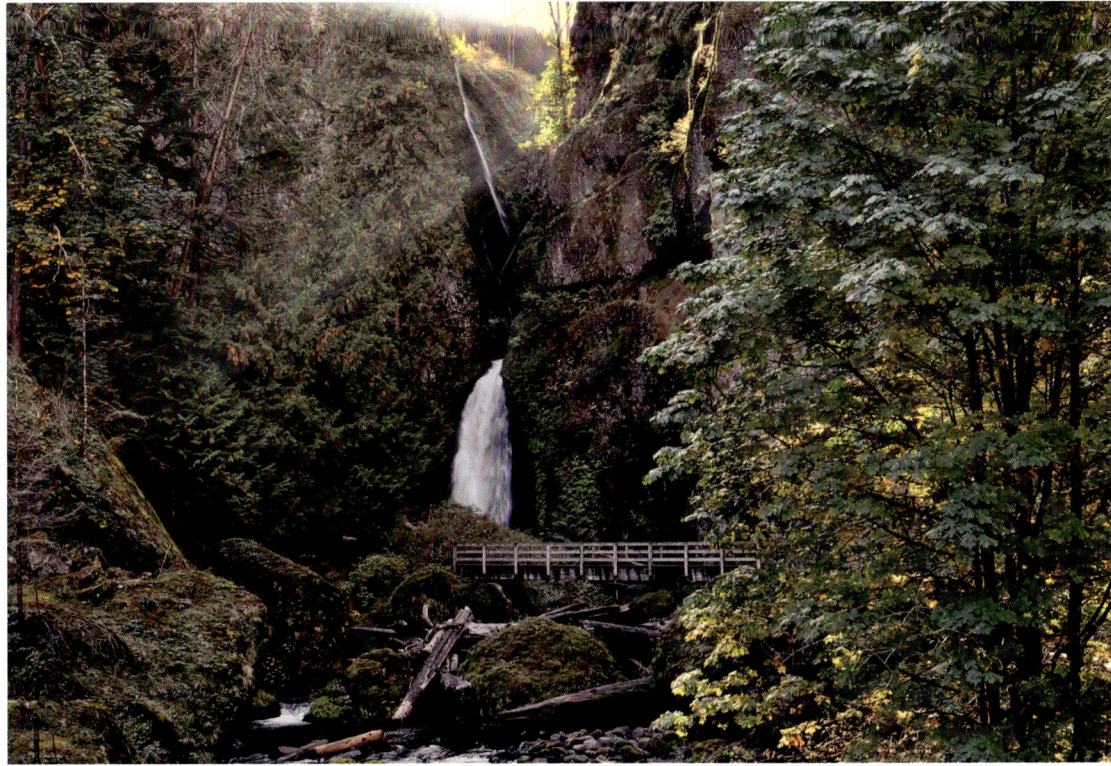

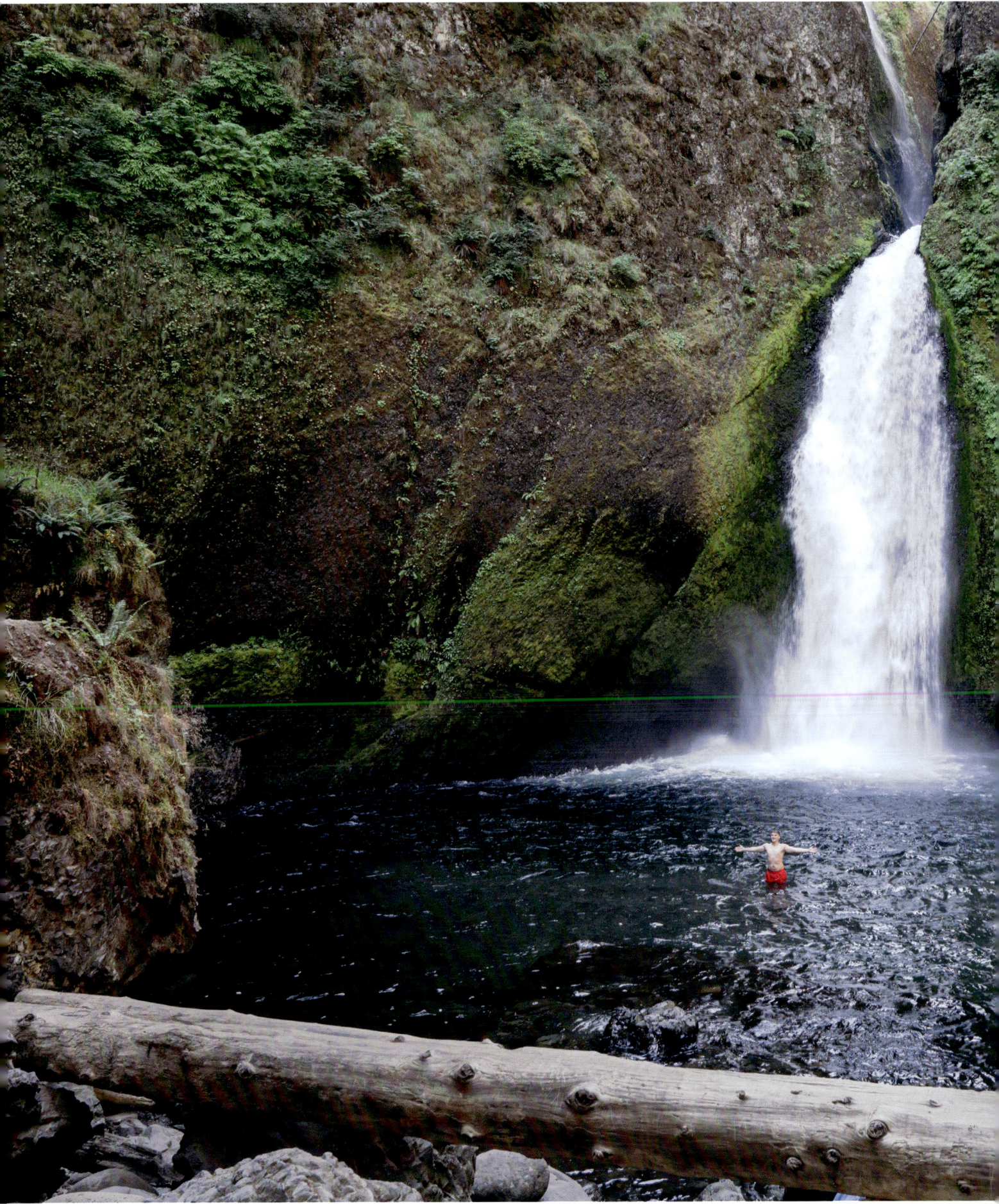

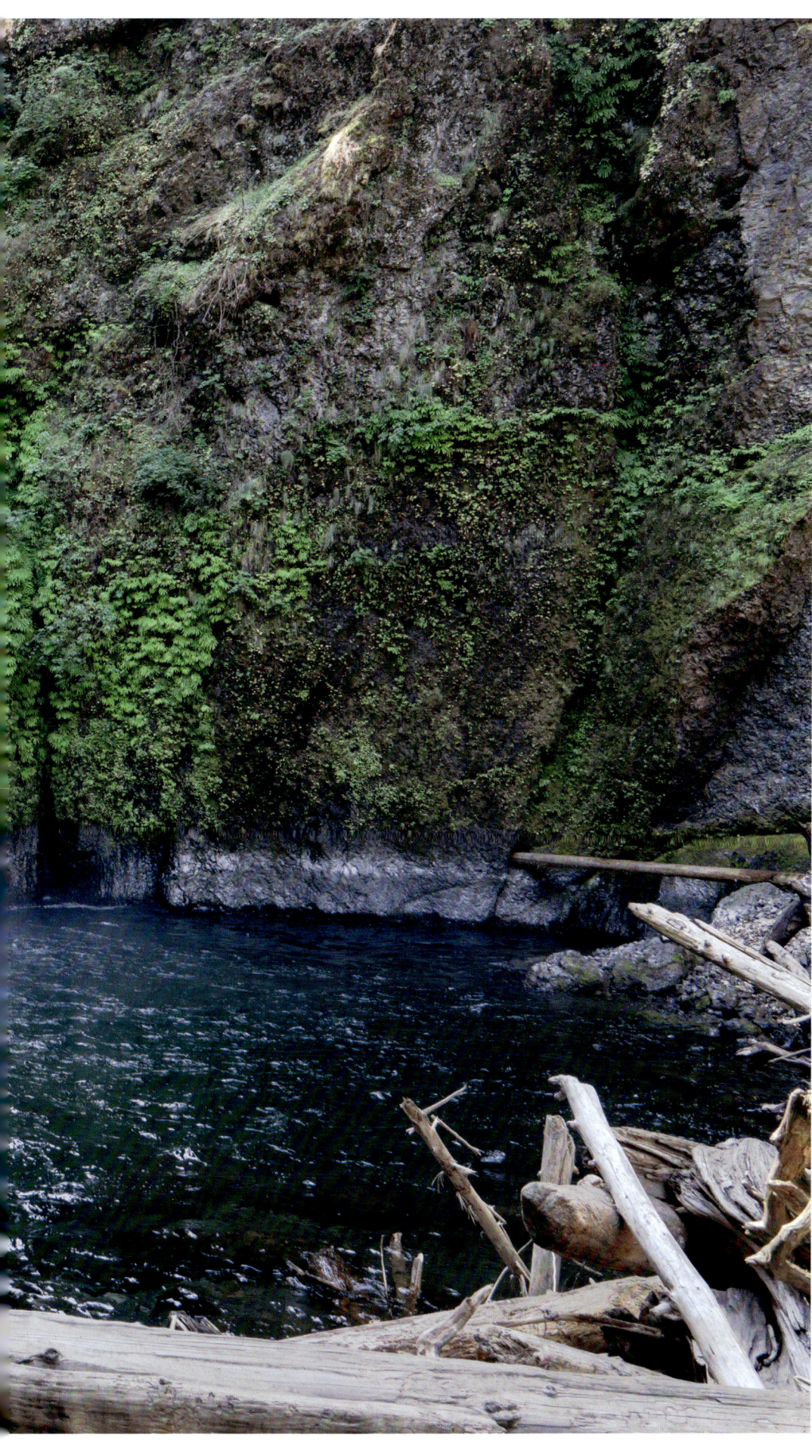

Wahclella Falls is the backdrop for a popular swimming hole. *Photo by Richard P. Handler*

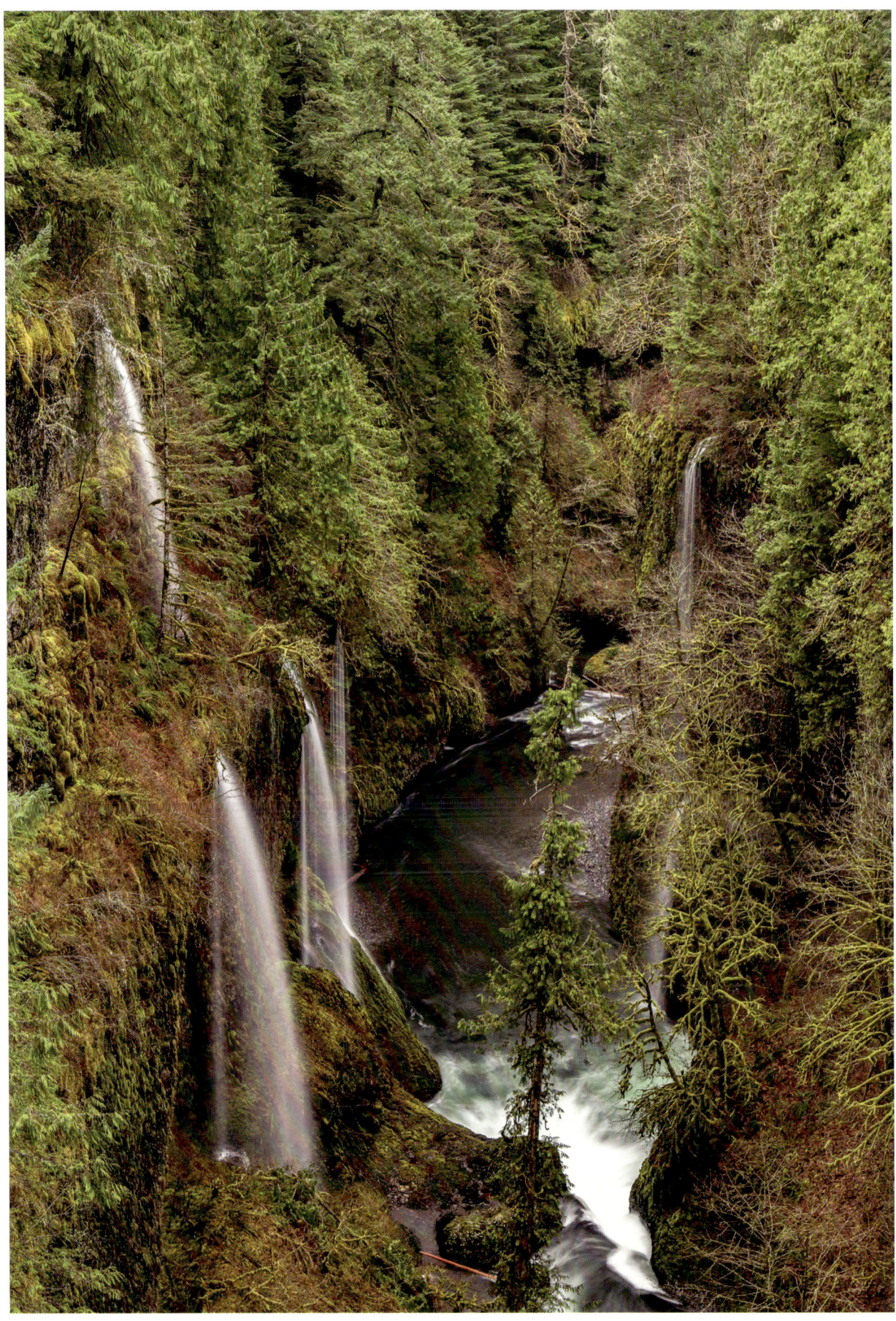

Weeping Walls. This seasonal and dramatic "weeping wall" is in the Eagle Creek Canyon, on the Wahclella Falls Trail. Water pours off the cliffsides, especially in spring. The trail was once in the middle of a lush green forest. Unfortunately, as of this writing, there may not be access. The area was destroyed by the 2017 Eagle Creek fire, so check before going. *Photo by Vldn Taylor*

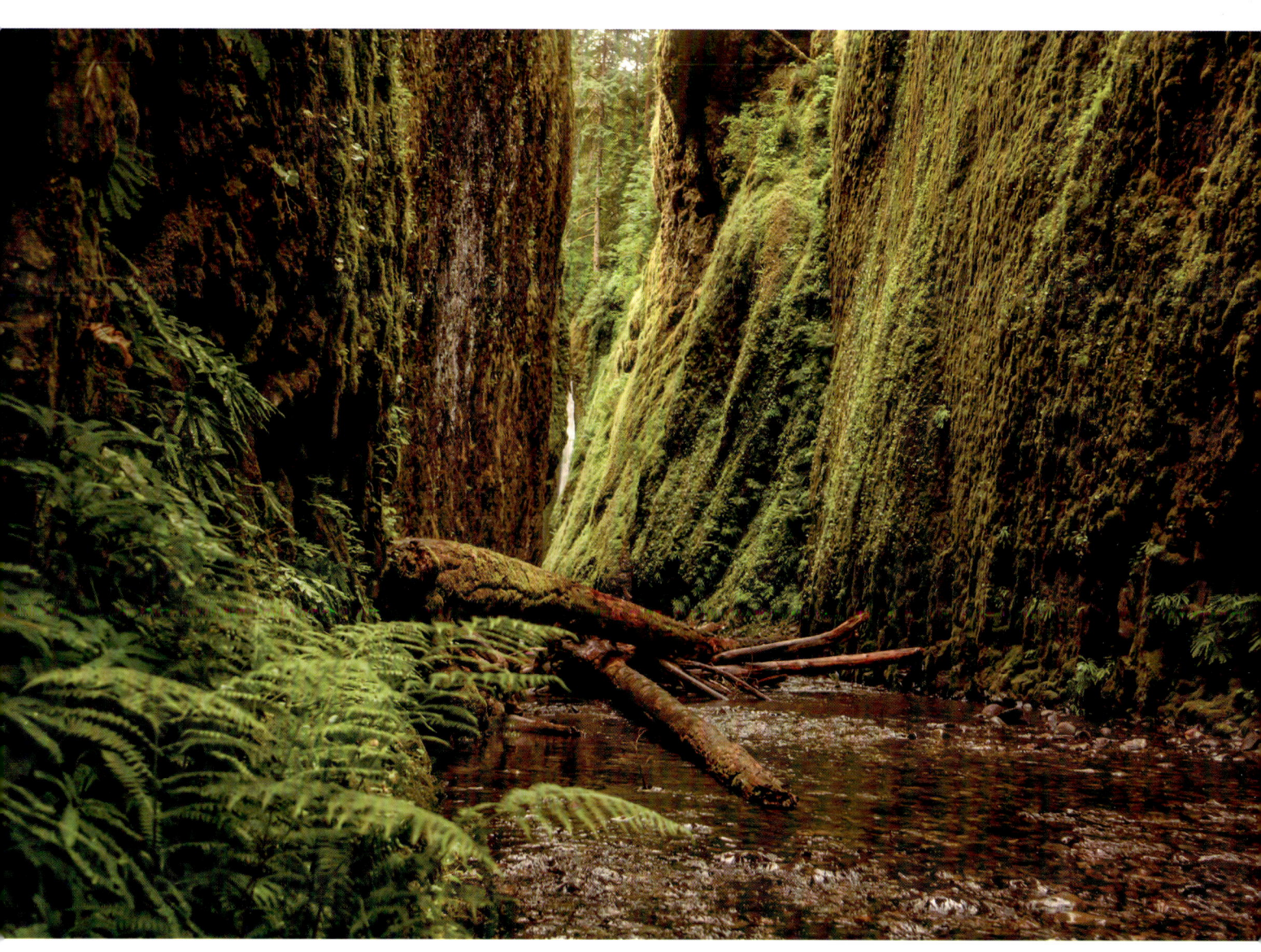

Oneonta Falls. The breathtaking Oneonta Gorge was once a popular destination in the Columbia River Gorge National Scenic Area. Oneonta Falls, seen in the background, plummets 100 feet into a pool below. Home to rare species of lichens, mosses, and ferns in a moss-draped slot canyon, it was a popular attraction. Unfortunately, the 2017 Eagle Creek fire changed all that, and as of this writing, debris, boulders, and other hazards have made it inaccessible to visitors. Check before going. *Photo by Hans Stroo*

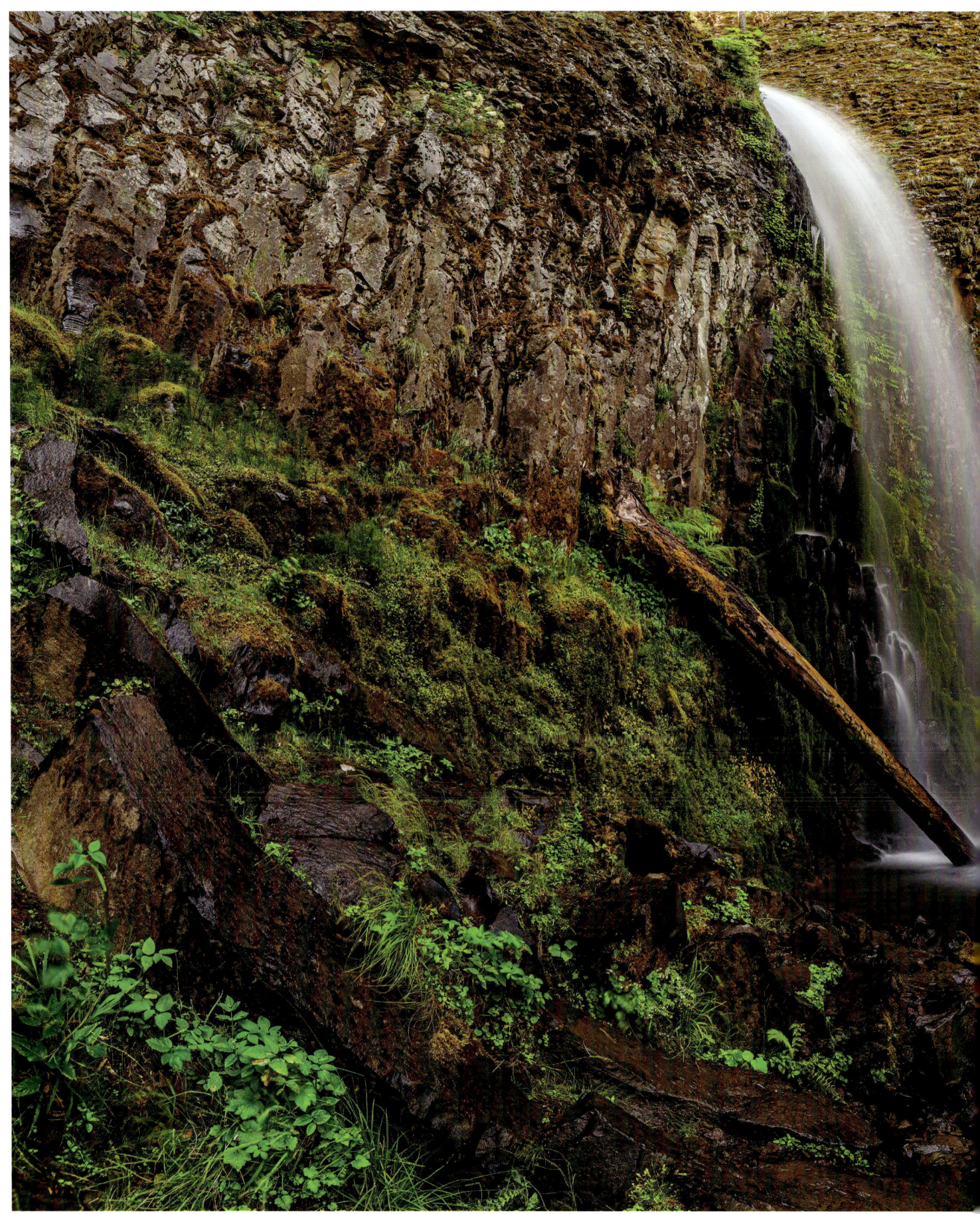

Dry Creek Falls. This waterfall is accessed along the Pacific Crest Trail. It is considered an easy, 4.4-mile-out-and-back hike, with a refreshing pool at the base of the falls to cool off. However, do check, since the trailhead may still be closed due to the Whiskey Creek fire. *Photo by David Joarnt*

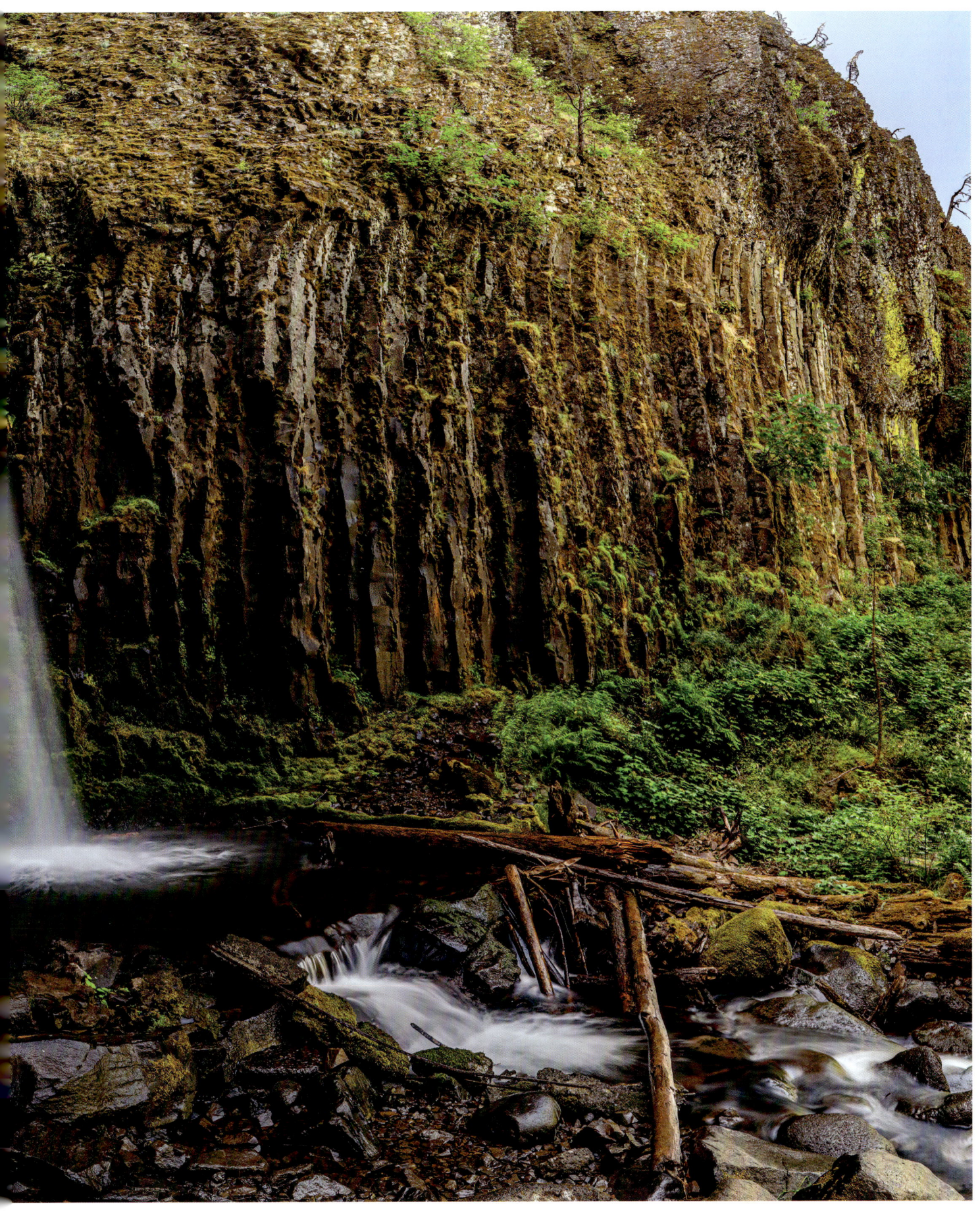

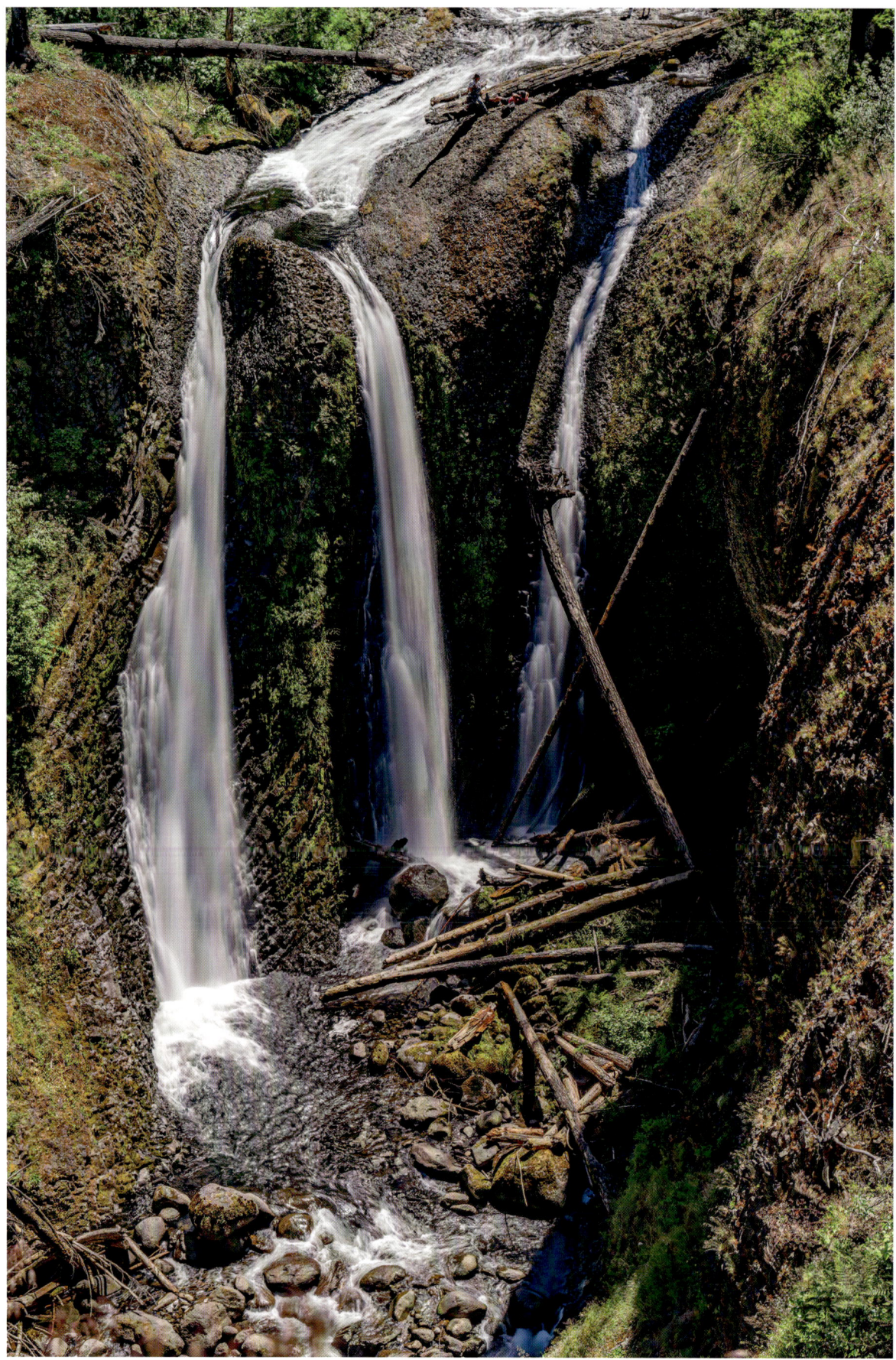

Triple Falls. To find the challenging route to these waterfalls, begin on Oneonta Trail and head through the woods just above the Columbia River Highway. This is generally considered the most demanding route up the mountain due to the steep grade, cliff edges, slick areas, and switchbacking weathered basalt cliffs. *Photo by David Joarnt*

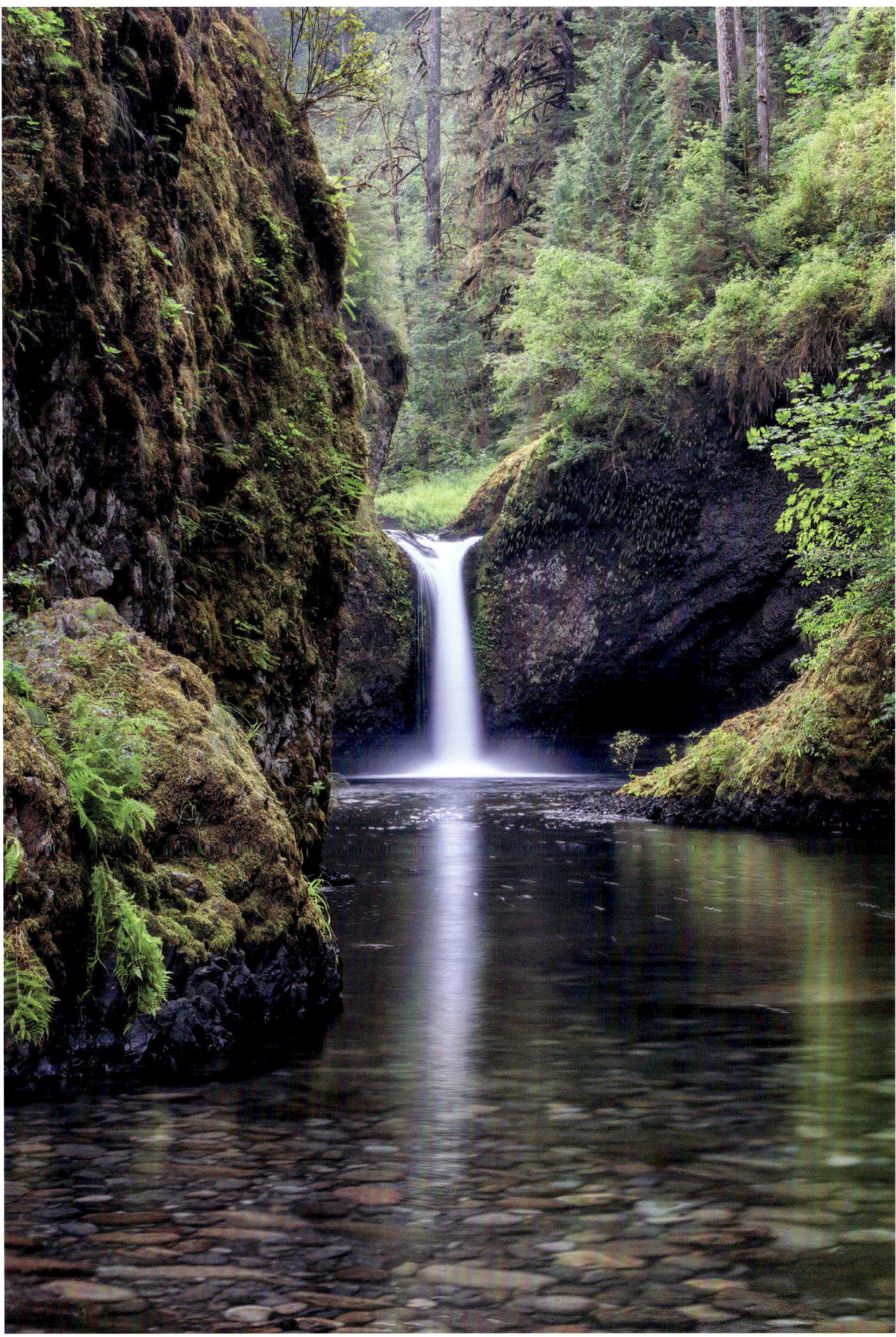

Punch Bowl Falls. Near Cascade Locks, along Eagle Creek, this is a moderately challenging, 4-mile-out-and-back popular trail. It is the first significant waterfall of Eagle Creek's spectacular series of 13 waterfalls within 5 miles. The path winds through old-growth forests with sheer cliffs and views of the canyon below. Due to a recent fire, the trail may still be inaccessible in places. There are striking views, but the hike is not recommended for small children. Bring water shoes and be prepared to scramble over some rocks and a logjam. *Photo by Gary Thurman*

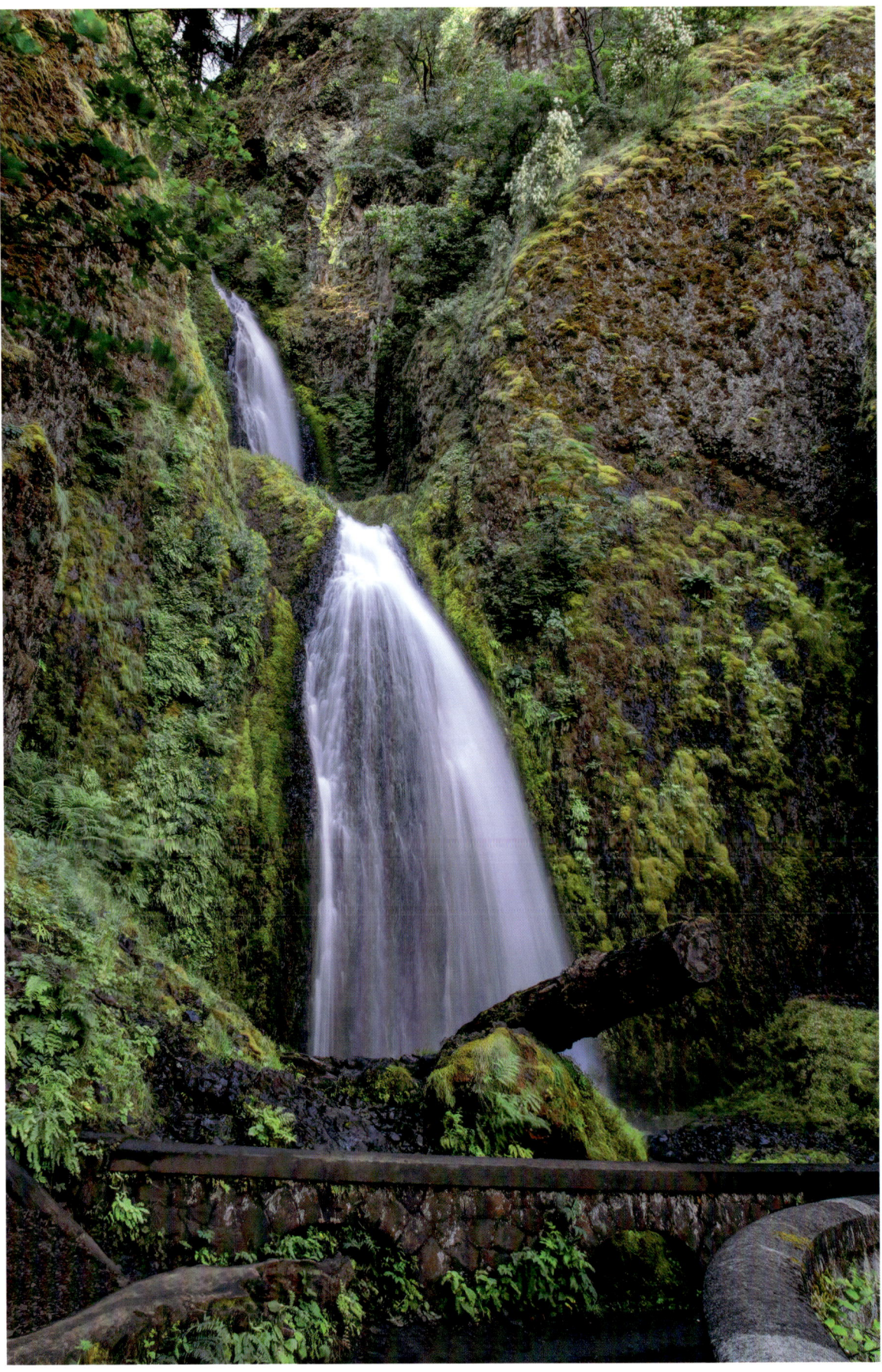

Shepperd's Dell Falls. This easy, 0.2-mile walk showcases an arched bridge built in 1914. The total height of Shepperd's Dell Falls is 220 feet, but upper tiers cannot easily be seen. What can be seen is the 45-foot drop of the hourglass-shaped falls above the bridge, and two 20-foot drops below the bridge. *Photo by Alana Starkweather*

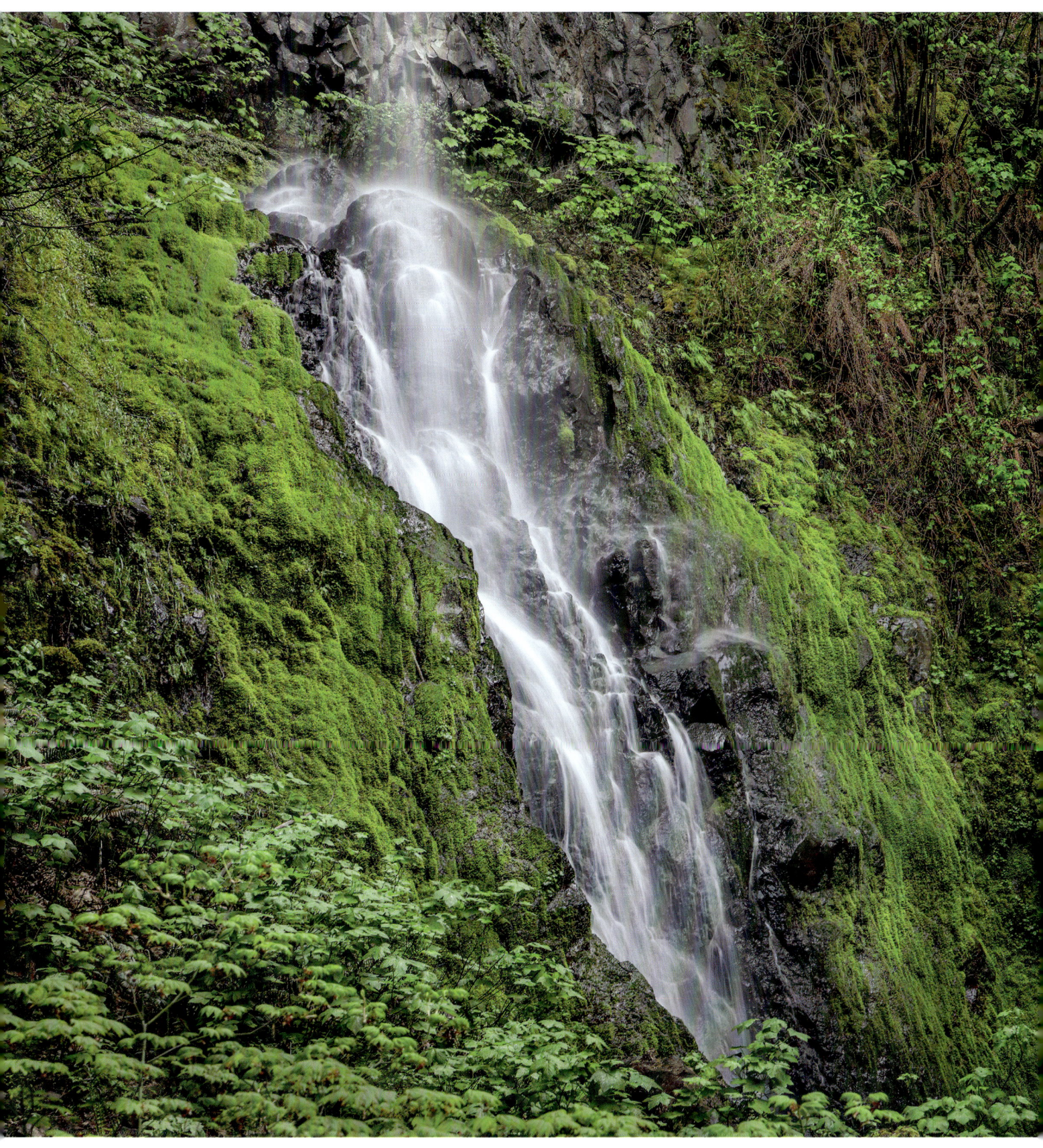

Lower Cabin Creek Falls. Cabin Creek Falls is located in Starvation Creek State Park. To view this two-tiered, 220-foot waterfall, take the easy 1.9-mile-out-and-back trail near Cascade Locks. It takes only about 46 minutes to complete. *Photo by John Christer Petersen*

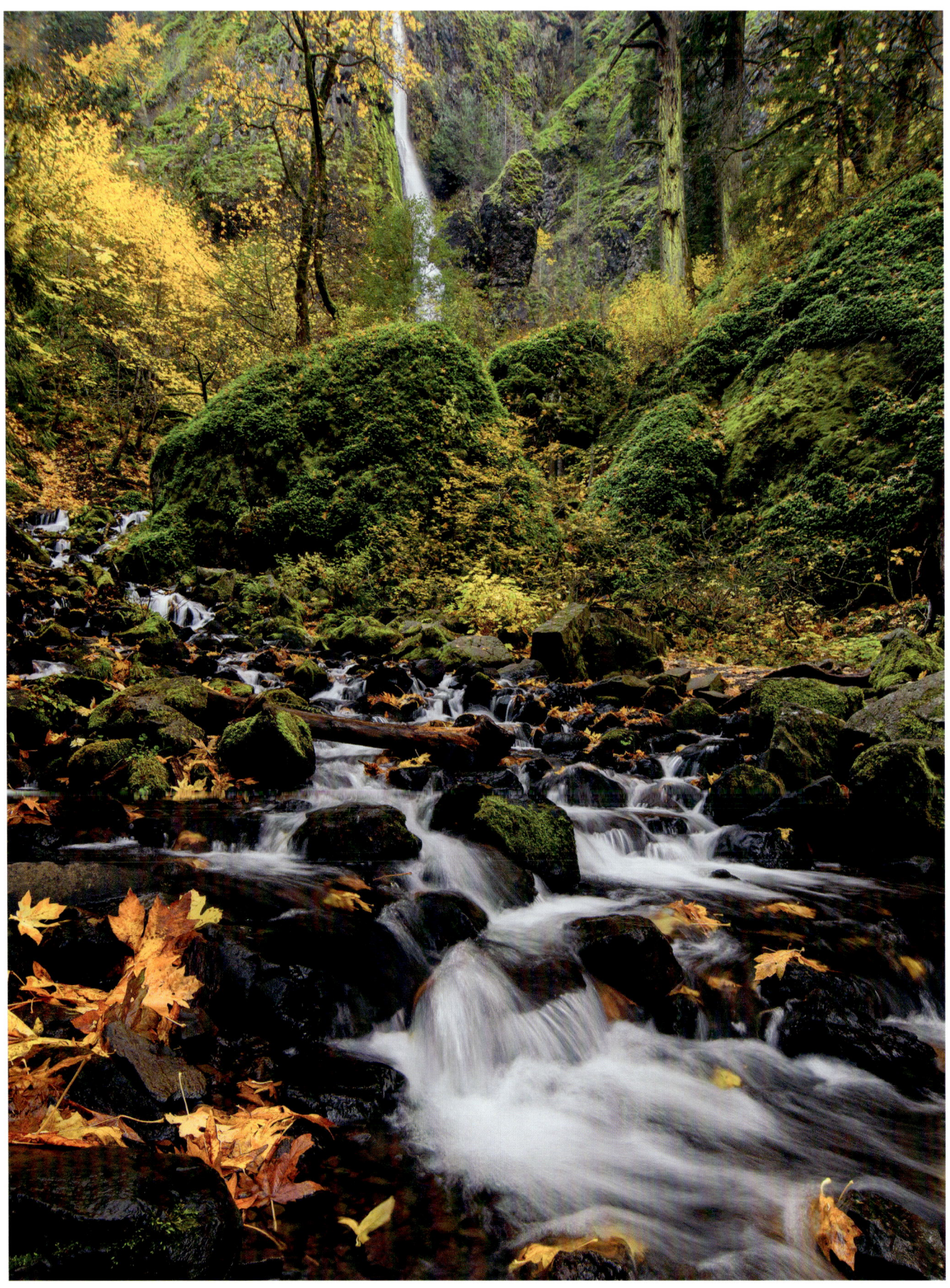

Starvation Creek Falls. This is a 190-foot, two-tiered waterfall, off I-84. The state park, river, and waterfall were so named after a blizzard and avalanche trapped a Union Pacific train in the winter of 1884-85. Though cold and hungry for two weeks, the passengers were kept from starvation by locals who shoveled and brought food supplies to the remote area on skis (hence its name). *Photo by Clem Paslack*

3 Willamette Valley

The lush Willamette Valley is a 150-mile-long valley in Oregon, nestled between the Cascade and Oregon Coast Mountain ranges. Known for its moderate rainfall and mild summer temperatures, the Willamette Valley produces rich soil, abundant crops and vineyards, and gorgeous seasonal flowers. Over half of the state's population is located in the valley. Most reside within the cities of Portland, Eugene, Gresham, Hillsboro and Salem, home of Oregon's state capital. Silver Falls State Park (with its "Trail of Ten" waterfalls) is considered the crown jewel of the Oregon parks system. Those 10 waterfalls are in a separate chapter in this book.

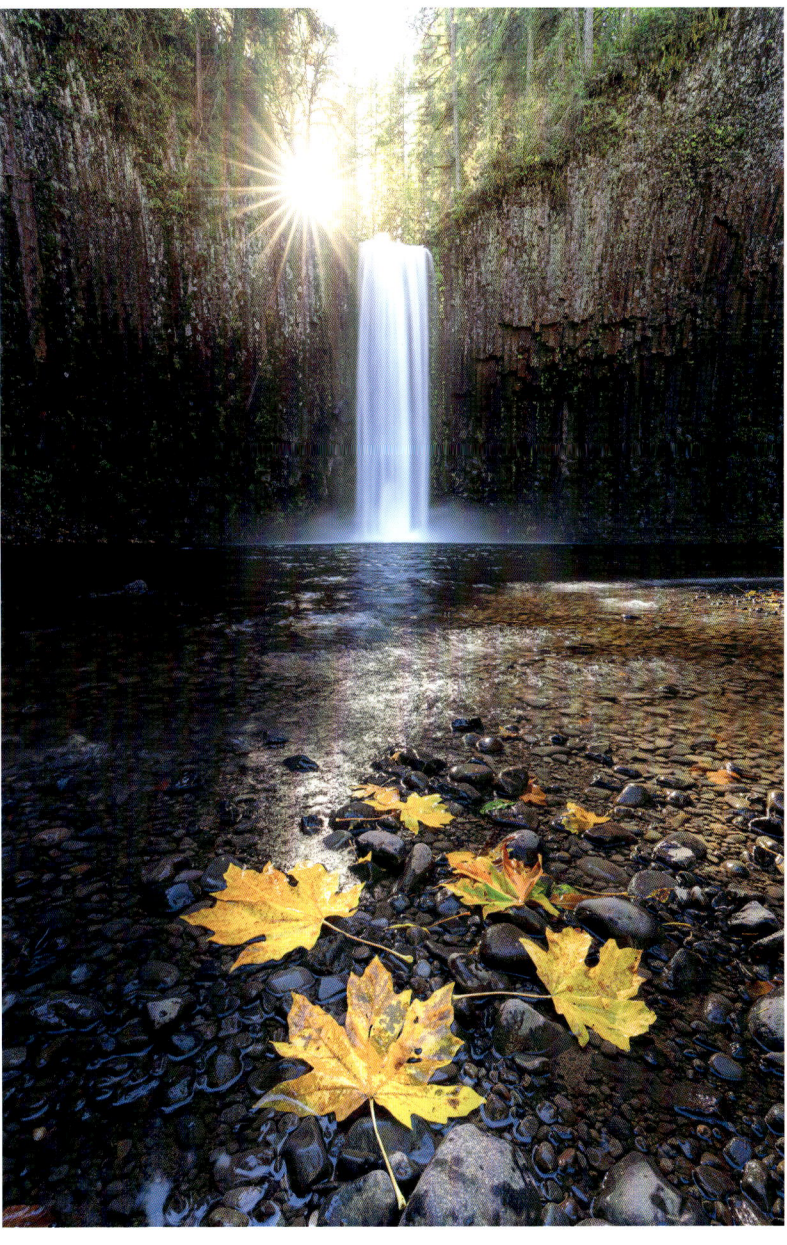

Abiqua Falls. Technically on private property, Abiqua Falls is owned by Mount Angel Abbey, a Benedictine monastery, which has graciously allowed the public access to it. There are sections of rope to guide one up and down the trail, and it's often necessary to climb over downed trees. It is approximately a 1.9-mile walk from parking to the trailhead down steep paths. *Photo by Annette Stiers Jones*

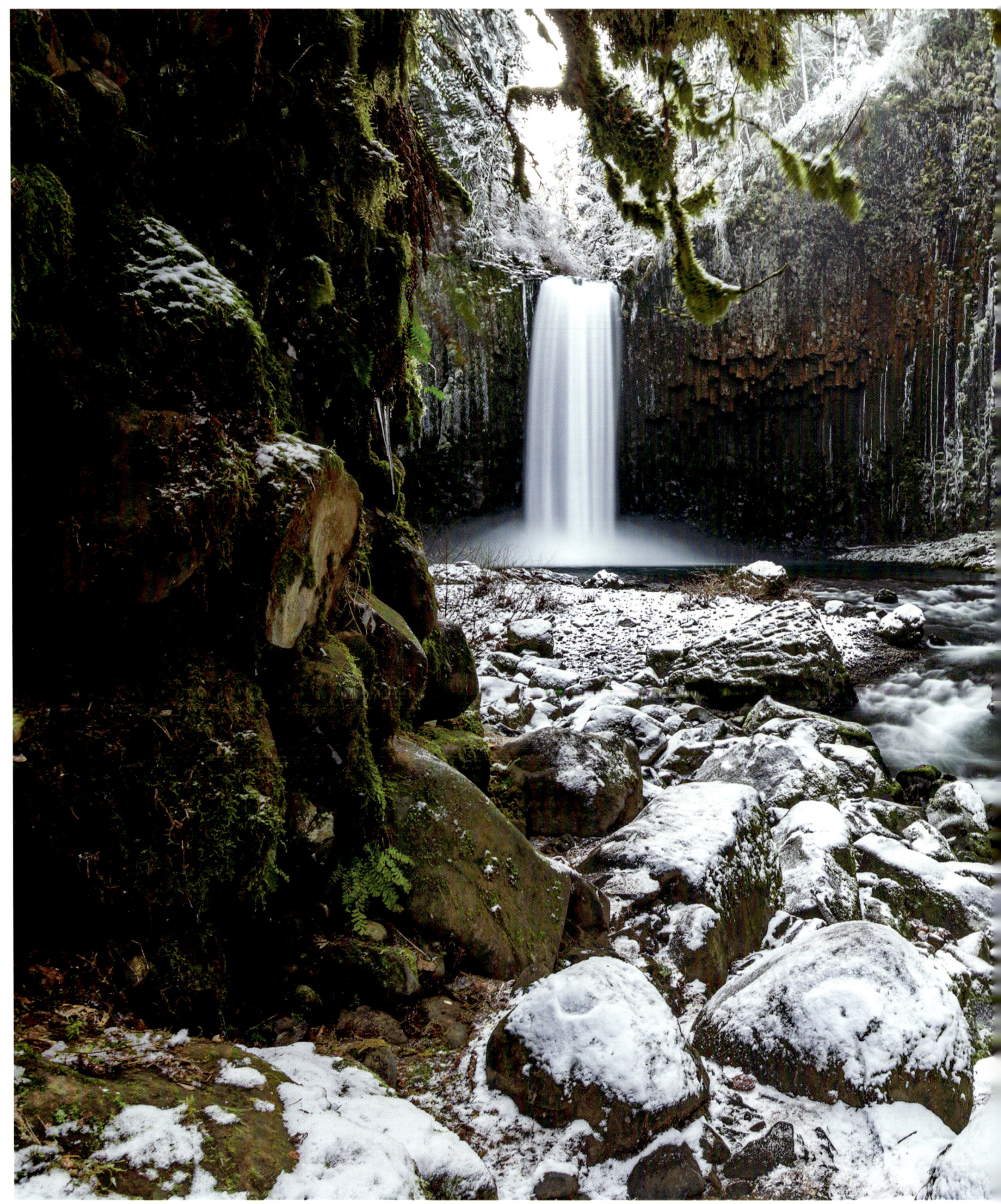

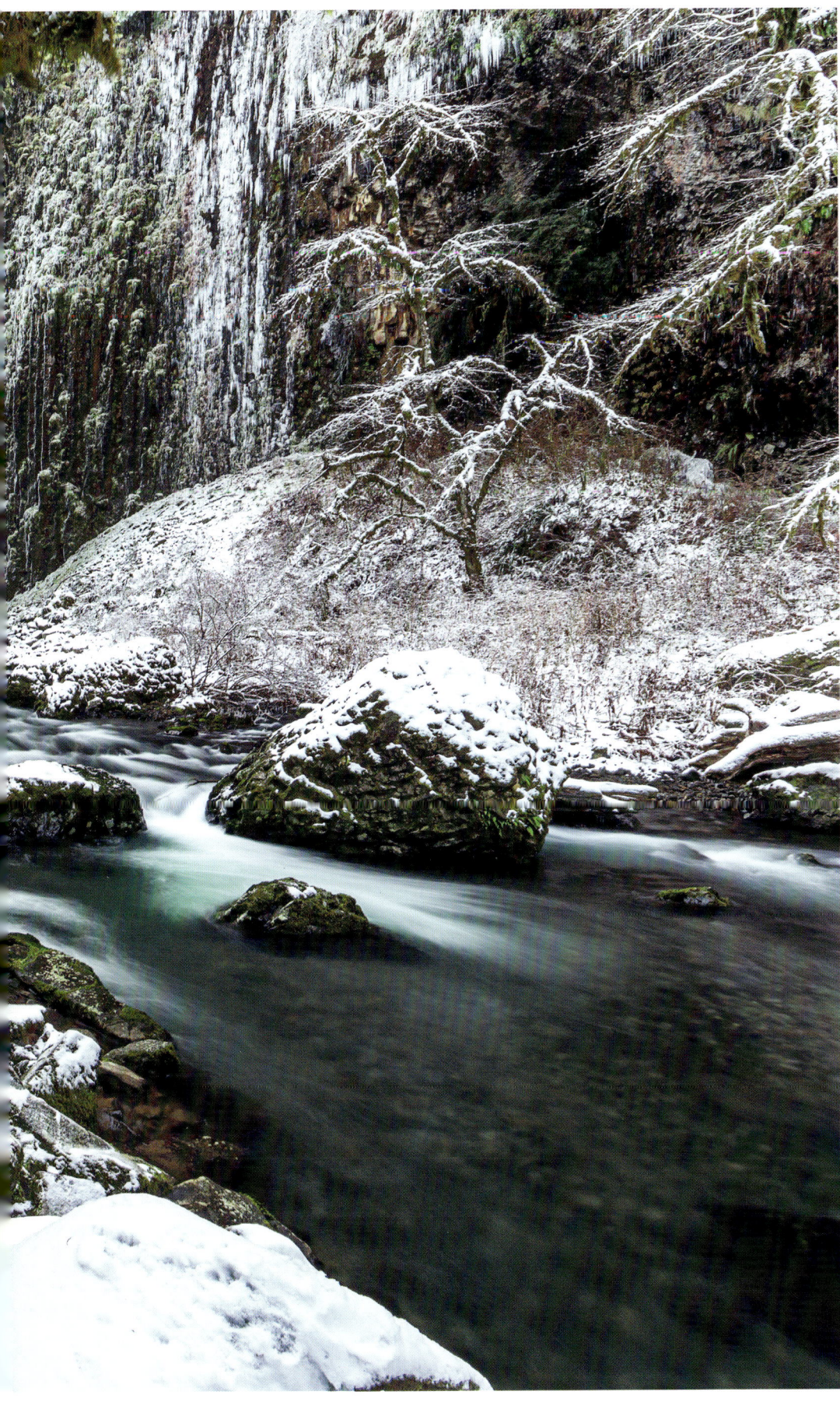

Abiqua Falls in winter. About an hour and a half away from Portland, on an unpaved road, Abiqua Falls is considered challenging to reach by foot or car in any season, especially in winter. The road is especially rocky, bumpy, and icy in the winter, meaning you may need to walk to the trailhead, a 5-mile round trip. However, the end result is a stunning 92-foot waterfall. *Photo by Vldn Taylor*

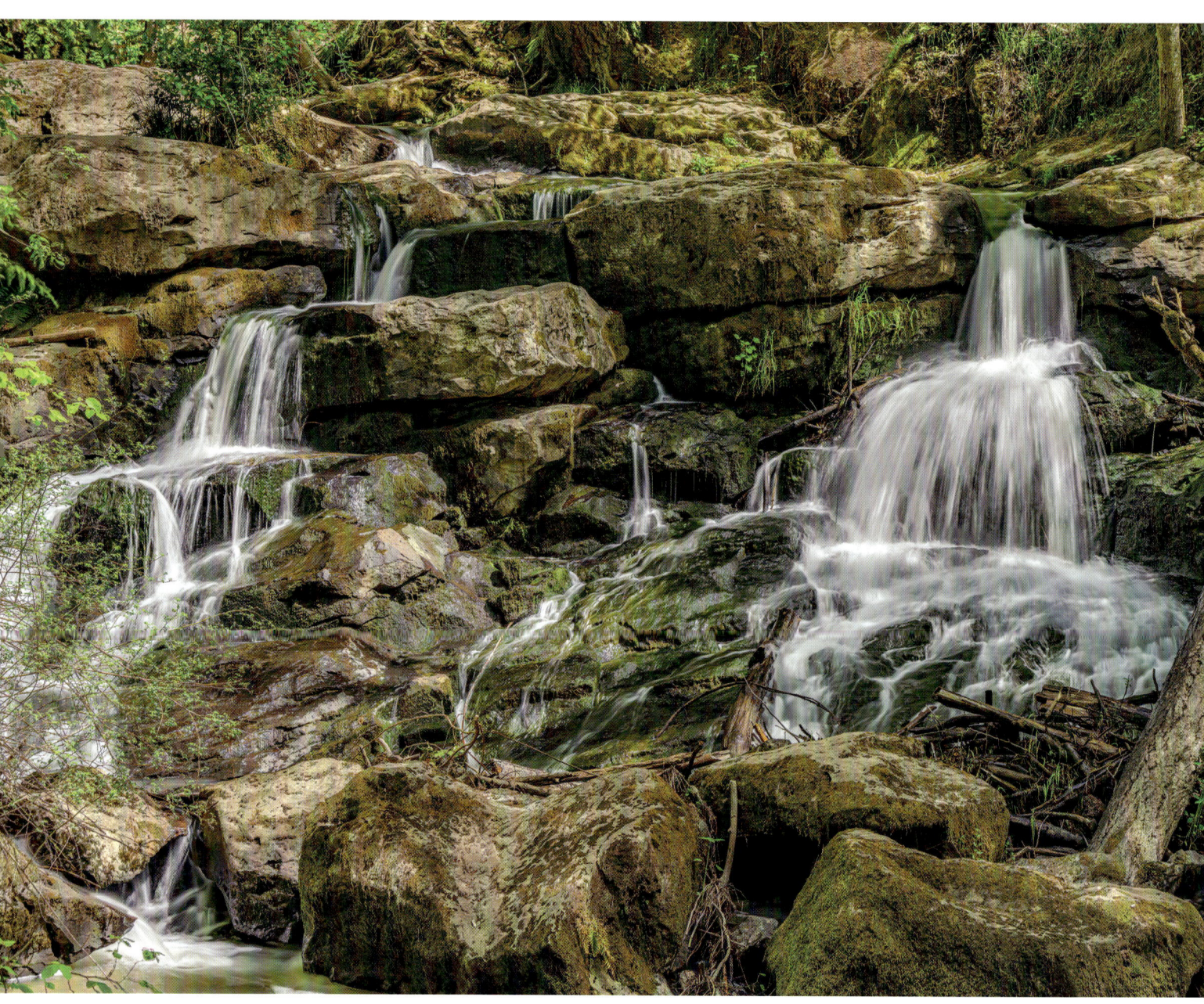

Cedar Mill Falls. Cedar Mill Falls is in Beaverton, a western suburb of Portland, not far from a busy road. The falls tumble down a rock ledge just below Cornell Road in Cedar Mill, named for the Jones Cedar Mill, which operated from 1855 to 1891. *Photo by David Joarnt*

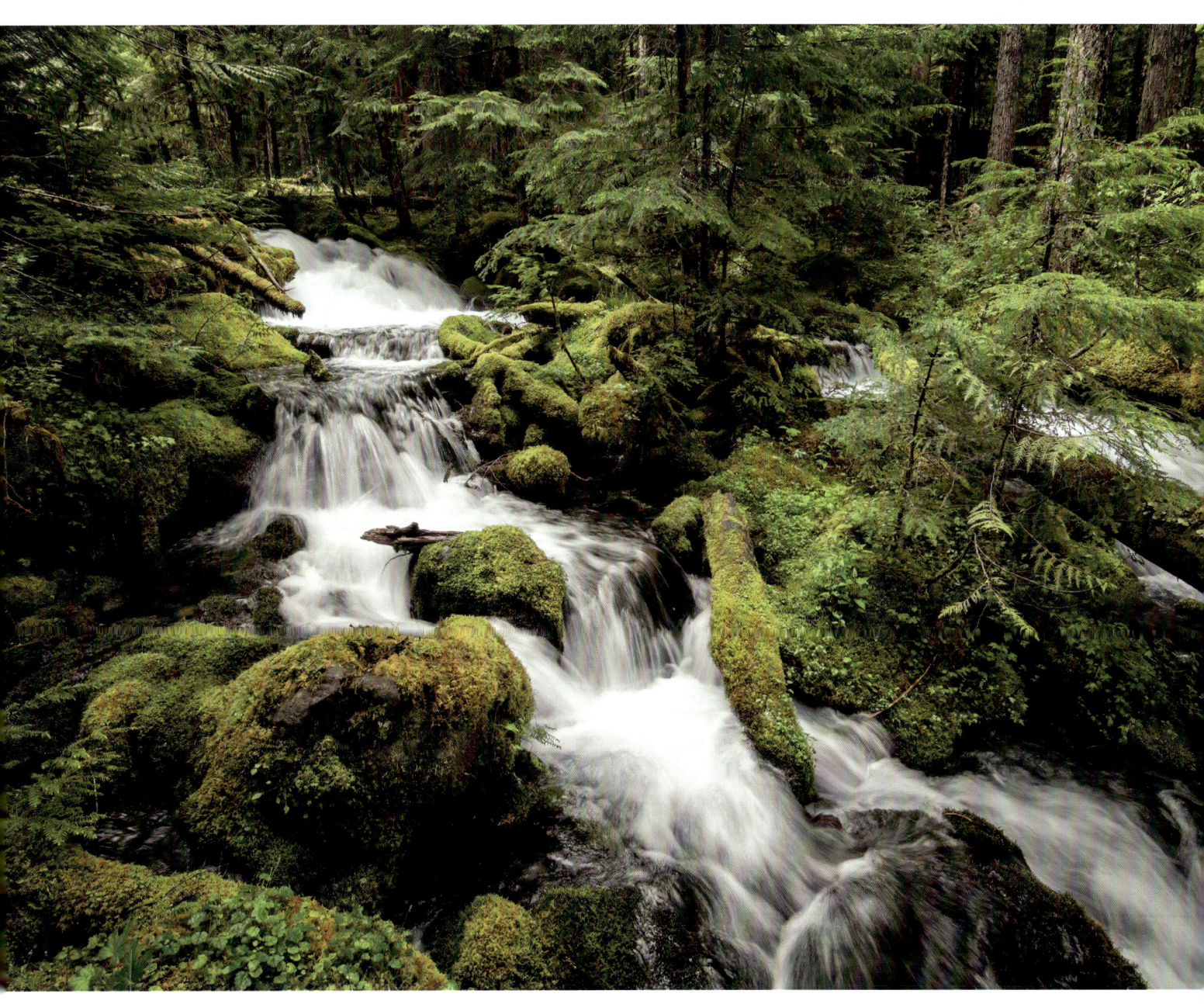

Downing Creek Falls. These mossy-green falls near Blue River, Oregon, are 35 feet tall. The 1.0-mile-out-and-back route is considered moderately challenging and takes about 33 minutes to complete. The road leading to the falls is very narrow, with room for only one car to pass at a time. *Photo by Gary Thurman*

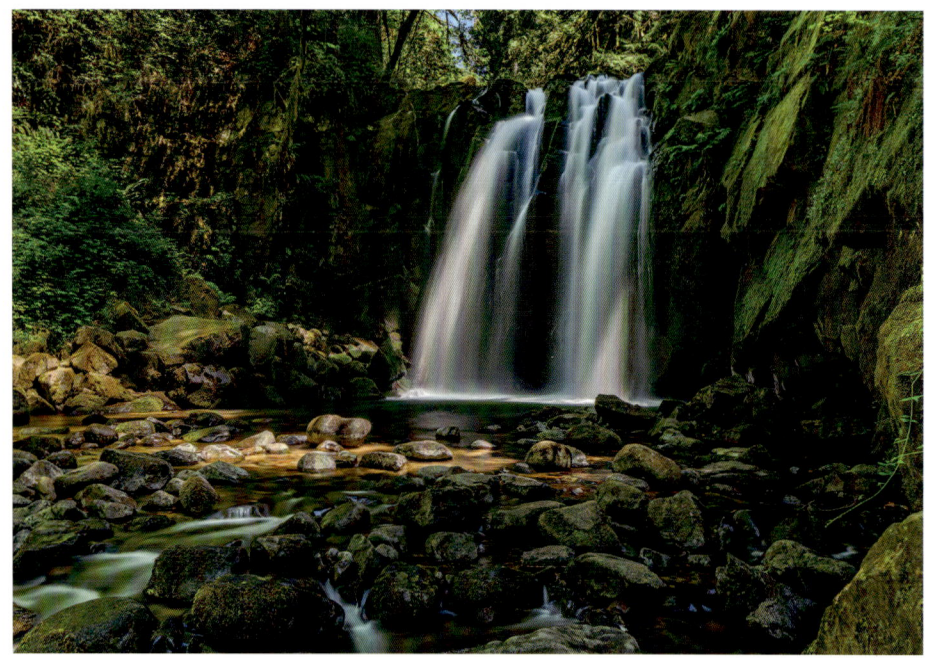

Majestic Falls. Majestic Falls, in McDowell Creek Falls County Park near Lebanon, Oregon, can be seen by climbing a wooden staircase to an observation deck. It's the largest of several waterfalls located within the park and drops 39 feet into a pool. *Photo by David Joarnt*

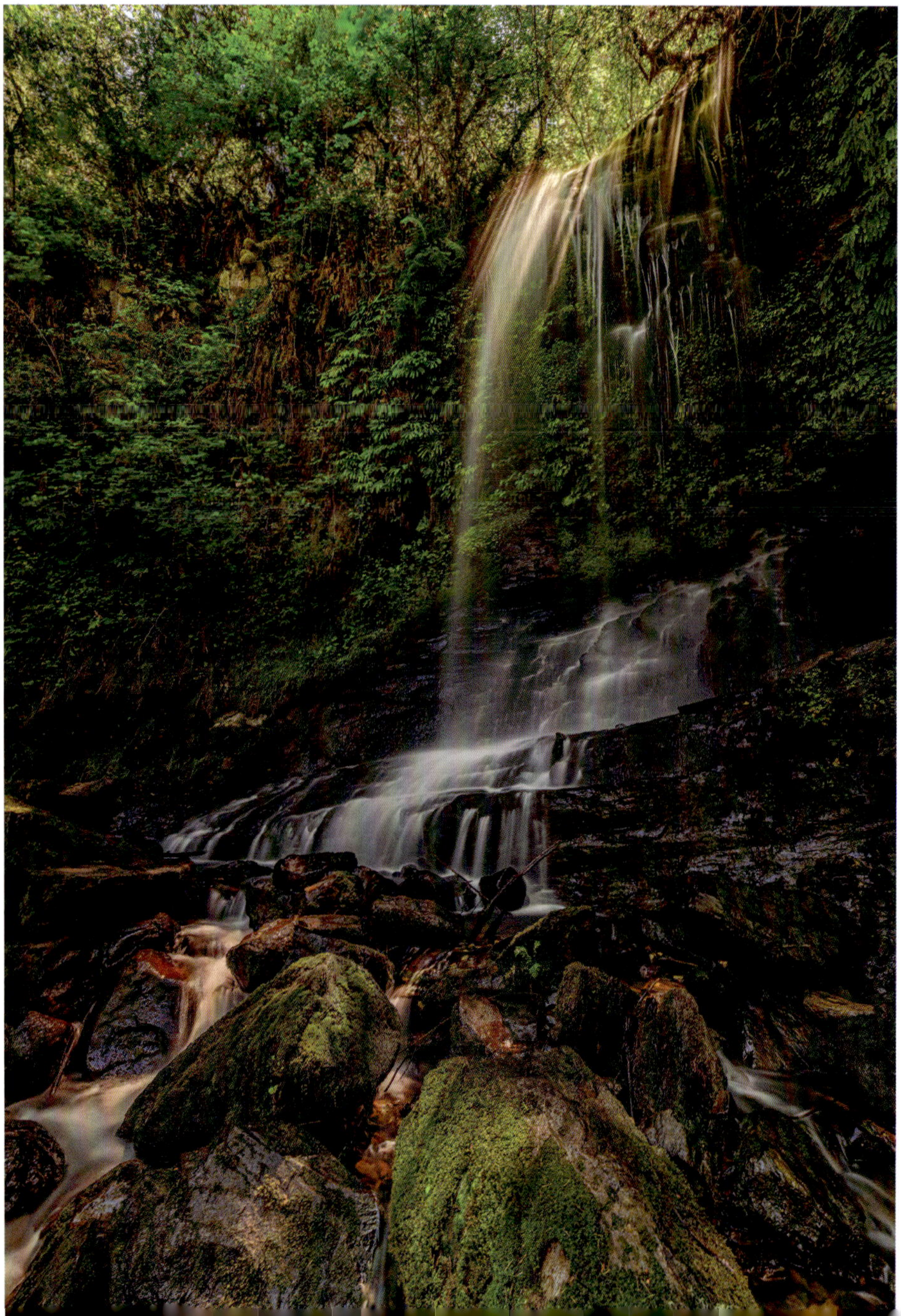

Royal Terrace Falls. This is a two-tiered waterfall, approximately 120 feet high in McDowell Creek Falls County Park. There are several other waterfalls within the park on a short hike. *Photo by David Joarnt*

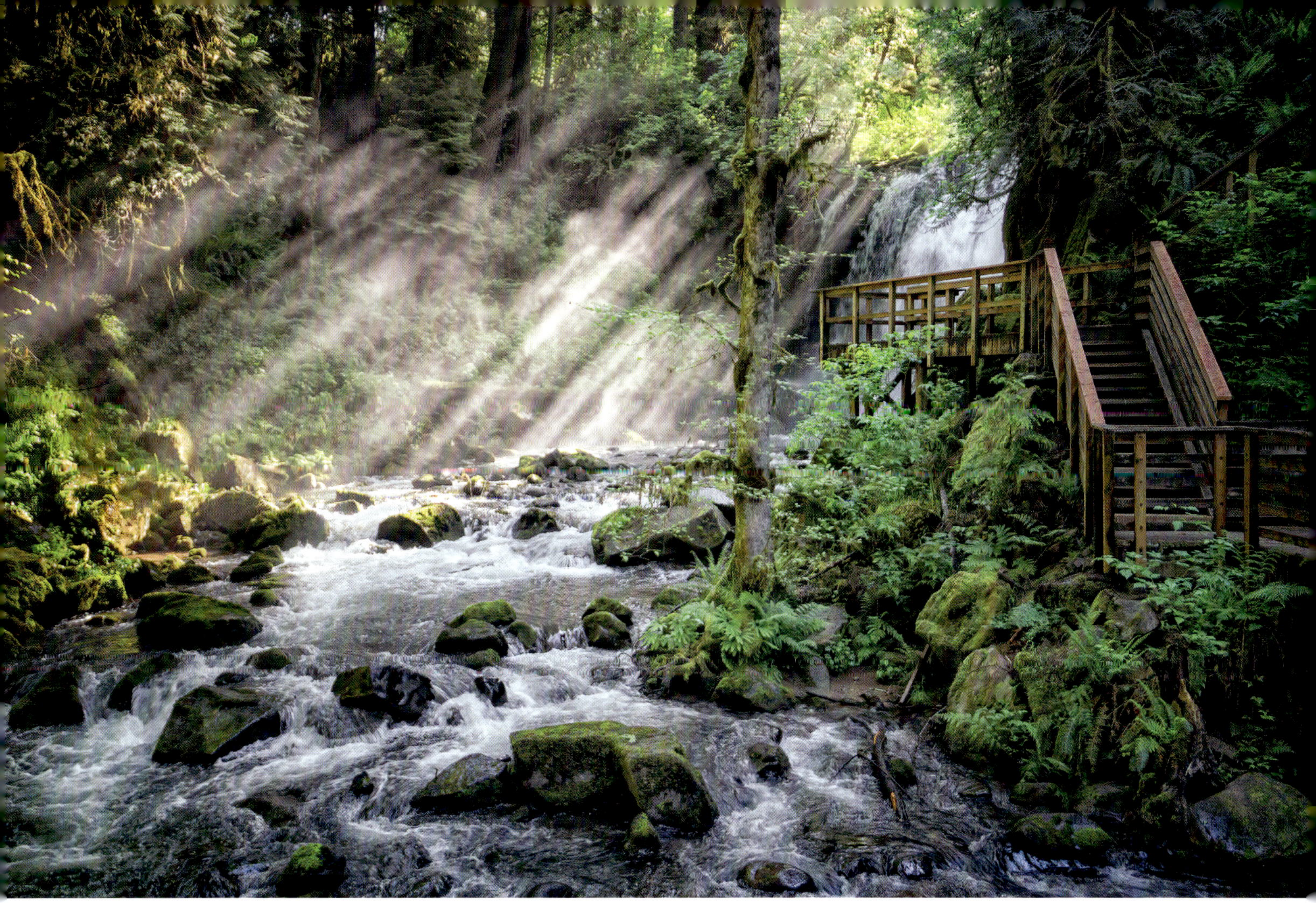

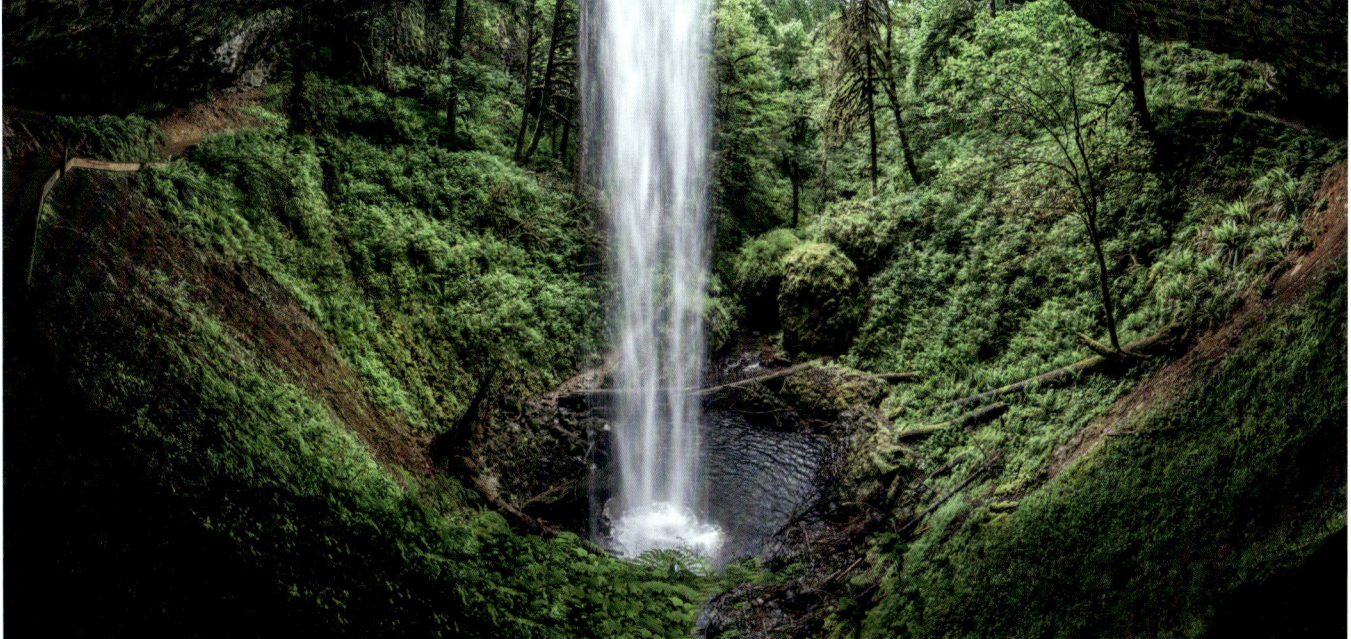

McDowell Creek Falls. There are several waterfalls in McDowell Creek Falls County Park near Lebanon, Oregon. They flow into the South Santiam River. The hiking trail to see the falls is considered moderate and takes about an hour to complete. One can hike a gradual ascent or take steep stairs. There are bridges and viewing decks along the trails. *Photo by Gary Thurman*

Shellburg Falls. Located near Mehama, Oregon, this is considered a moderately challenging 2-mile route on a narrow gravel trail, with abundant wildflowers in spring. Some areas may still not be accessible due to a recent fire. Note that it is not recommended to walk behind the falls. *Photo by Susan Sheets*

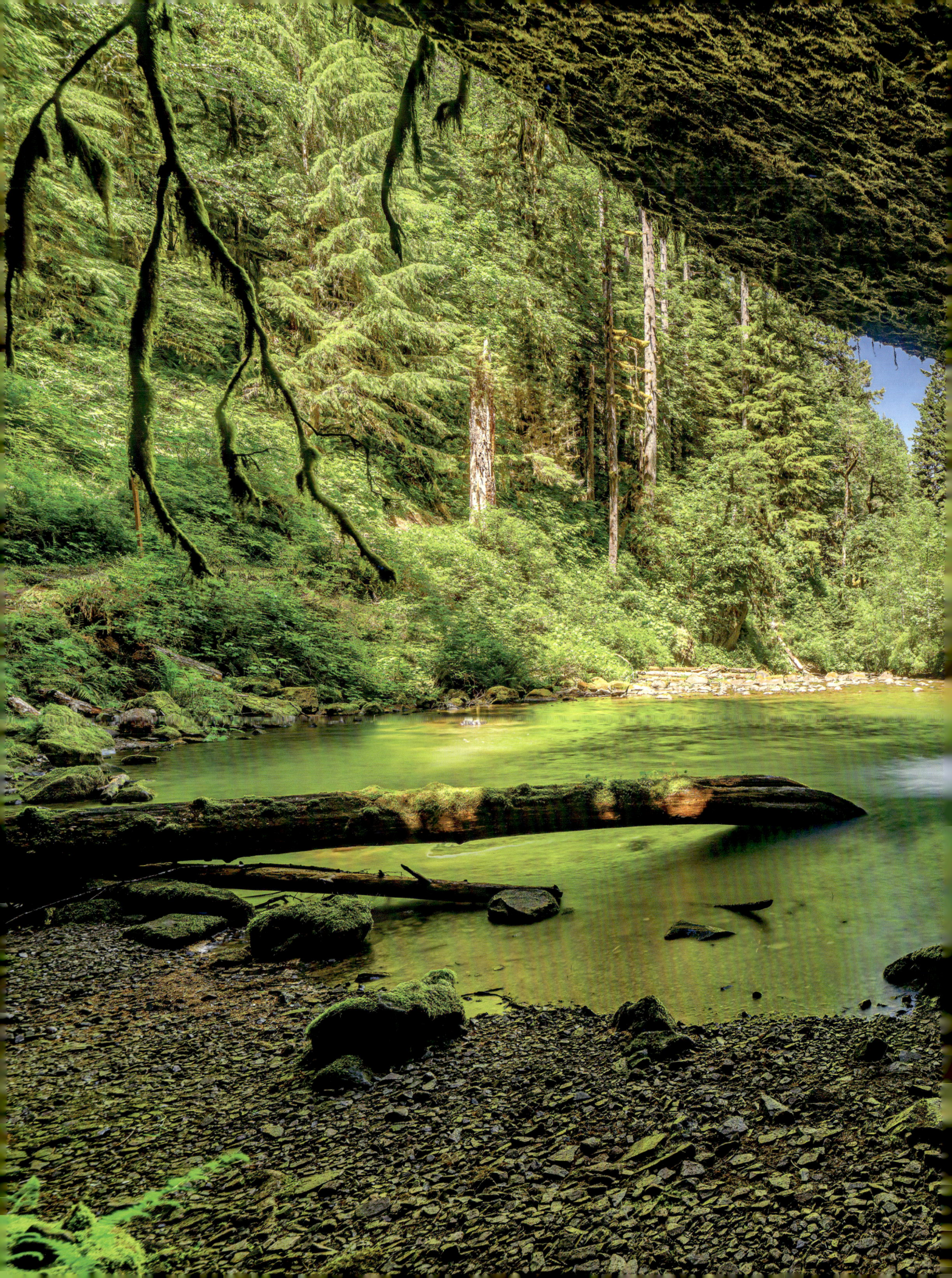

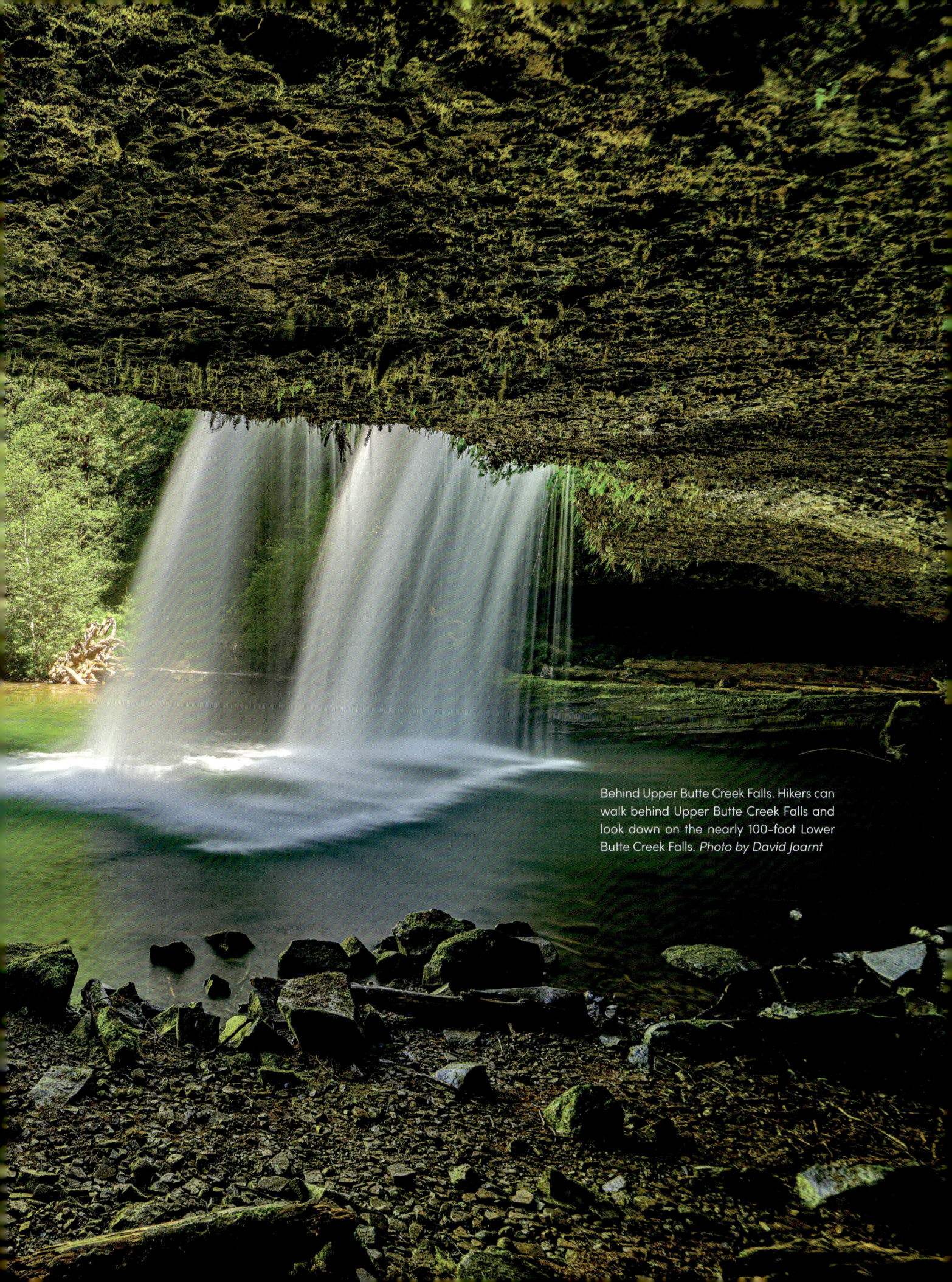

Behind Upper Butte Creek Falls. Hikers can walk behind Upper Butte Creek Falls and look down on the nearly 100-foot Lower Butte Creek Falls. *Photo by David Joarnt*

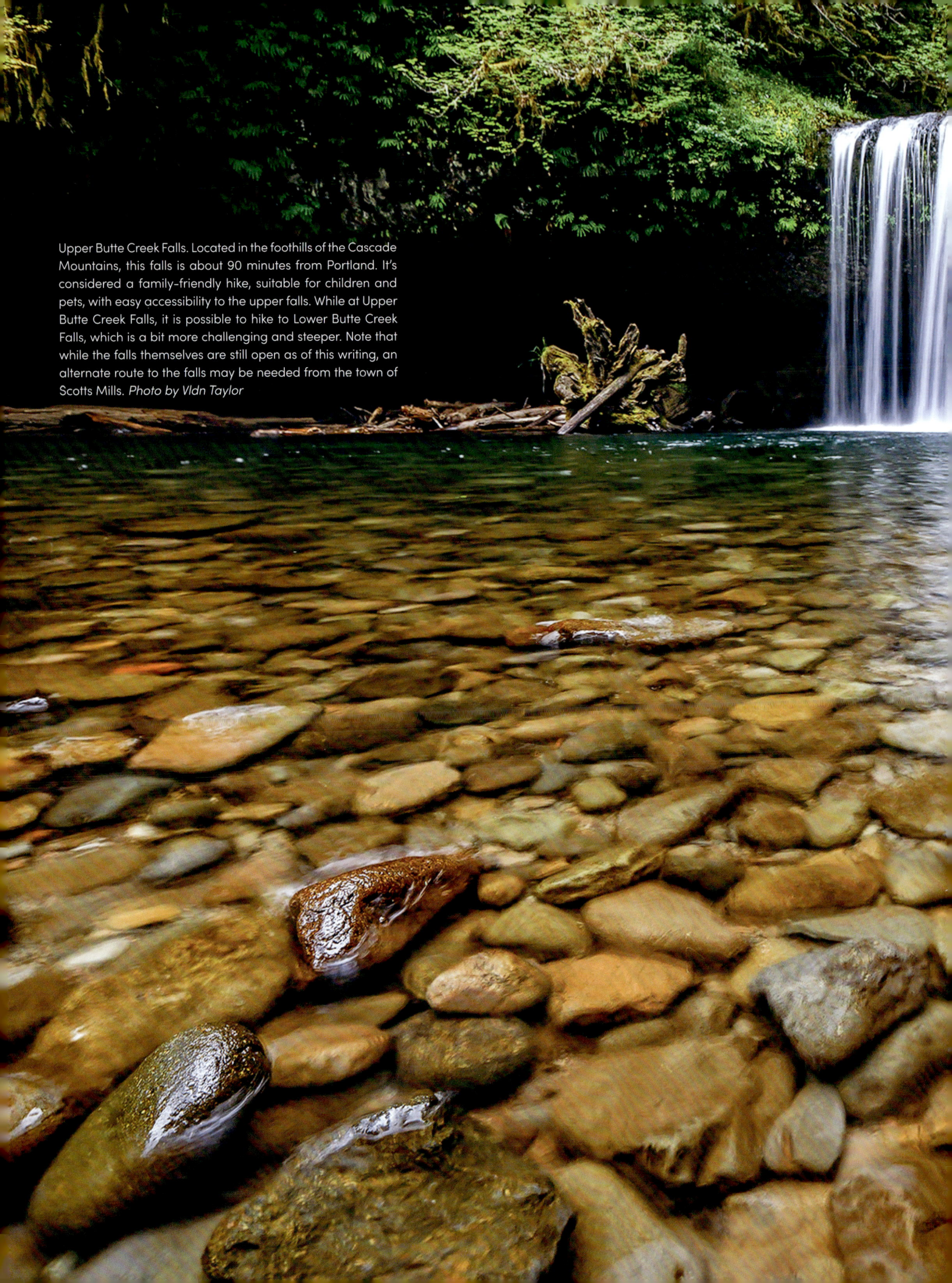

Upper Butte Creek Falls. Located in the foothills of the Cascade Mountains, this falls is about 90 minutes from Portland. It's considered a family-friendly hike, suitable for children and pets, with easy accessibility to the upper falls. While at Upper Butte Creek Falls, it is possible to hike to Lower Butte Creek Falls, which is a bit more challenging and steeper. Note that while the falls themselves are still open as of this writing, an alternate route to the falls may be needed from the town of Scotts Mills. *Photo by Vldn Taylor*

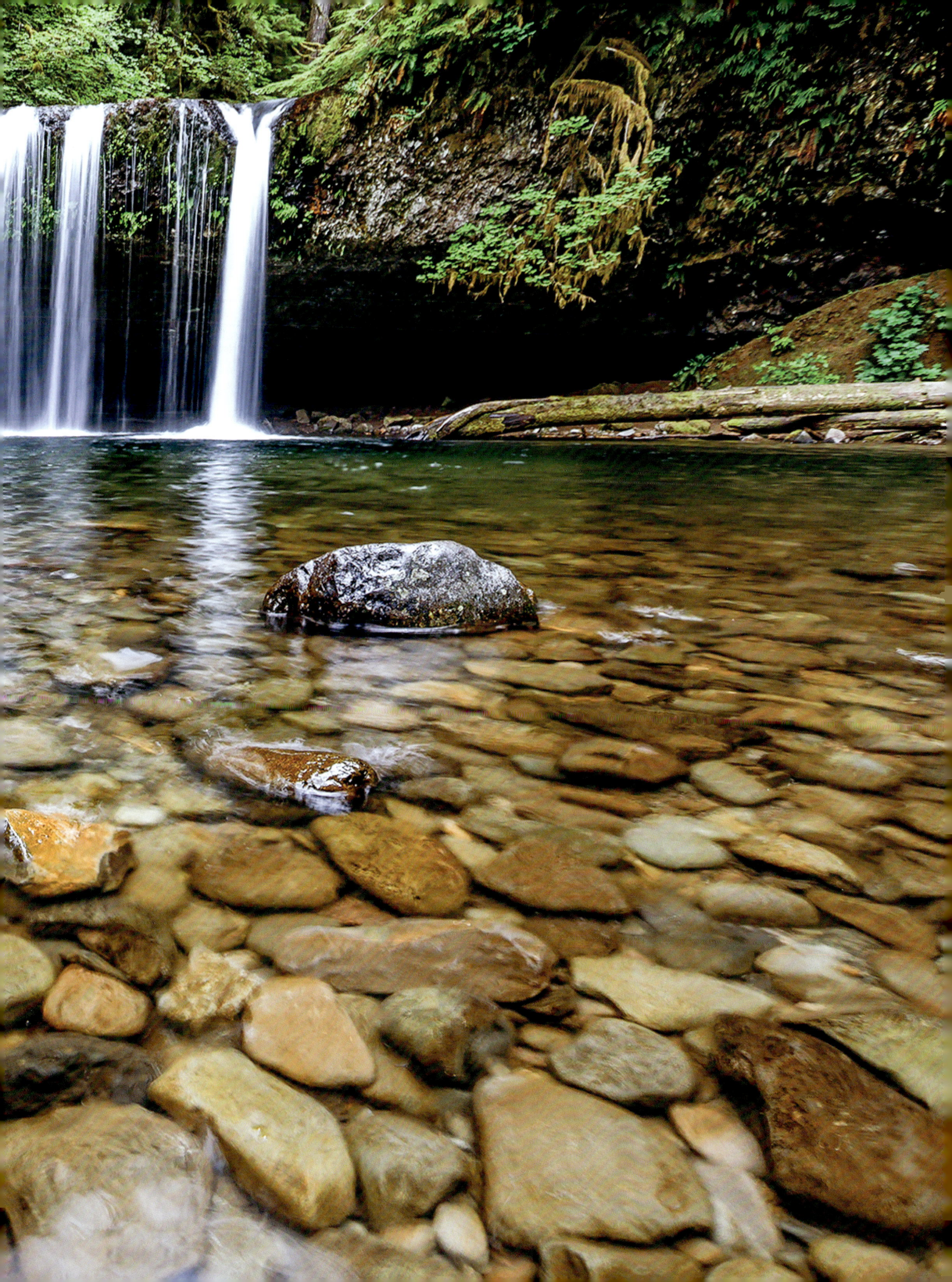

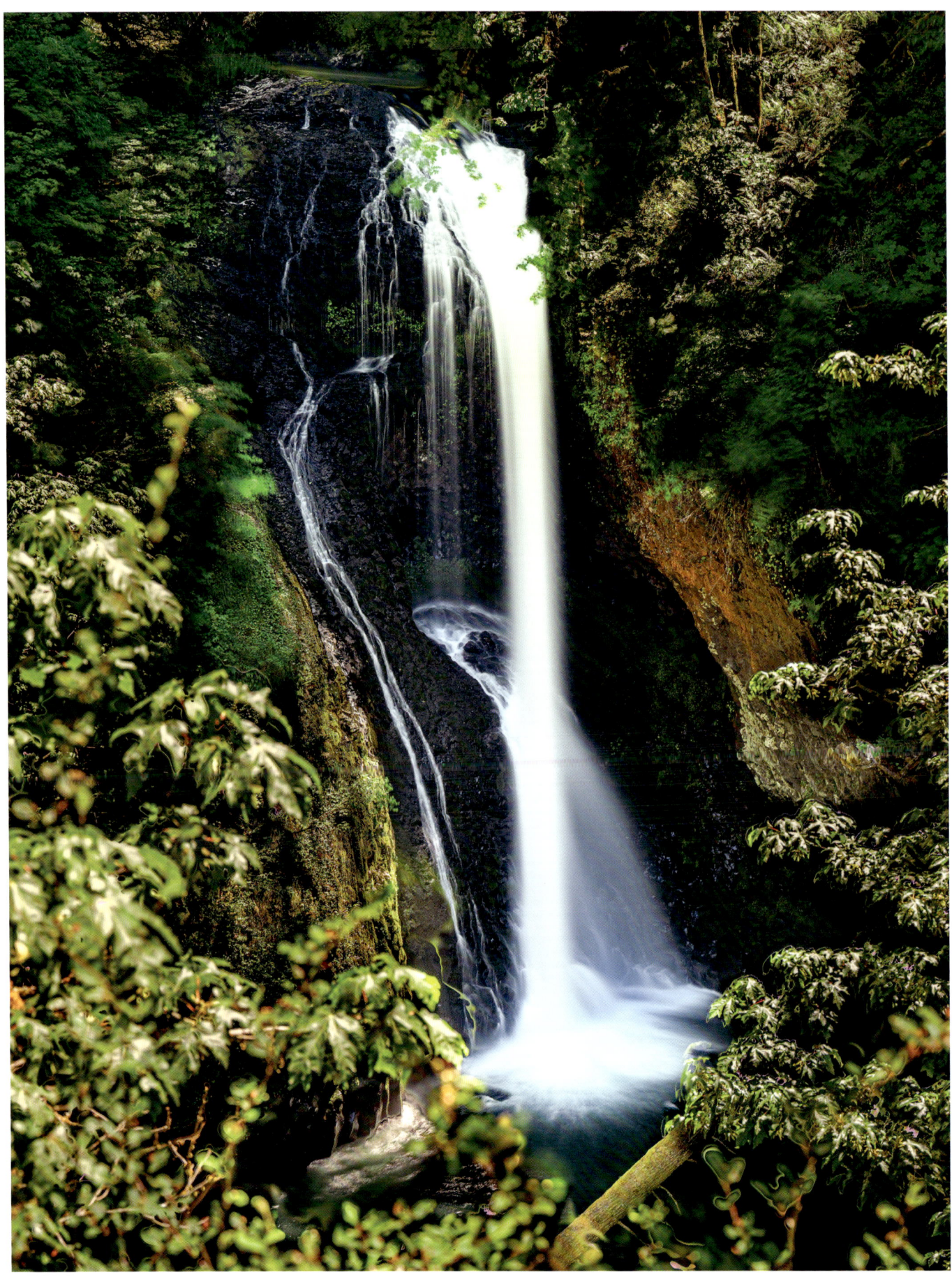

Lower Butte Creek Falls. The Butte Creek Falls Trail is located outside Scotts Mills, Oregon, 90 minutes from Portland, where hikers will be treated to two waterfalls. The trail to the Lower Butte Creek Falls is more challenging than its sister falls, Upper Butte Creek Falls. *Photo by David Joarnt*

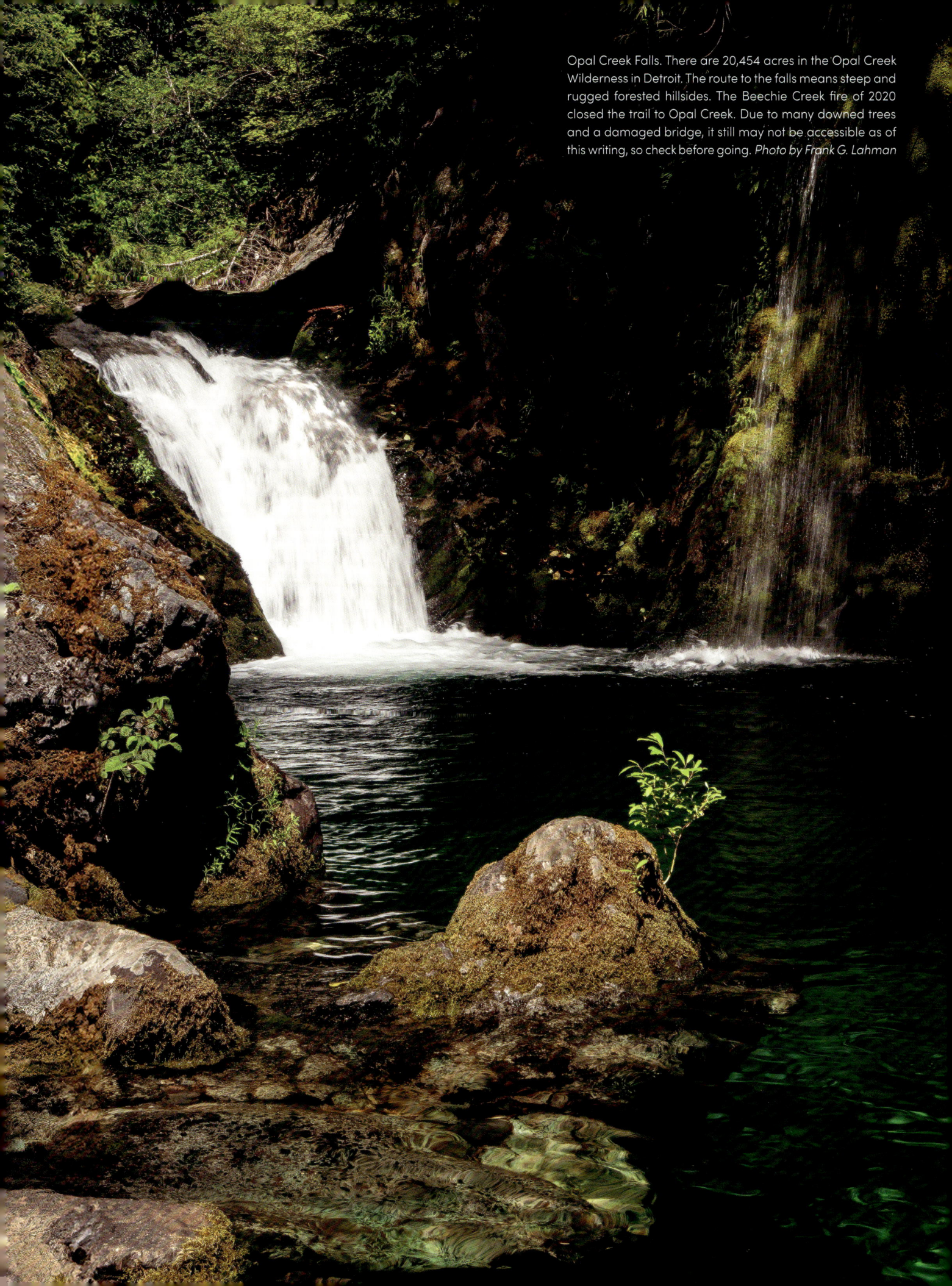

Opal Creek Falls. There are 20,454 acres in the Opal Creek Wilderness in Detroit. The route to the falls means steep and rugged forested hillsides. The Beechie Creek fire of 2020 closed the trail to Opal Creek. Due to many downed trees and a damaged bridge, it still may not be accessible as of this writing, so check before going. *Photo by Frank G. Lahman*

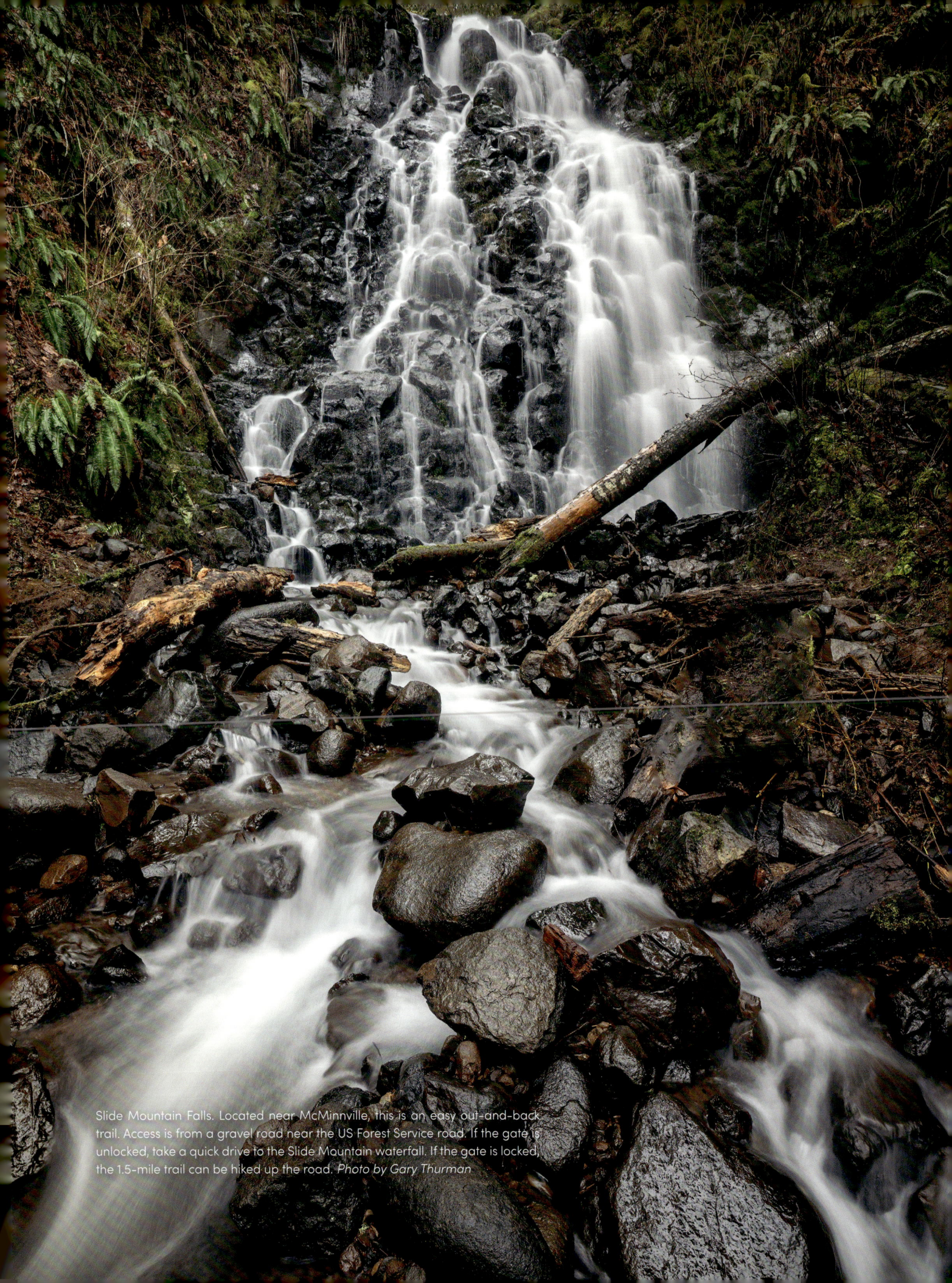

Slide Mountain Falls. Located near McMinnville, this is an easy out-and-back trail. Access is from a gravel road near the US Forest Service road. If the gate is unlocked, take a quick drive to the Slide Mountain waterfall. If the gate is locked, the 1.5-mile trail can be hiked up the road. *Photo by Gary Thurman*

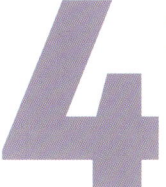

Silver Falls State Park in the Willamette Valley

"The Trail of Ten"

Some of the most prolific and popular waterfalls outside the Columbia River Gorge region are at Silver Falls State Park in the Willamette Valley. The park is the largest state park in Oregon, at 9,200 acres. It includes 35 miles of backcountry trails. The trails and campground were built by the Civilian Conservation Corps (CCC) during the Depression era in the 1930s and early 1940s. Silver Falls State Park is often called the "crown jewel" of the Oregon State Parks system. The 7-mile loop boasts the "Trail of Ten Falls," which can be seen in a day. The hike is considered moderate. One can even walk behind four of the falls (South Falls, Lower South Falls, Middle North Falls, and North Falls). An 11th falls, Frenchie Falls, is seasonal and dries up in summer. Other small, unofficial seasonal falls can occasionally be found within the park.

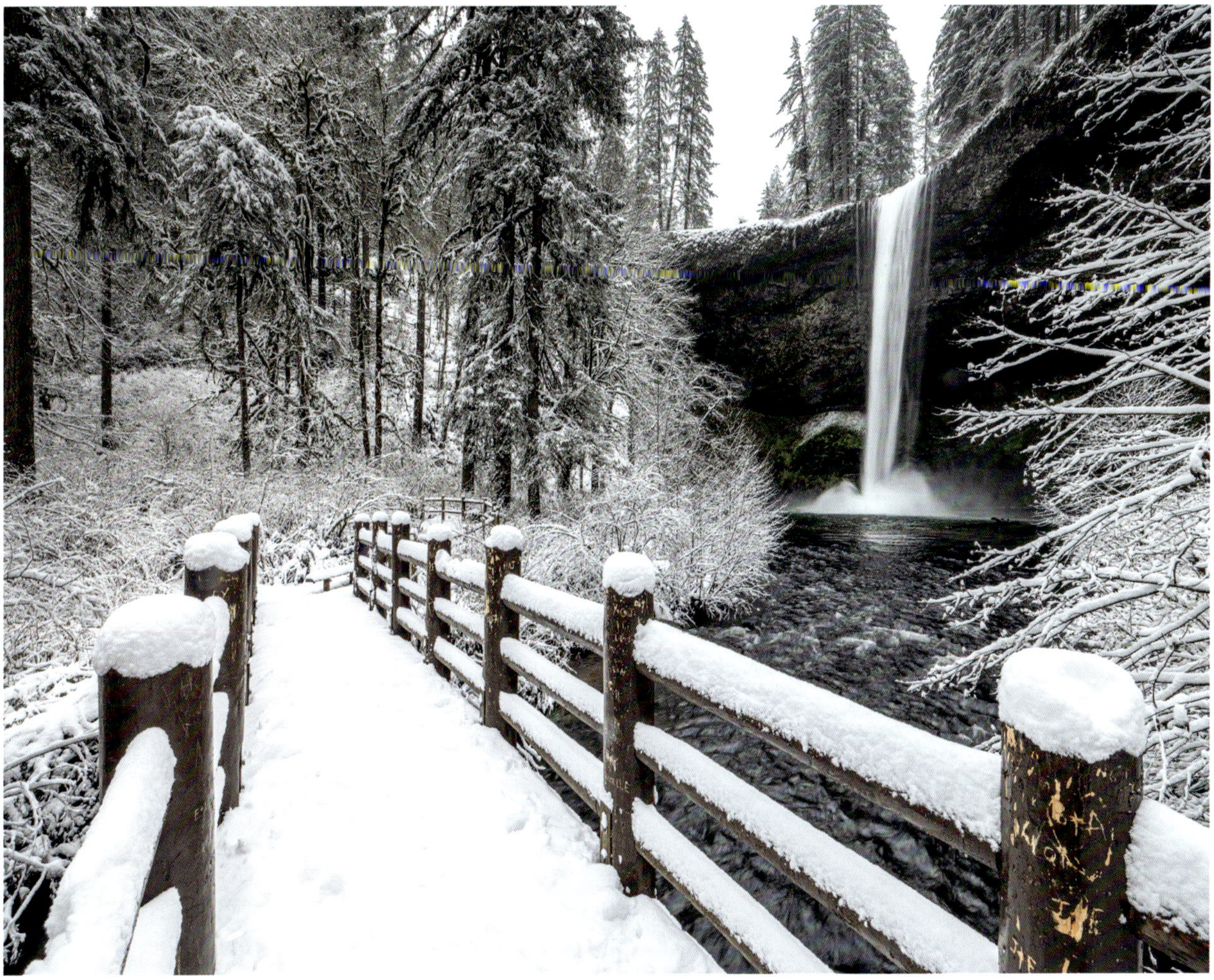

South Falls in winter. The water from South Falls flows off a basalt shelf. Flow is at its peak January through April. This is the most visited waterfall in Silver Falls State Park. The CCC built several bridges at the park, including footbridges and a vehicle bridge. *Photo by Vldn Taylor*

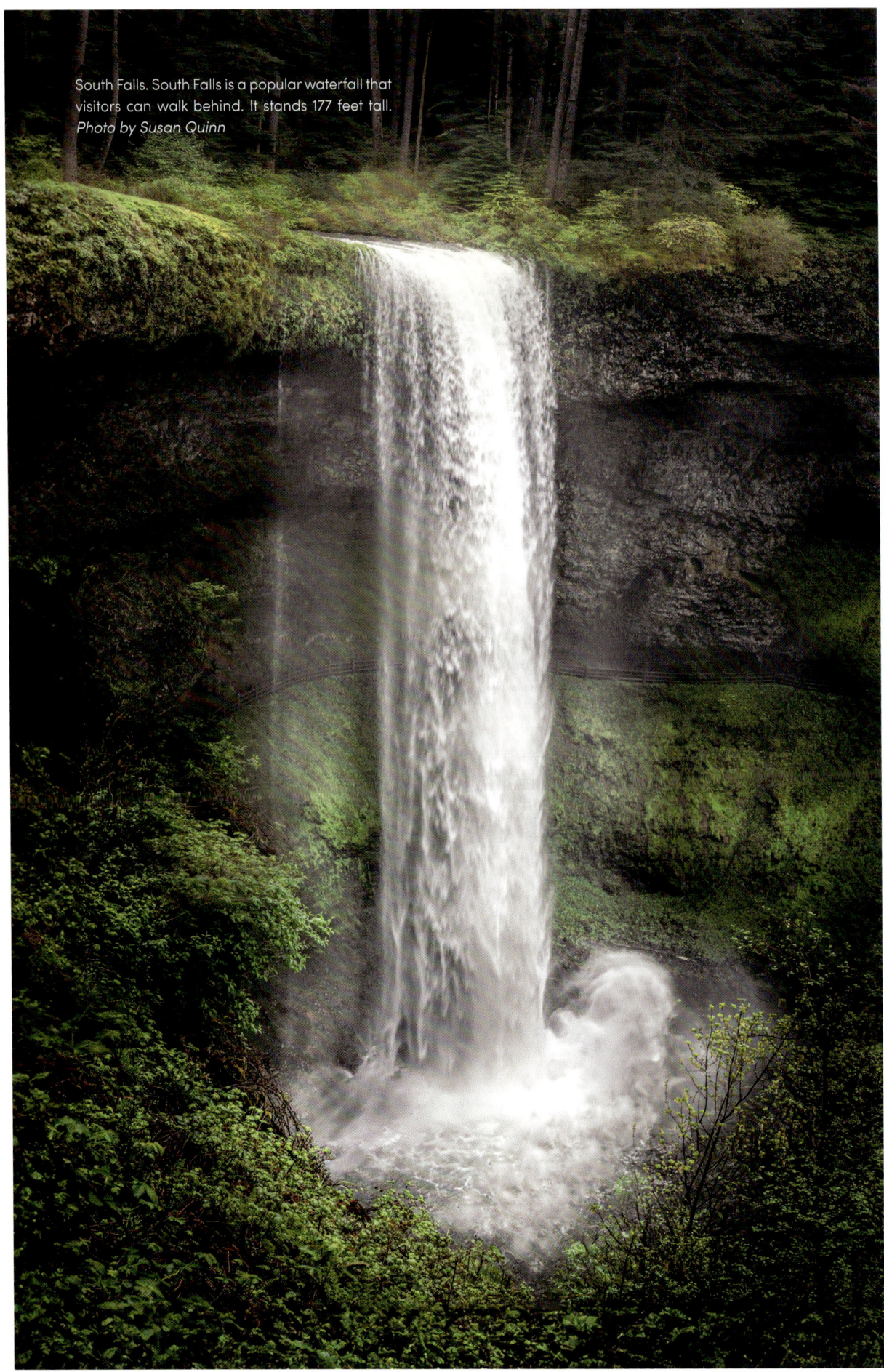

South Falls. South Falls is a popular waterfall that visitors can walk behind. It stands 177 feet tall.
Photo by Susan Quinn

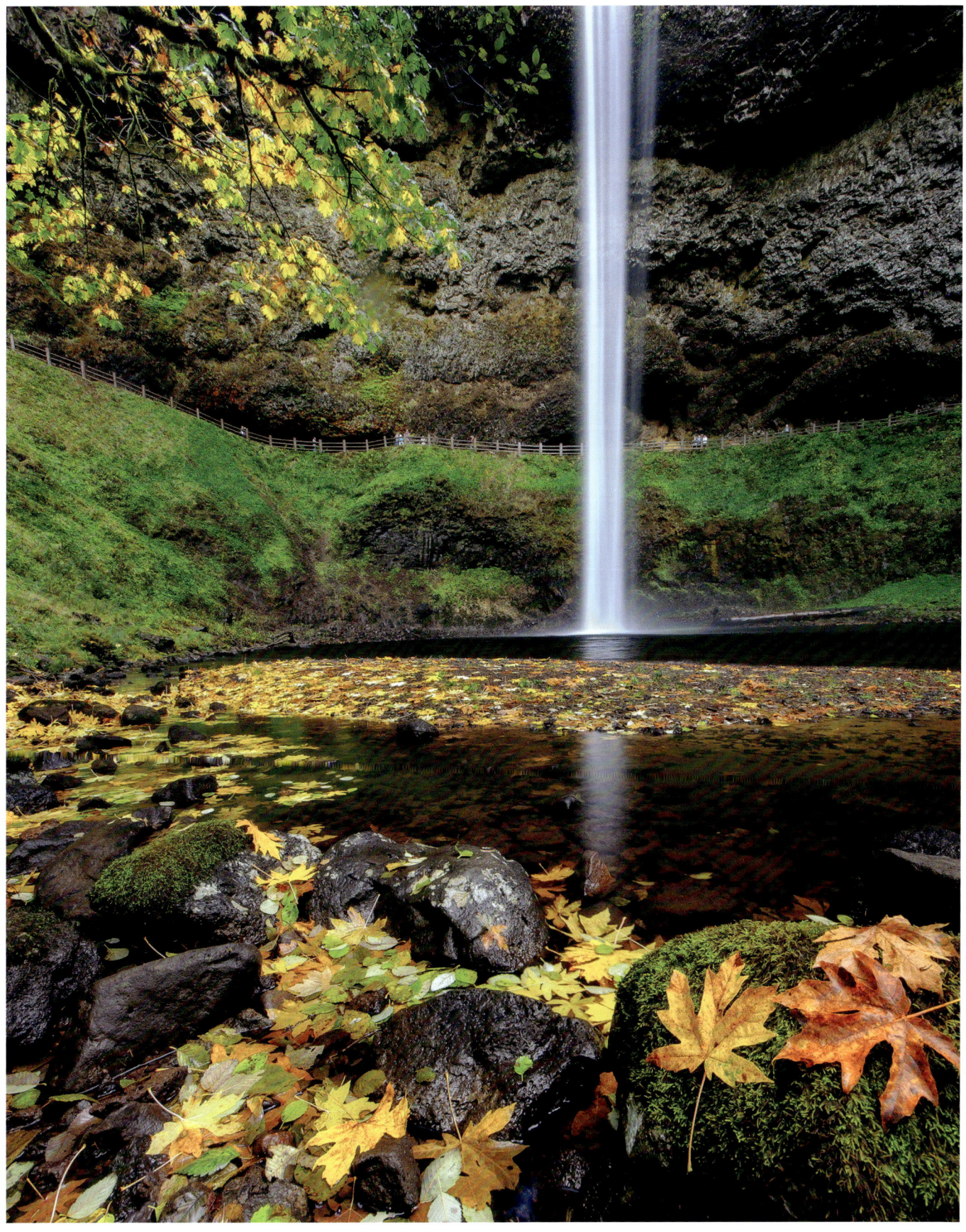

South Falls. Open year-round, South Falls is spectacular in any season but especially colorful in the fall. *Photo by Clem Paslack*

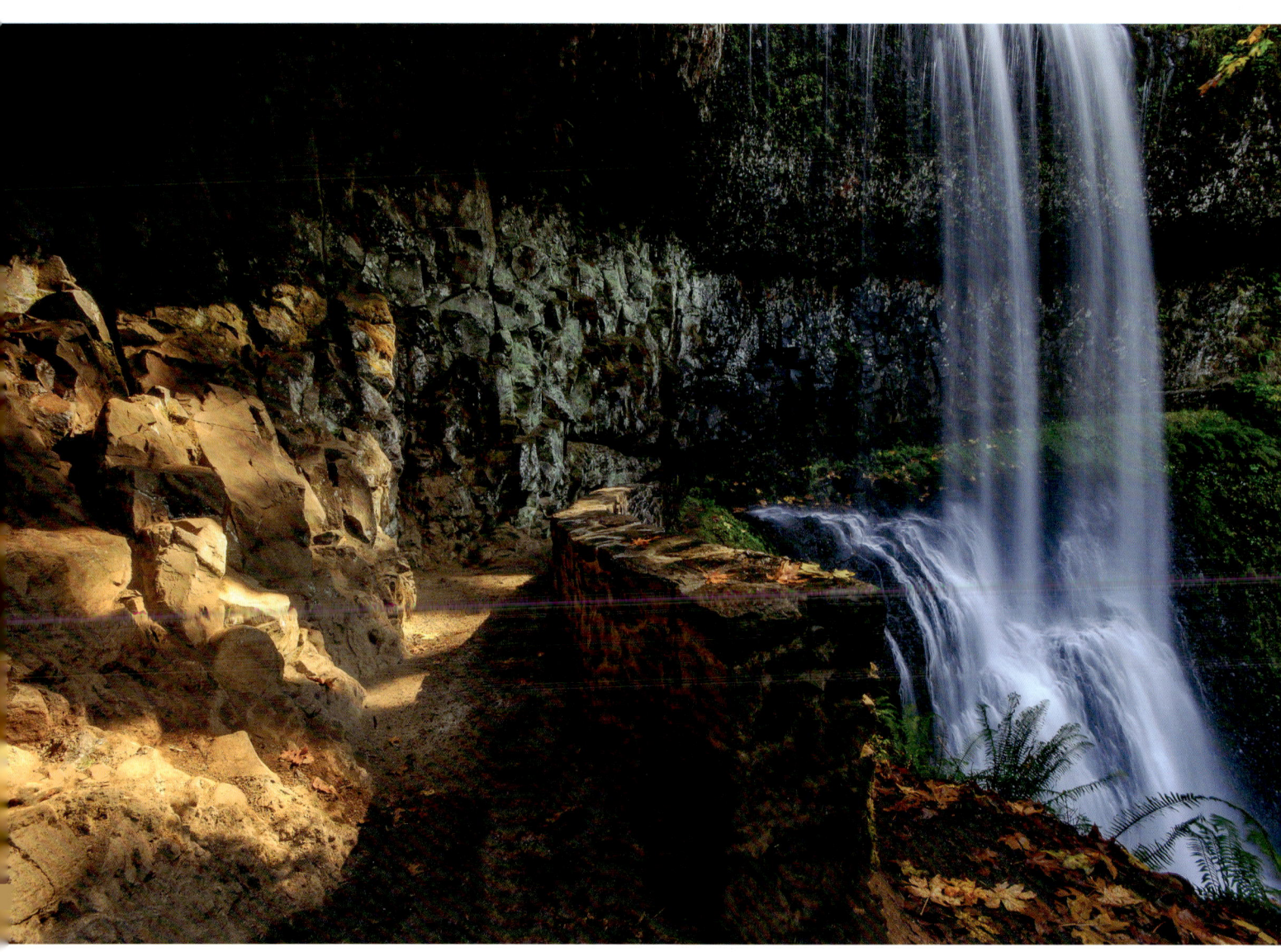

Lower South Falls. One of the four waterfalls one can walk behind is Lower South Falls. It is also one of the larger waterfalls in the park, at 93 feet. *Photo by Clem Paslack*

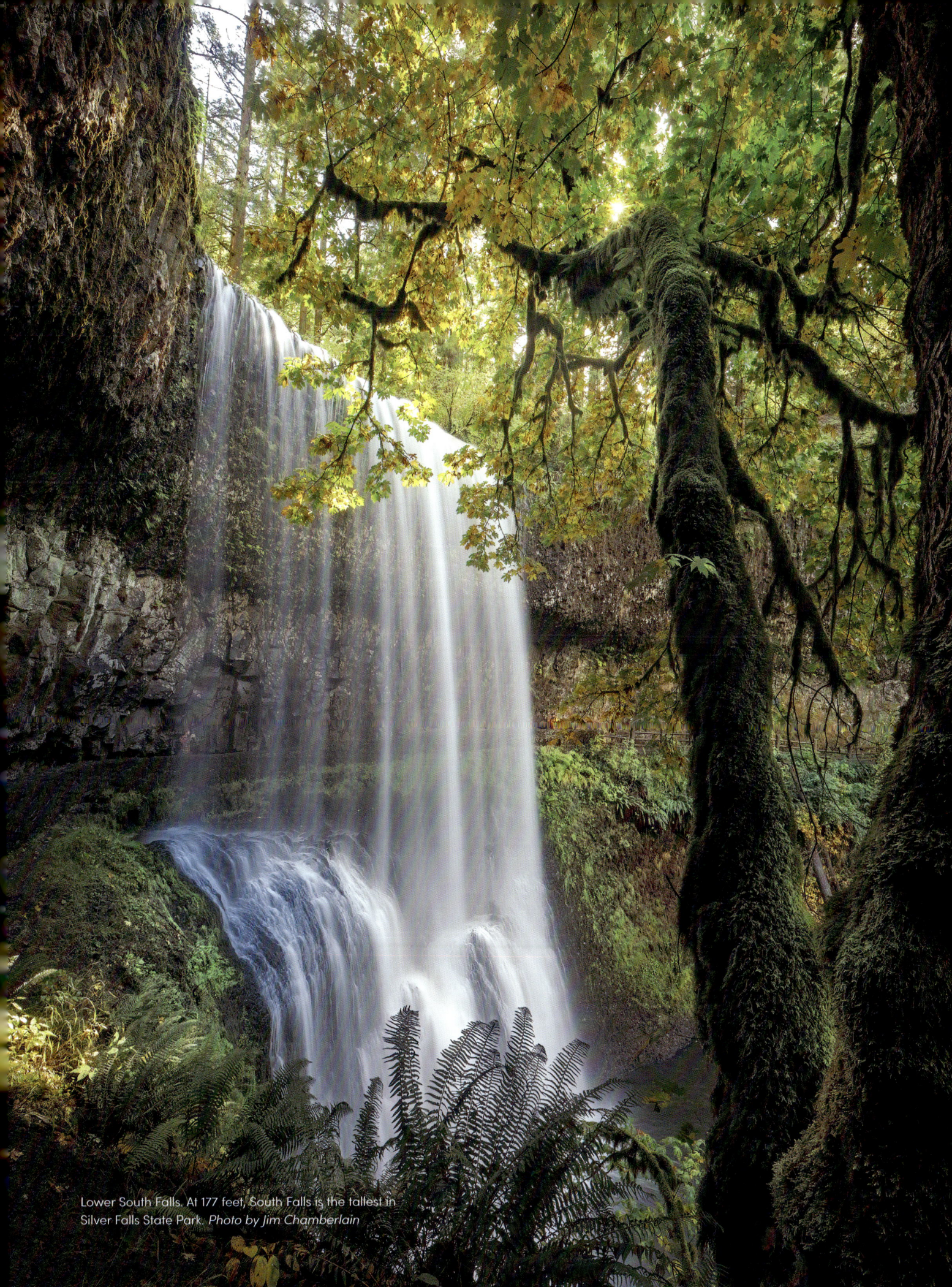

Lower South Falls. At 177 feet, South Falls is the tallest in Silver Falls State Park. *Photo by Jim Chamberlain*

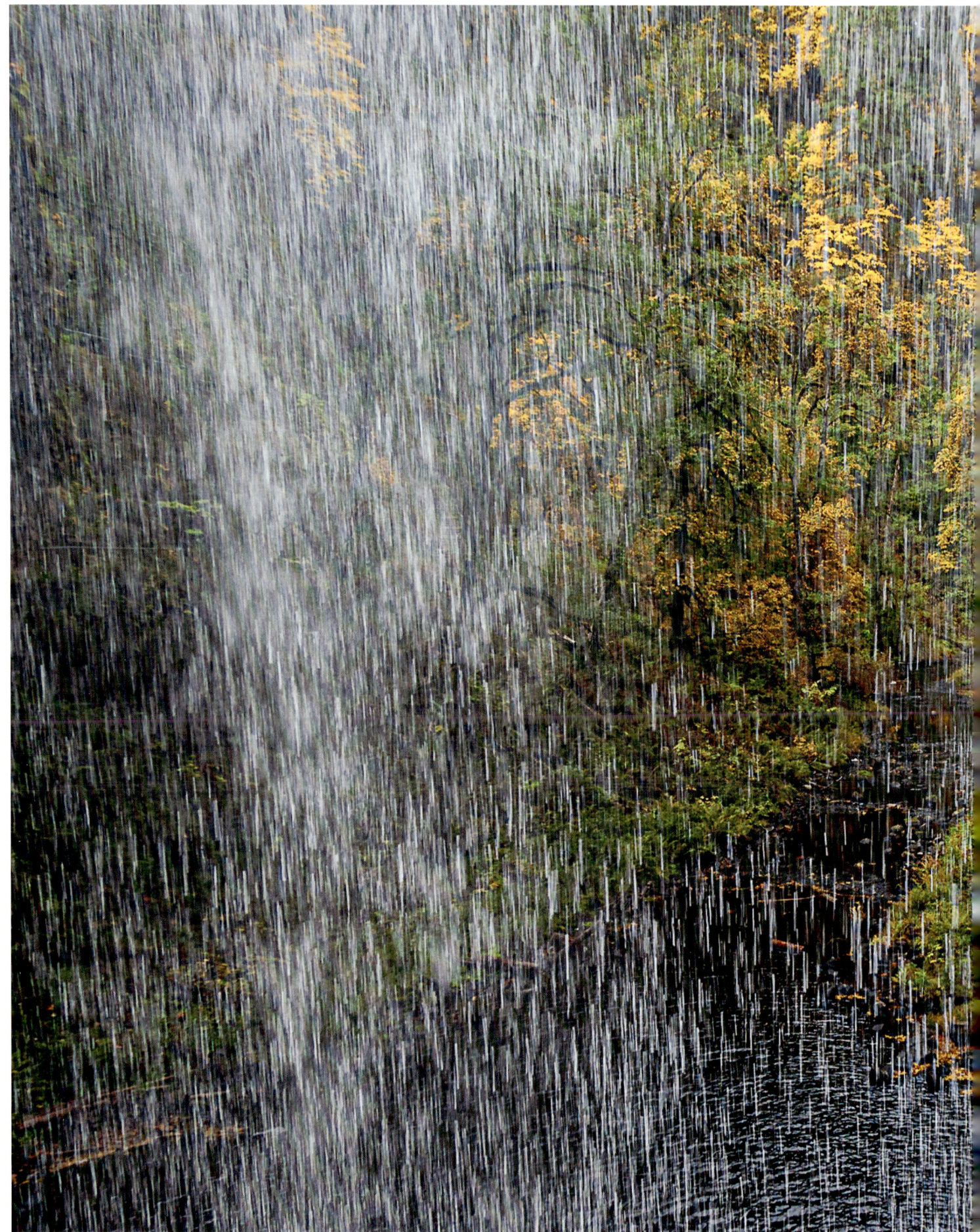

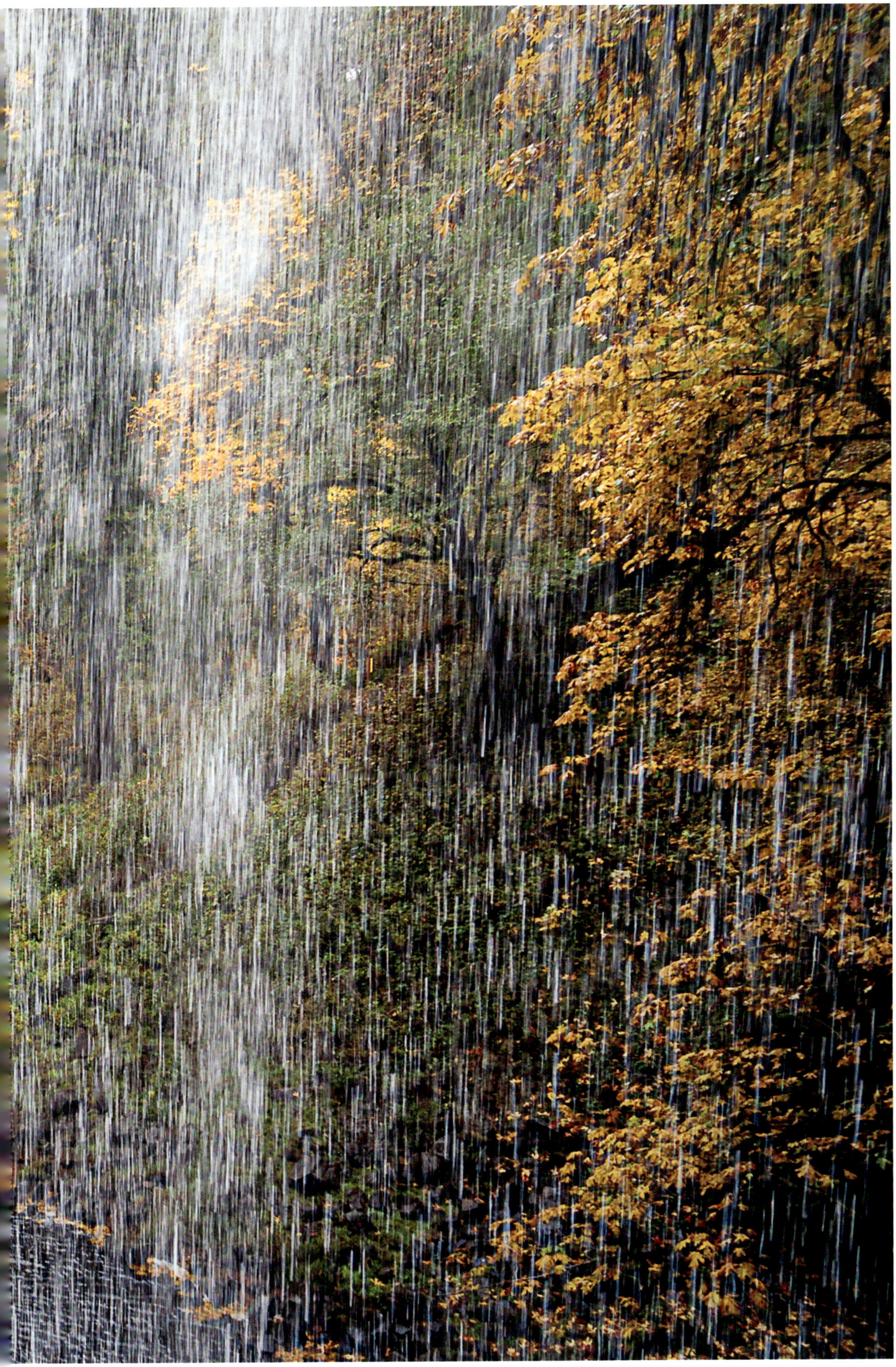

Behind Lower South Falls. South Falls is one of the most photographed waterfalls in Oregon. *Photo by Frank G. Lehman*

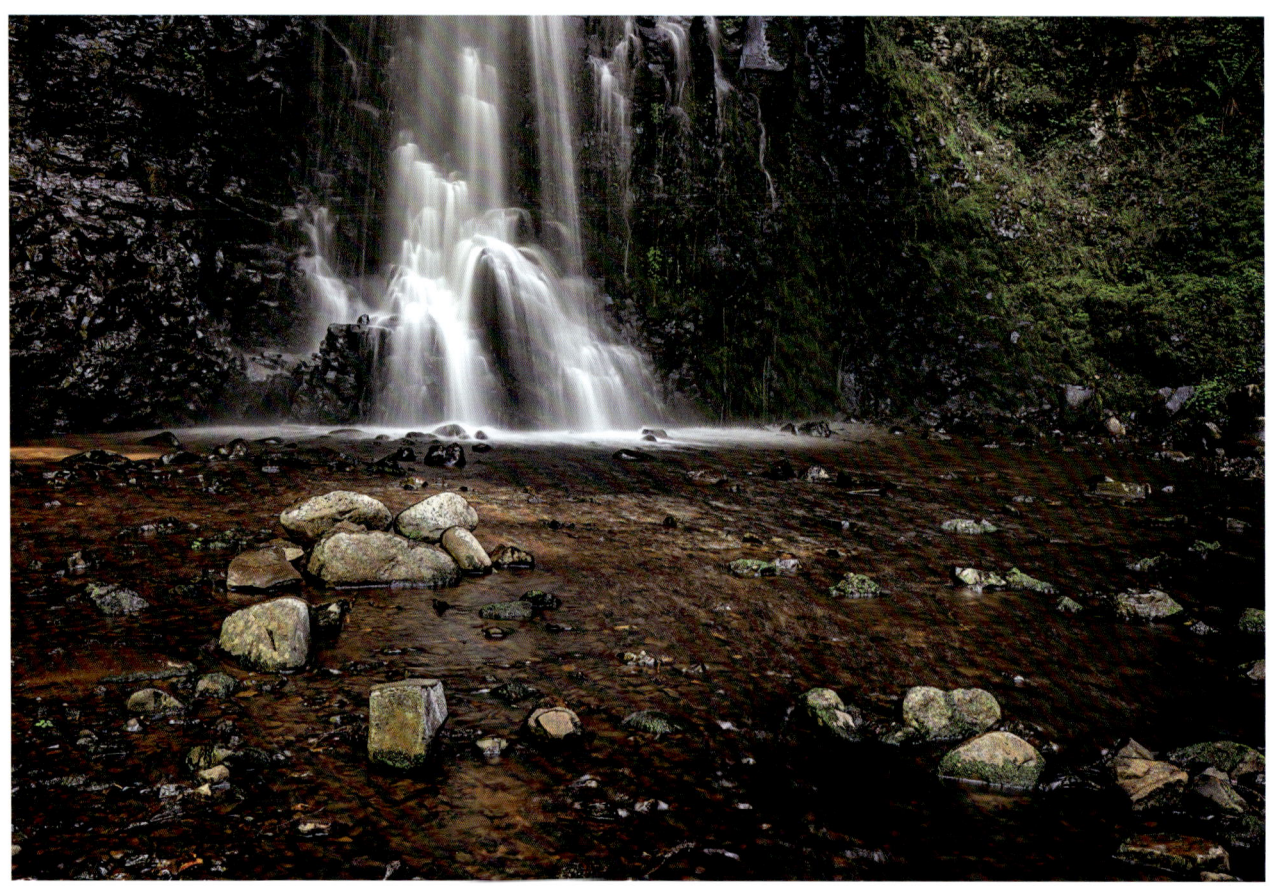

Double Falls. This impressive waterfall is a seasonal, tiered waterfall with two drops that total 178 feet in height. *Photo by Jim Chamberlain*

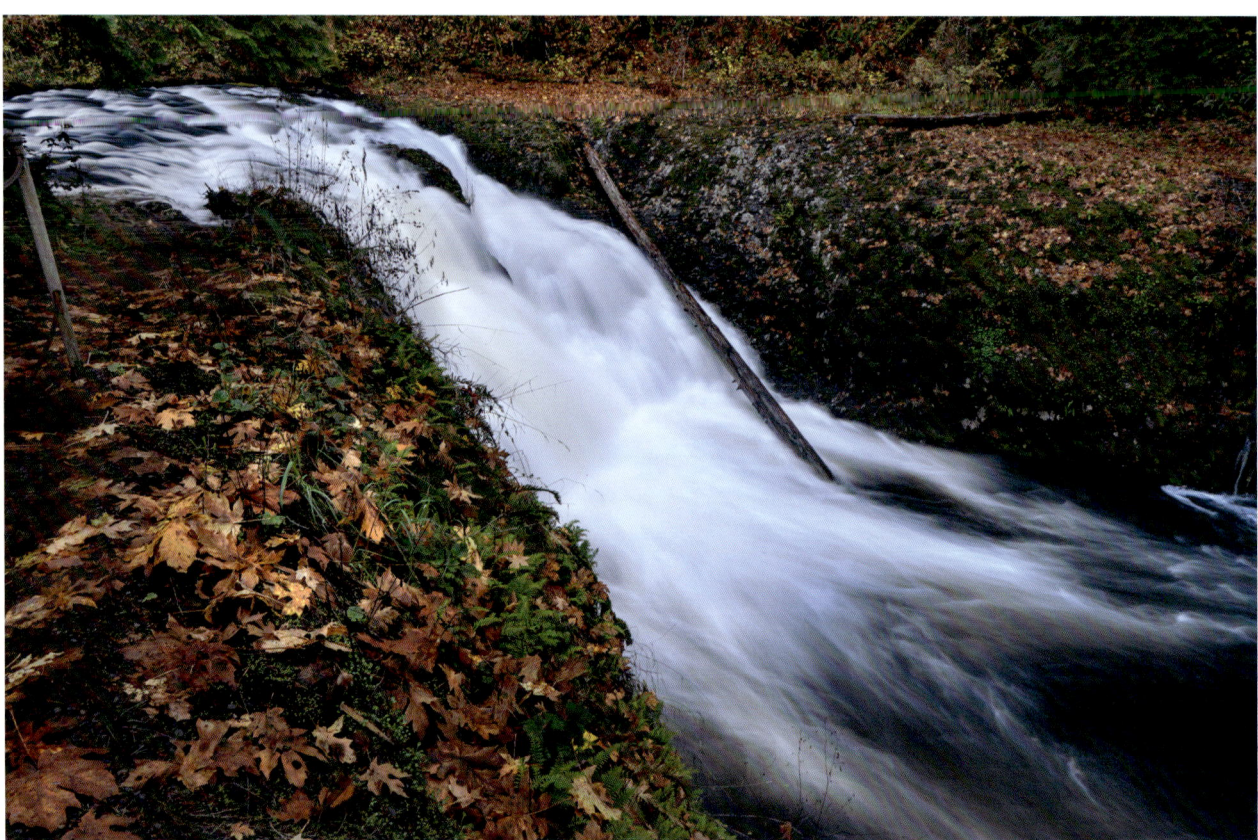

Twin Falls. This is one of the smaller waterfalls in Silver Falls State Park. A large rock splits the flow into two channels; hence its name. Due to an abundance of trees, it may be harder to photograph than others in the park. *Photo by Adam Marland*

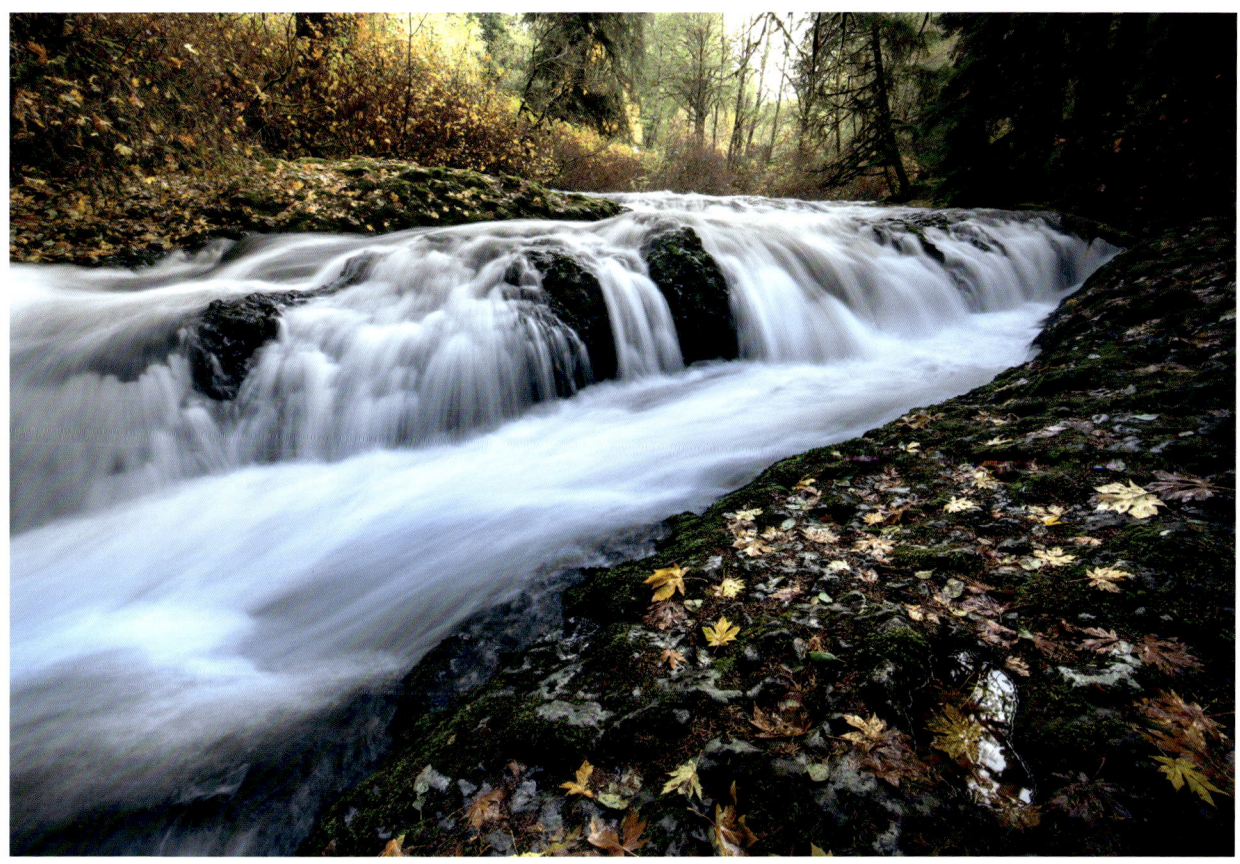

Unnamed waterfall in Silver Falls. Like almost any area in Oregon with abundant water flow, small unofficial falls sometimes crop up, like this one in Silver Falls State Park. *Photo by Adam Marland*

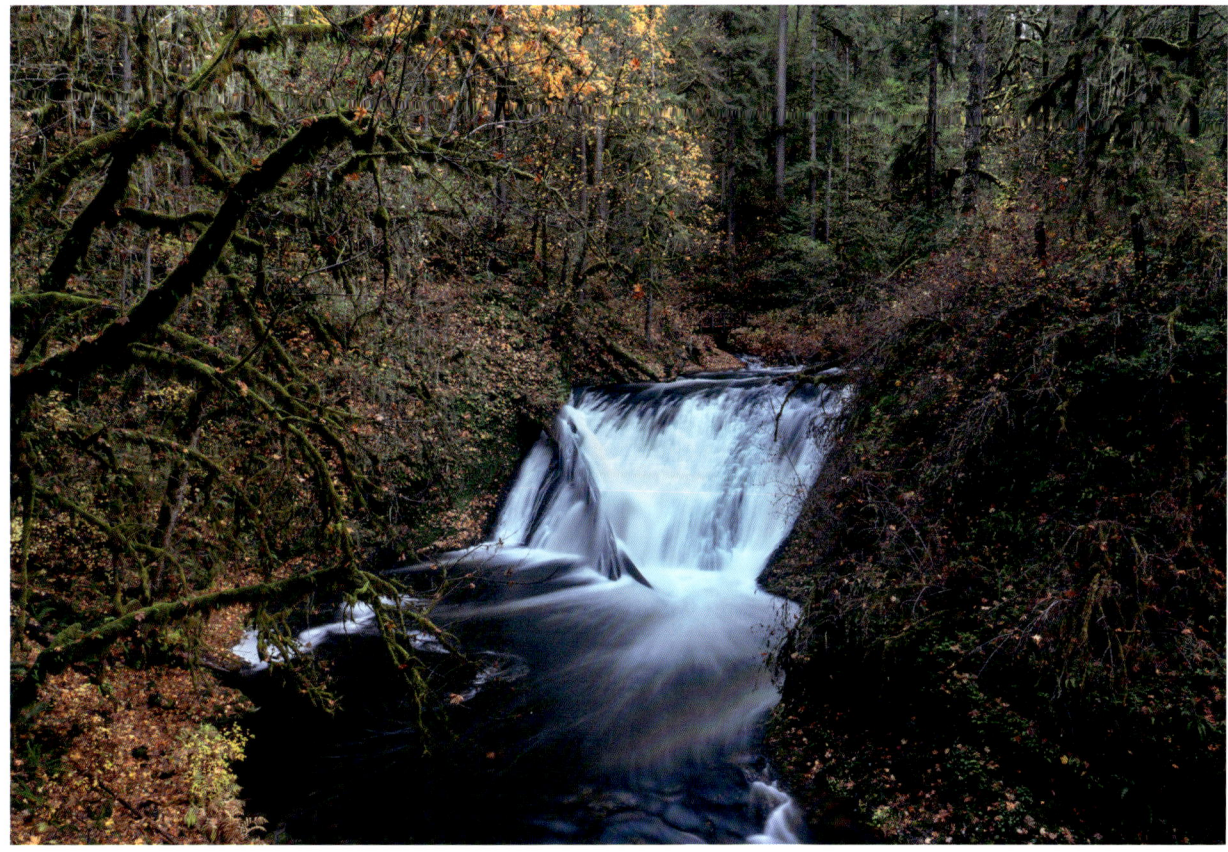

Drake Falls. At 27 feet, this waterfall is the shortest of the waterfalls on the Trail of Ten Falls. It is named after June Drake, a local photographer who discovered and named the waterfalls in the late 1880s and helped establish the park. *Photo by Adam Marland*

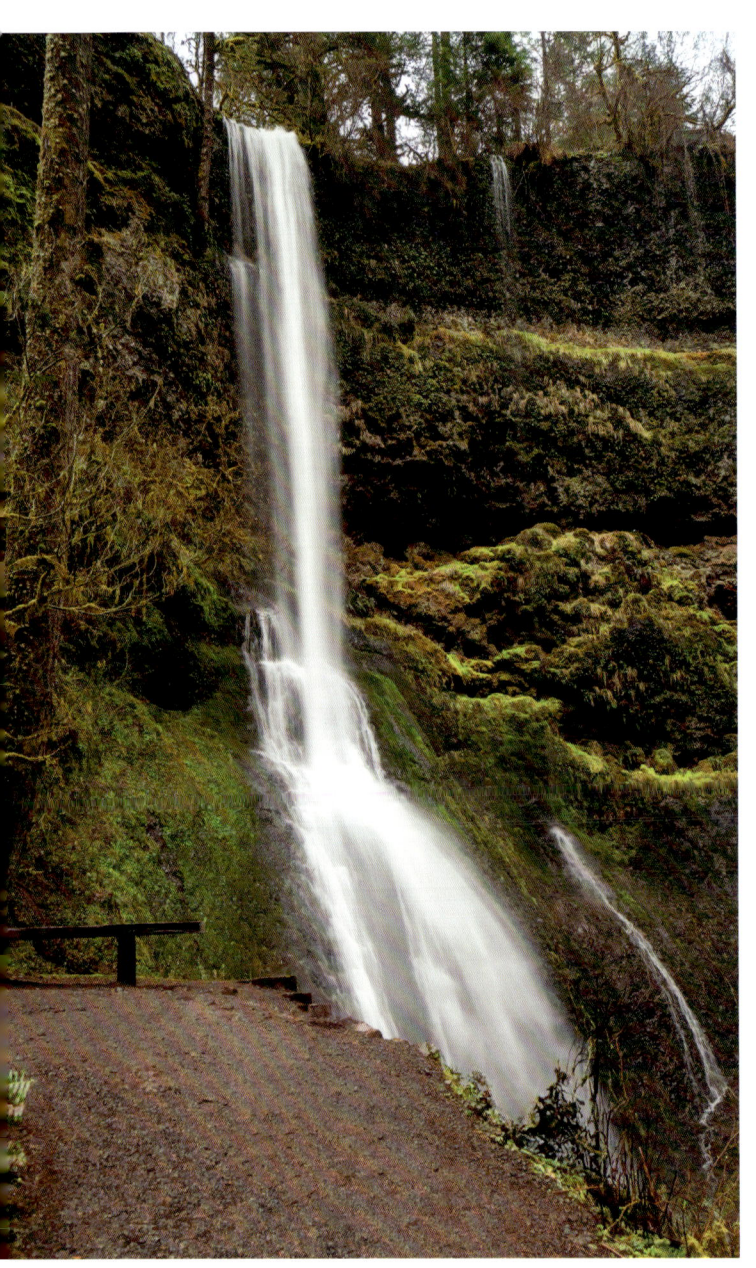

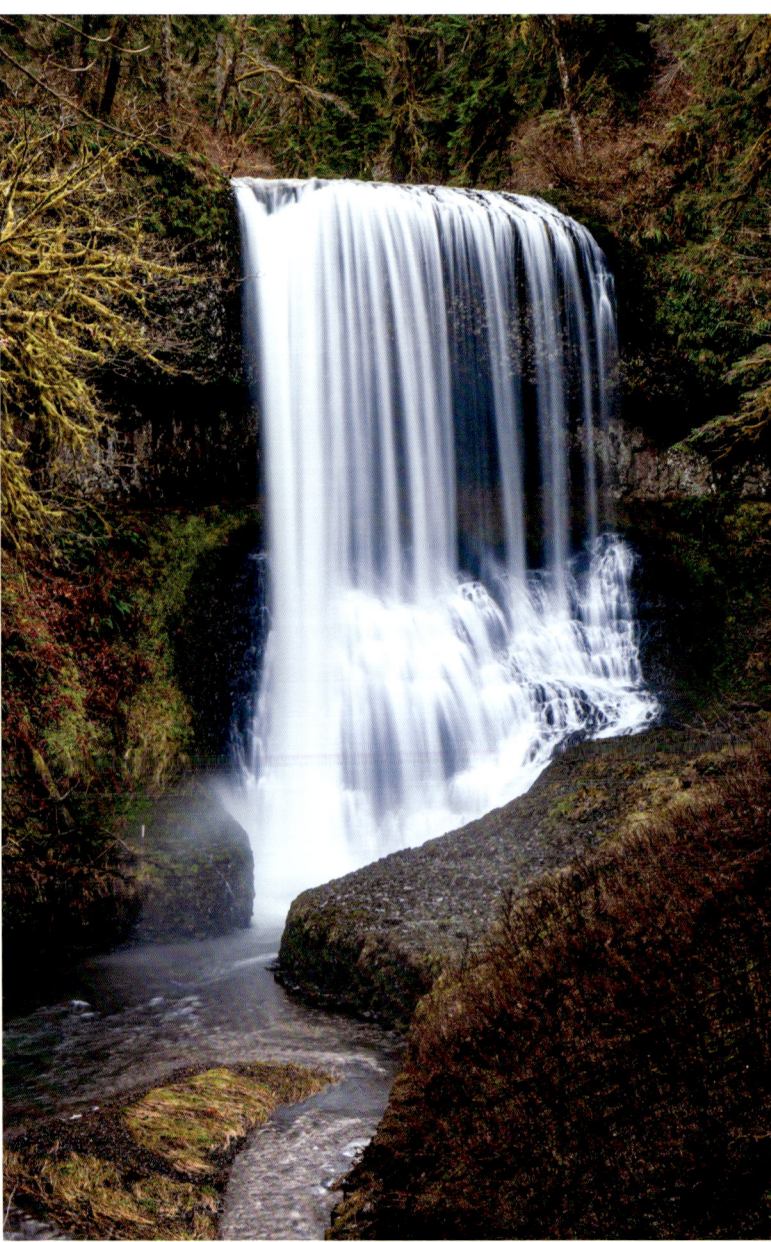

Winter Falls. This waterfall trail is considered a moderately challenging route due to the elevation gain and takes over two hours to complete. Winter Falls is a 134-foot waterfall, best seen in the winter and the spring. *Photo by Alana Starkweather*

Middle North Falls. Considered one of the most majestic waterfalls in Silver Falls State Park, Middle North Falls is moderately challenging due to its steepness. *Photo by Frank G. Lahman*

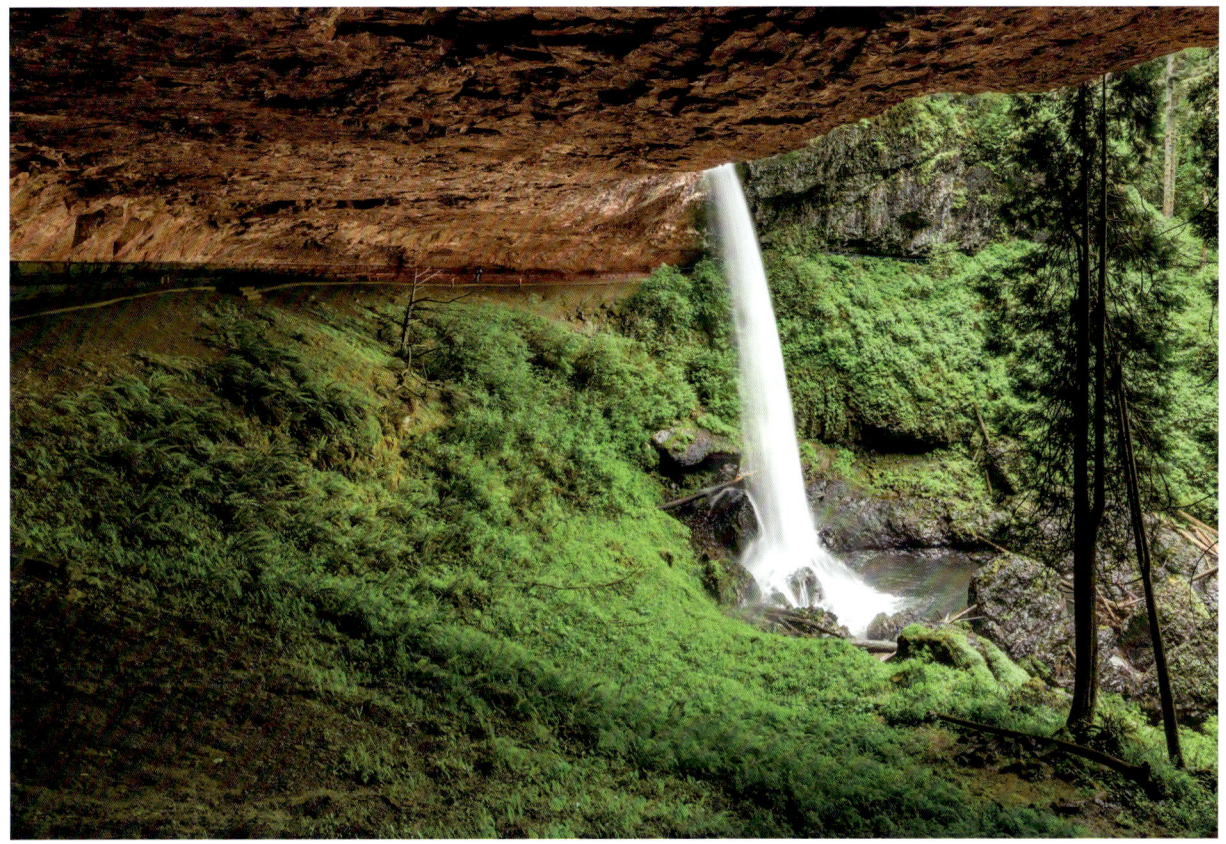

North Falls overhang. There are 78 stairs leading to this large rock overhang at North Falls. Hikers can walk behind it.
Photo by Frank G. Lahman

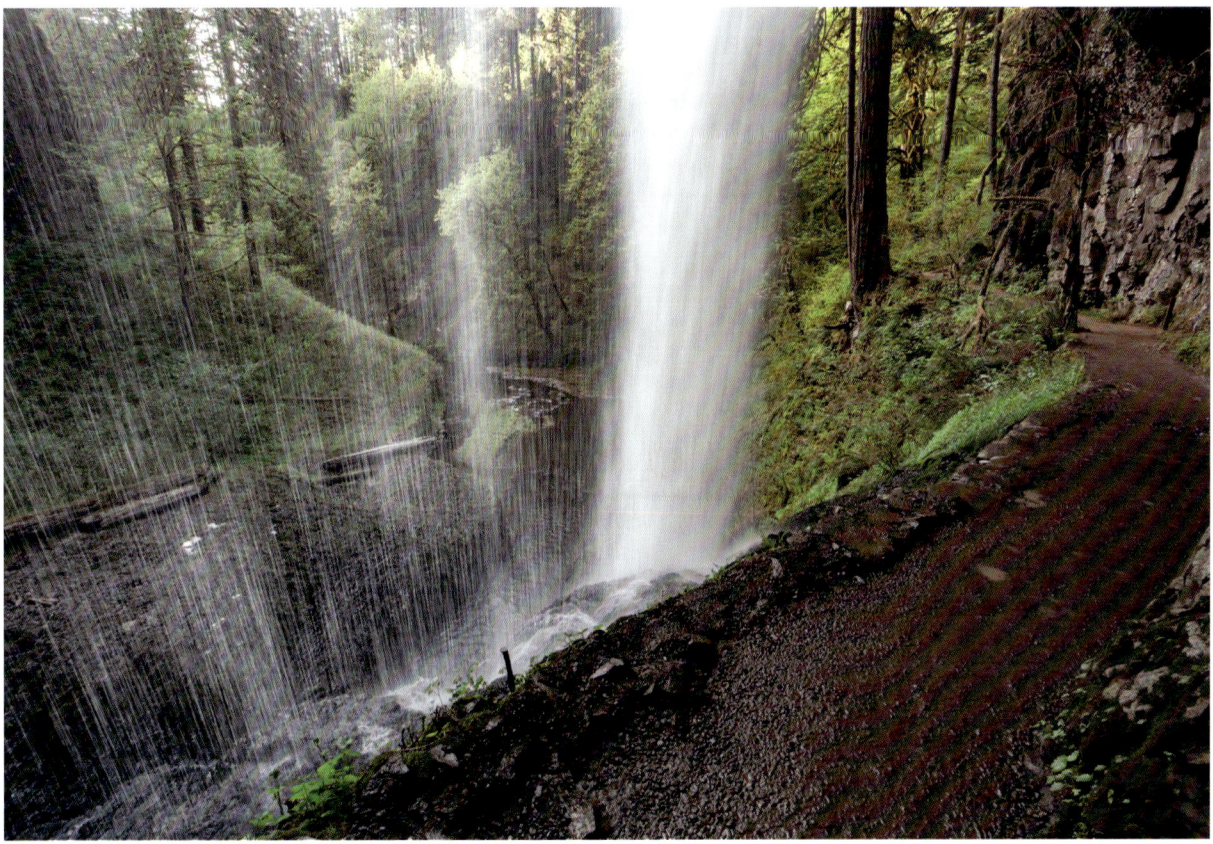

Behind Middle North Falls. Be prepared to feel a little spray! The hike to Middle North Falls is worth it. *Photo by Jim Chamberlain*

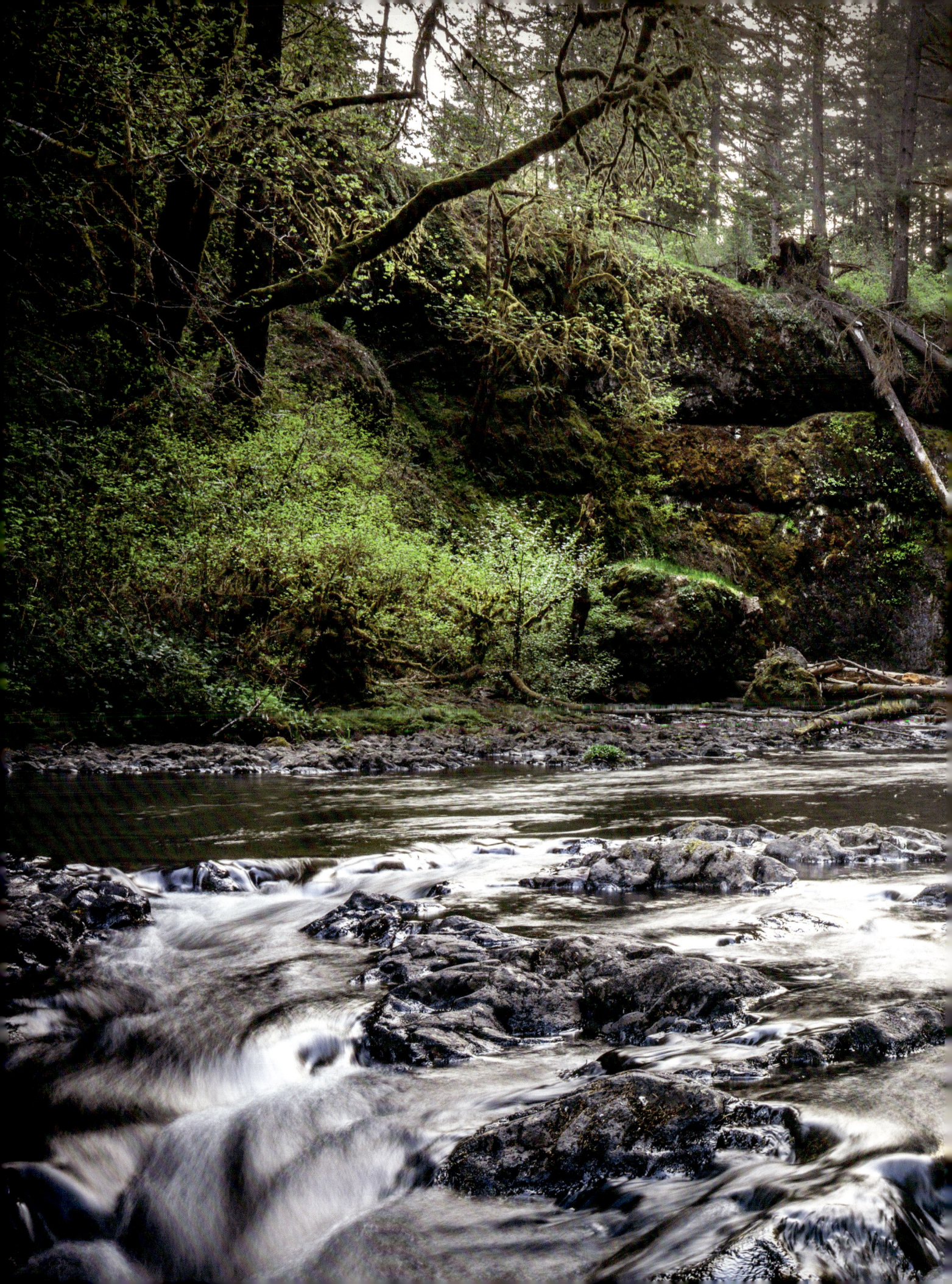

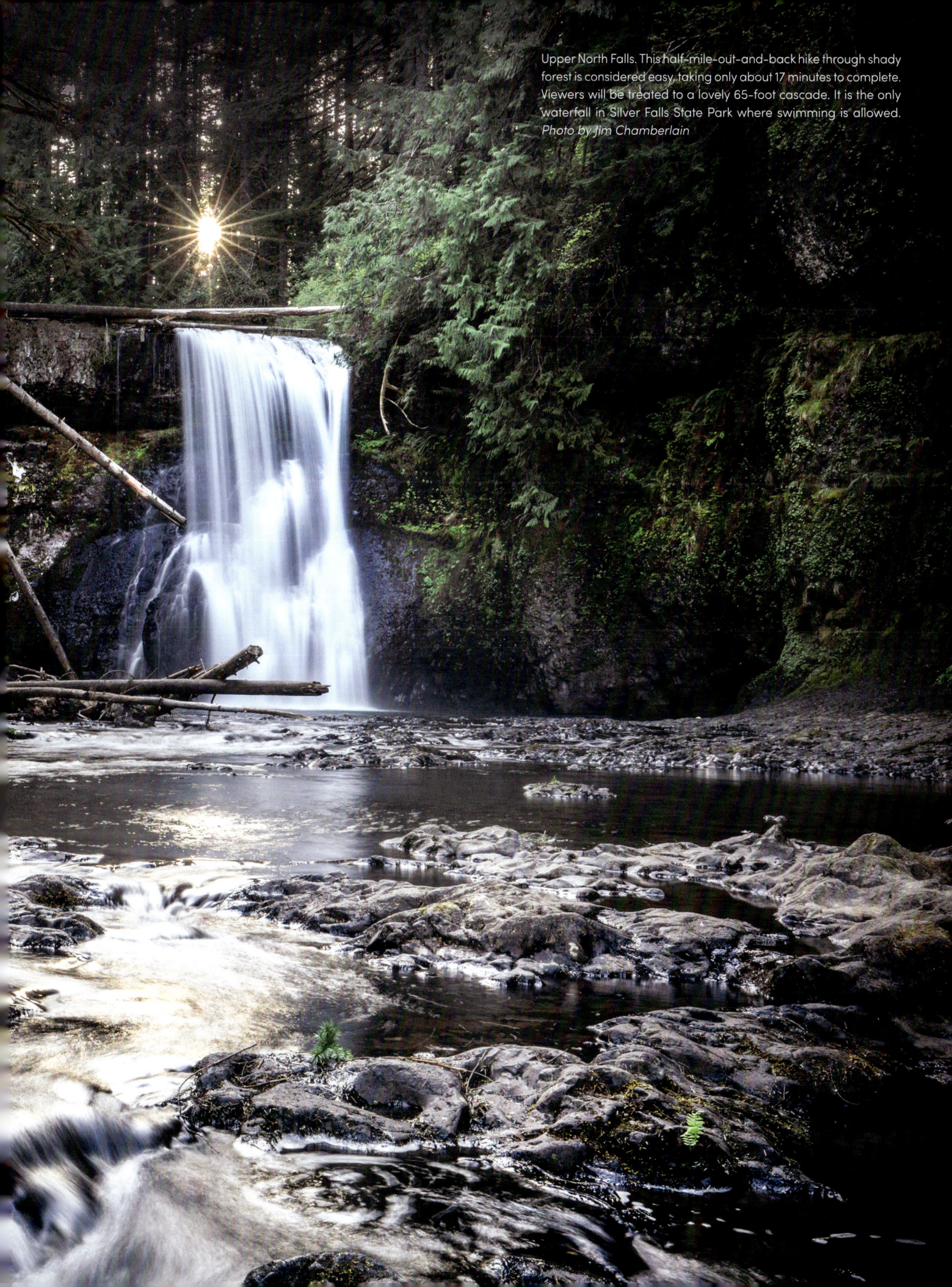

Upper North Falls. This half-mile-out-and-back hike through shady forest is considered easy, taking only about 17 minutes to complete. Viewers will be treated to a lovely 65-foot cascade. It is the only waterfall in Silver Falls State Park where swimming is allowed. *Photo by Jim Chamberlain*

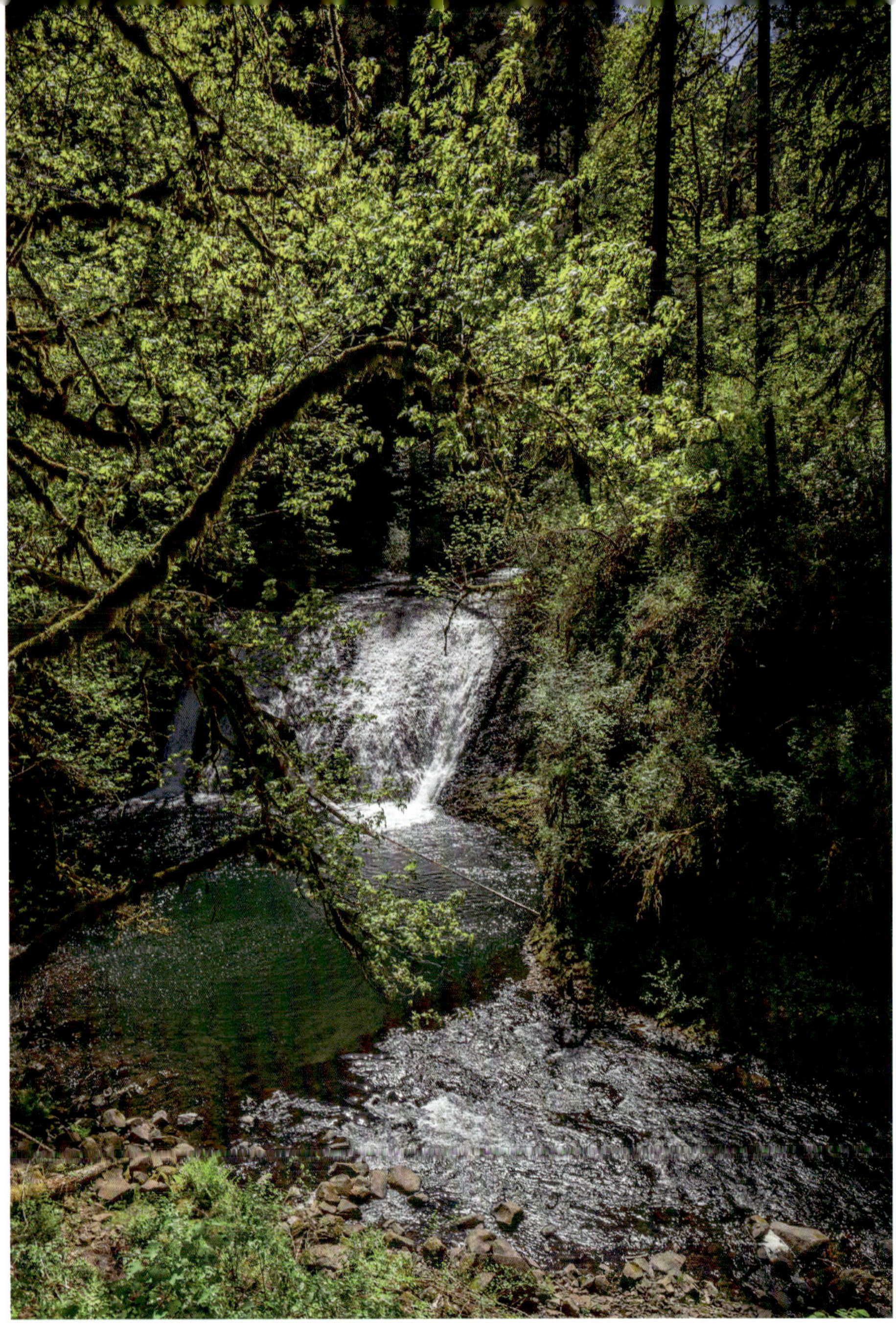

Lower North Falls. Lower North Falls is the farthest from the Silver Falls State Park Trail of Ten Falls. It's a quarter of a mile north of Drake Falls. This spot is in one of the more serene stretches along the trail. *Photo by Jim Chamberlain*

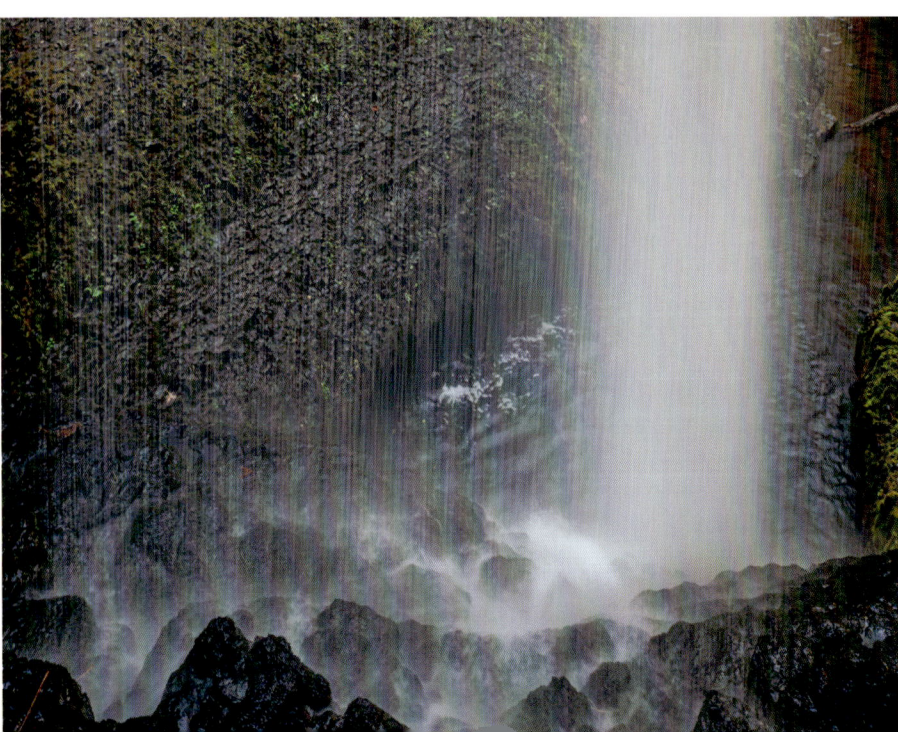

Detail of Lower North Falls. This 30-foot plunge-type waterfall is considered one of the most photogenic waterfalls in Silver Falls State Park. *Photo by George F. Peterson*

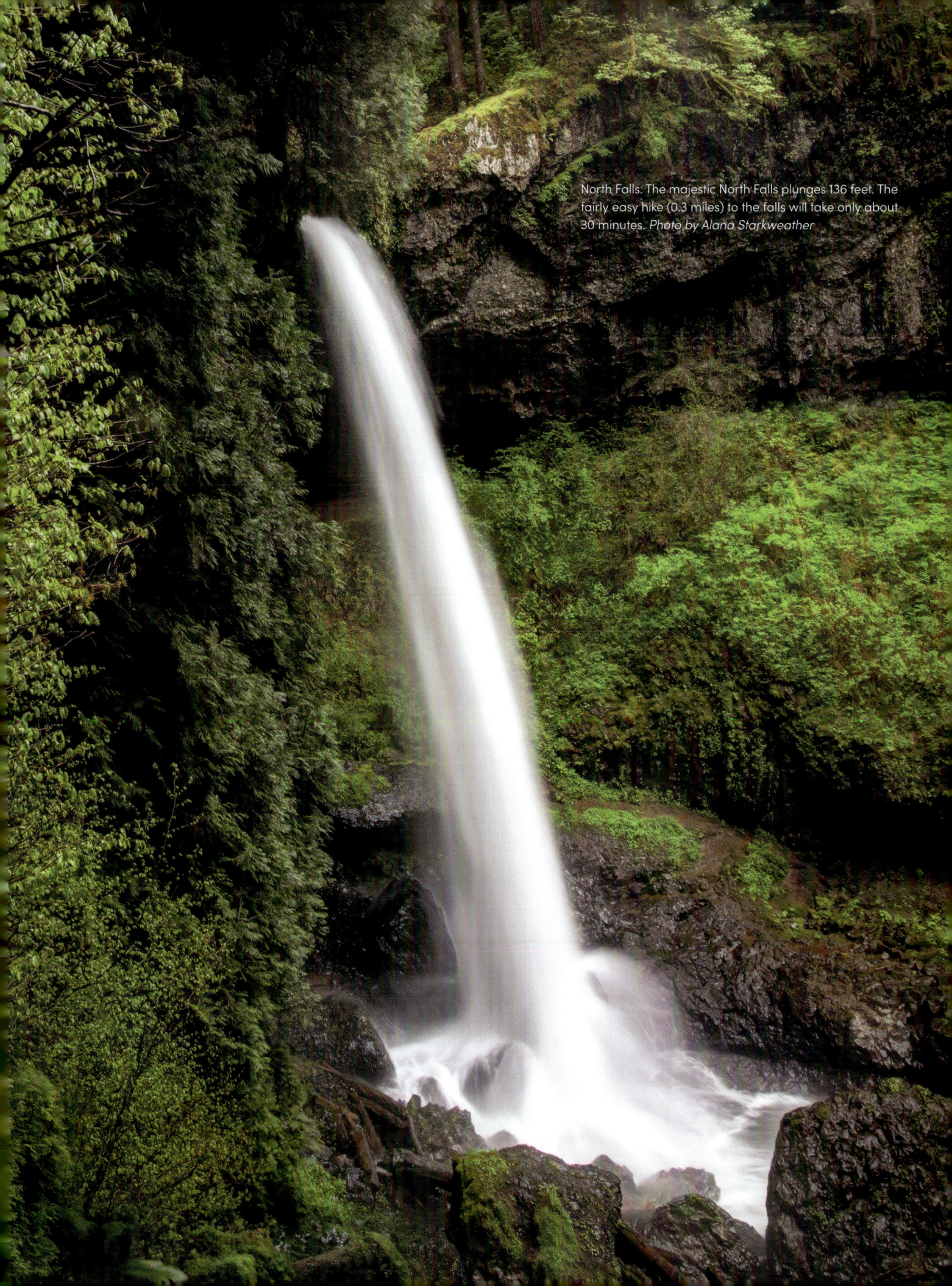

North Falls. The majestic North Falls plunges 136 feet. The fairly easy hike (0.3 miles) to the falls will take only about 30 minutes. *Photo by Alana Starkweather*

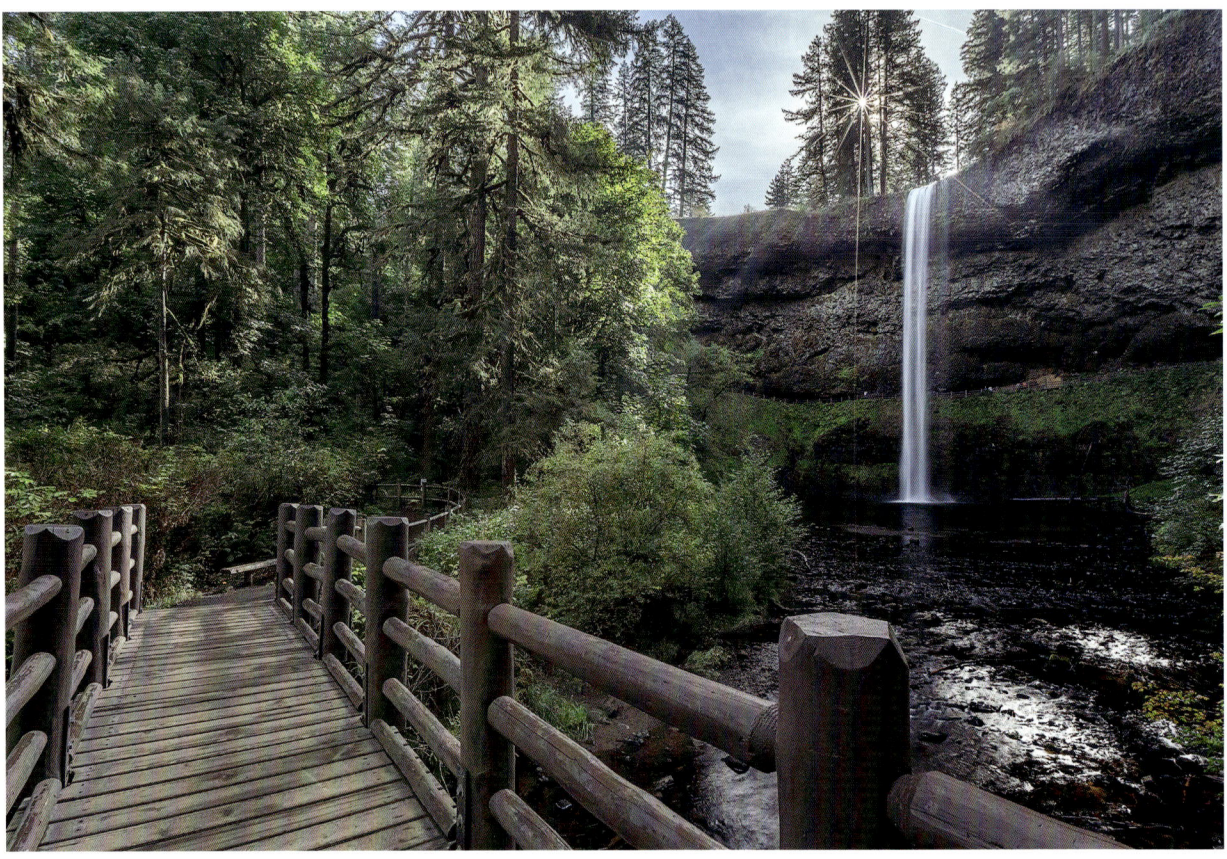

South Falls. The South Falls Loop Hike is the most popular in Silver Falls State Park. Hikers can be seen on a trail behind the falls. The CCC built trails, buildings, walls, picnic shelters, and bridges in the 1930s that still stand today. *Photo by Vldn Taylor*

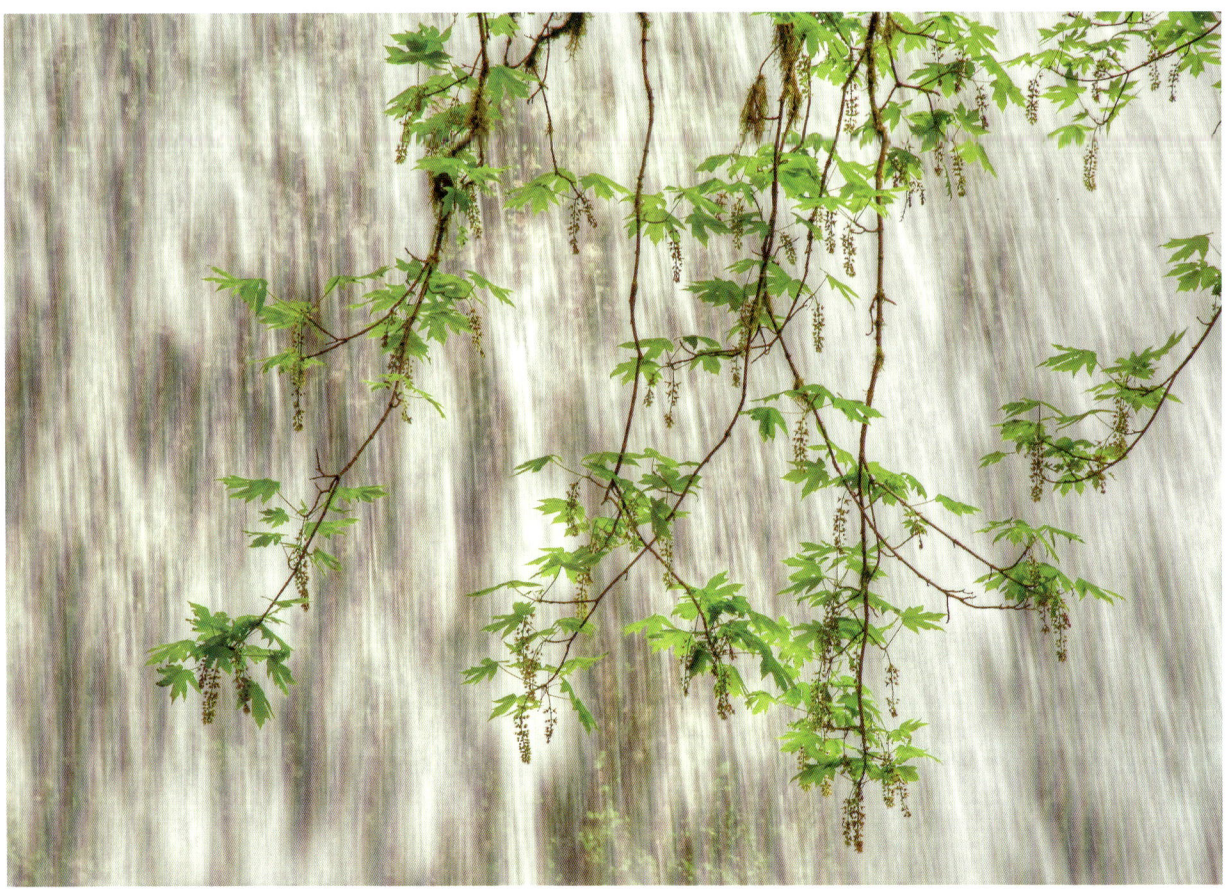

Detail of waterfall in Silver Falls State Park. *Photo by Sue Newman*

5 Central Oregon Cascades

The Cascade Range was named after the Cascade Rapids in the Columbia River. They were often-unsurmountable barriers to Lewis and Clark and other early pioneers. The surrounding mountains became known as the "Cascades." There are several spectacular falls to be found in the Cascade Mountains of central Oregon along or near the Deschutes River. The Cascade Range covers about 17,000 square miles and is almost entirely volcanic in origin. Many falls are in proximity to Bend, Oregon. Some, such as Tumalo Falls, 30 minutes from Bend, are breathtaking in any season, including winter hikes through snow and ice. Steelhead Falls, closer to Terrebonne, can be combined with a visit to the picturesque Smith Rock. The Metolius River, with its green-turquoise water, also won't disappoint! The rapids there cascade delicately, forming mini waterfalls. To see cliffs and waterfalls formed by hot ash and pumice from 75,000 years ago, head to Paulina Falls, with its 80-foot drop.

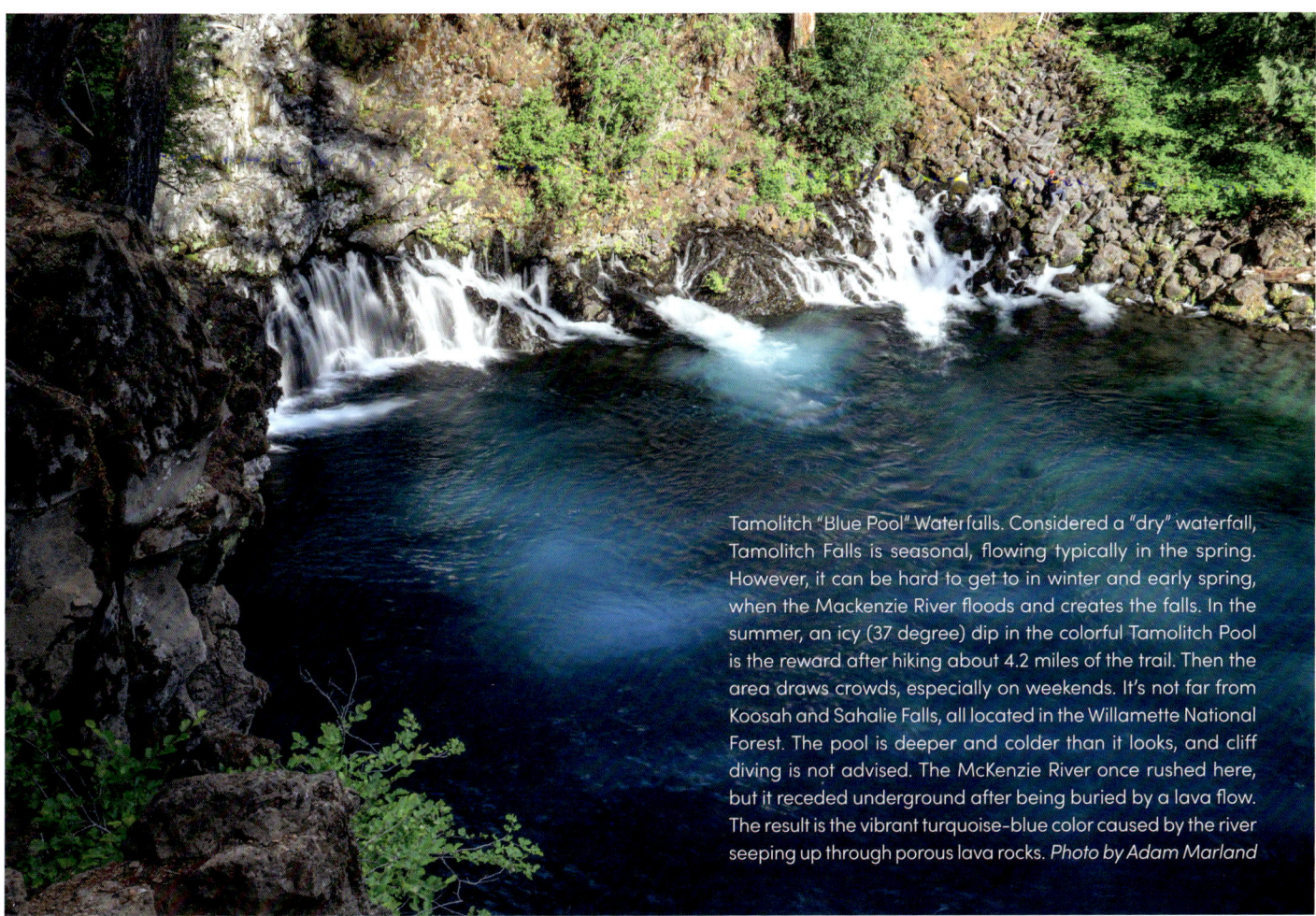

Tamolitch "Blue Pool" Waterfalls. Considered a "dry" waterfall, Tamolitch Falls is seasonal, flowing typically in the spring. However, it can be hard to get to in winter and early spring, when the Mackenzie River floods and creates the falls. In the summer, an icy (37 degree) dip in the colorful Tamolitch Pool is the reward after hiking about 4.2 miles of the trail. Then the area draws crowds, especially on weekends. It's not far from Koosah and Sahalie Falls, all located in the Willamette National Forest. The pool is deeper and colder than it looks, and cliff diving is not advised. The McKenzie River once rushed here, but it receded underground after being buried by a lava flow. The result is the vibrant turquoise-blue color caused by the river seeping up through porous lava rocks. *Photo by Adam Marland*

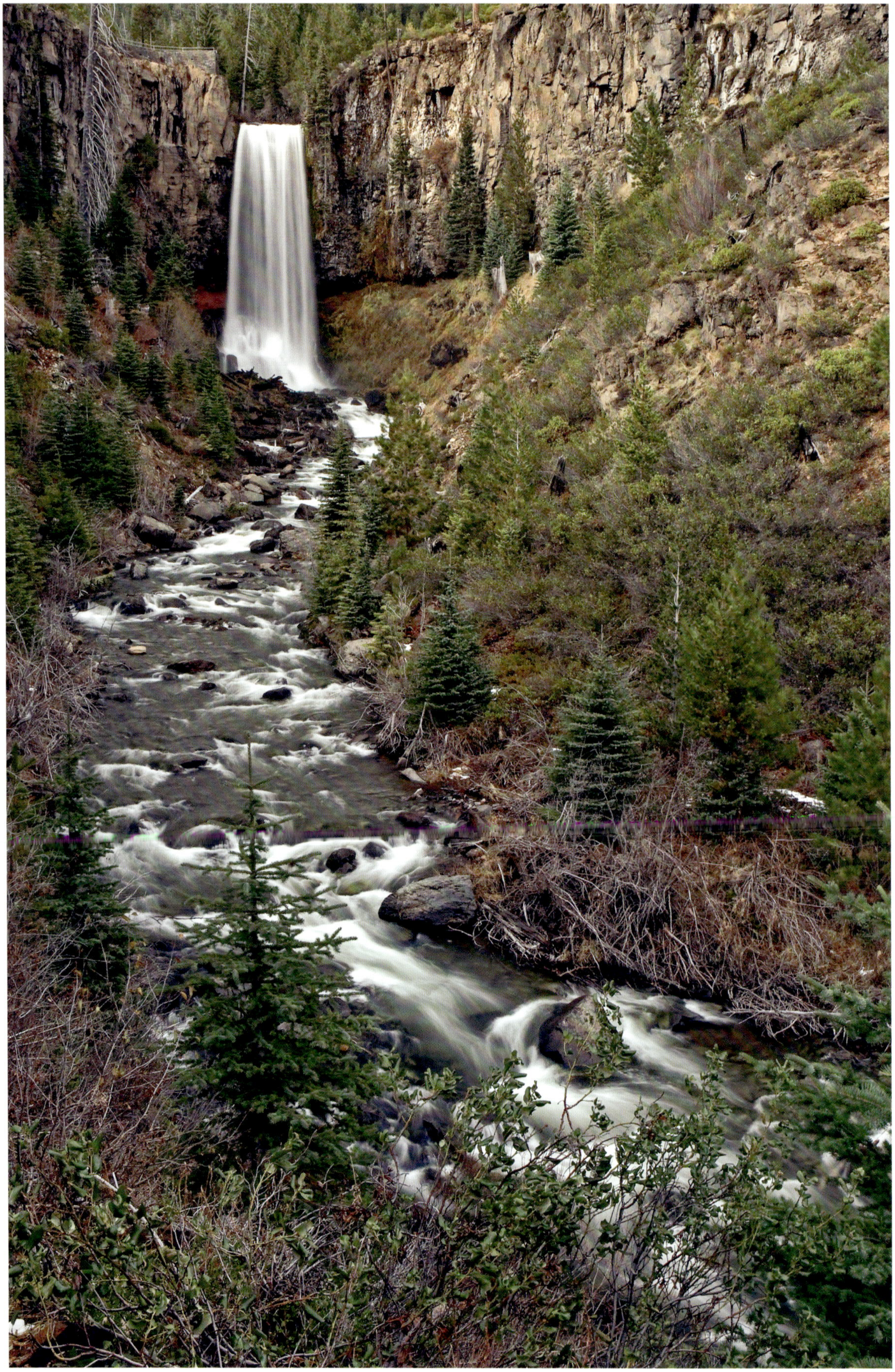

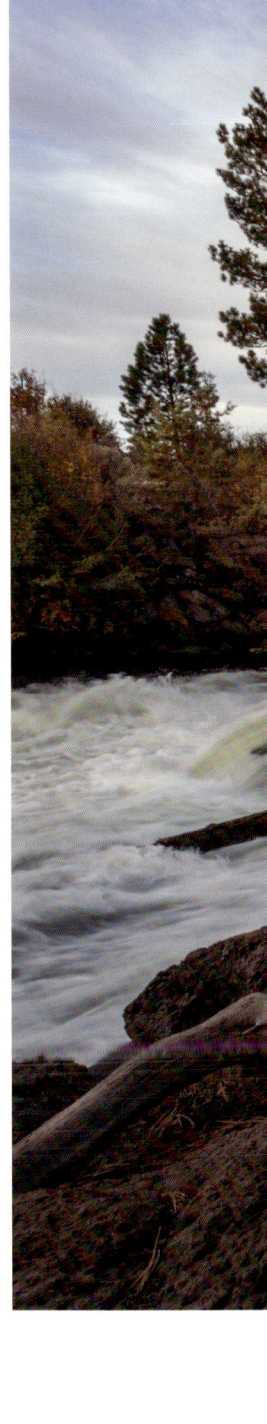

Tumalo Falls. Located in the Deschutes National Forest, Tumalo Falls measures 97 feet tall. The moderately challenging hike to the falls takes an average of 2.5 hours to complete. *Photo by Jay Newman*

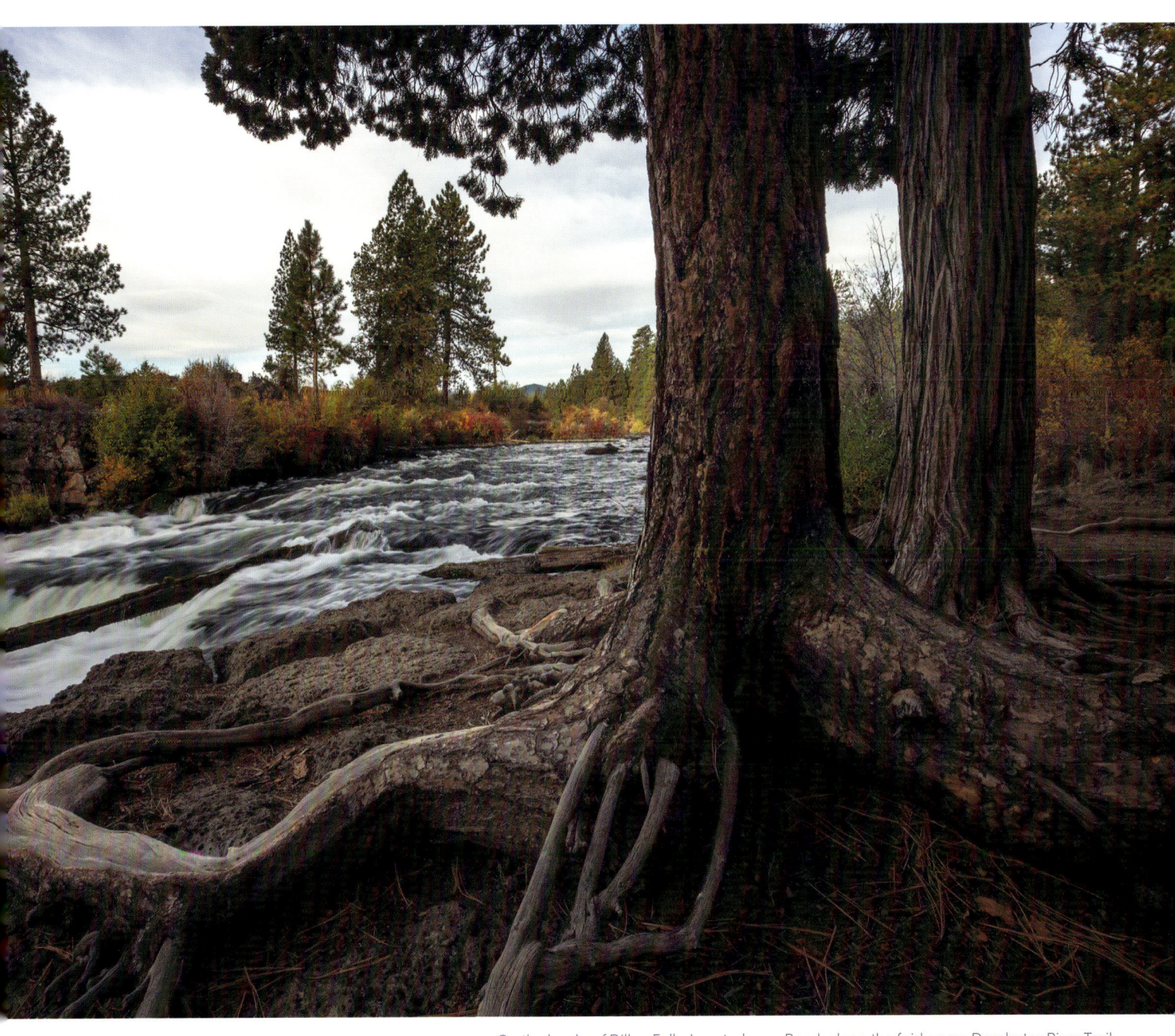

On the banks of Dillon Falls. Located near Bend, along the fairly even Deschutes River Trail, these powerful but flat falls become class 5 rapids. *Photo by Sean Bagshaw*

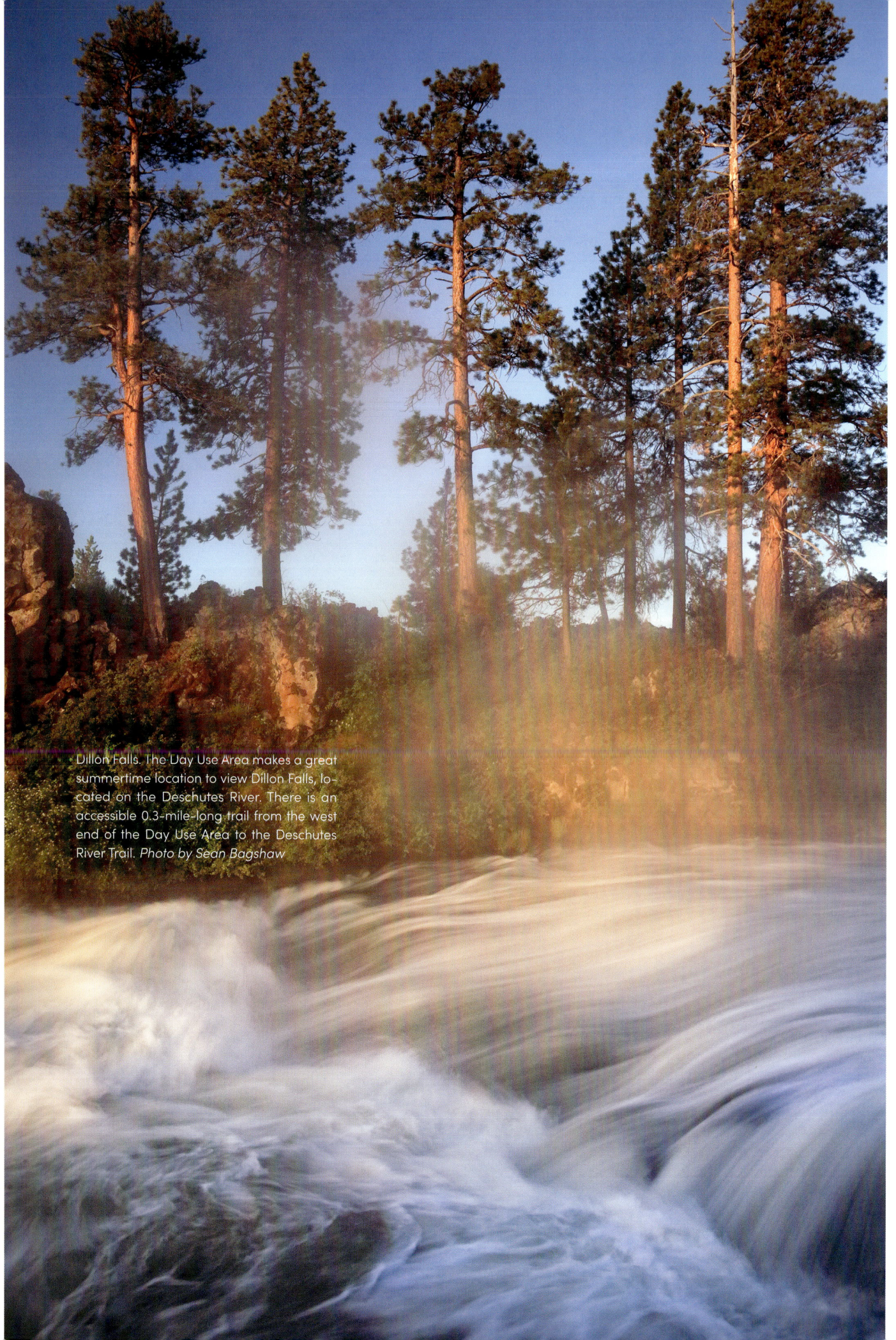

Dillon Falls. The Day Use Area makes a great summertime location to view Dillon Falls, located on the Deschutes River. There is an accessible 0.3-mile-long trail from the west end of the Day Use Area to the Deschutes River Trail. *Photo by Sean Bagshaw*

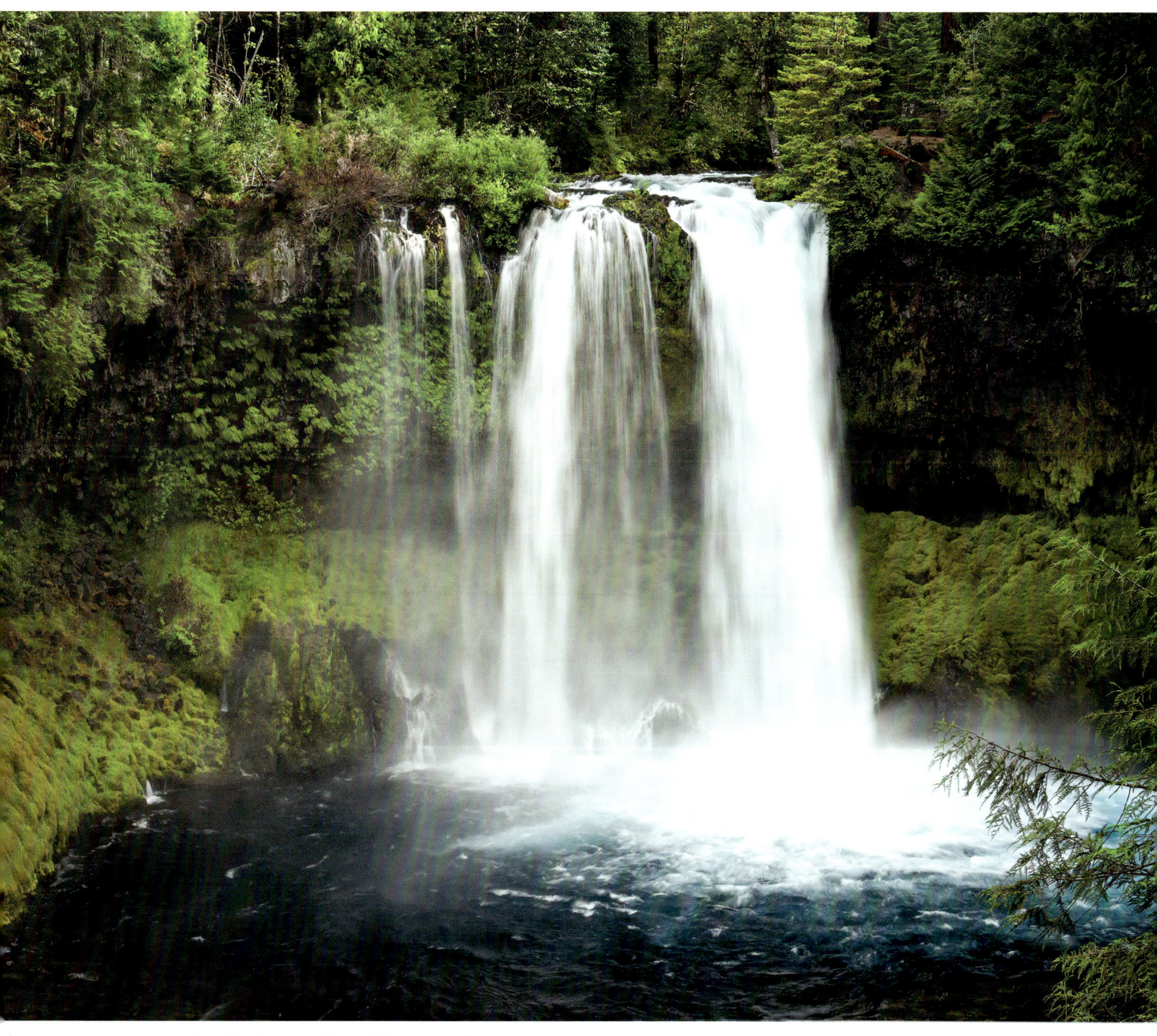

Koosah Falls. The name "Koosah" means"sky" in the Chinook language. Over 3,000 years ago, Koosah Falls was formed when a basalt lava flow dammed up Clear Lake. Both Koosah and its sister, Sahalie Falls, are located on the McKenzie River, along an easy-to-follow trail. Koosah Falls drops over 70 feet into a deep pool. *Photo by Gary Thurman*

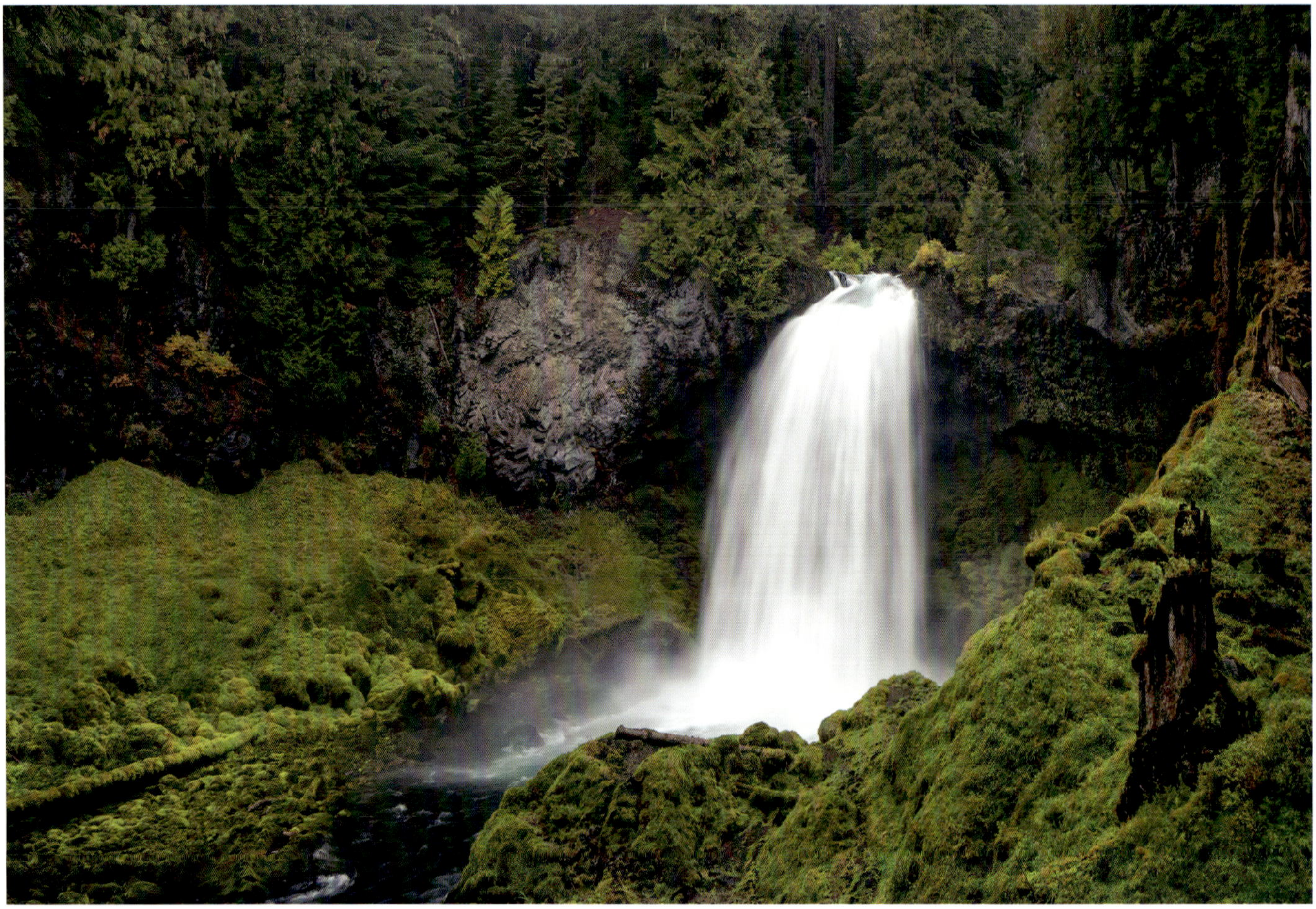

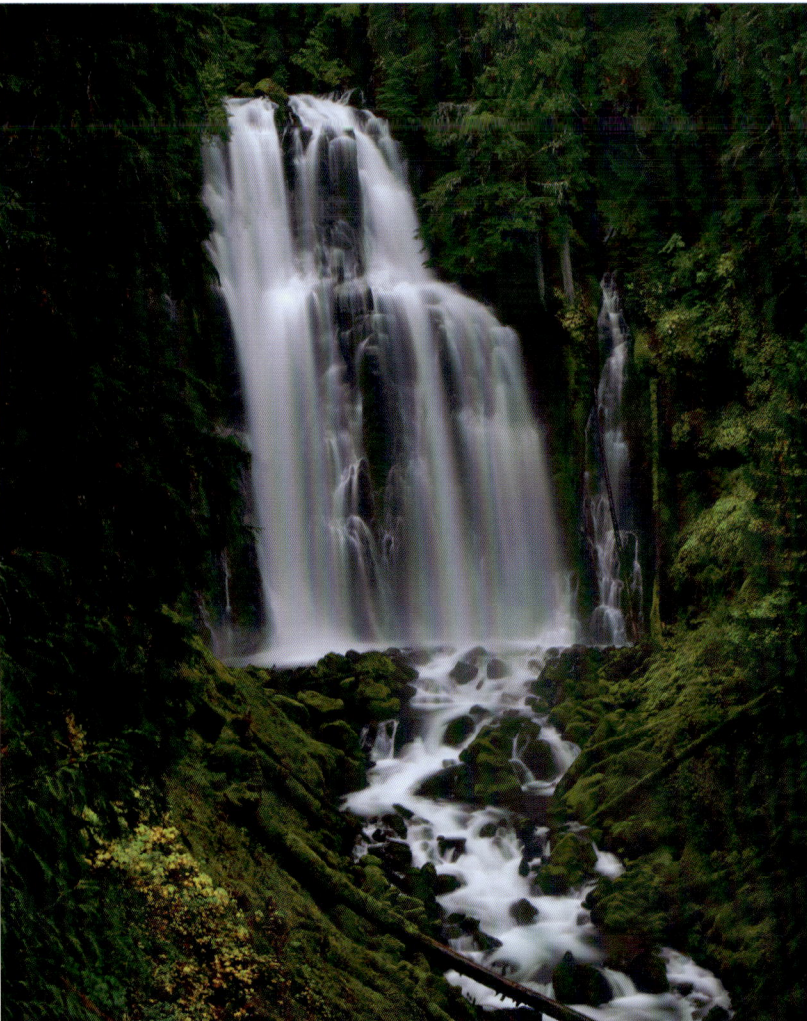

Sahalie Falls. "Sahalie" is a Native American word meaning, aptly, "waterfall." Sahalie Falls, on the McKenzie River, plunges 100 feet over a natural lava dam. The trail to both Sahalie and Koosah is along a 2.4-mile easy path. There is also a wheelchair-accessible observation deck. *Photo by Gary Thurman*

Linton Falls. Considered a moderately challenging route through the Three Sisters Wilderness Area, the hike to Linton Falls is short but very steep. Linton is one of the tallest Oregon waterfalls, at 615 feet, almost as tall as Multnomah Falls. *Photo by Clem Paslack*

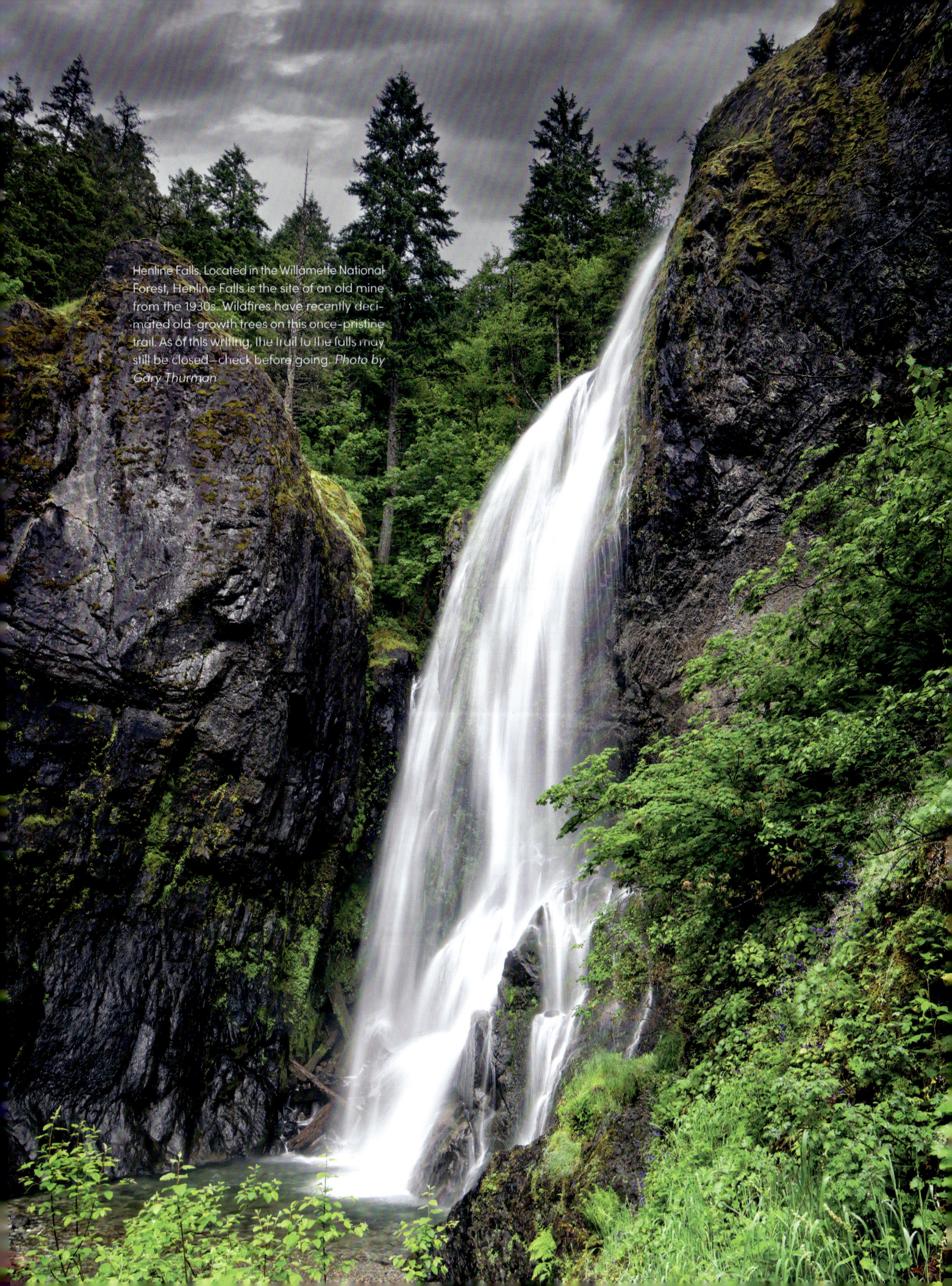

Henline Falls. Located in the Willamette National Forest, Henline Falls is the site of an old mine from the 1930s. Wildfires have recently decimated old-growth trees on this once-pristine trail. As of this writing, the trail to the falls may still be closed—check before going. *Photo by Gary Thurman*

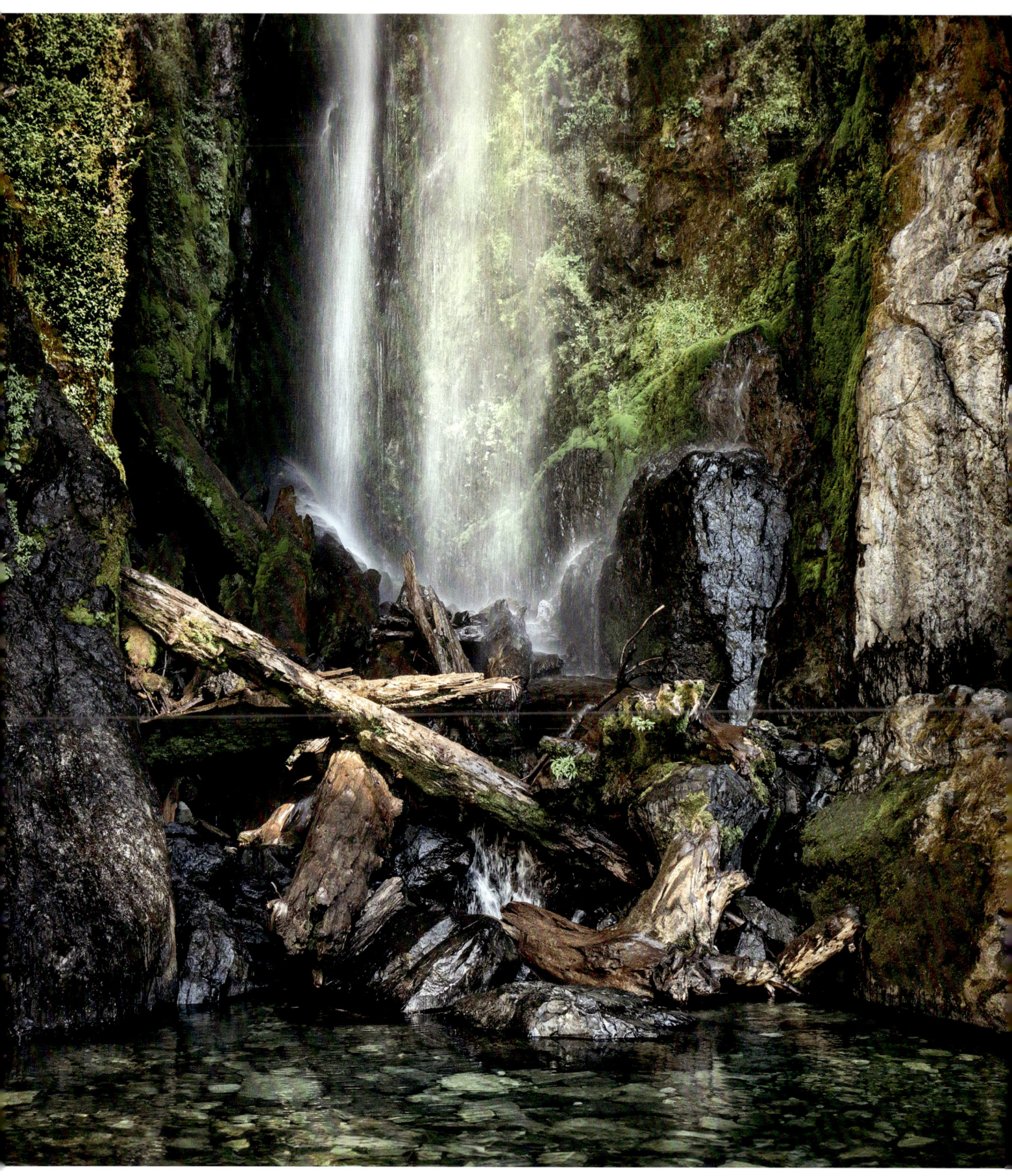

Henline Falls. Henline Falls is a waterfall in the Opal Creek Wilderness, with a height of 126 feet and a width of 50 feet. Named for Henline Mountain, Henline Creek supplies the flow of water to the falls. *Photo by Susan Sheets*

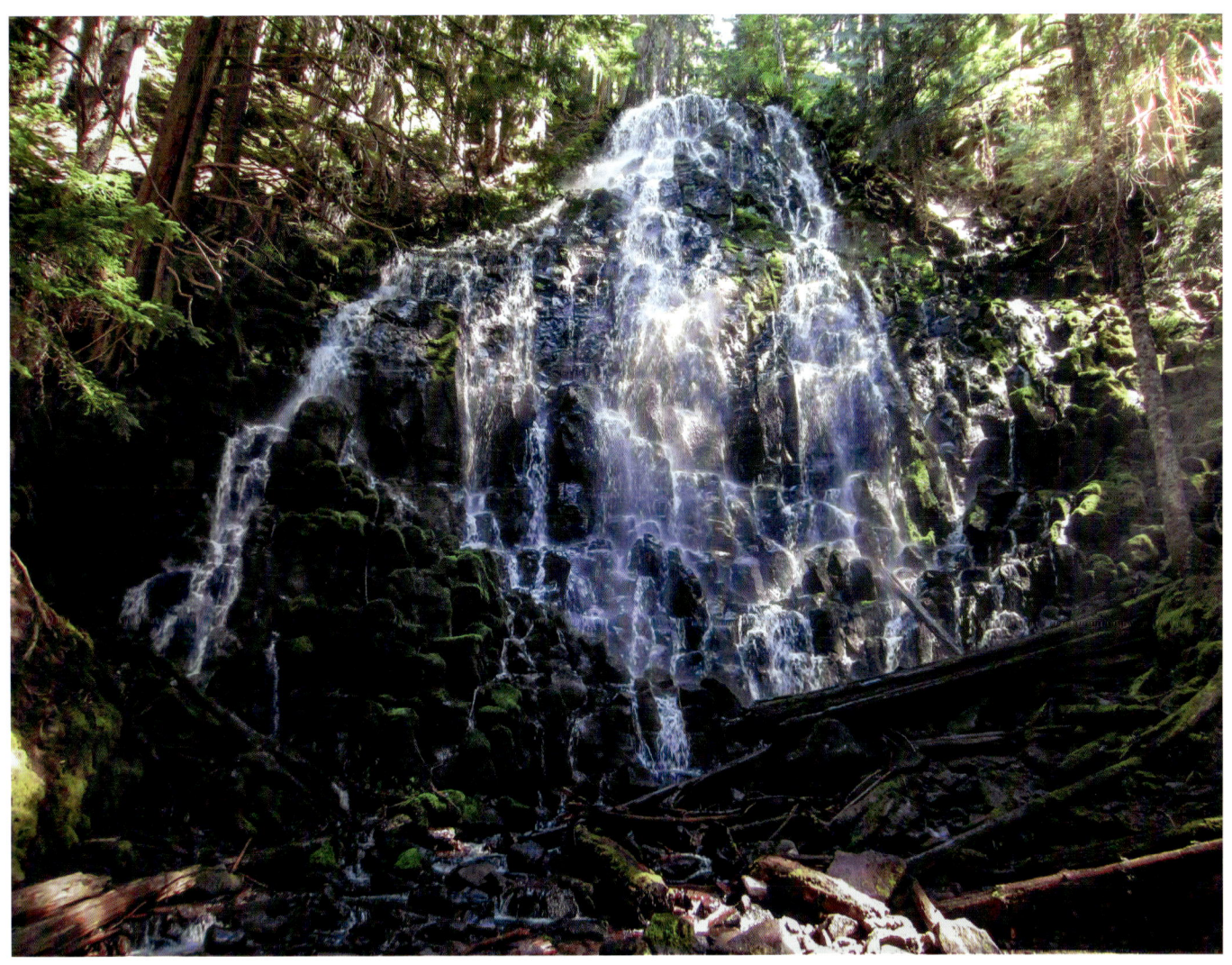

Ramona Falls. The trail to see this jewel on the upper Sandy River near Mount Hood is considered challenging. The distinctive horsetail-type waterfall is located about 30 minutes from Timberline Lodge and an hour and a half from Portland. The 7-mile-round-trip hike to see the falls can be strenuous, especially since the bridge is washed out. One has to wade through the river and walk across logs. The reward is seeing these striking falls as well as a view of Mount Hood. *Photo by Adam Marland*

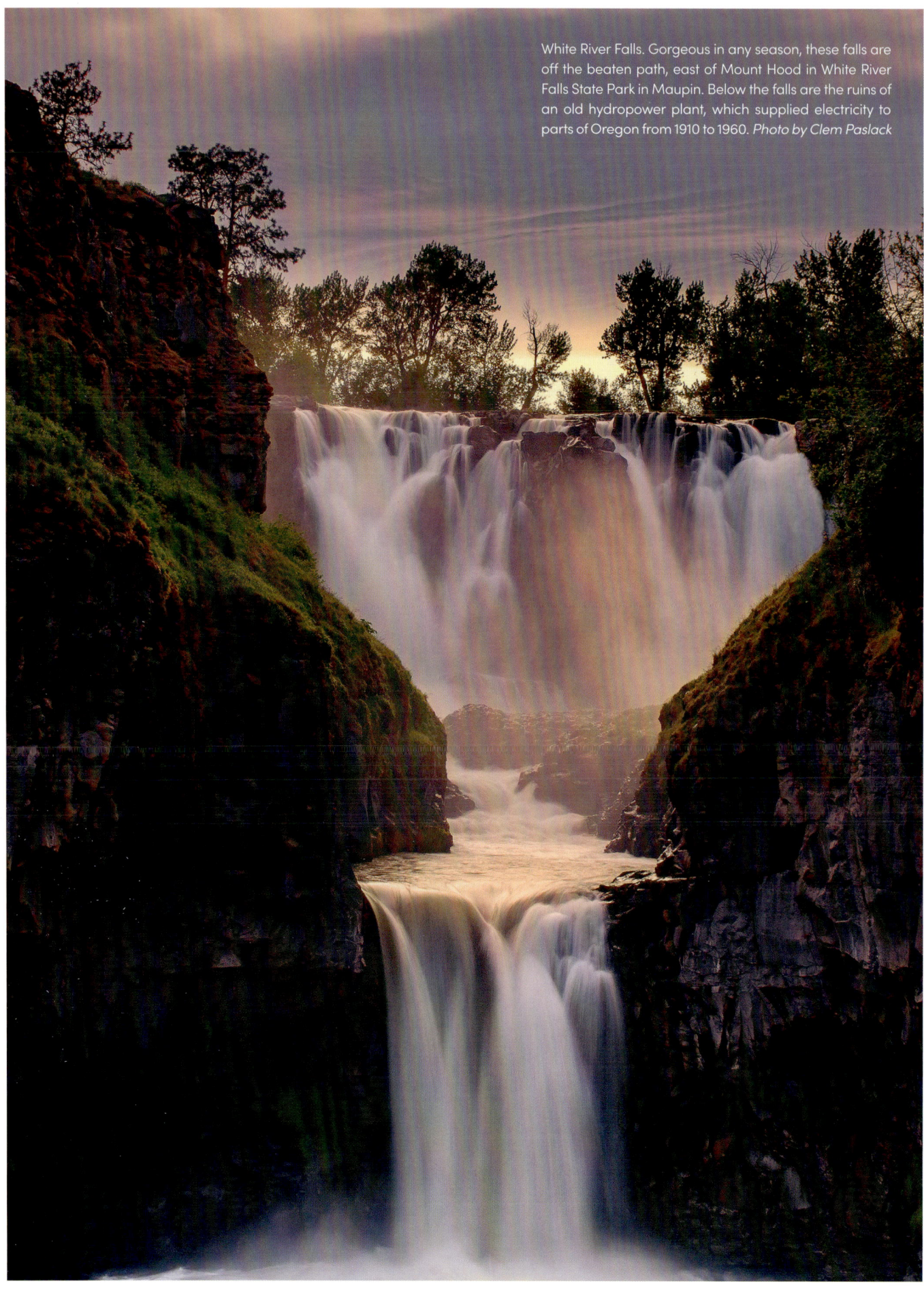

White River Falls. Gorgeous in any season, these falls are off the beaten path, east of Mount Hood in White River Falls State Park in Maupin. Below the falls are the ruins of an old hydropower plant, which supplied electricity to parts of Oregon from 1910 to 1960. *Photo by Clem Paslack*

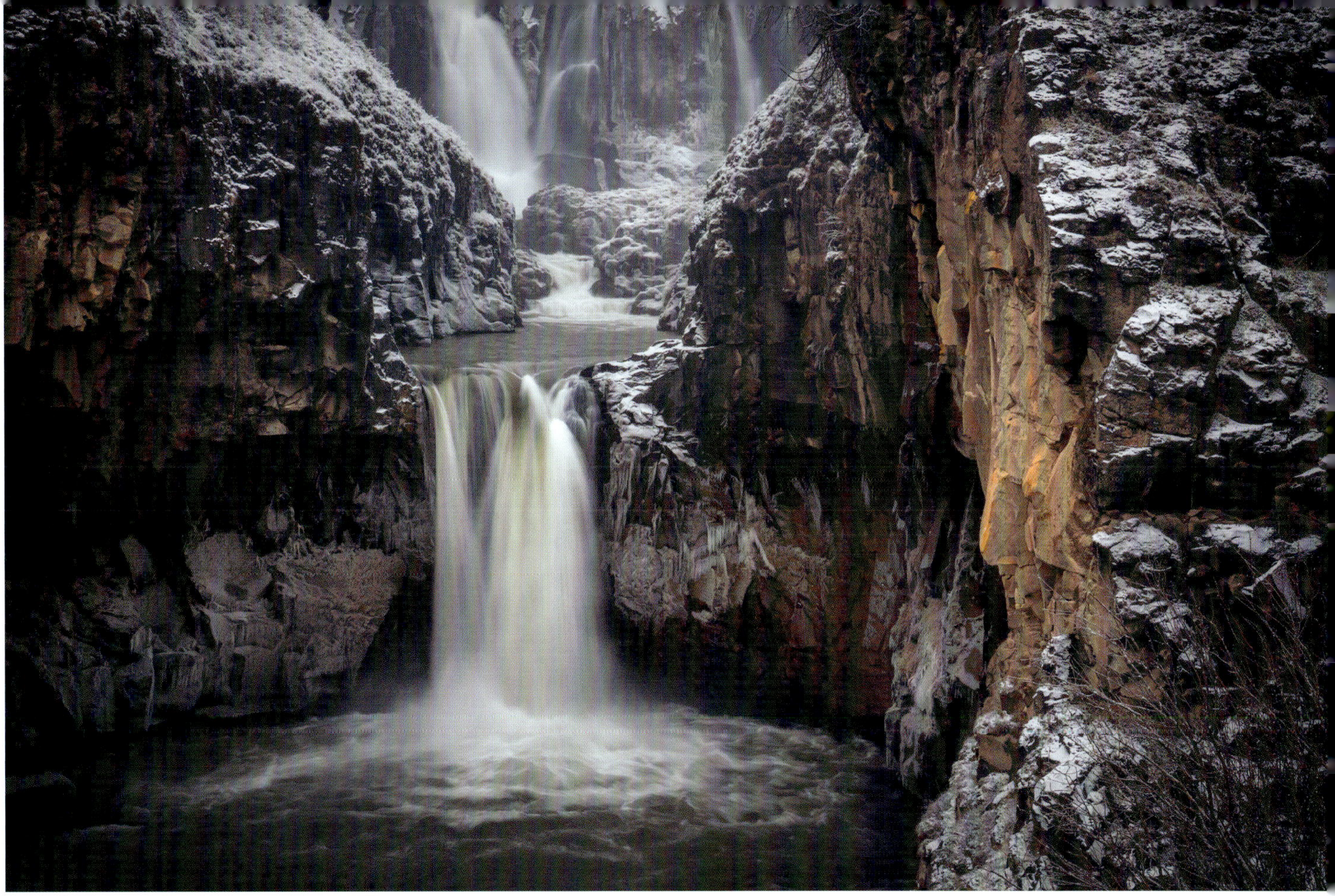

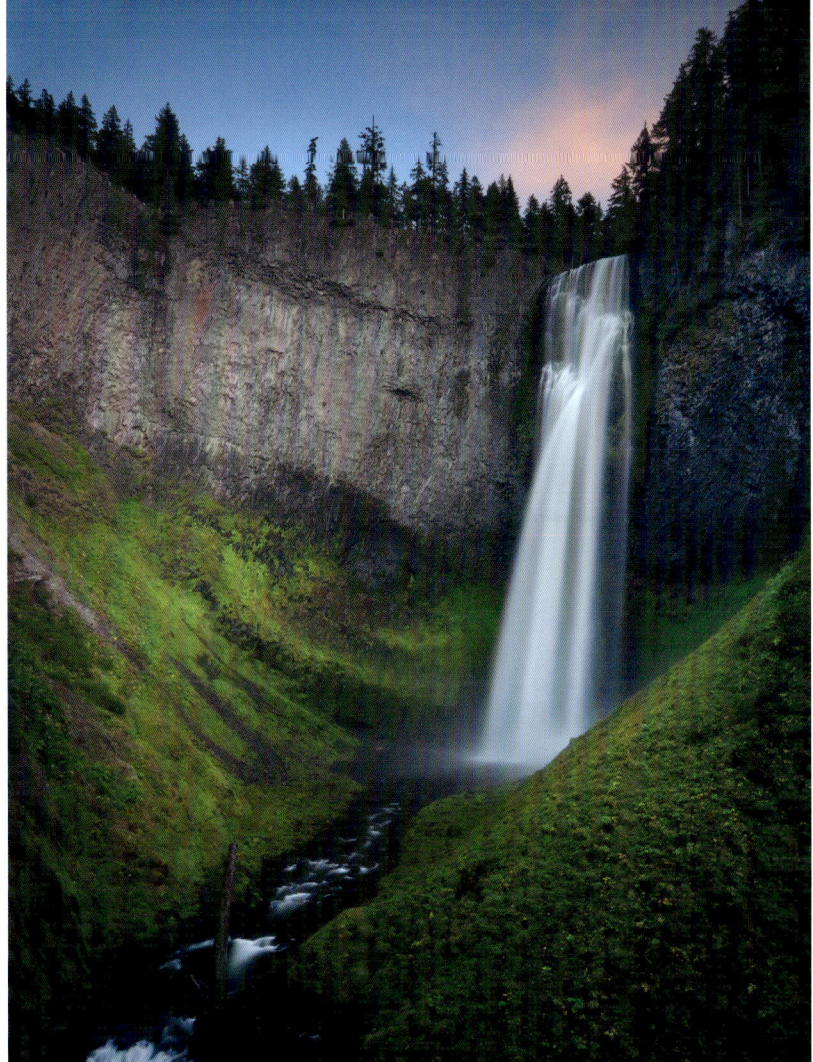

White River Falls. In winter, the White River plunges dramatically 90 feet over the falls from a basalt shelf. *Photo by Sean Bagshaw*

Salt Creek Falls. Salt Creek Falls is located in the Willamette National Forest of the South Cascades. It is Oregon's second-highest single-drop waterfall, plunging 286 feet. There is a wheelchair-accessible platform available, with impressive views of the falls. *Photo by Sean Bagshaw*

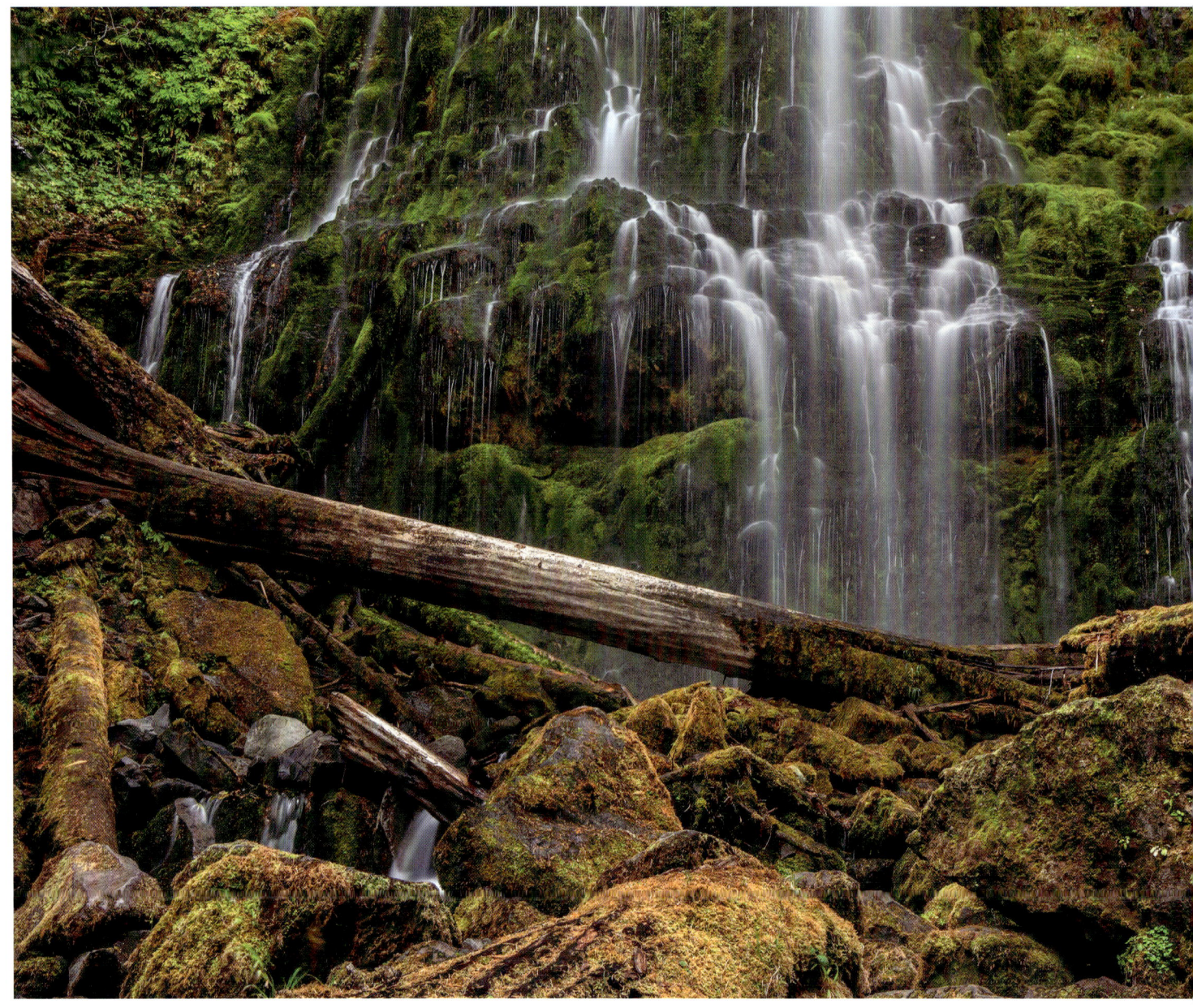

Lower Proxy Falls. Both Upper and Lower Proxy Falls, located on a loop trail near the McKenzie Pass, are doable in one trip and are not to be missed. The Lower Proxy Falls is the bigger of the two. *Photo by Sue Newman*

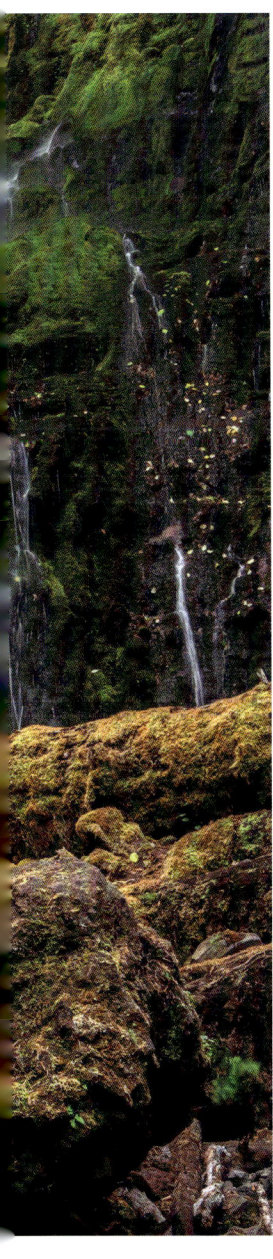

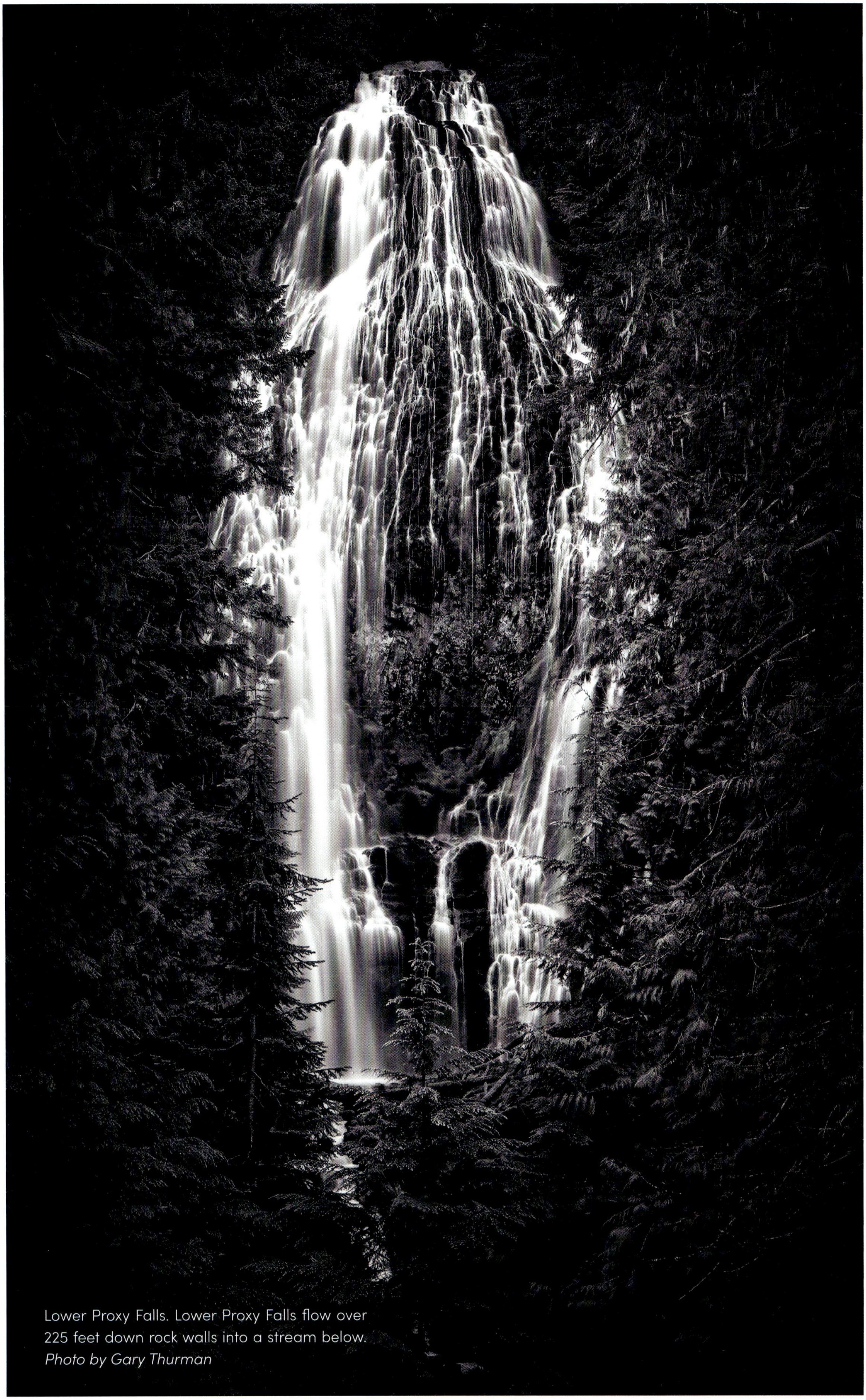

Lower Proxy Falls. Lower Proxy Falls flow over
225 feet down rock walls into a stream below.
Photo by Gary Thurman

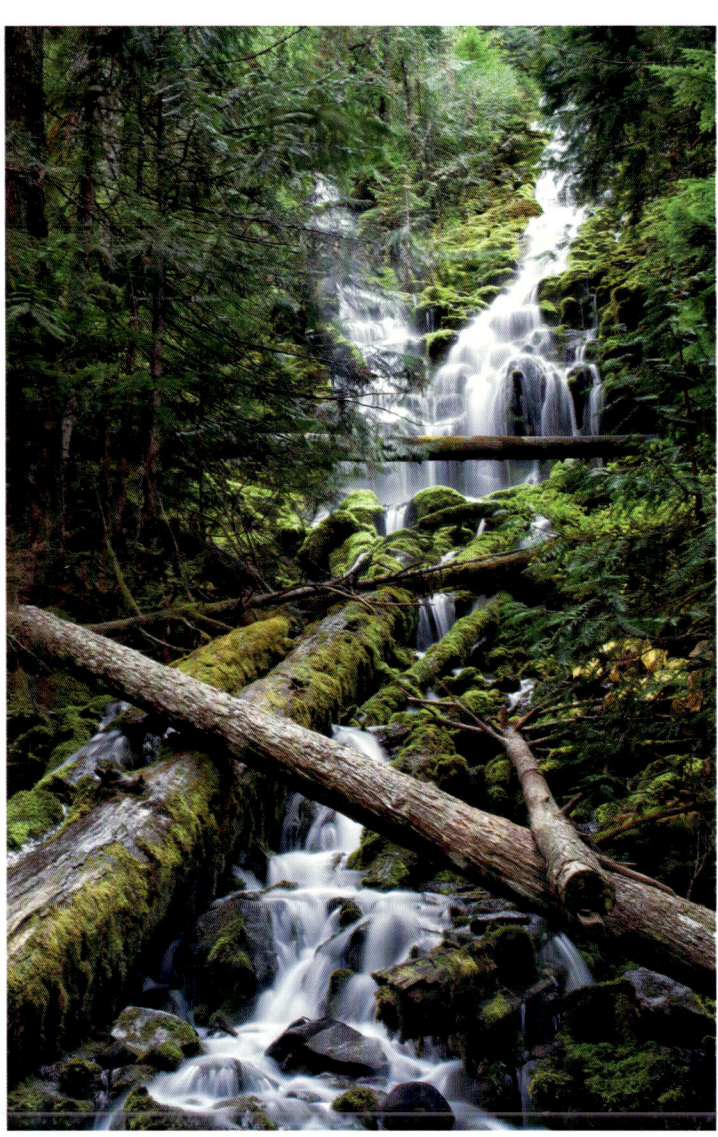

Upper Proxy Falls. The smaller of the two Proxy Falls, these falls drain into lava rocks and disappear underground. The lava fields where the falls are located were cut by glaciers over 6,000 years ago. *Photo by Gary Thurman*

Steelhead Falls. Located on the Deschutes River near Terrebonne, this dramatic waterfall lies in a triangle formed by the towns of Madras, Redmond, and Sisters. There's a reasonably easy path to find the falls, and the brave can even swim here. *Photo by Larry Pollock*

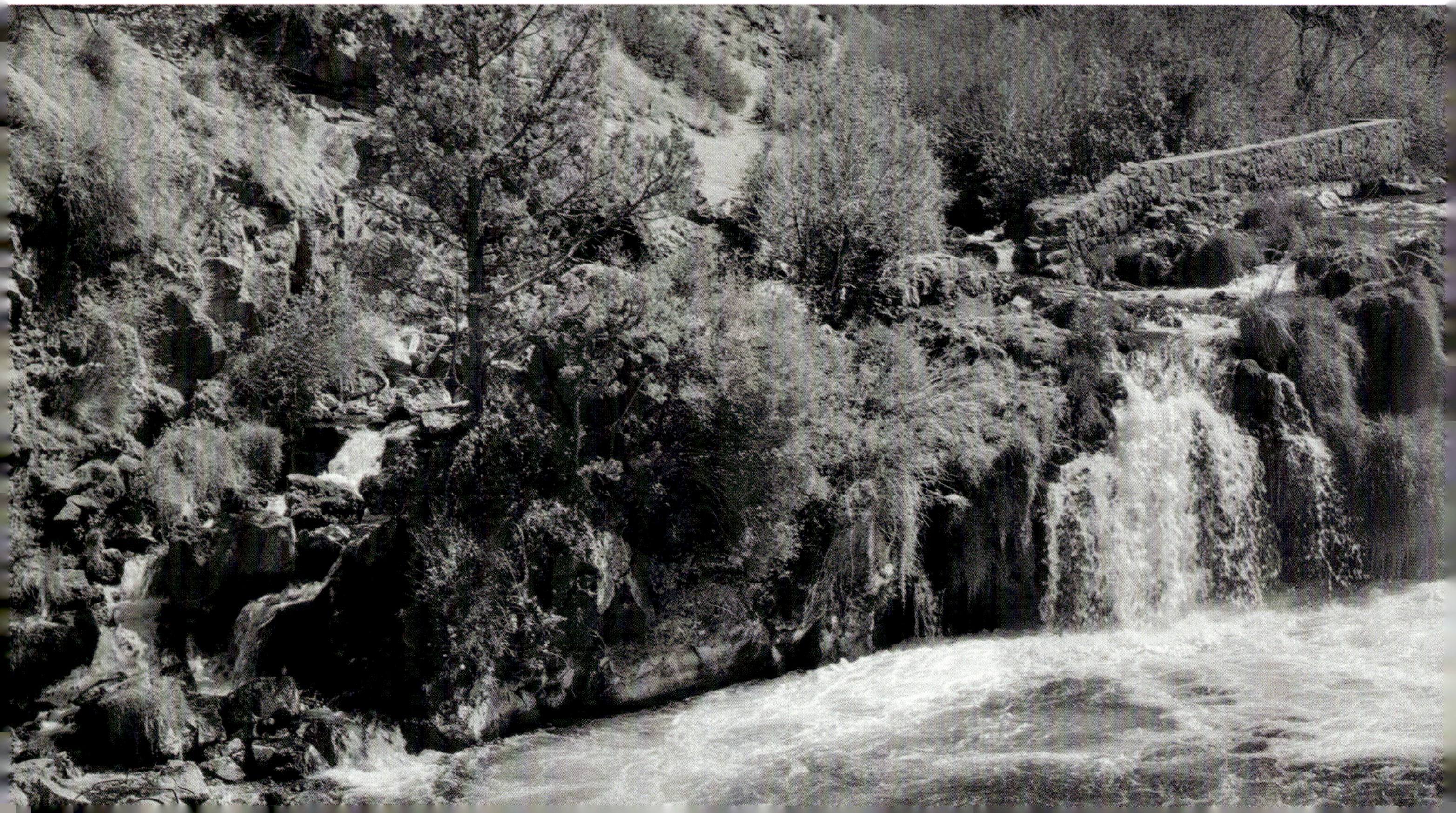

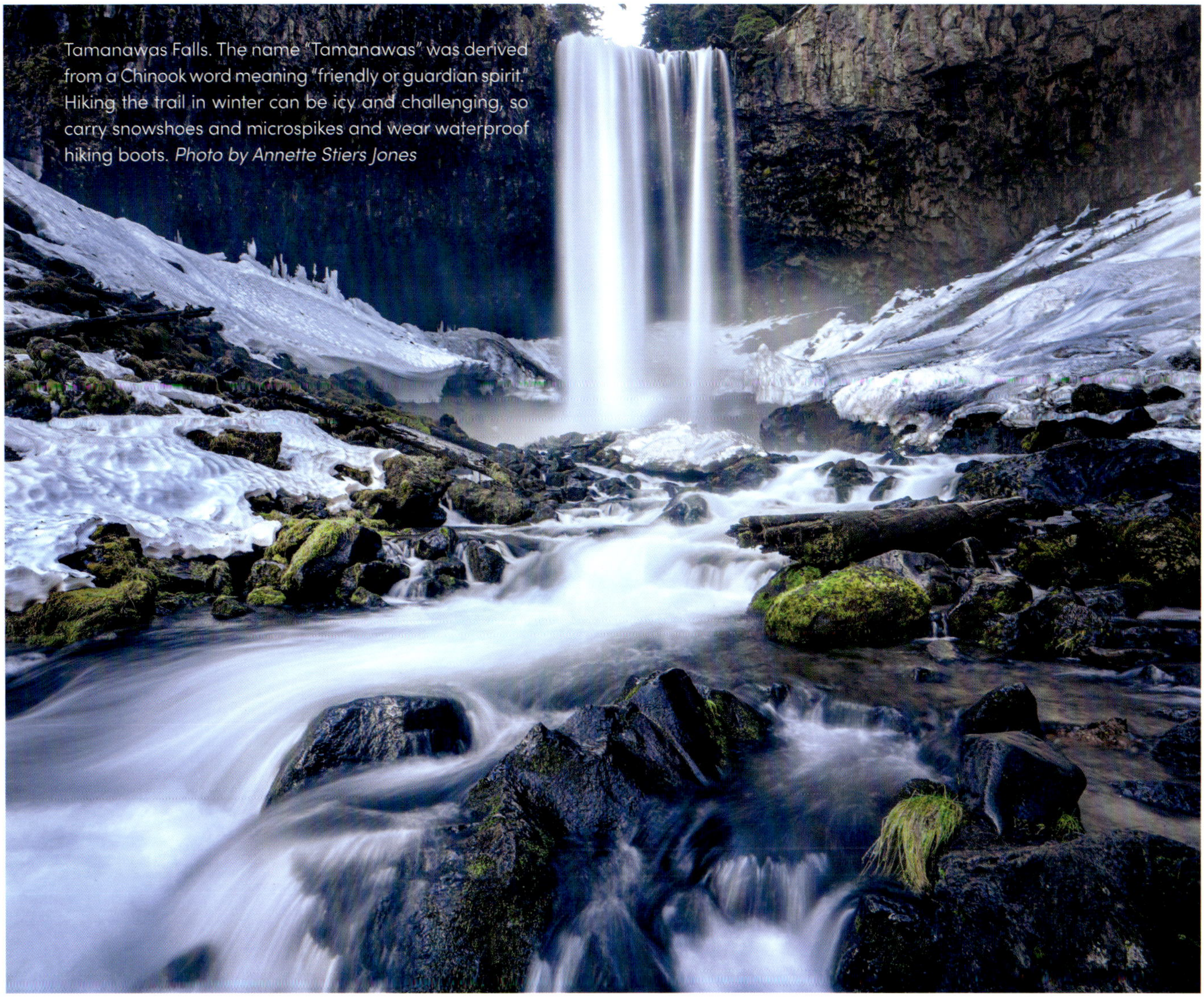

Tamanawas Falls. The name "Tamanawas" was derived from a Chinook word meaning "friendly or guardian spirit." Hiking the trail in winter can be icy and challenging, so carry snowshoes and microspikes and wear waterproof hiking boots. *Photo by Annette Stiers Jones*

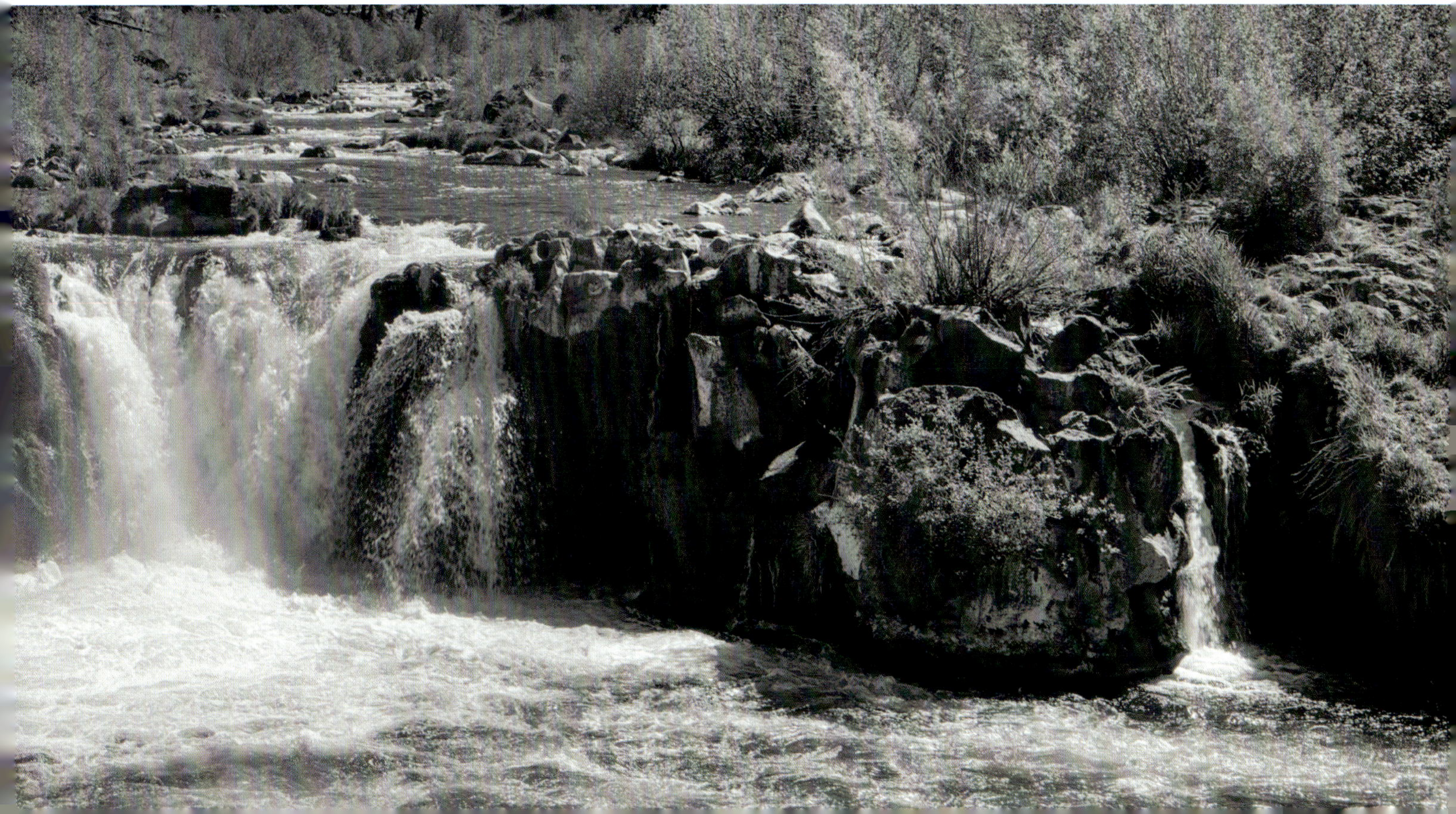

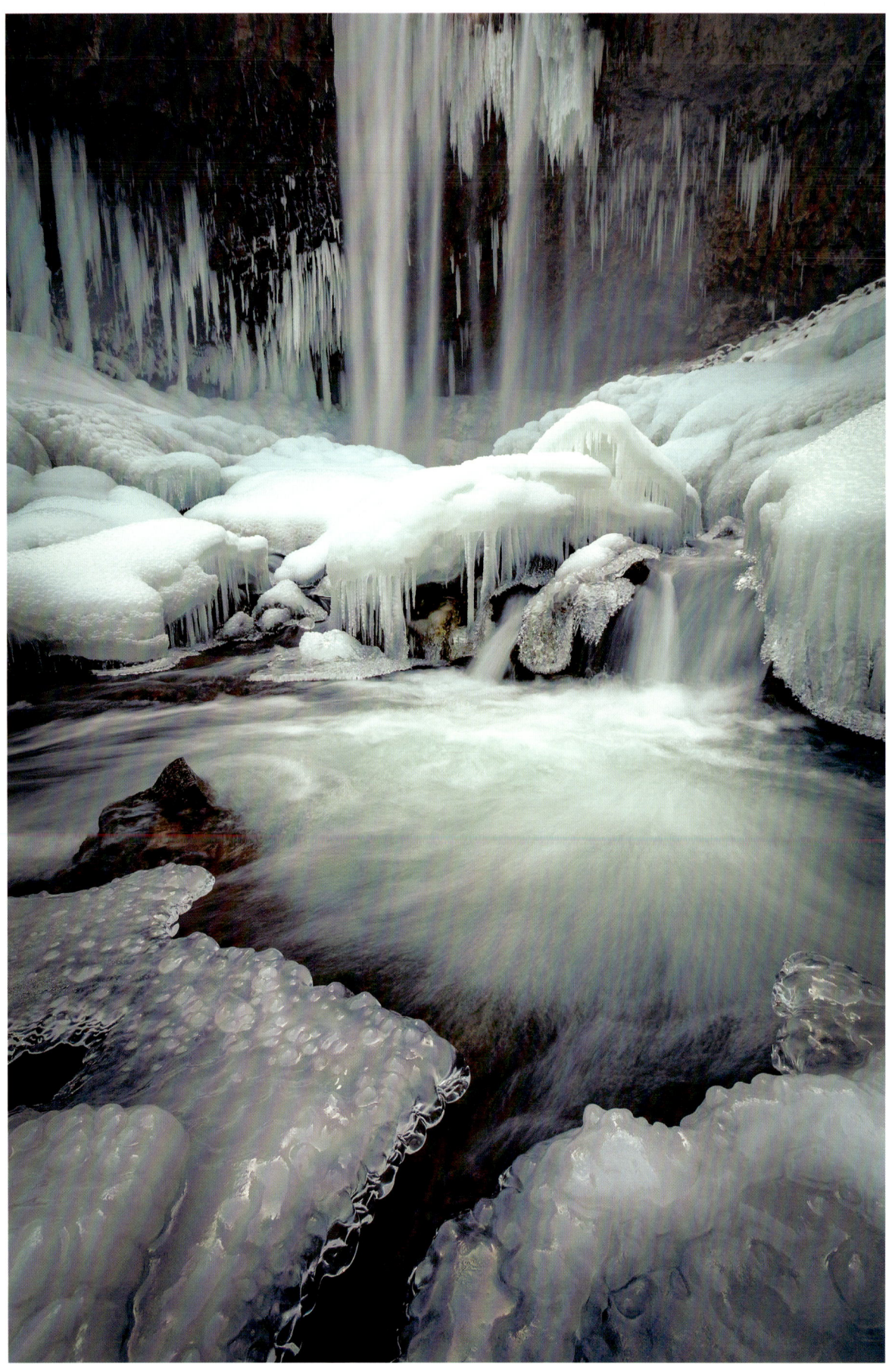

Tamanawas Falls. This dramatic waterfall is found on the east slope of Mount Hood, on a 3.4-mile, moderately challenging, out-and-back trail, especially in winter. Follow the trail alongside Cold Spring Creek. The falls are approximately 100 feet high and 40 feet wide. *Photo by Vldn Taylor*

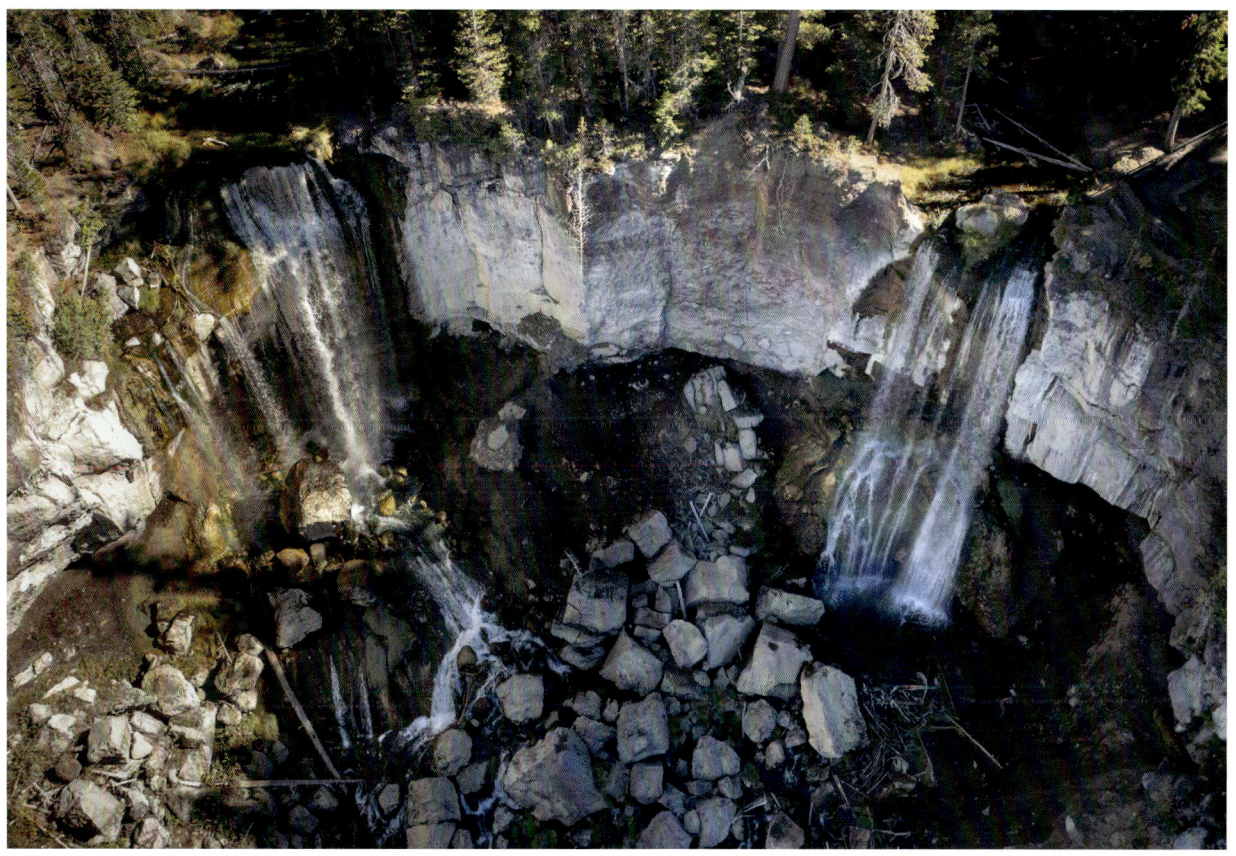

Paulina Creek Falls. Located in La Pine, Oregon, 22 miles south of Bend, in the Newberry National Volcanic Monument. It's only a short hike to see the double falls, which drop 80 feet from the top. *Photo by Adam Marland*

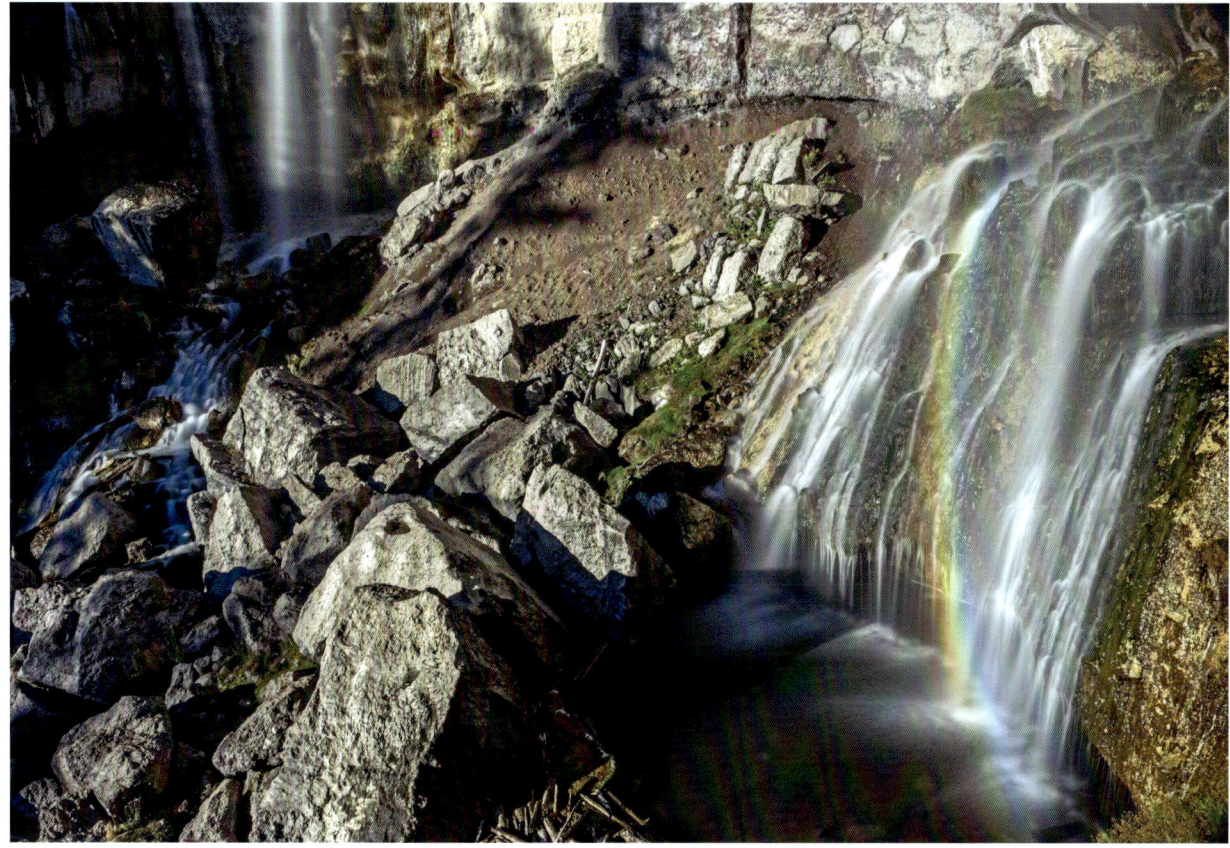

Paulina Creek Falls. Just west of Paulina Lake, outside the Newberry Caldera, this popular, moderately challenging, half-mile-out-and-back trail takes about 16 minutes to complete. *Photo by Sue Newman*

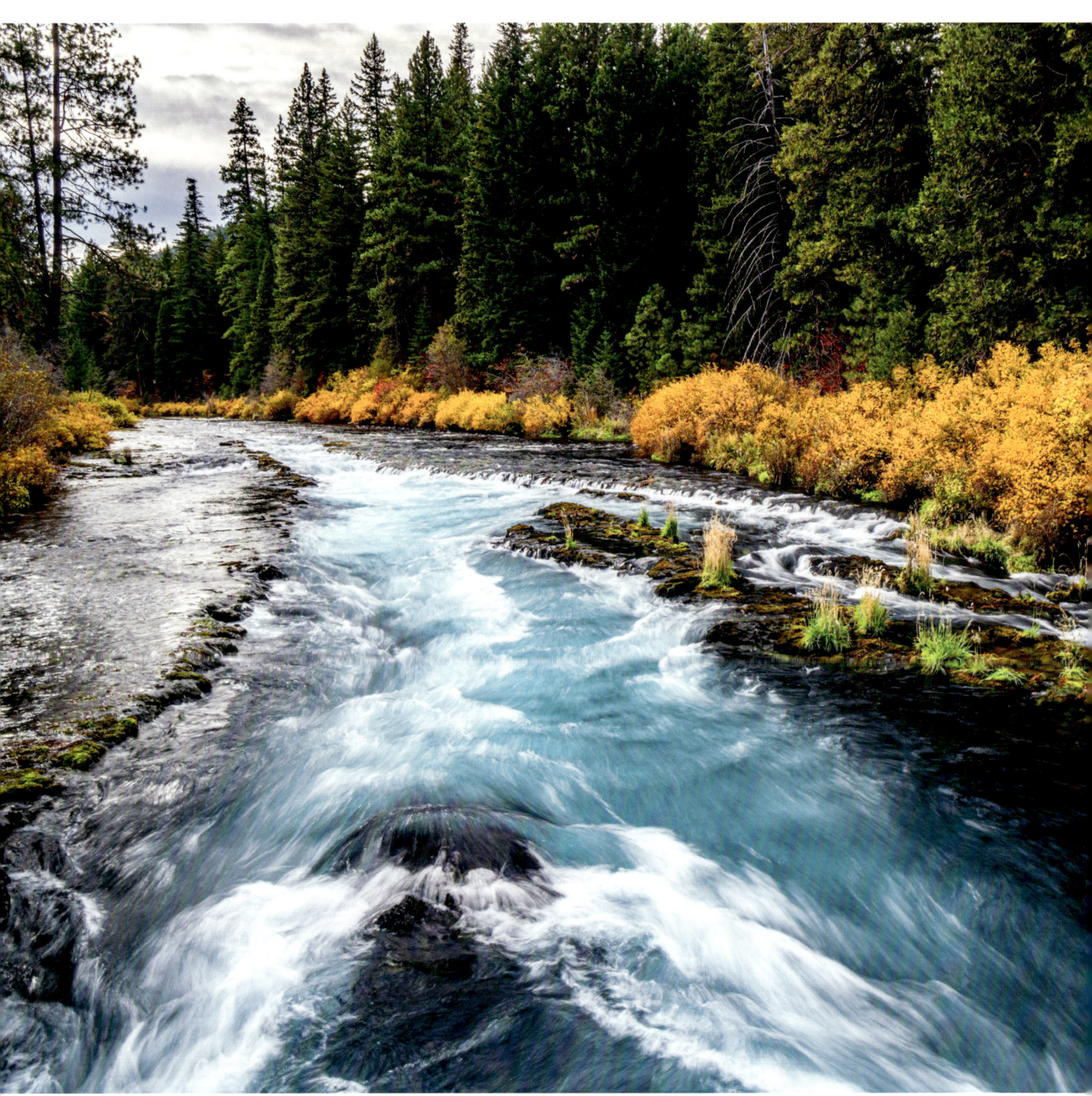

Wizard Falls. Located on the Metolius River, Wizard Falls is located about 40 miles northwest of Bend in the Deschutes National Forest. The river is also a popular fly-fishing destination. *Photo by Frank G. Lahman*

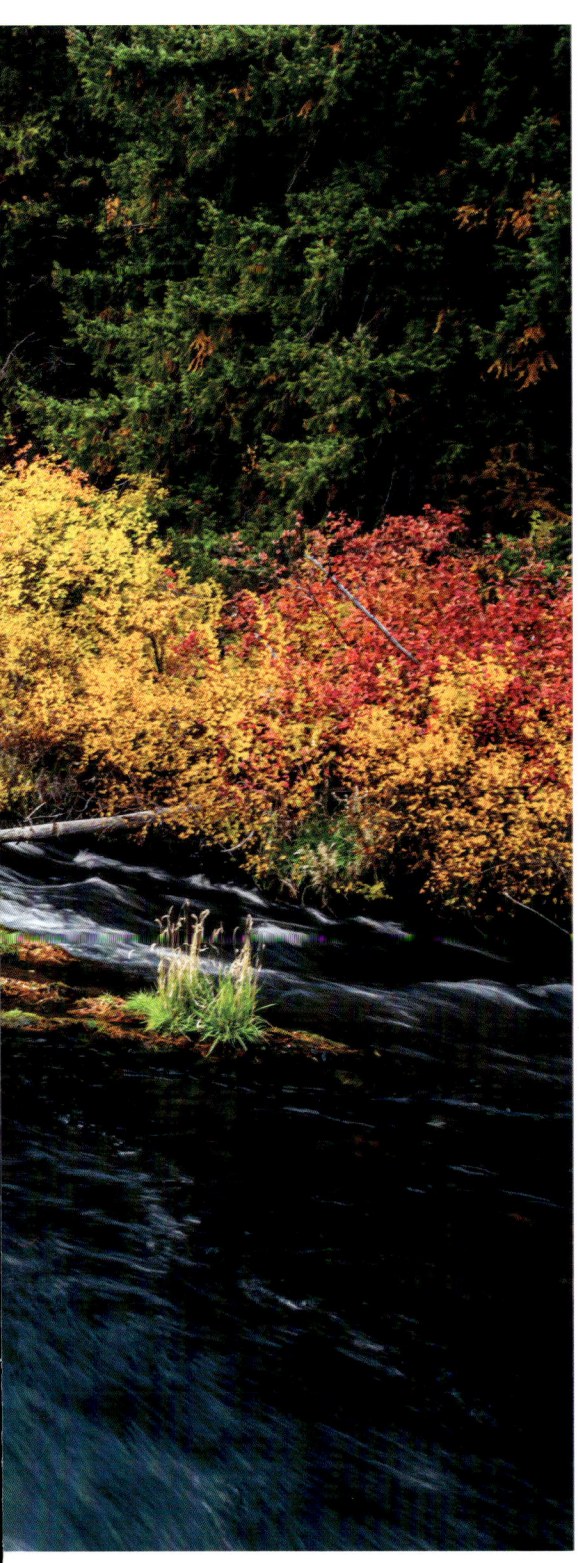

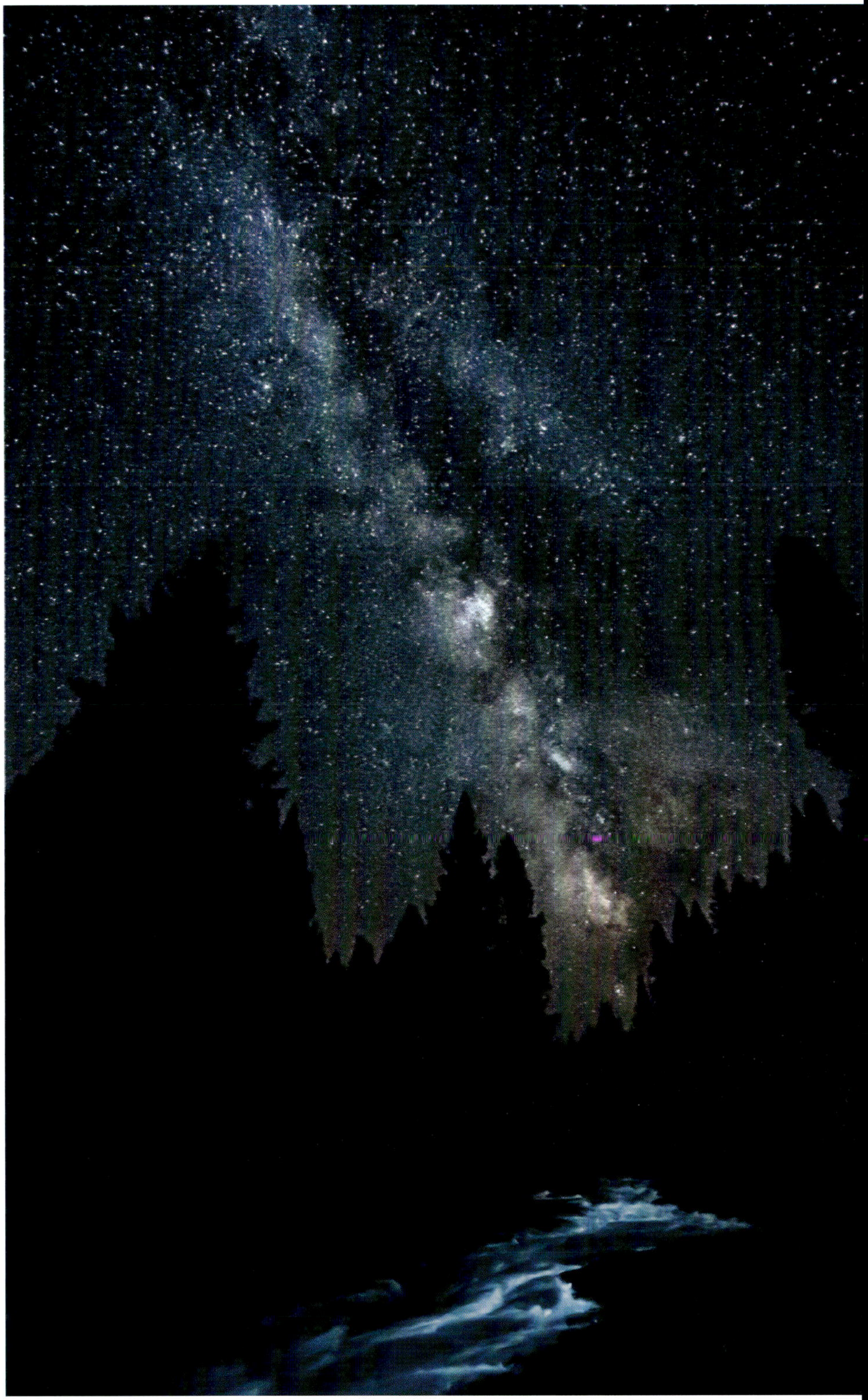

Wizard Falls. Seen here at night under the Milky Way, Wizard Falls was once a 12-foot-high waterfall. In 1948 the water was diverted for a fish hatchery. Today, the waterfall, which runs along the Metolius River, does not flow unless the hatchery is shut down completely for cleaning or maintenance. *Photo by Frank G. Lahman*

6

Southern Oregon

There are several popular waterfalls in southern Oregon. This chapter includes only waterfalls from the California border as far north as Grants Pass and west through the Applegate Valley. (Be sure to also check out other southern Oregon waterfalls in the Umpqua Valley and Prospect to Crater Lake chapters in this book.) While not as dramatic as other waterfalls throughout Oregon, many of these smaller southern Oregon waterfalls are favorites for locals. In the southeastern part of the state, there is only one lonely and remote waterfall near Lakeview, called Deep Creek Falls.

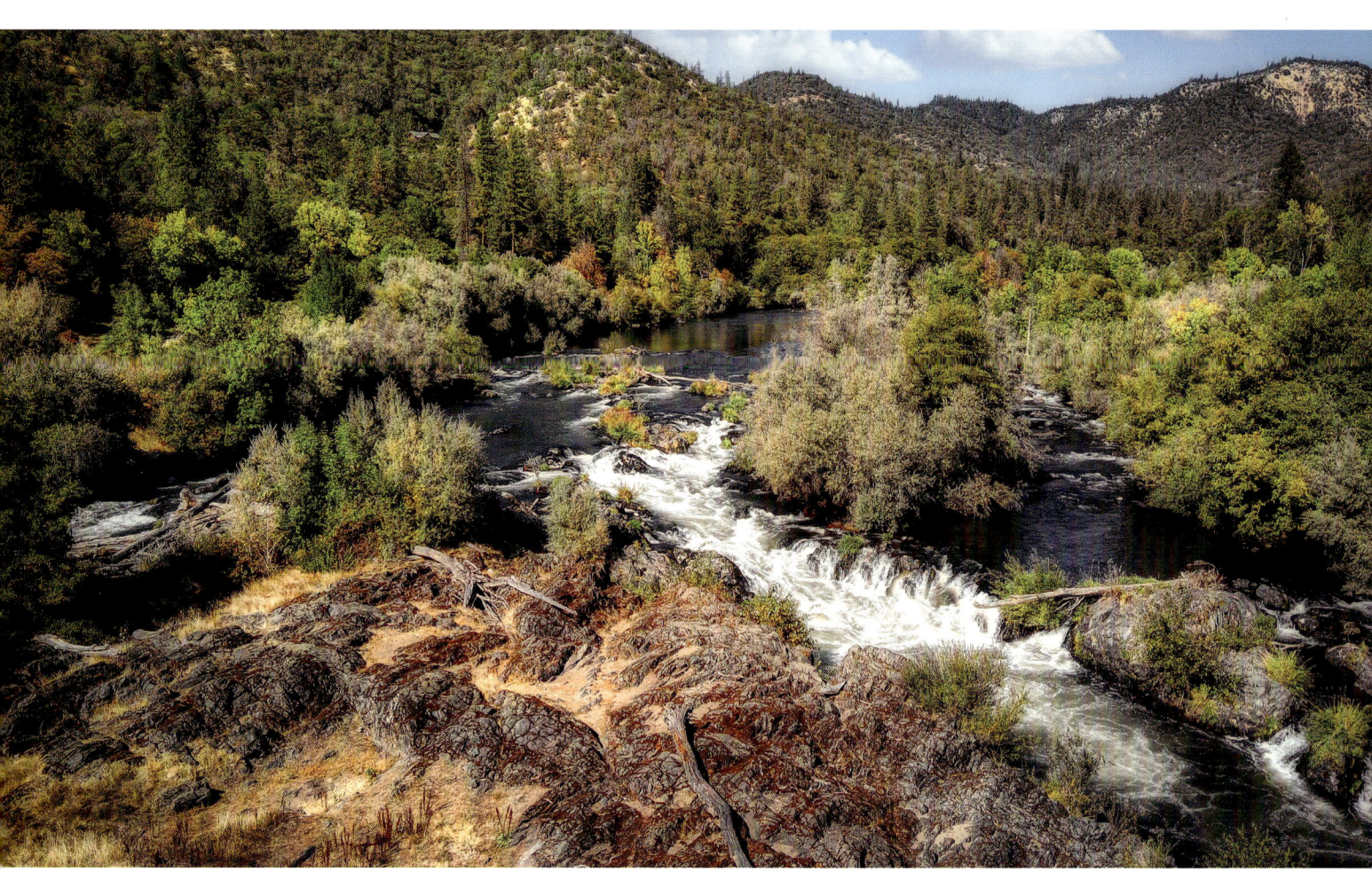

Ti'lomikh Falls. More of a series of rapids than falls, Ti'lomikh Falls near Gold Hill is a challenging spot for rafters and kayakers alike. It is a historic area where the Takelma tribe once prospered. Known as "People of the River" until 1856, the area was once a thriving Native village. Thanks to the work of the late Agnes Pilgrim (Grandma Aggie), the culture and traditions of her people continue during the annual Salmon Ceremony. It's an easy 2.7-mile-round-trip hike to view the falls from a parking area off Highway 234. *Photo by Tony Kilcollins*

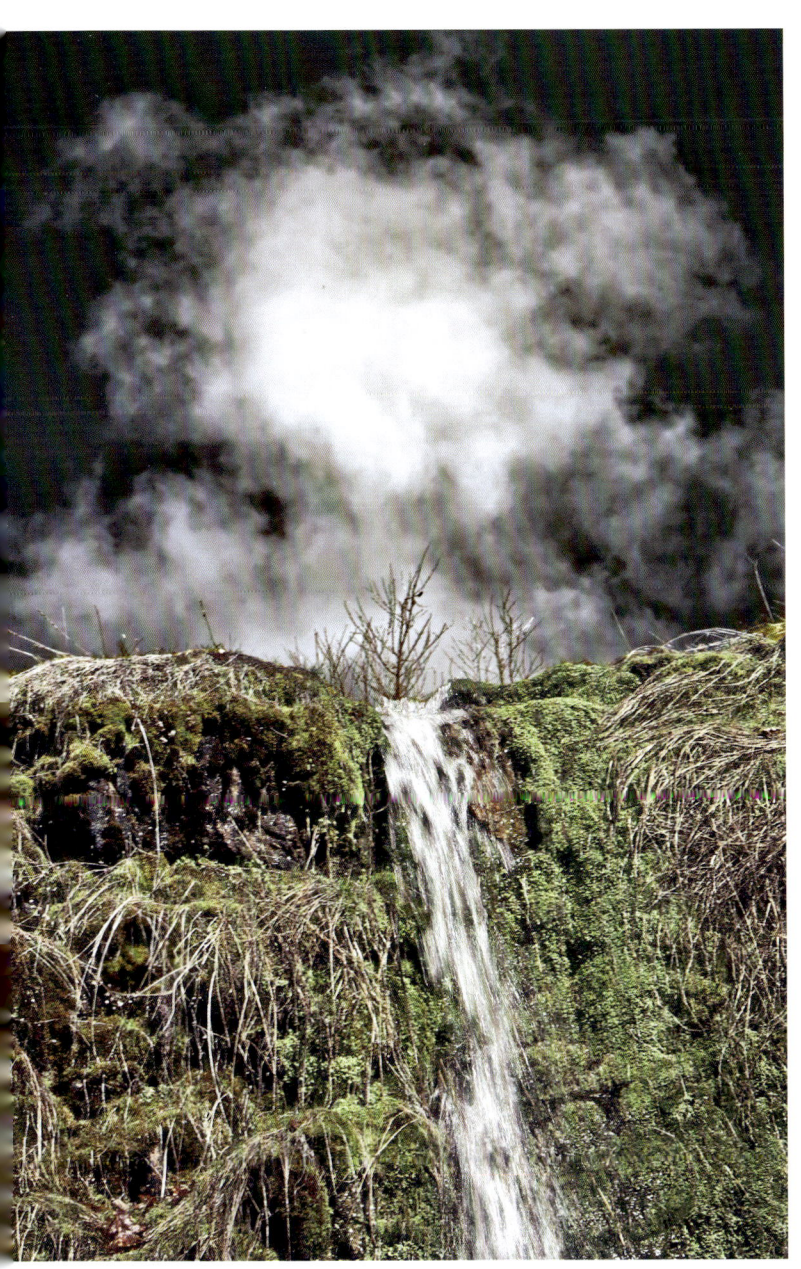

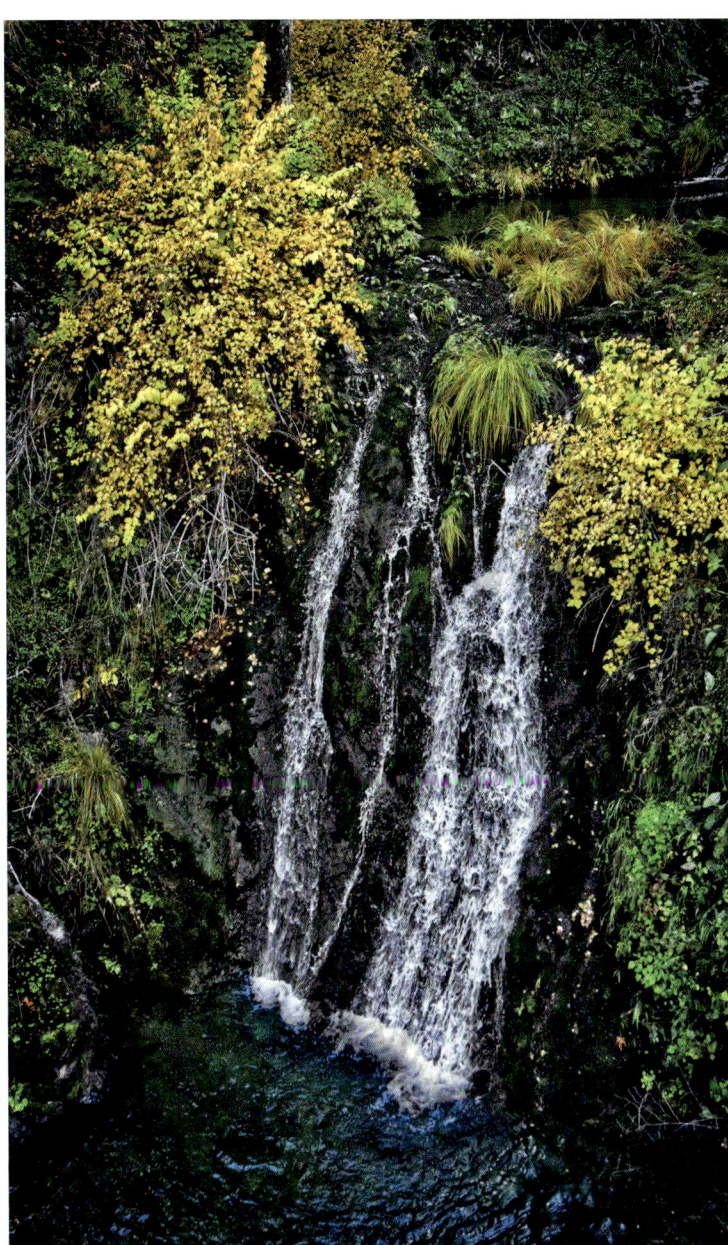

Granite Falls. This is located in Jacksonville's Forest Park along the 1.5-mile Pipsissewa Trail, and the hike to the seasonal Granite Falls is considered challenging. Pipsissewa is the name of a medicinal herb found along the trail. The granite walls also feature hanging fern gardens. *Photo by Matt Witt*

Burnt Timber Falls. Located about an hour from Grants Pass along Taylor Creek Trail, this quarter-mile hike, along unofficial narrow footpaths, can be challenging. There is a sharp drop-off at the viewpoint, so be cautious. There is also a lower unofficial and equally challenging trail to the bottom of the falls. *Photo by Matt Witt*

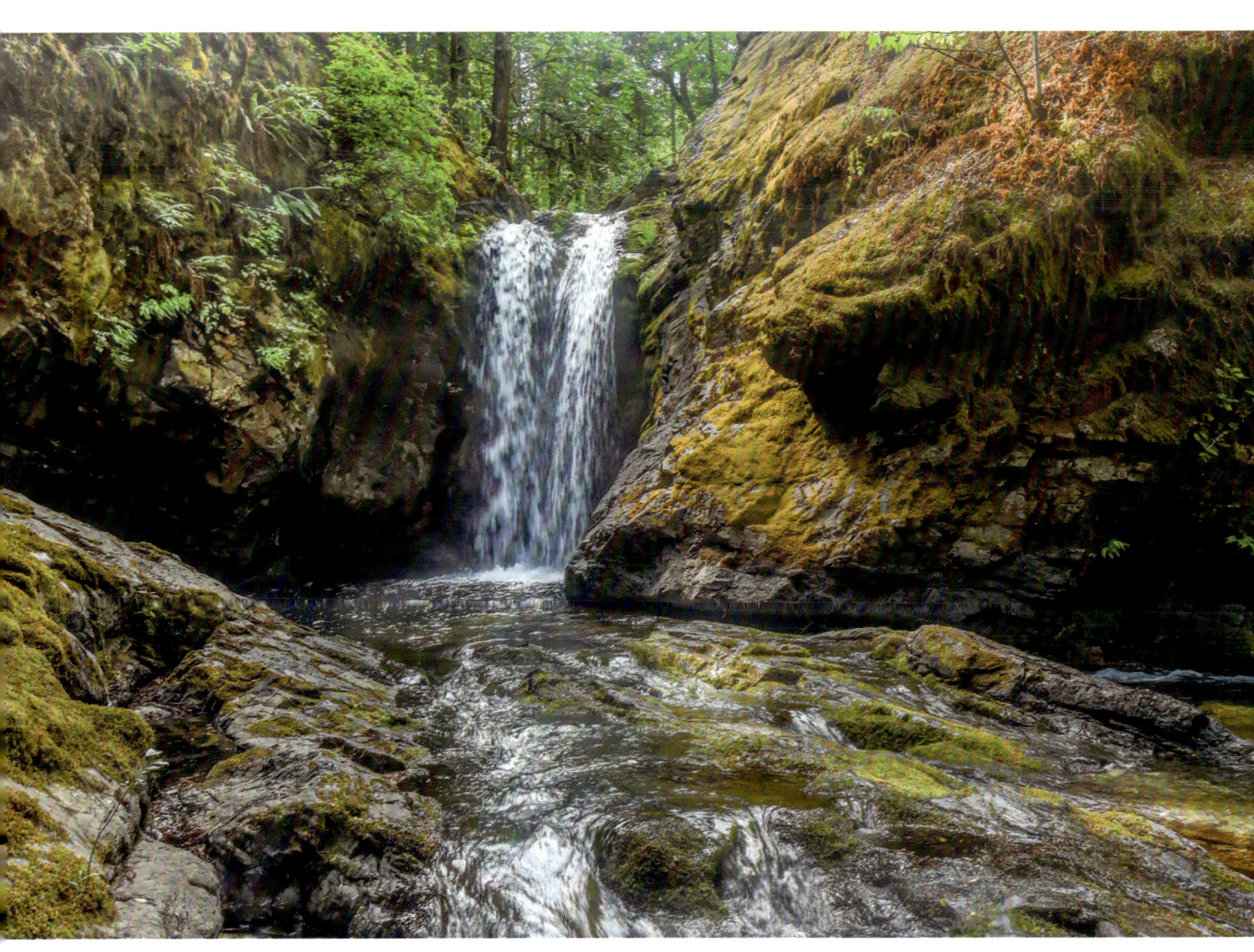

Middle Fork Falls. After crossing the Carberry Bridge near Applegate Lake and after a short hike through a shady forest, this small, unofficial waterfall can be found. It's not far from the California state line. *Photo by Jessica King*

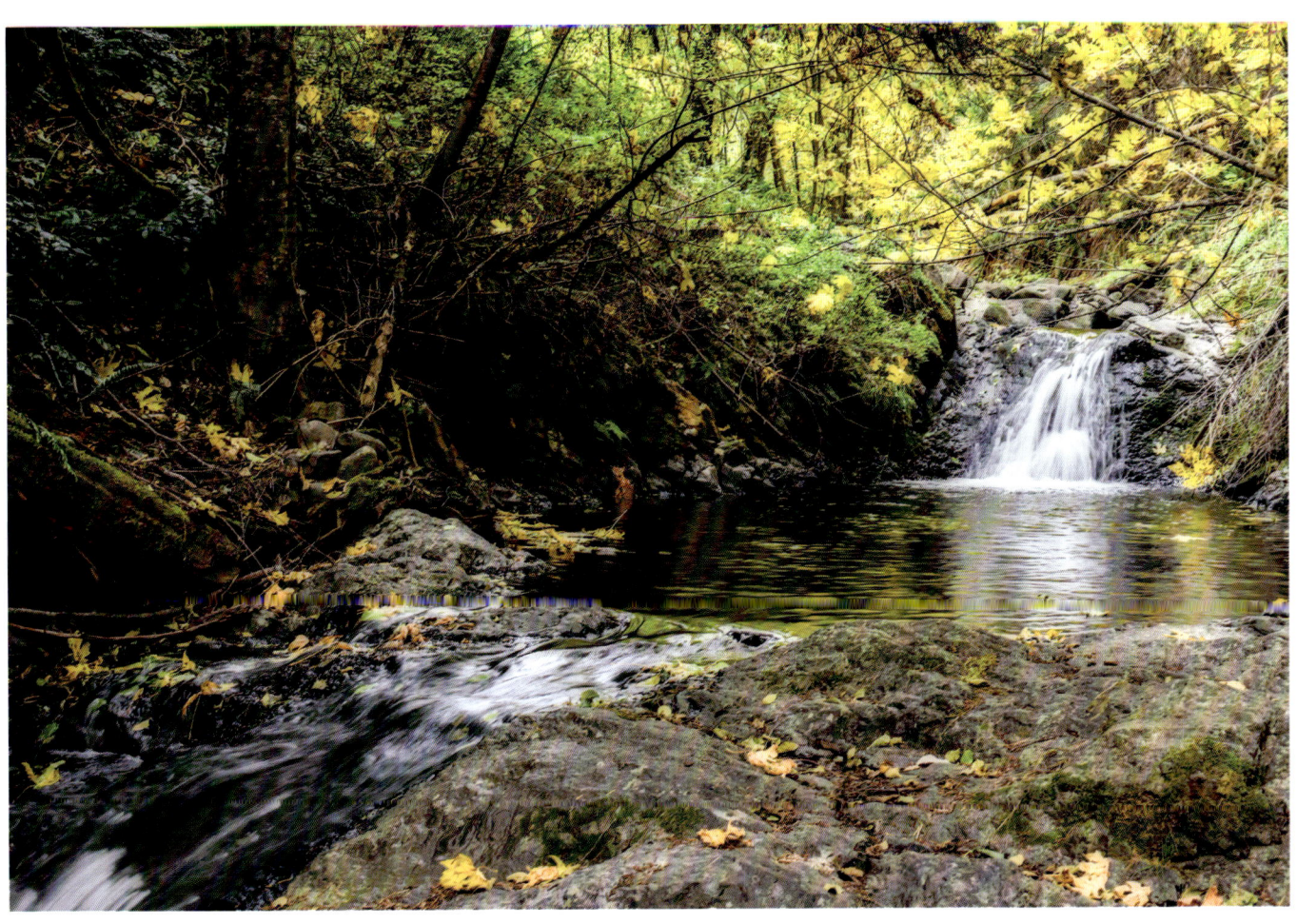

Carberry Creek Falls. This Applegate Lake spot is popular during the summer for fishing or cooling off. Carberry Creek cascades into Applegate Lake, creating this small, unofficial waterfall. *Photo by Nomeca Hartwell*

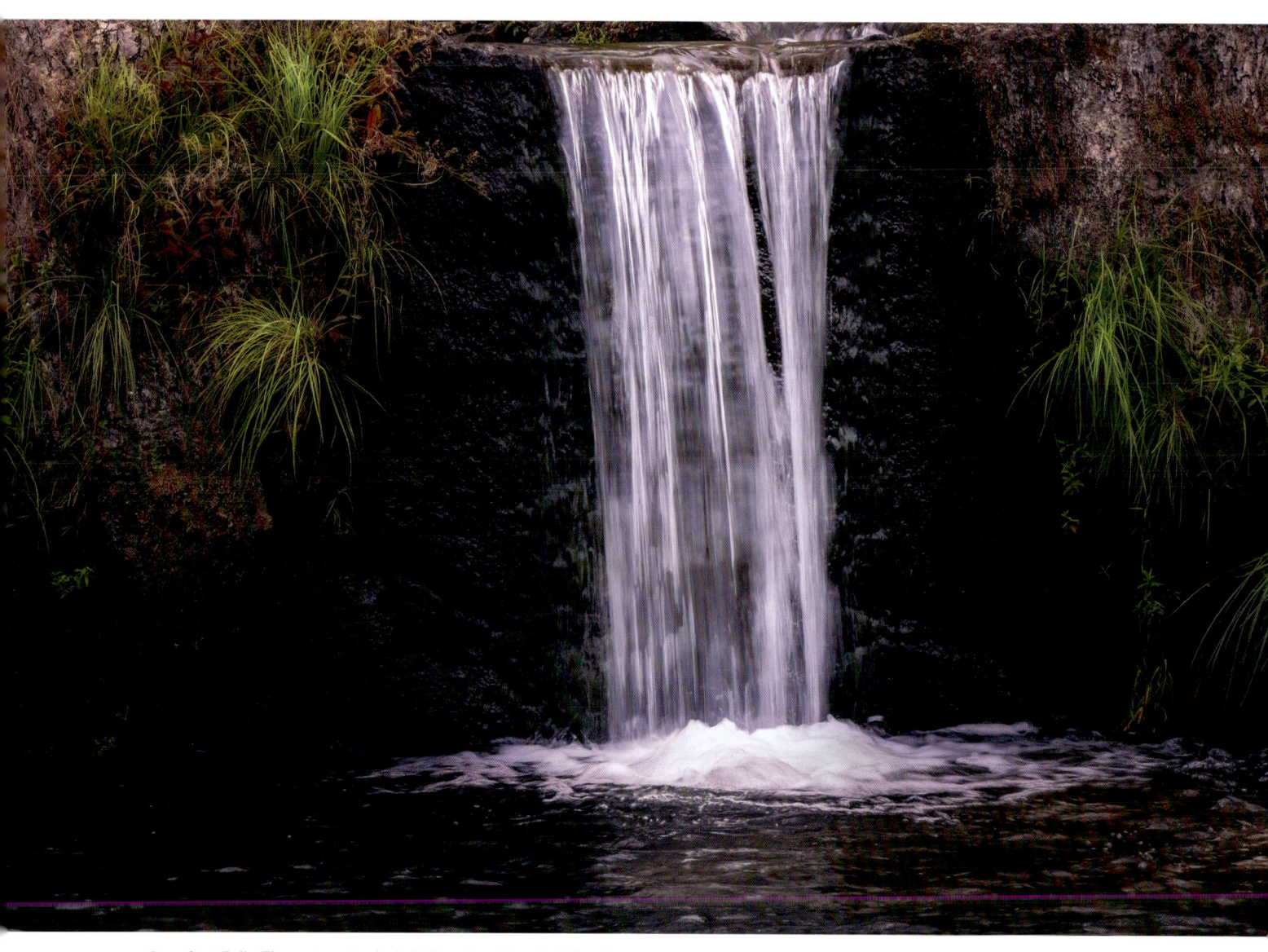

Crowfoot Falls. The swimming hole below Crowfoot Falls has been a popular area for cool dips on a hot day. However, recent access to the falls may be restricted. *Photo by Tony Kilcollins*

Crowfoot Falls. This popular and refreshing waterfall is south of Lost Creek Lake on Big Butte Creek near Trail, Oregon, about 30 minutes north of Medford. It measures only about 10 feet high and 80 feet wide. Check before heading out, since current access may be on private property. *Photo by Patty Albin*

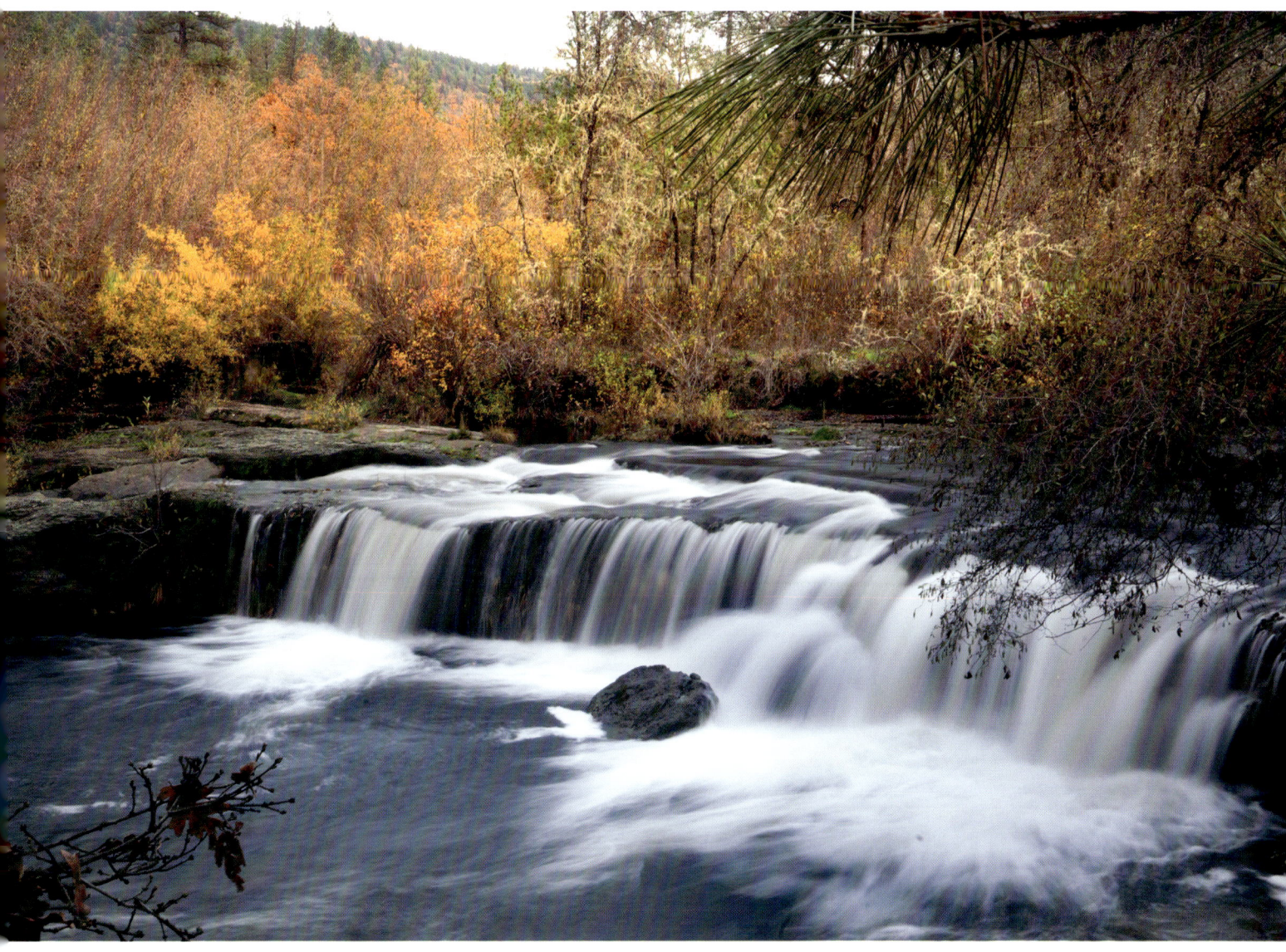

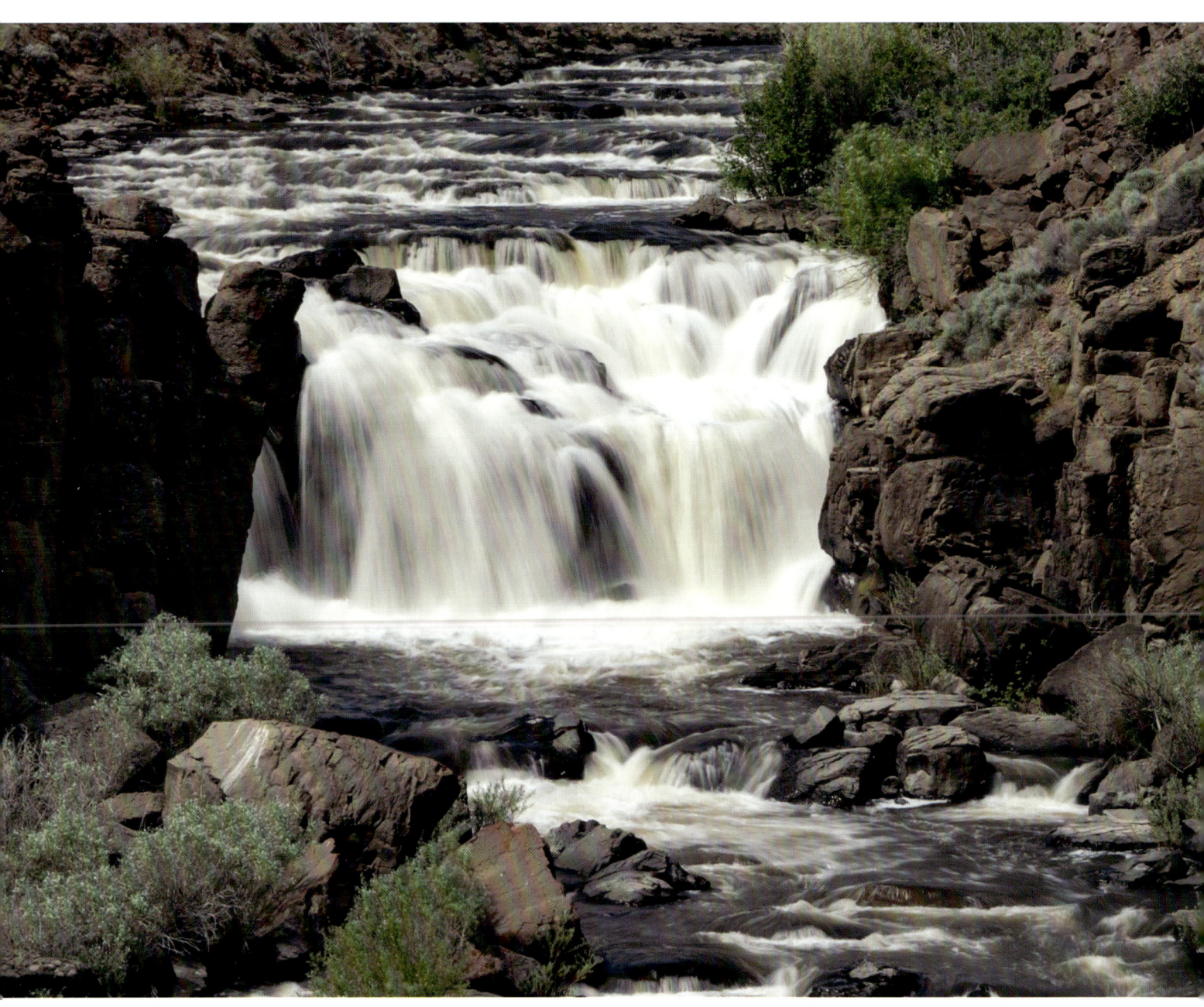

Deep Creek Falls. The falls are situated close to the three borders of Oregon, California, and Nevada. They run along the Oregon Outback Scenic Bikeway in the East Cascades and are easily visible from Highway 140. *Photo by Patty Albin*

Deep Creek Falls in autumn. One doesn't expect waterfalls in the high desert country of southeastern Oregon, especially in early fall. There are no other Oregon waterfalls within 100 miles of Deep Creek Falls, located east of Lakeview along Gibson Canyon on the south end of Warner Valley. The closest town is the small town of Adel, population 39. *Photo by Terry Fisher*

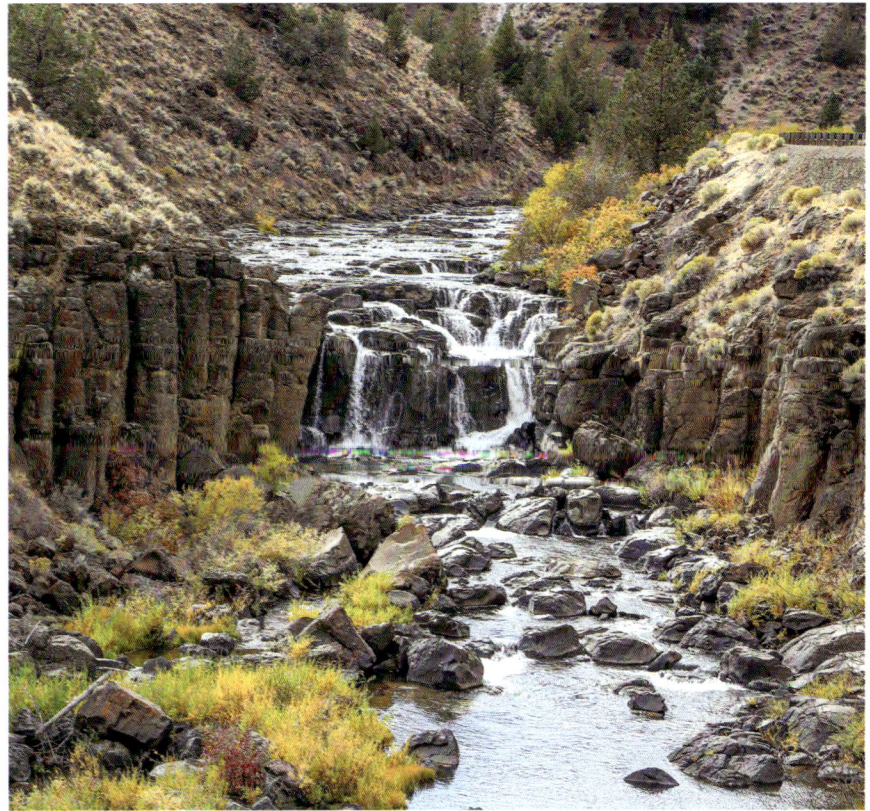

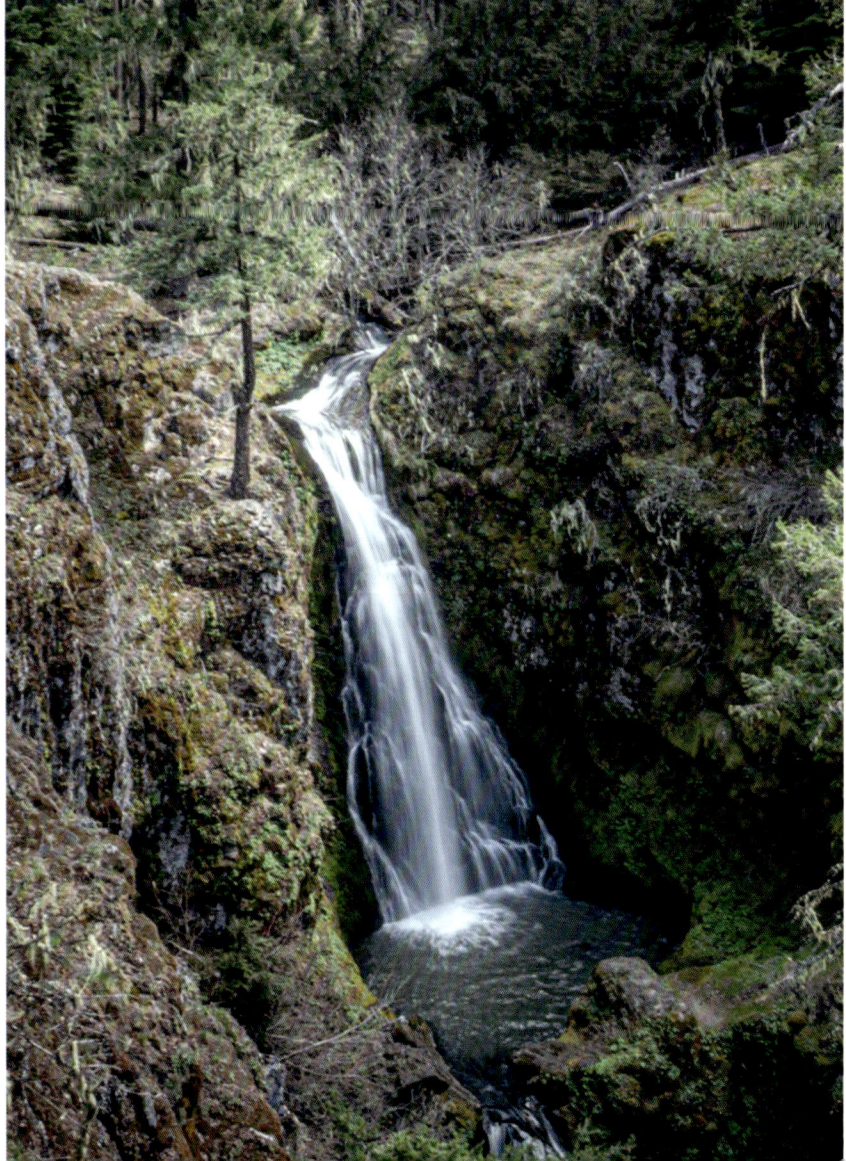

Lost Creek Falls, Ashland. A secluded, hidden, and hard-to-find waterfall in Ashland behind Grizzly Peak, Lost Creek Falls is not well marked. Access to the bottom of the falls may require a treacherous climb down. The hike to the top of the trail may include a creek crossing and the use of fixed ropes down a steep descent. Research before heading out, and don't rely on GPS or Google Maps, since the drive to find it can be perplexing. This fall is not to be confused with the equally challenging Lost Creek Falls in Coos County. *Photo by Randy Bryan*

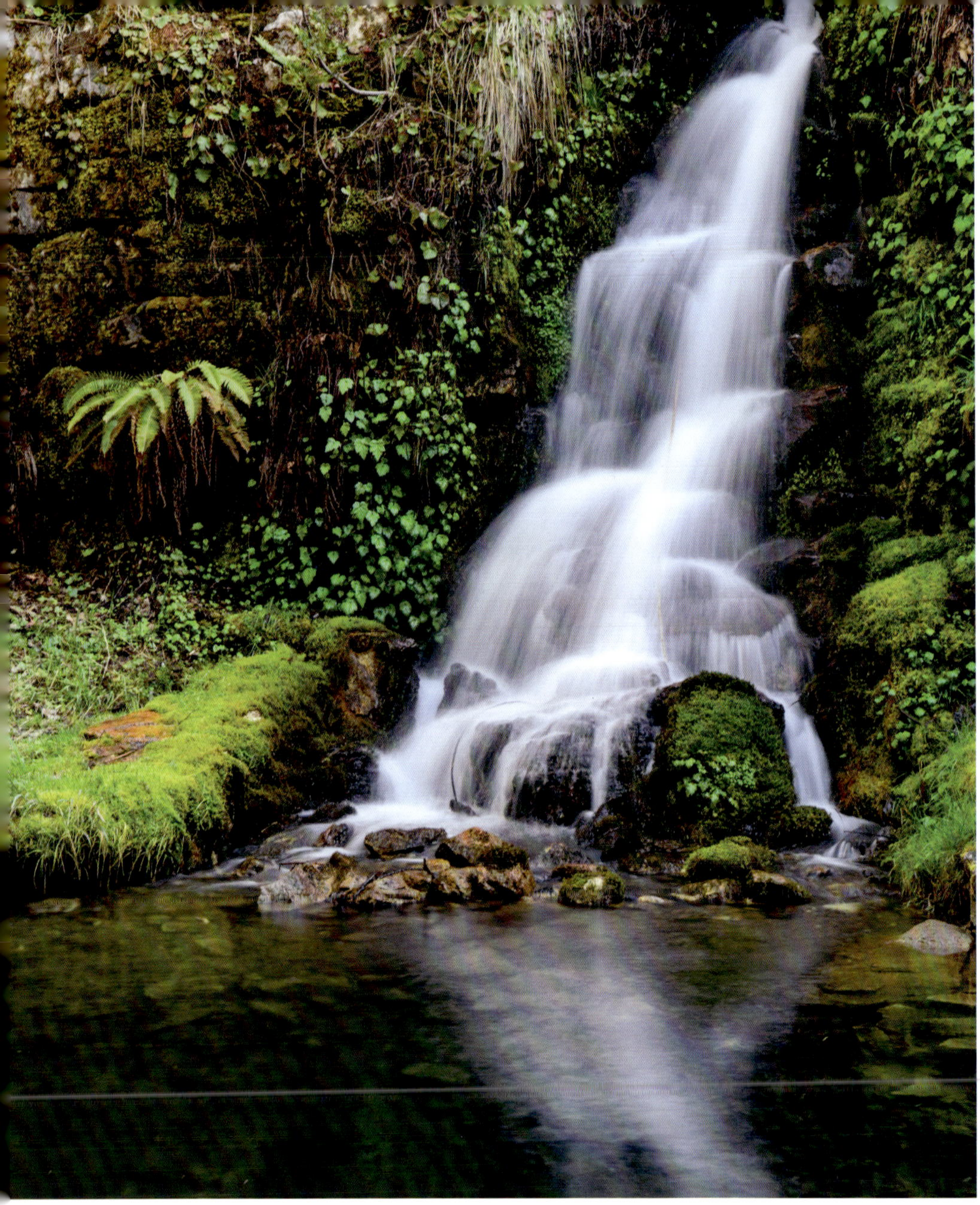

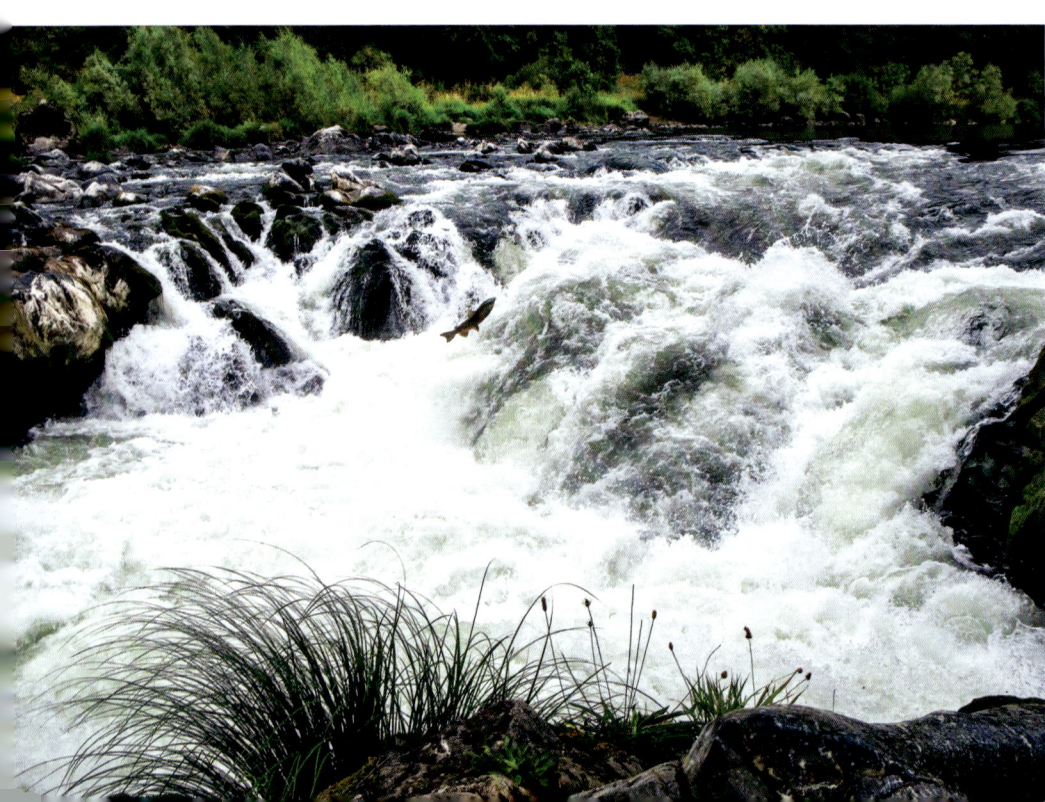

Cave Creek Falls. This is considered a more challenging trail, and hikers who visit the Oregon Caves National Monument may wish to take time to experience this 3.4-mile-out-and-back route. The charming waterfall is in the Siskiyou Mountains range near Cave Junction. It's located off Highway 99 (Redwood Highway), which is a popular route from southern Oregon to the Oregon coast. *Photo by Frank G. Lahman*

Rainie Falls. This rocky and challenging 1.8-mile trail runs parallel to the Rogue River. The trail was recently reopened after a 2022 fire. The falls themselves are considered class 5 rapids rather than a waterfall. Rafters can often be seen floating by, as well as salmon jumping (like the one in this photo!). *Photo by Nomeca Hartwell*

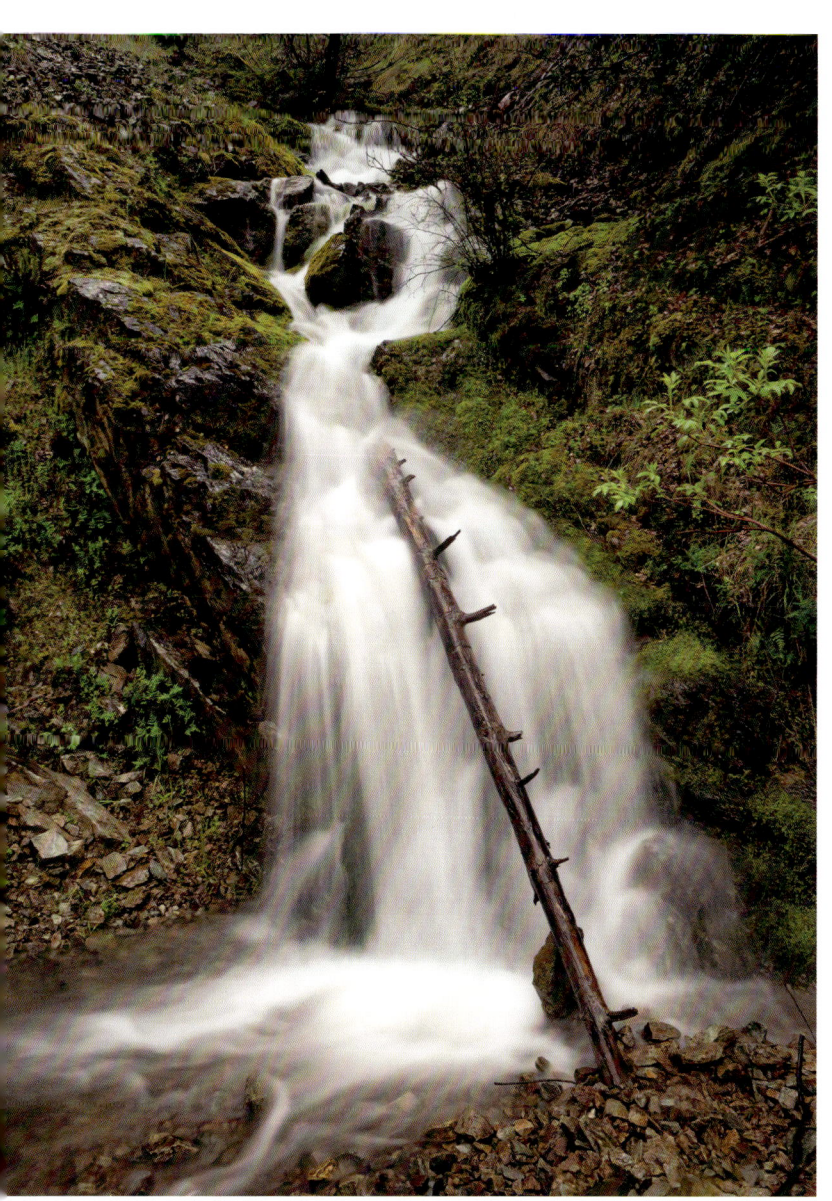

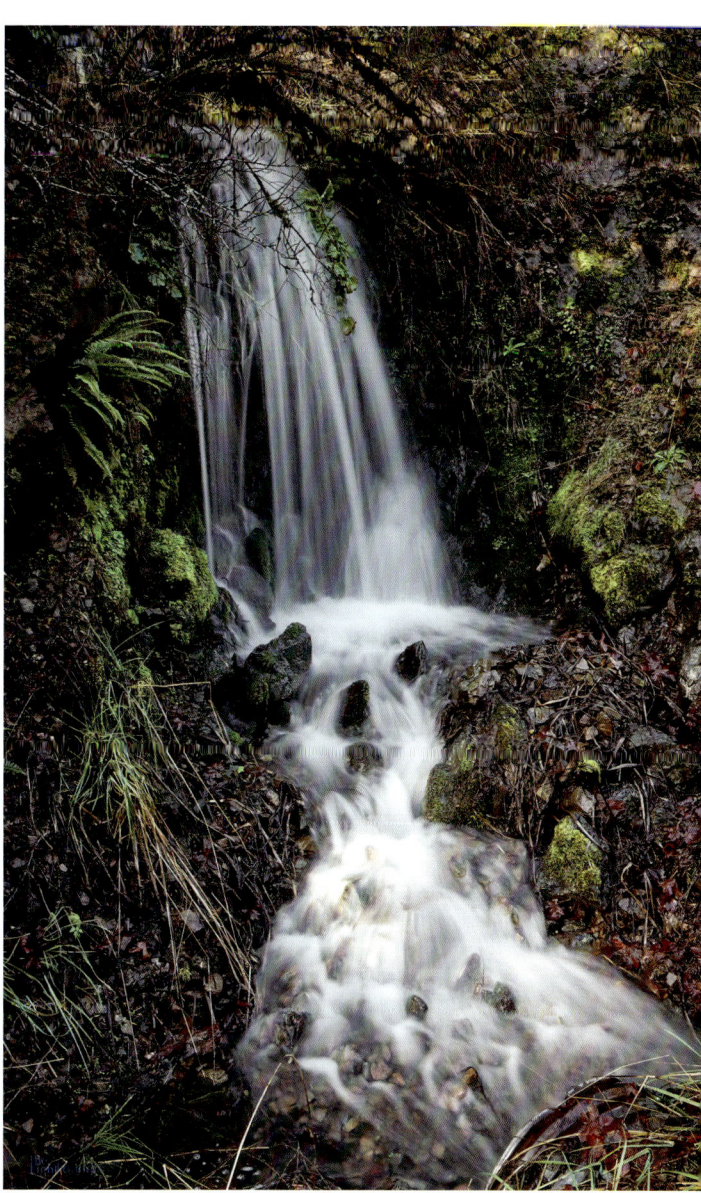

Rogue River Side Falls. This small seasonal waterfall, downriver from Galice, is a Rogue River side falls. The nearby Taylor Creek Trail, west of Grants Pass near Merlin, is a picturesque 5.1-mile-out-and-back trail. *Photo by Larry Pollock*

Taylor Creek Falls. There are many small seasonal falls along Taylor Creek Road like this one. *Photo by Larry Pollock*

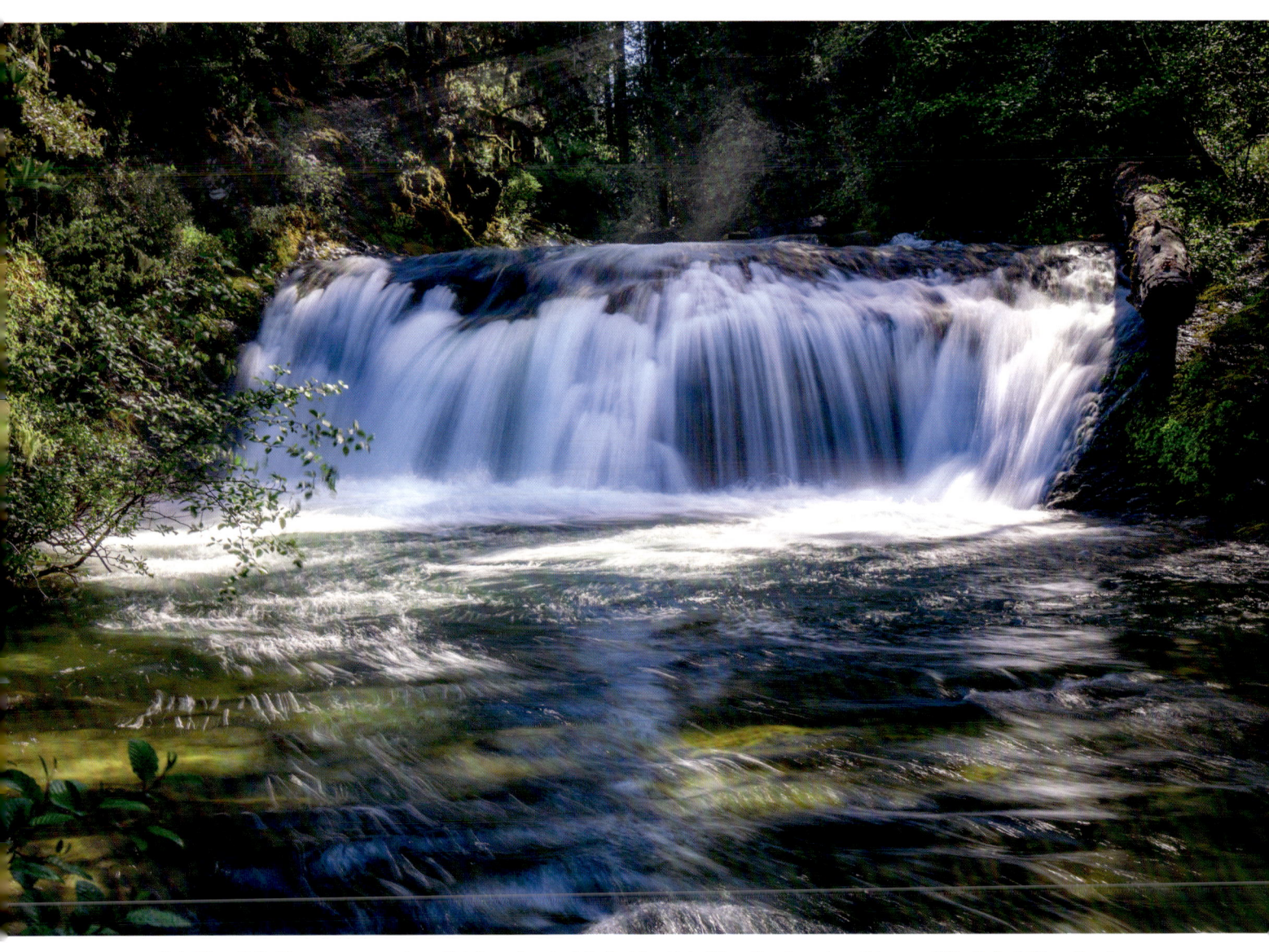

Little Silver Falls. There are several unofficial small waterfalls that feed into Silver Creek, such as this one off North Fork Silver Creek Road. It is approximately 8 miles up Bear Camp Road. *Photo by Nomeca Hartwell*

Silver Creek side falls. This little side falls is an offshoot of Silver Creek Falls in Josephine County. It is off Bear Camp Road.
Photo by Susan Sheets

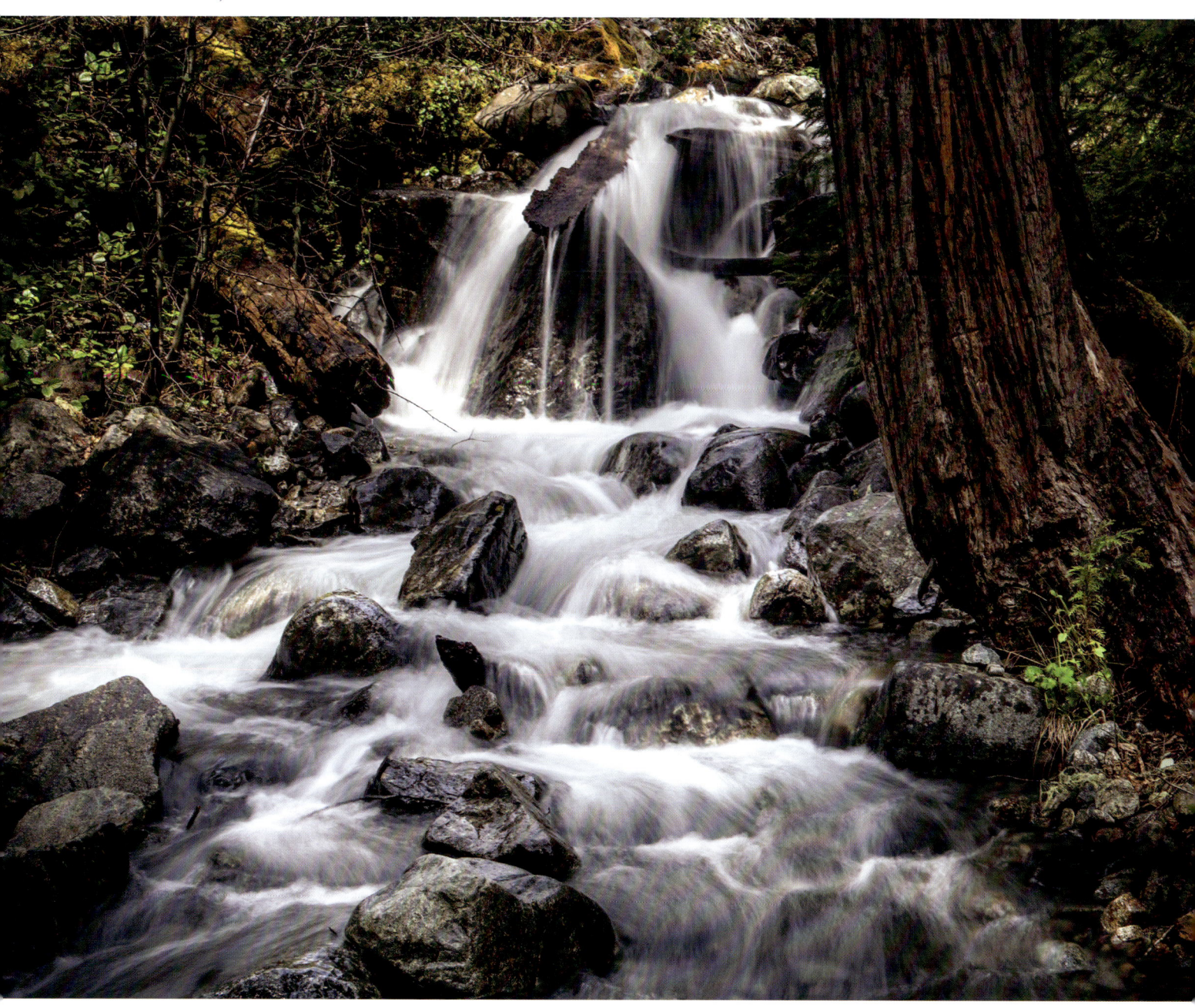

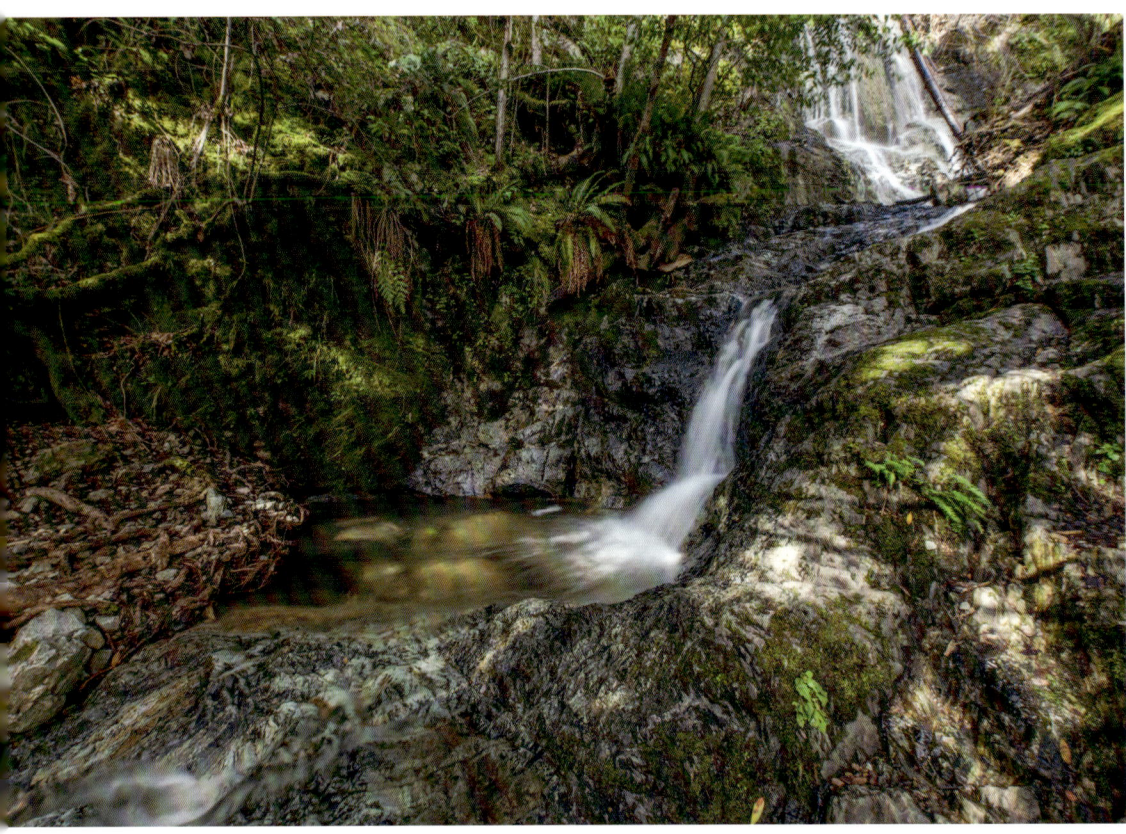

Mouse Creek Falls. This charming seasonal and unofficially named waterfall is in a creek a short distance off Galice Road in Josephine County. *Photo by Earshel Hogan*

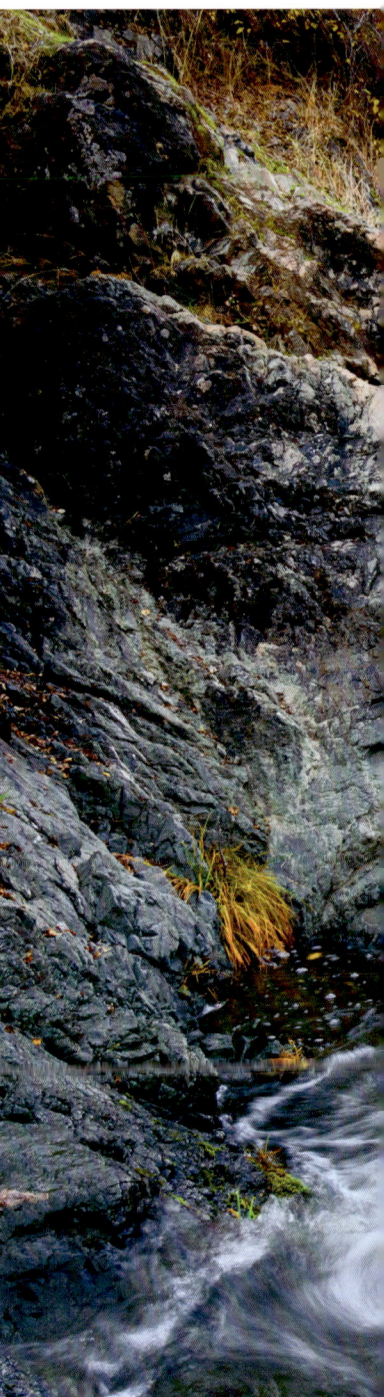

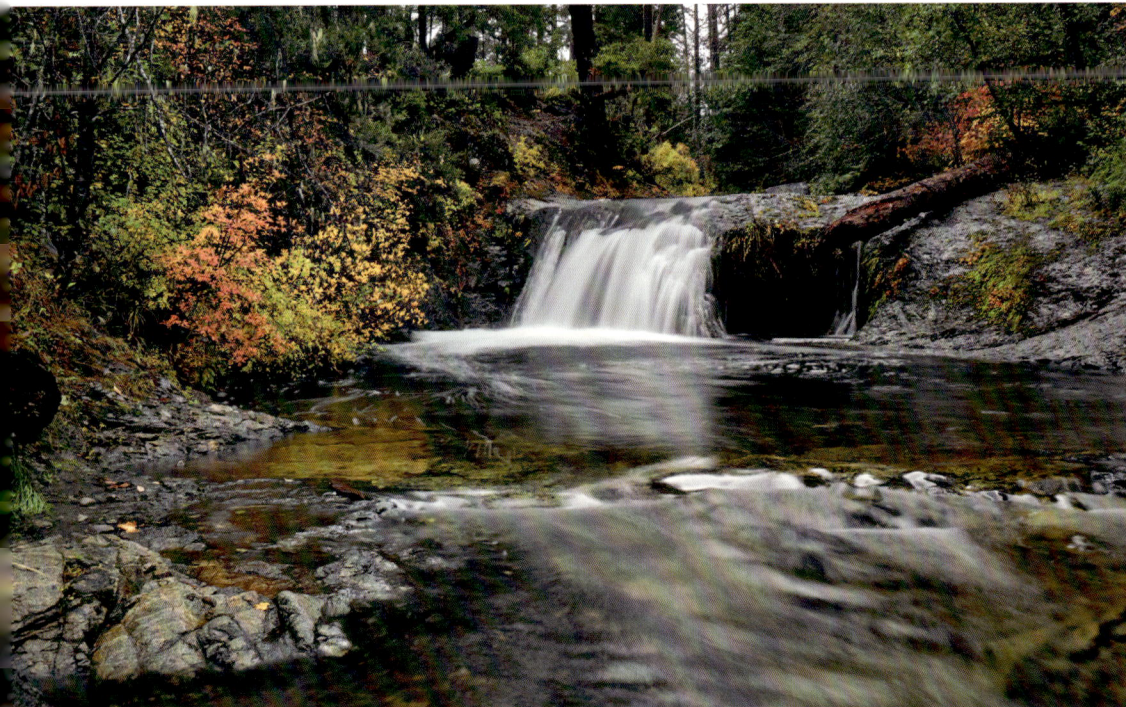

North Fork Silver Creek. An unofficial small waterfall that feeds into Silver Creek. *Photo by Larry Pollock*

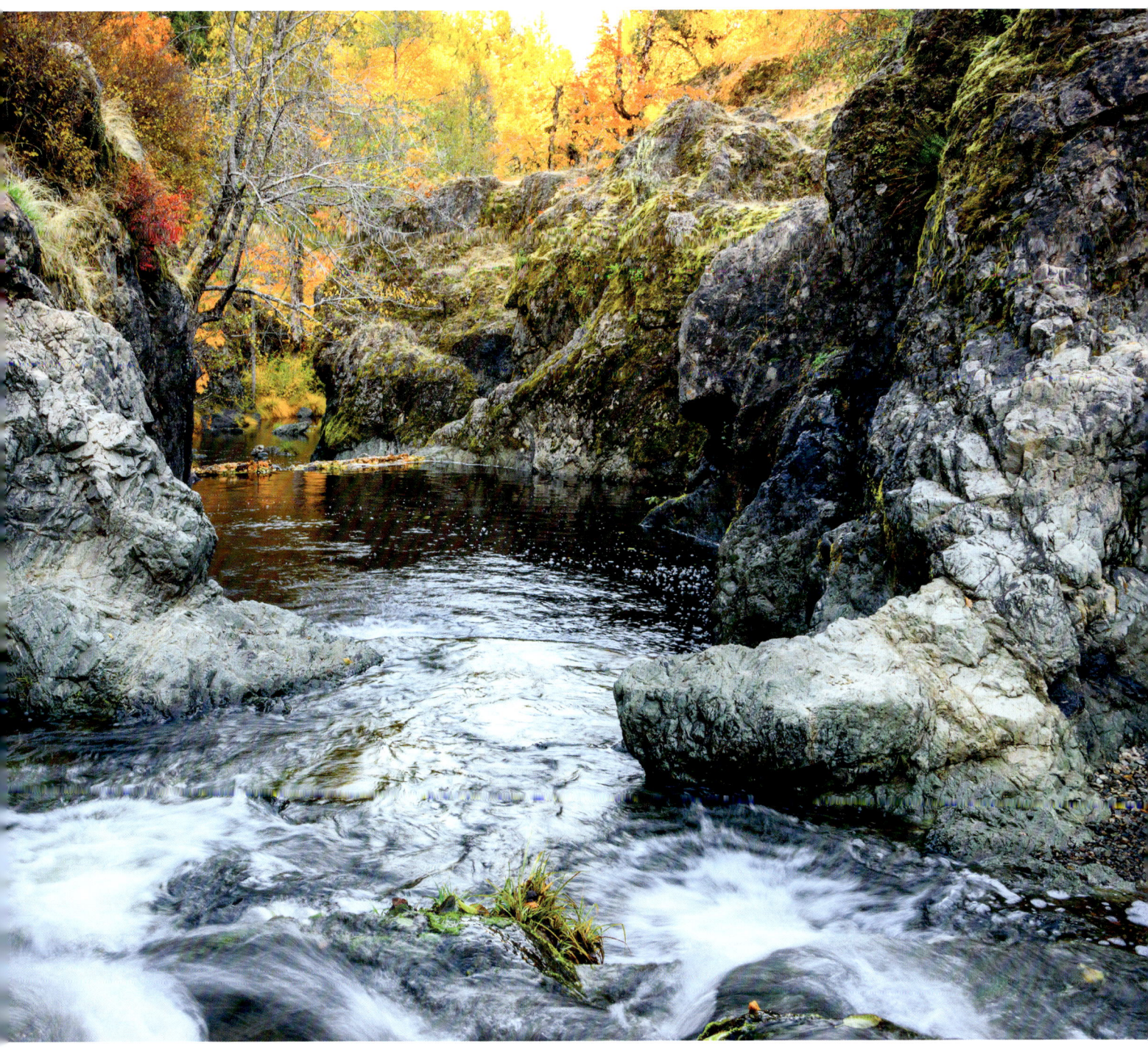

Taylor Creek step falls. Picturesque Taylor Creek, near Grants Pass and Merlin, has several no-name step falls, on and off the trail. This charming low falls runs alongside Taylor Creek Road, midway up to Big Pine Campground. *Photo by Nomeca Hartwell*

7 Umpqua Valley
"The Highway of Waterfalls"

Dubbed the "Highway of Waterfalls," Highway 138 (the Rogue-Umpqua Scenic Byway) in southern Oregon has dozens of waterfalls to enjoy. If Crater Lake is a destination, driving along Highway 138 from Roseburg will allow visitors to see multiple waterfalls along the route, many with easy access from the road. In addition to impressive and distinctive waterfalls, the North Umpqua River is also revered for its 30 miles of steelhead fishing. Located in the lush Umpqua National Forest, many of these Oregon waterfall gems are easily seen on a day trip.

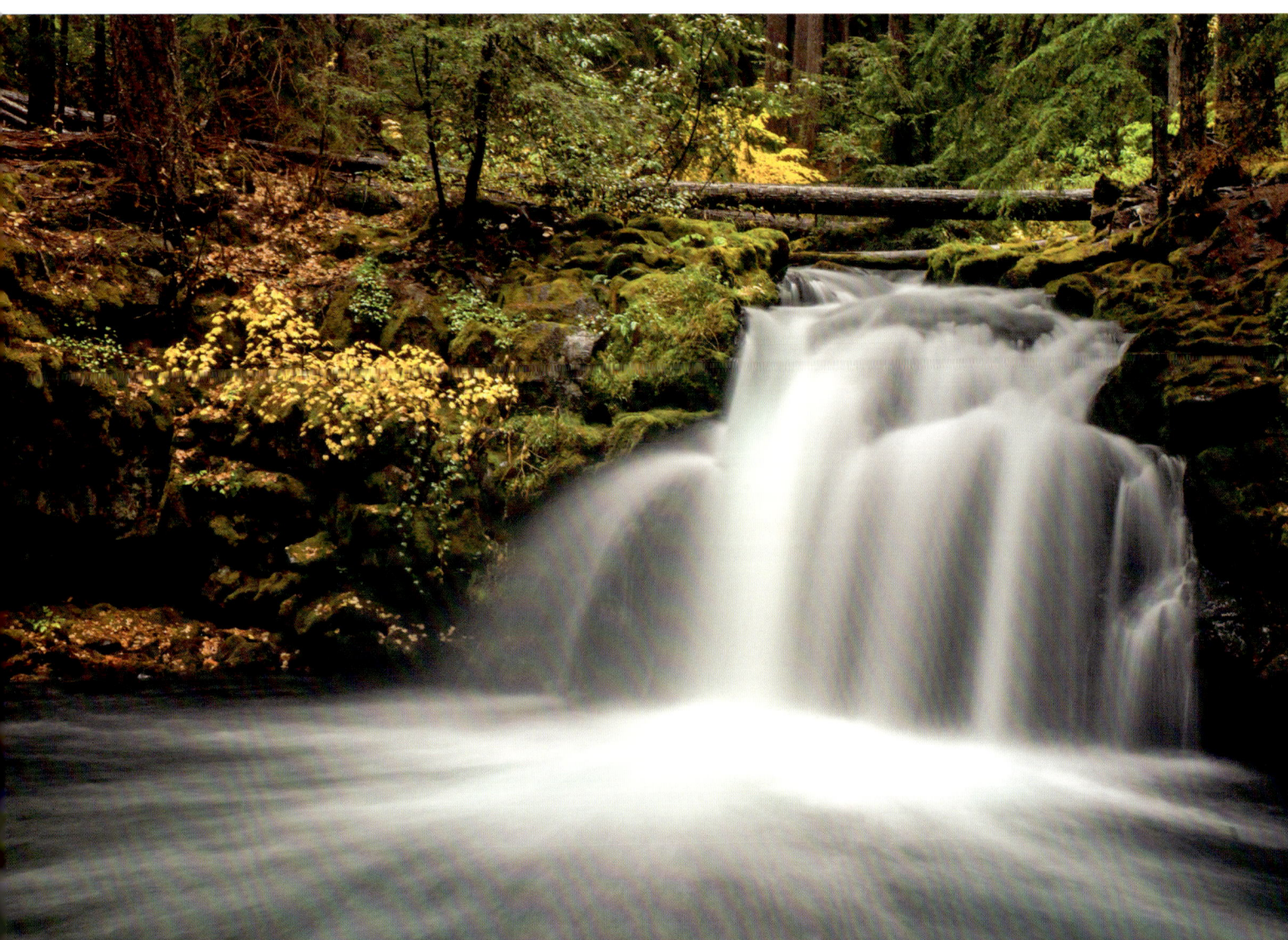

Whitehorse Falls. The family-friendly trail to this lacy "punchbowl" waterfall is lush, short, and very easy to hike. While there, visit other Umpqua Valley waterfalls such as Clearwater Falls, Watson Falls, and Toketee Falls. *Photo by Jay Newman*

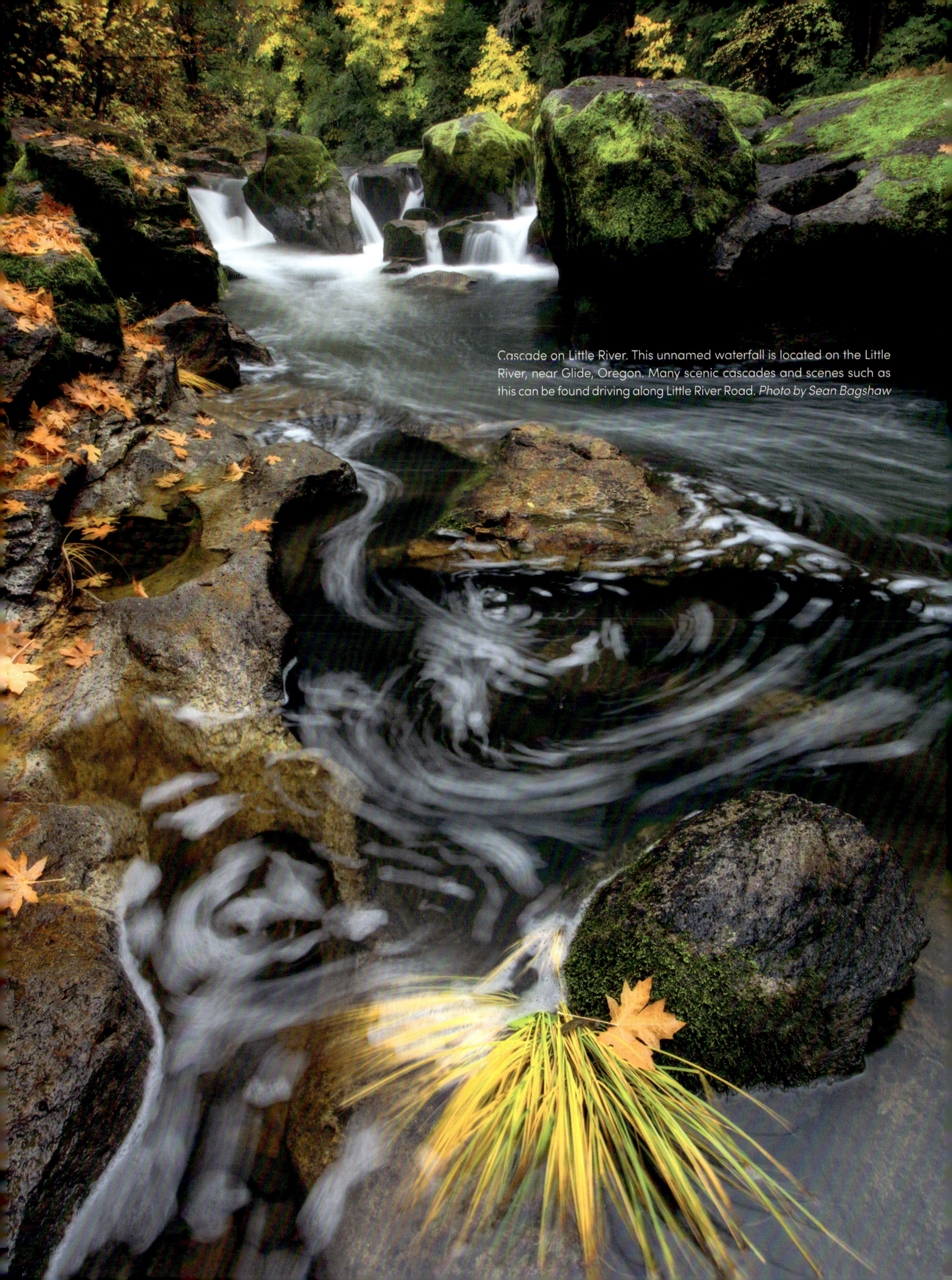

Cascade on Little River. This unnamed waterfall is located on the Little River, near Glide, Oregon. Many scenic cascades and scenes such as this can be found driving along Little River Road. *Photo by Sean Bagshaw*

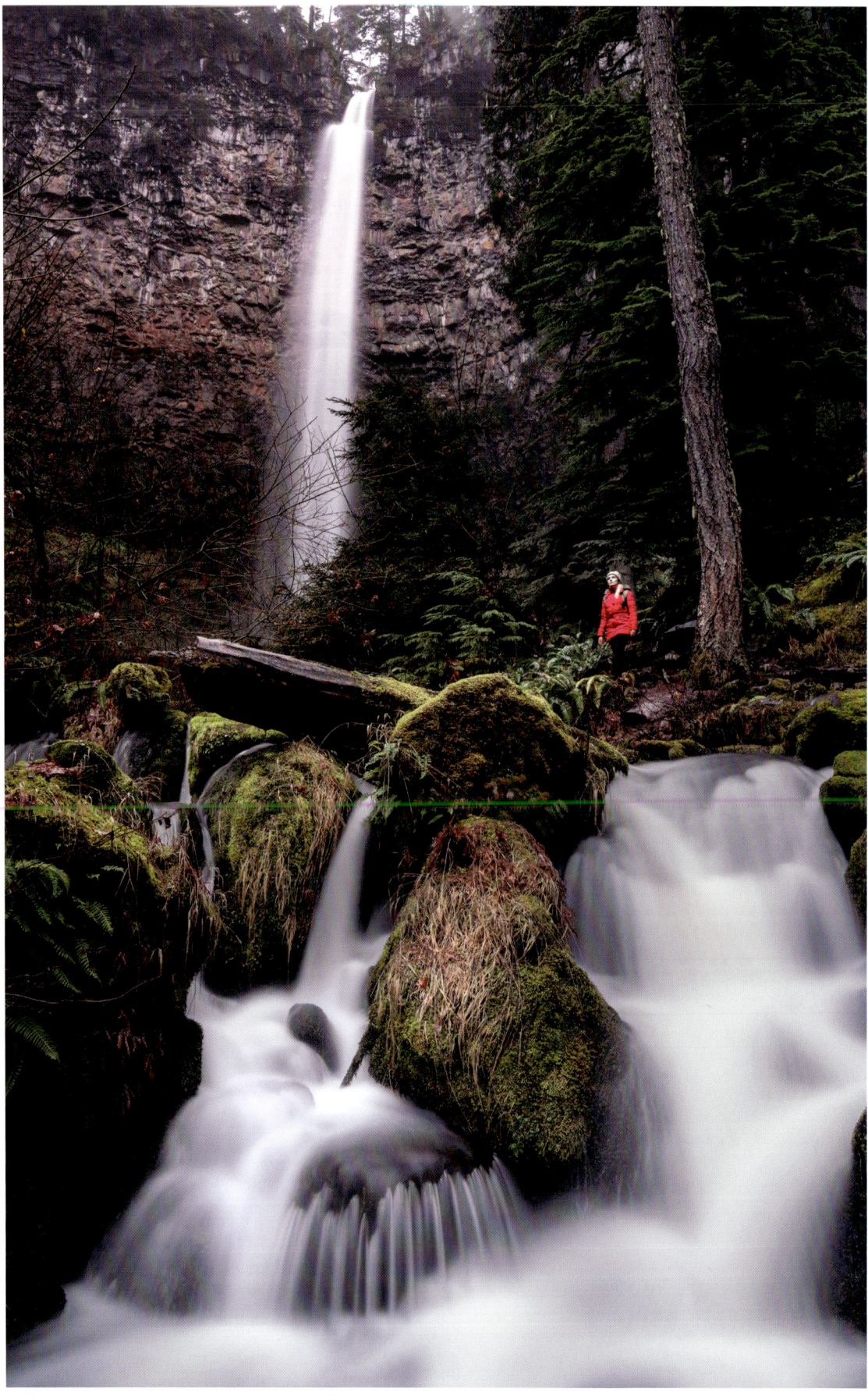

Watson Falls. This thundering waterfall is Oregon's third-tallest waterfall and the highest in the Umpqua Valley. It's easily accessible on a well-maintained trail over a wooden bridge that crosses Watson Creek. The falls majestically plunge 272 feet over the edge of basalt lava flow rocks on a cliff. The falls can also be viewed from the parking lot. *Photo by Adam Marland*

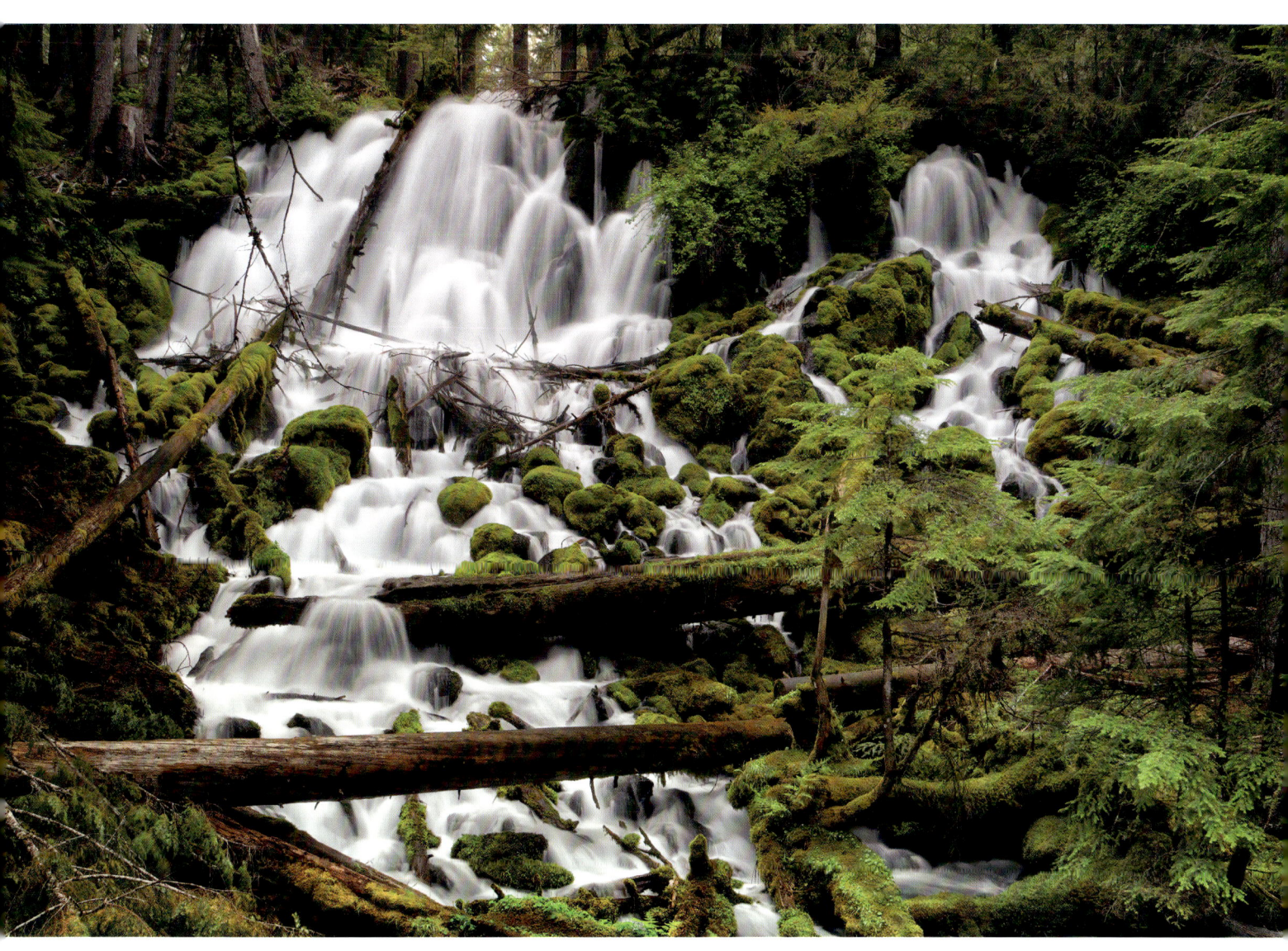

Clearwater Falls. A hike to this tiered waterfall is considered easy and takes only about five minutes from the parking lot. The falls cascade 30 feet over moss-covered rocks and logs. While in the area, visit nearby Whitehorse Falls, Watson Falls, or Toketee Falls. Clearwater Falls also has a parking/viewing area for handicapped individuals. *Photo by Gary Thurman*

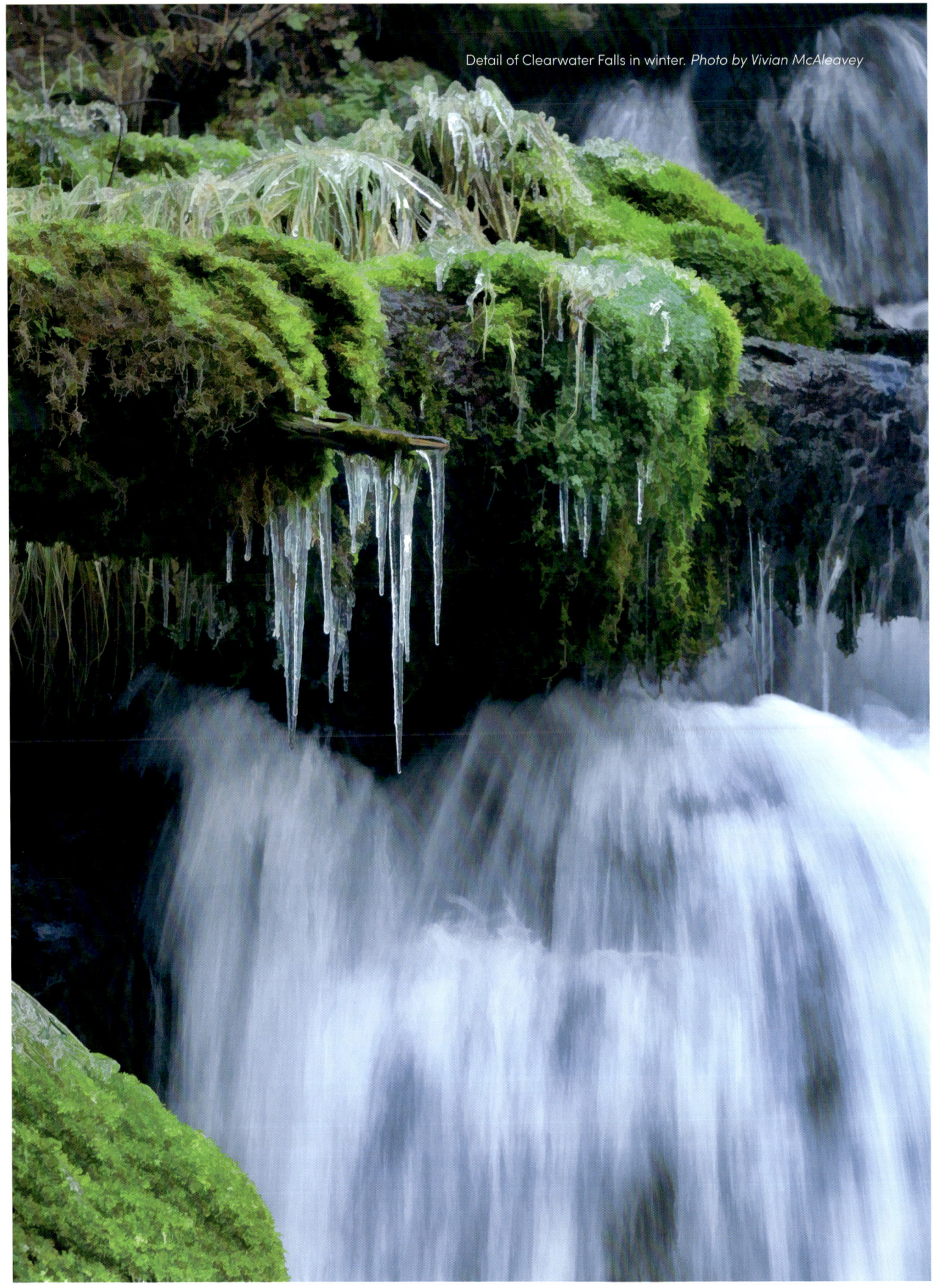

Detail of Clearwater Falls in winter. *Photo by Vivian McAleavey*

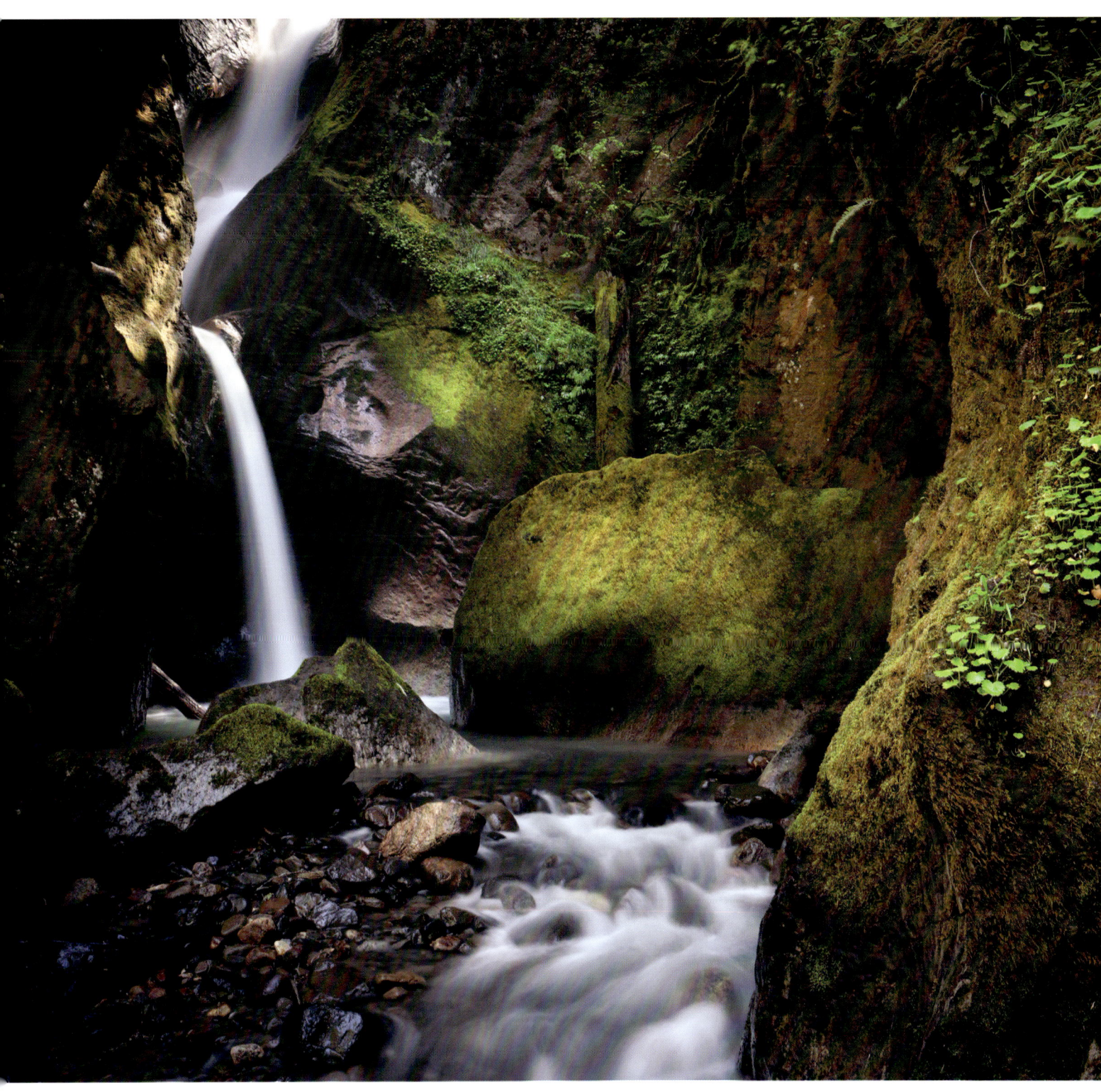

Shadow Falls. This triple-tiered waterfall is on Cavitt Creek. It stands 100 feet tall. Its name is apt because it rarely receives direct sunlight. The trail is flat until the last 0.2 miles, where one descends to the viewing area. Wildflowers bloom in spring. *Photo by Sean Bagshaw*

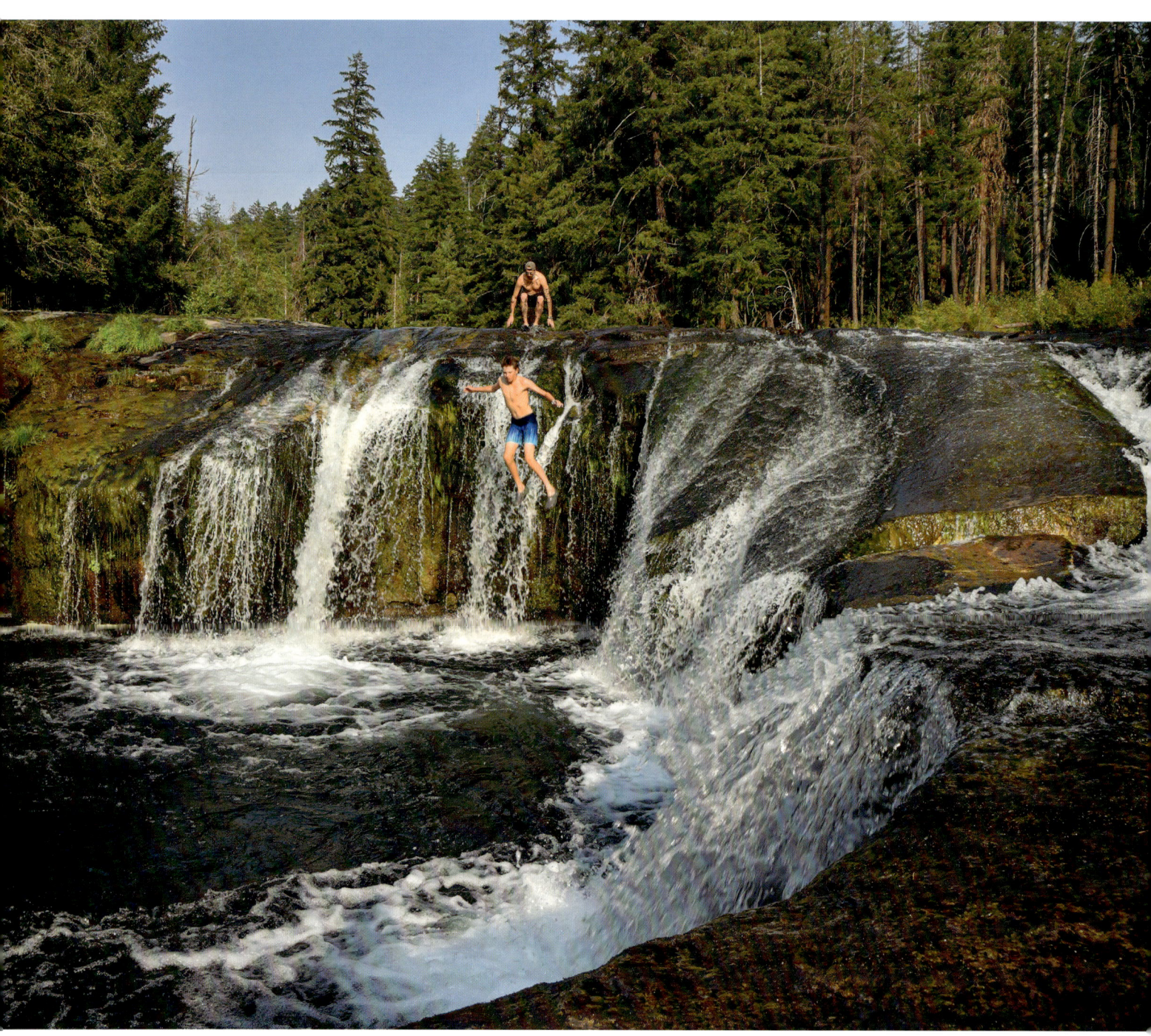

South Umpqua Falls. The natural water slides make it a perfect spot for swimming in the summer for the whole family.
Photo by Jessica King

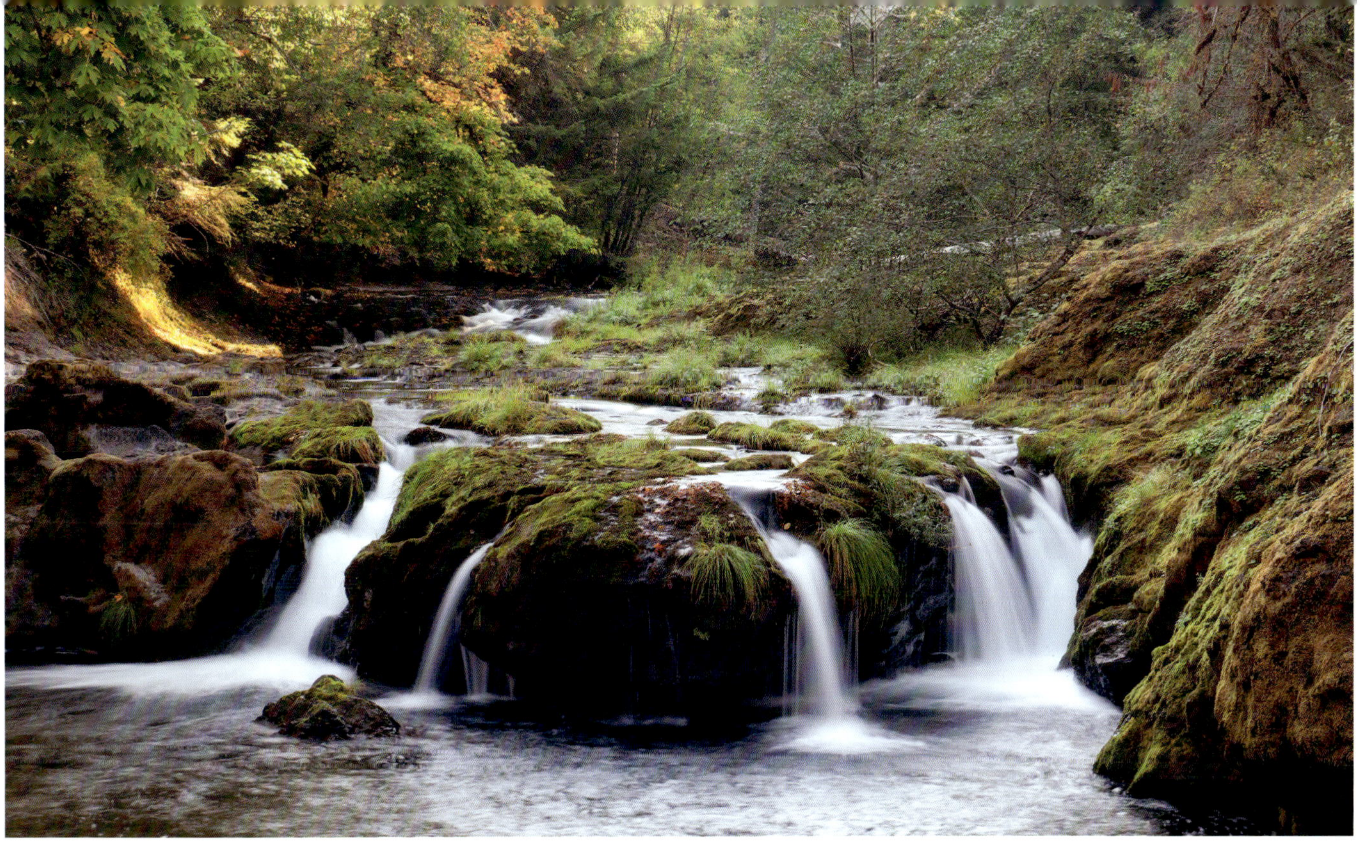

South Umpqua Falls. The National Forest Service considers the South Umpqua Falls Campground a "taste of Yosemite tucked away in the Umpqua Valley." It's only a quarter-mile hike down to the base of the waterfall. *Photo by Sean Bagshaw*

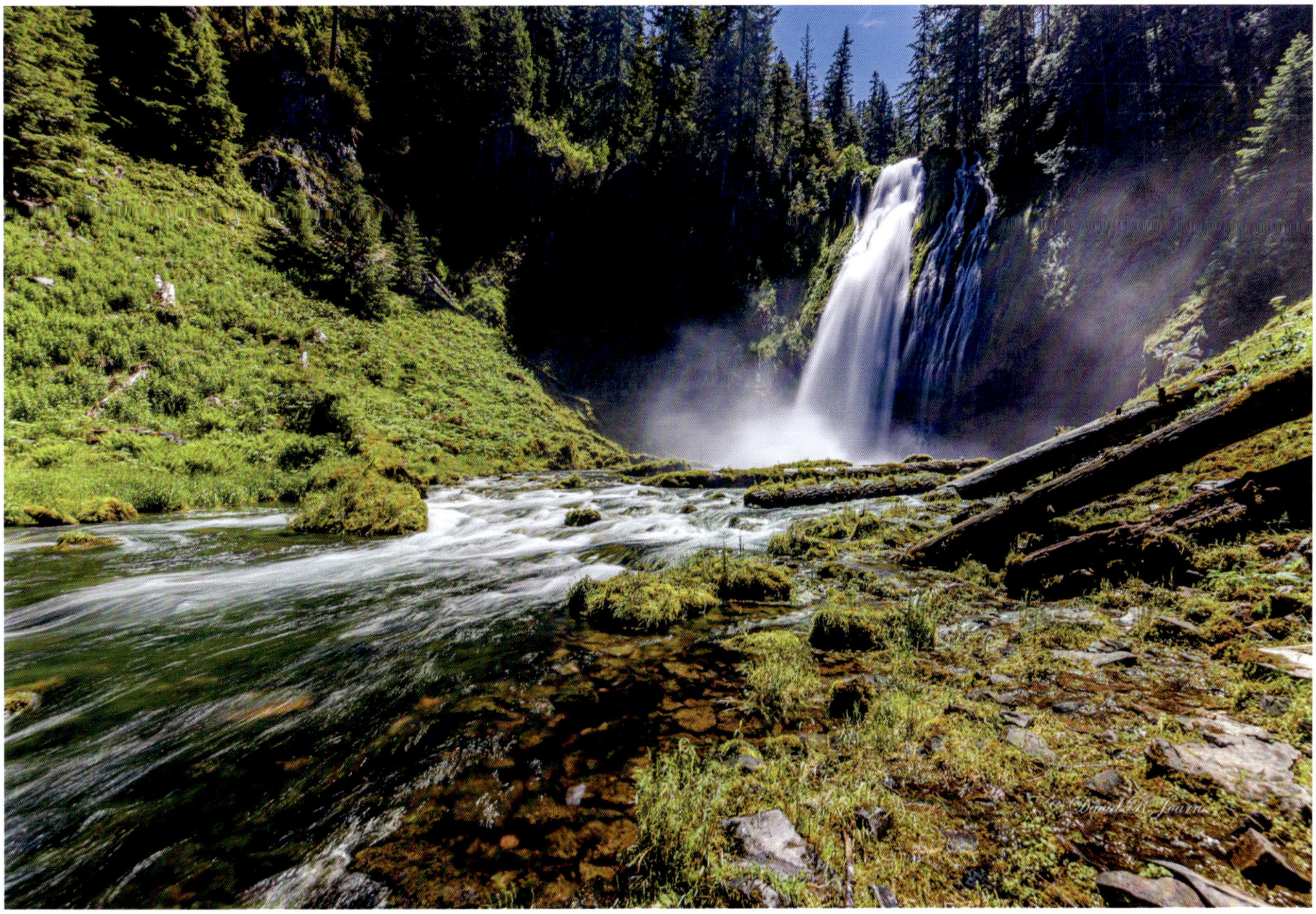

Lemolo Falls. About a 20-minute drive from Diamond Lake, and not far from Warm Springs Falls, Lemolo Falls' height is disputed. Some consider it the tallest waterfall on the North Umpqua River, at 165 feet, while a US Forest Service estimate is 102 feet. It is an example of a striking horsetail-type waterfall. The raging water drops over a cliff of columnar basalt into a canyon below. The hike to the falls is moderate to difficult. The word "Lemolo" is a Chinook Indian term meaning "wild" or "untamed." *Photo by David Joarnt*

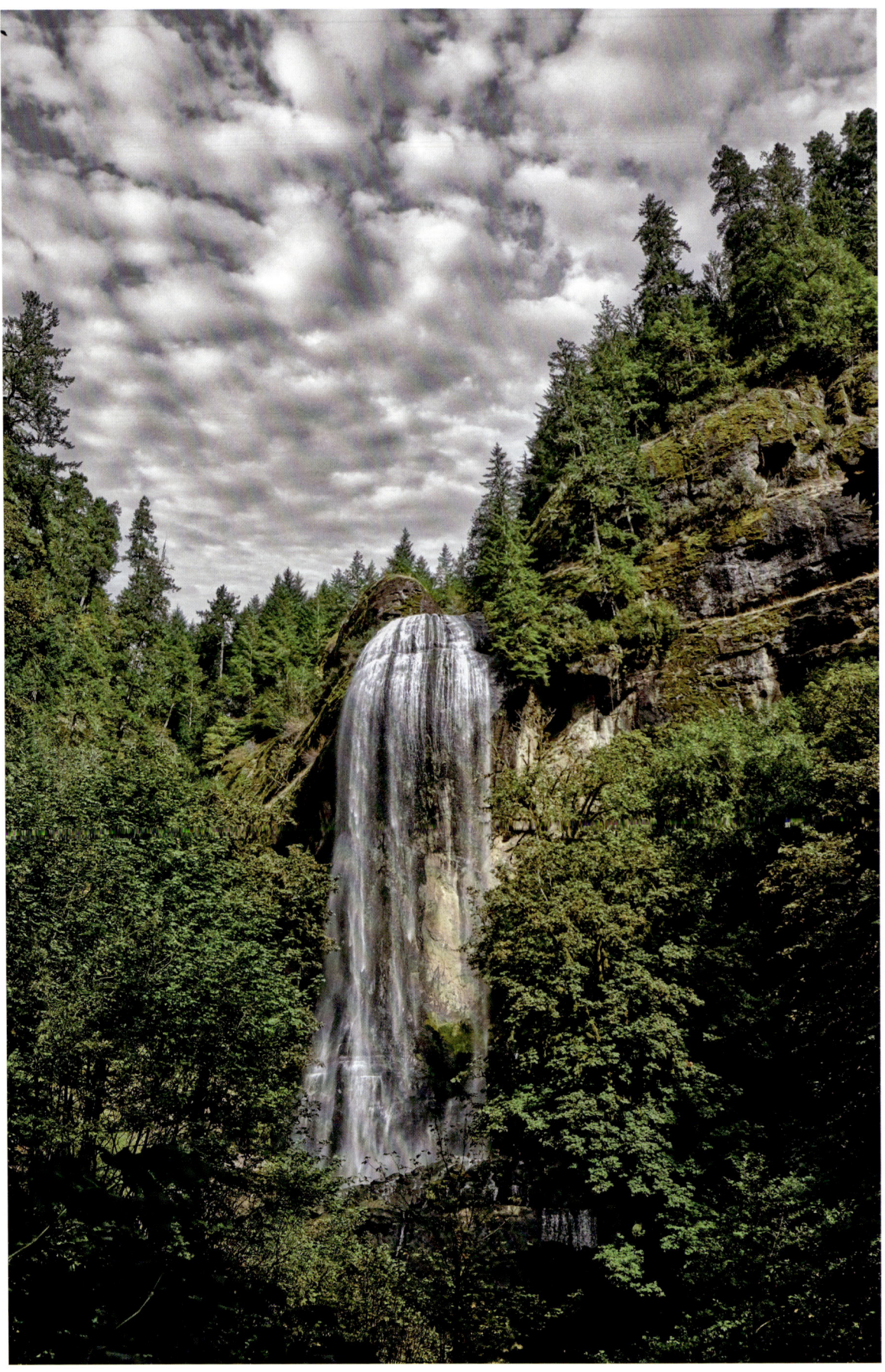

Spirit Falls. There is a fairly easy and short downhill trail to reach the falls along lovely Alex Creek, with occasional switch-backs. It tumbles 60 feet over mossy rock. Like many Oregon waterfalls, the flowing water is more plentiful in the spring. *Photo by Richard Krieger*

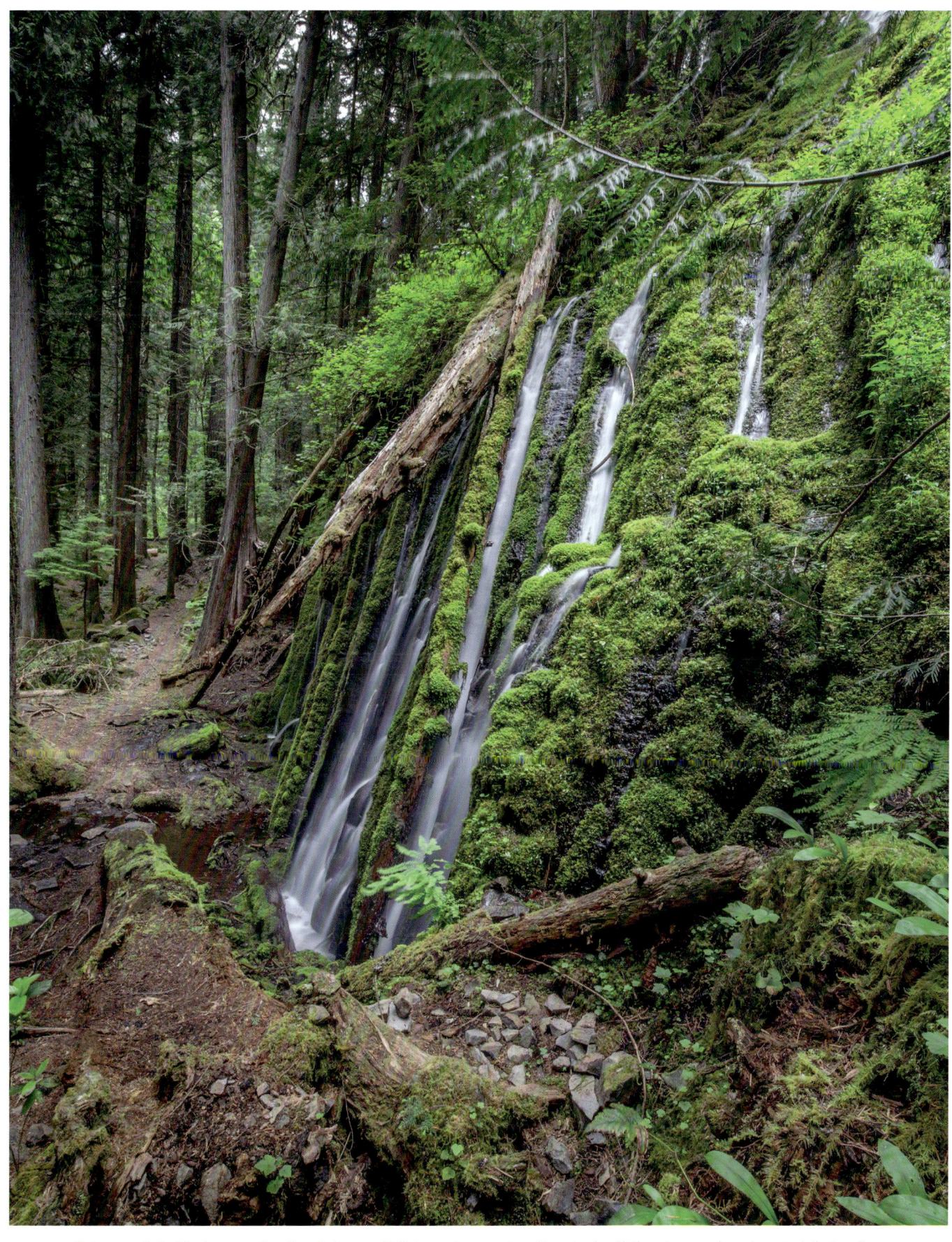

Columnar Falls. Like its name implies, Columnar Falls is a unique series of hundreds of little columnar-basalt waterfalls that flow between moss-covered rock columns. *Photo by Jim Chamberlain*

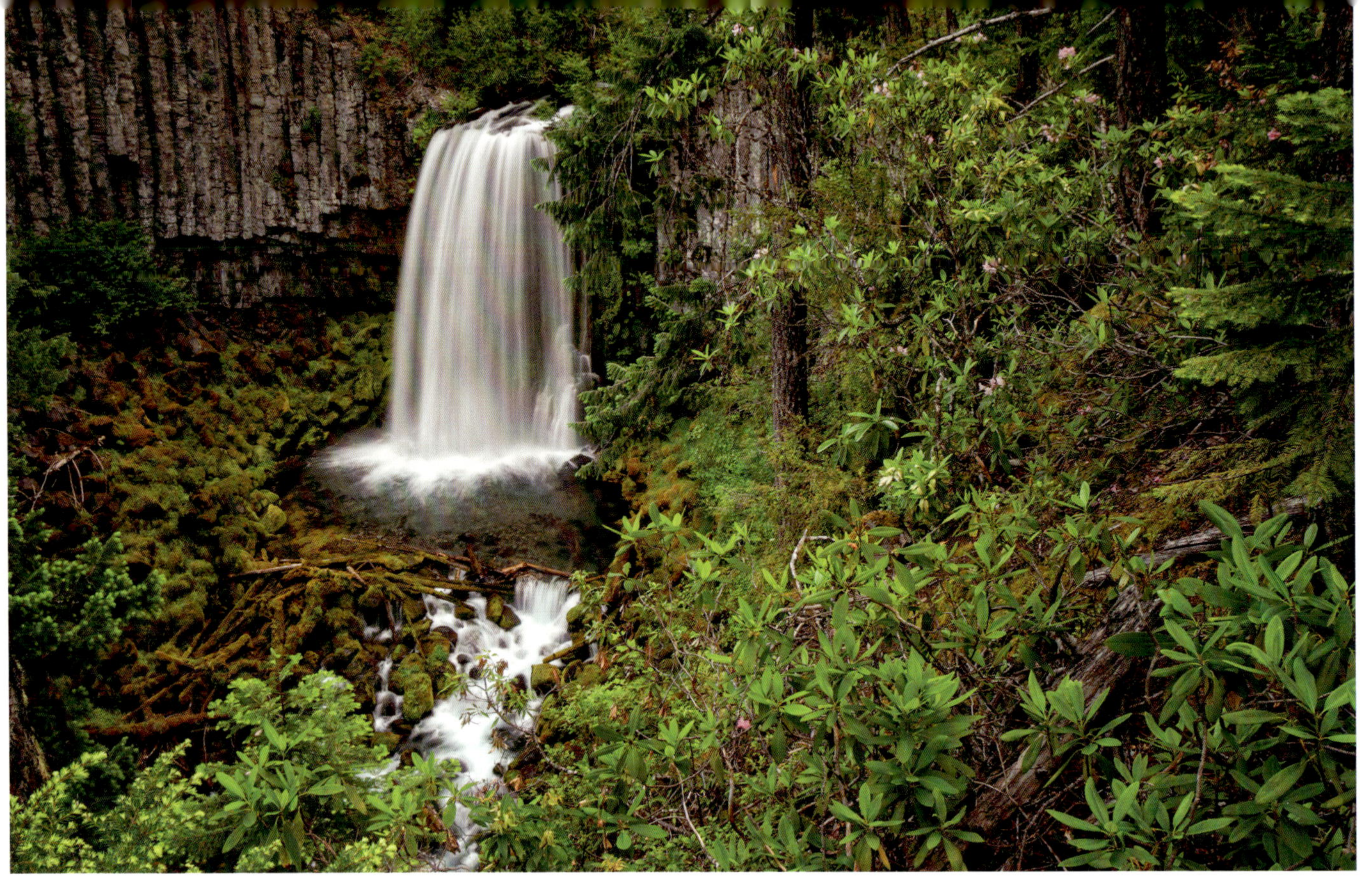

Warm Springs Falls. A 0.3-mile paved trail winds through Douglas fir and lodgepole pine to a viewing platform. There is no access to the base of the falls, and no guardrails. The falls thunder over a 70-foot drop, down columns of basalt. In spring, rhododendrons are in bloom. *Photo by Susan Sheets*

Warm Springs Falls. The base of Warm Springs Falls after a 70-foot drop. This waterfall is not far from Lemolo Falls. *Photo by Vivian McAleavey*

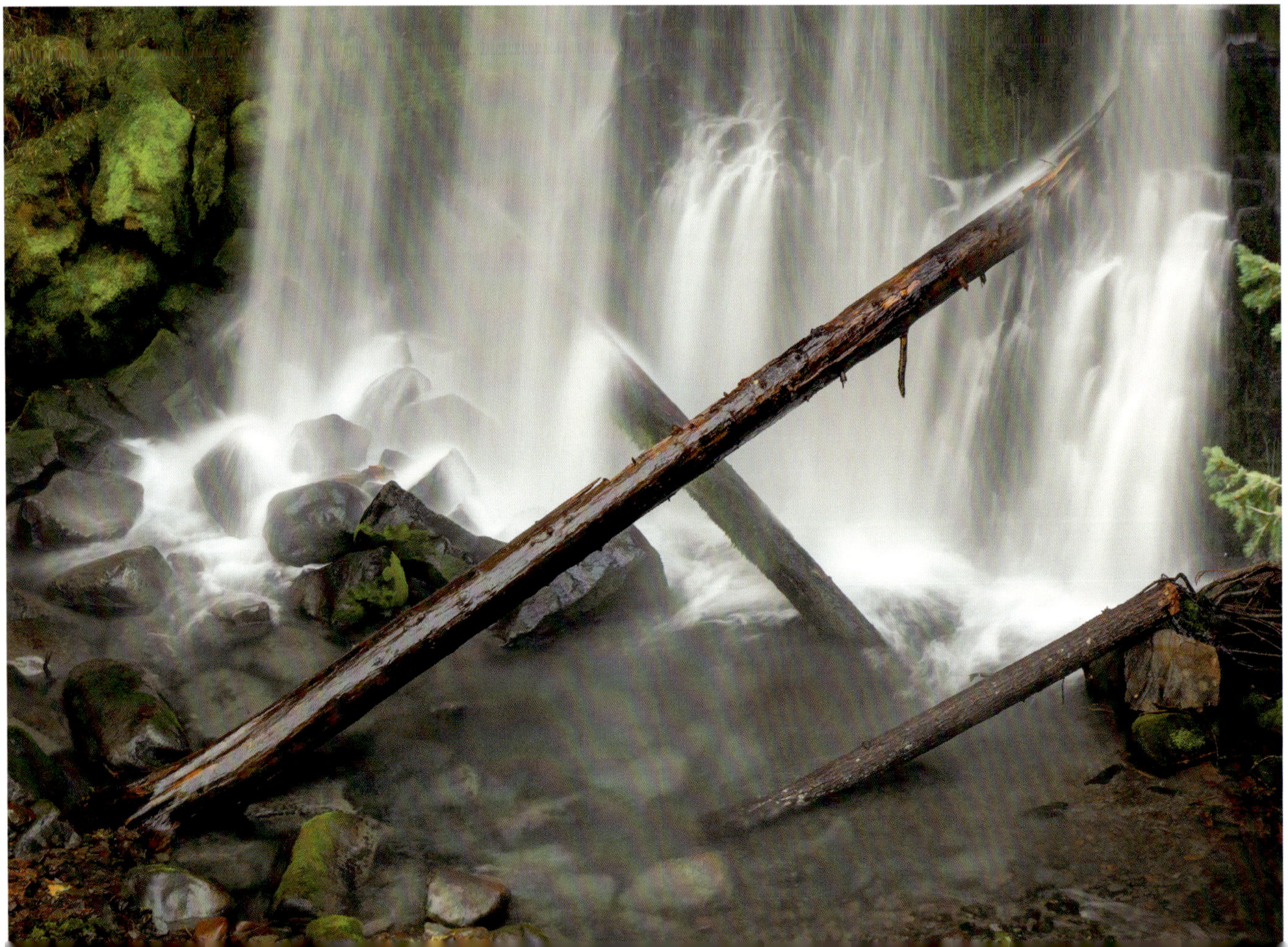

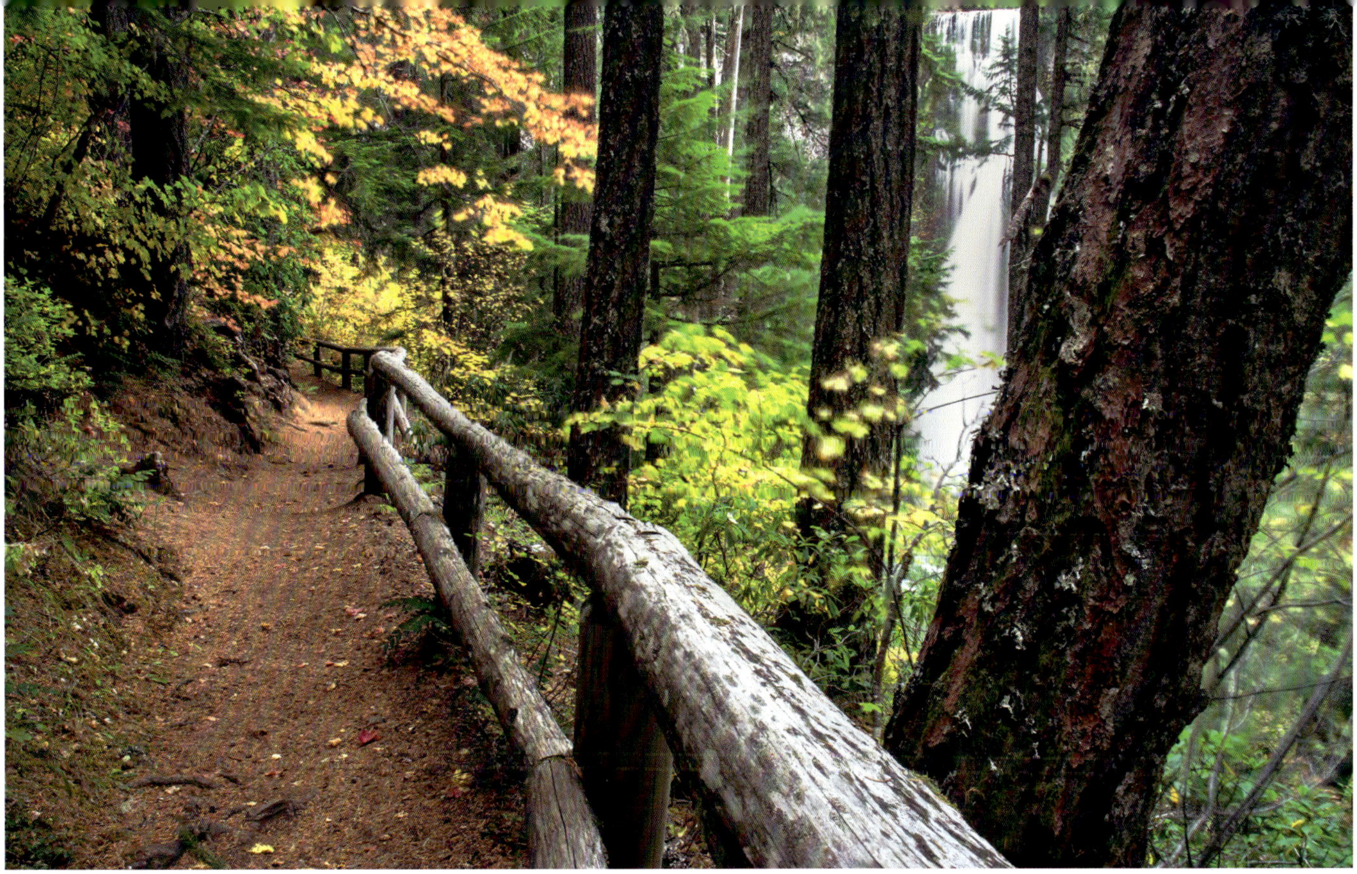

Trail to Fall Creek Falls. This is a family-friendly 1.5-mile-out-and-back trail near Idleyld Park. *Photo by Jay Newman*

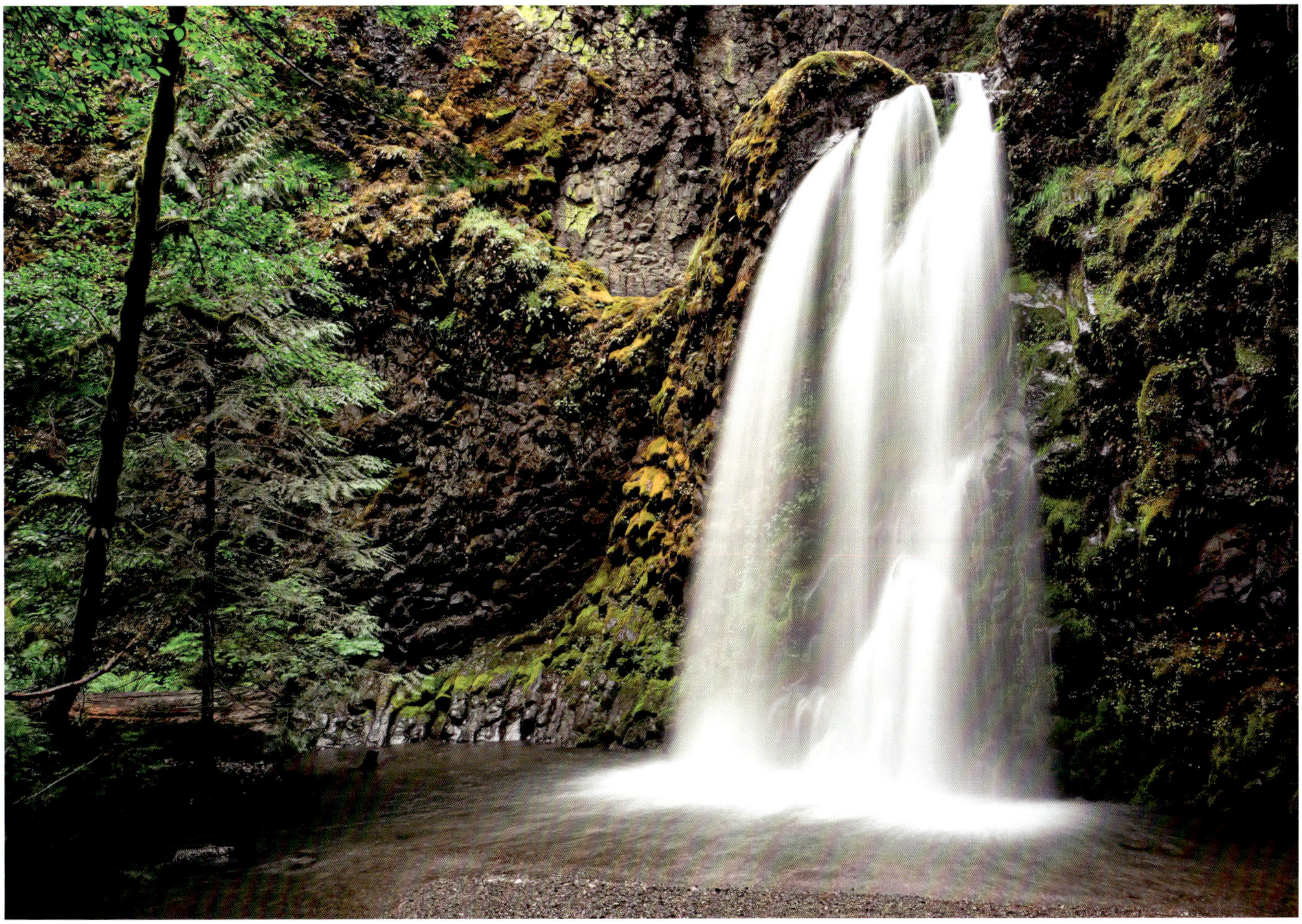

Fall Creek Falls. East of Roseburg in a canyon on the north side of the Umpqua River lies a 1-mile trail to Fall Creek Falls, a multitiered waterfall. The Archie Creek fire a few years ago burned over 130,000 acres and has left its scar. *Photo by Larry Pollock*

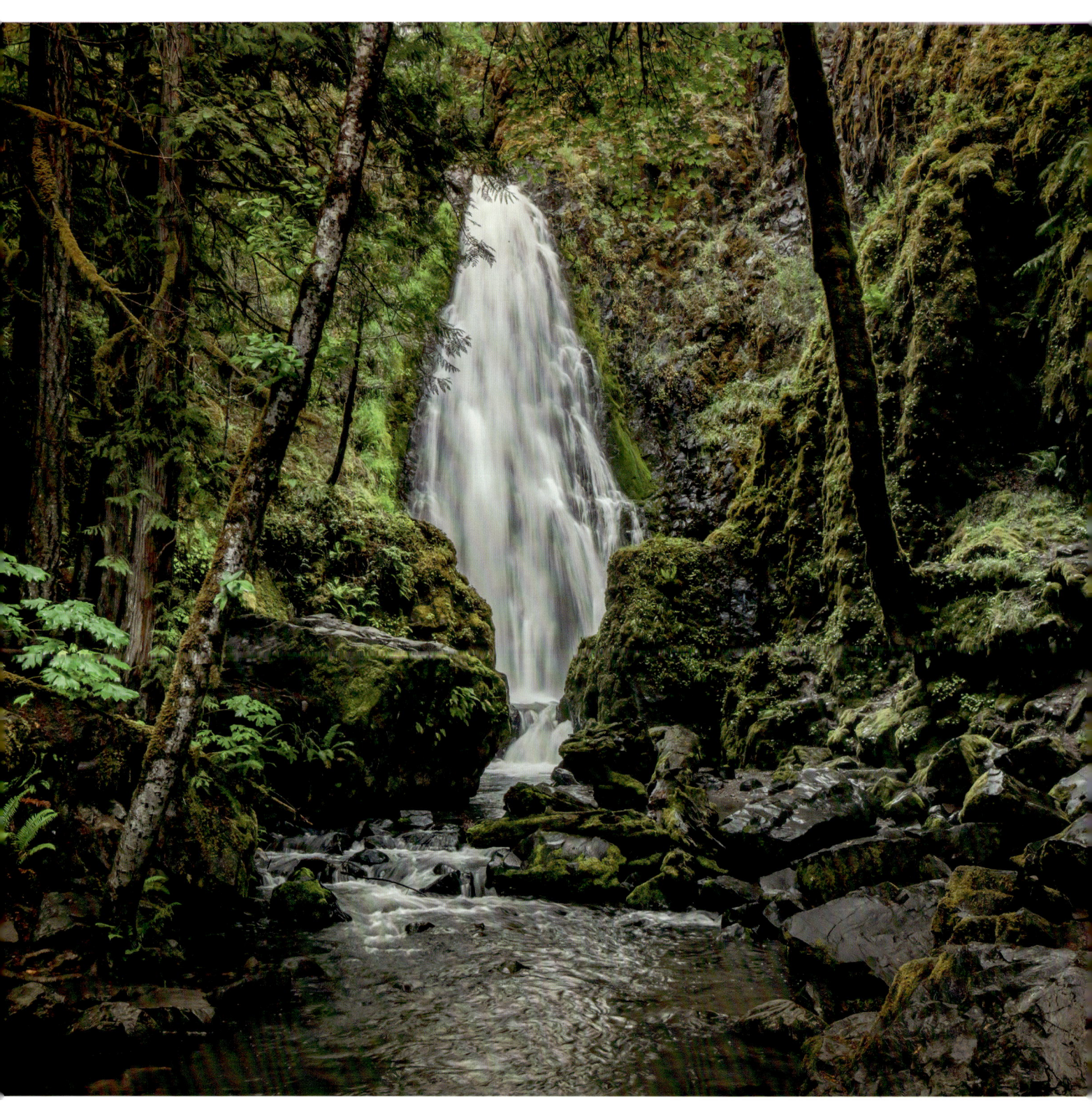

Susan Creek Falls. The fall drops 50 feet over moss-lined rock cliffs. A recent fire destroyed some of the surrounding landscape, but there are signs of regrowth. *Photo by Susan Sheets*

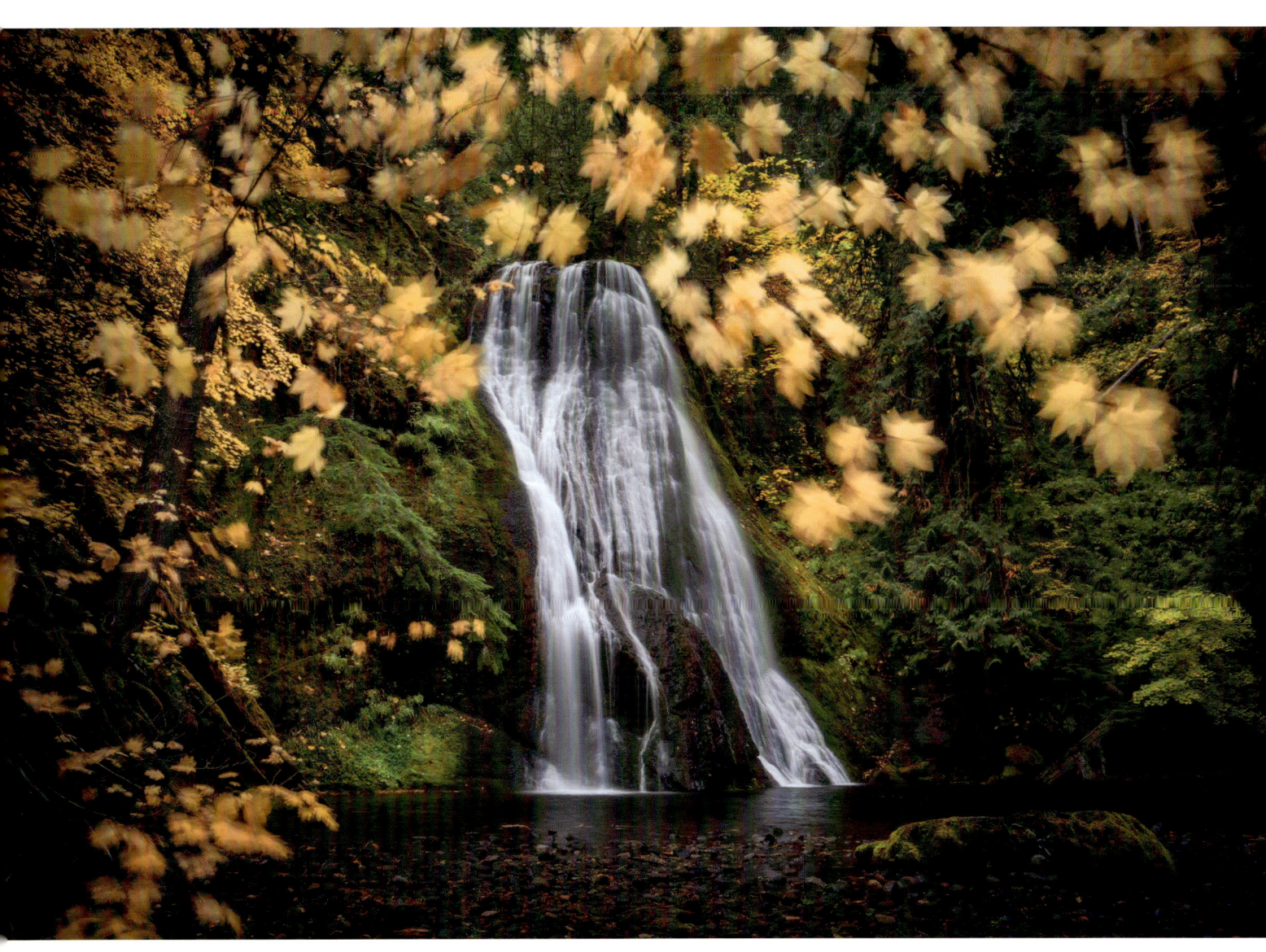

Yakso Falls. In the Chinook language, the name of this waterfall means "hair of a woman." The short and easy trail leads to a delicate falls that drops 70 feet over massive rocks. Wildflowers and rhododendrons are often seen in spring. *Photo by Sean Bagshaw*

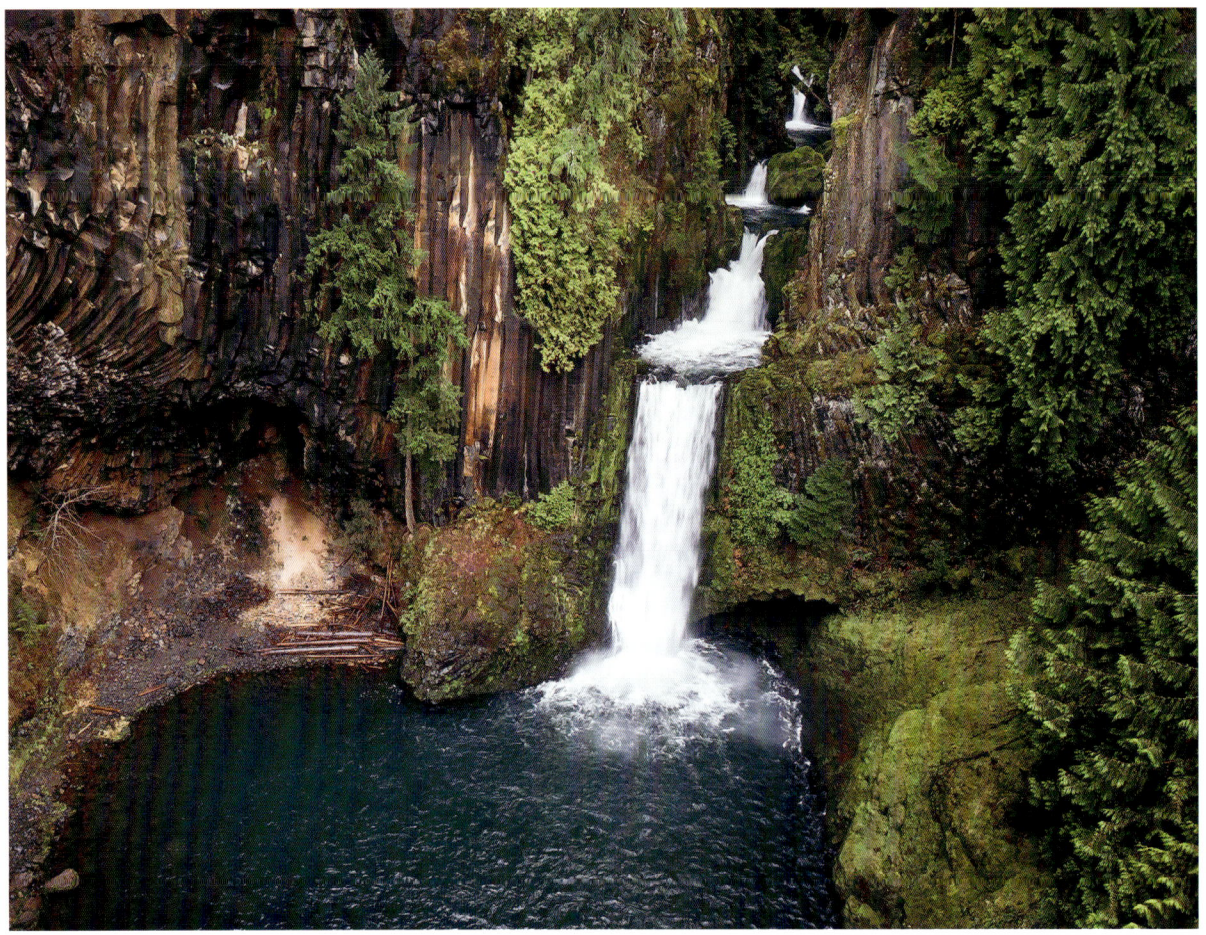

Toketee Falls. The word "Toketee" means "pretty" or "graceful" in the Chinook language. This is a stunning two-tiered waterfall amid an old-growth forest on the Rogue-Umpqua Scenic Byway. There is a 200-step moderate hike to the wooden viewing platform. *Photo by Adam Marland*

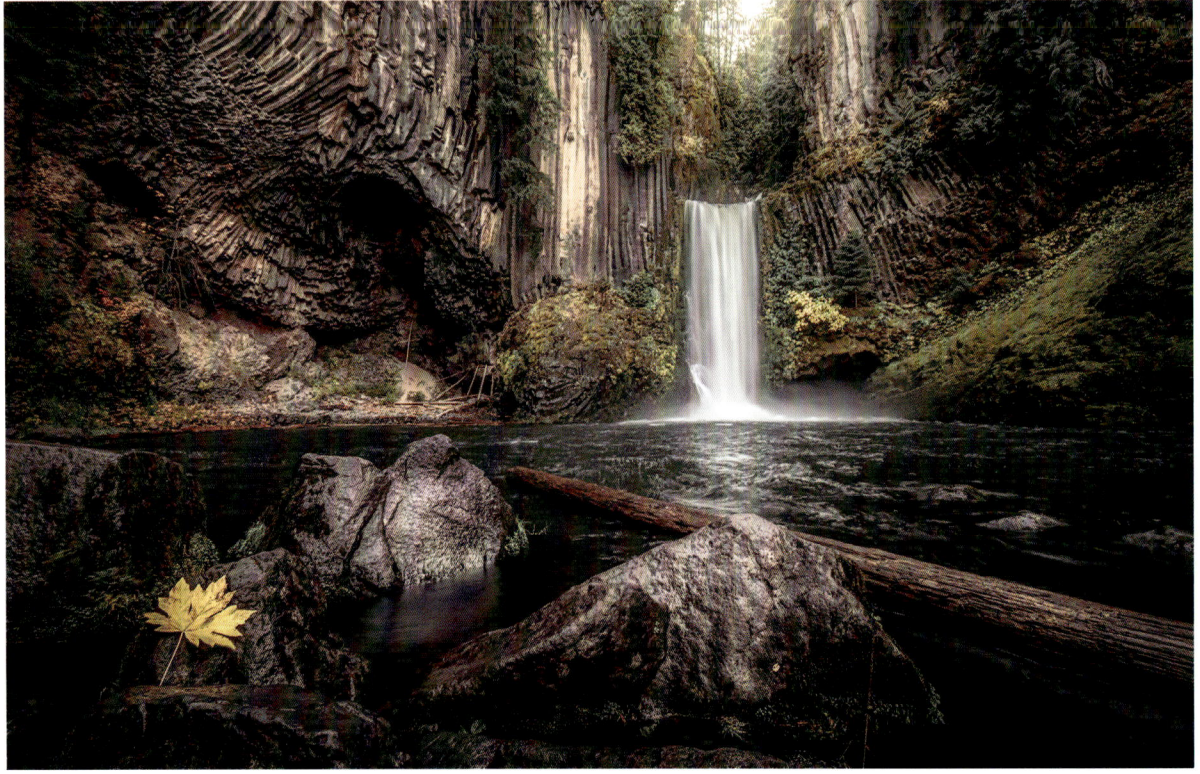

Toketee Falls. The North Umpqua River flows below this waterfall through a narrow gorge. Nearby waterfalls are also worth a visit while at Toketee Falls: Clearwater Falls, Whitehorse Falls, and Watson Falls. *Photo by Ricardo Barrera*

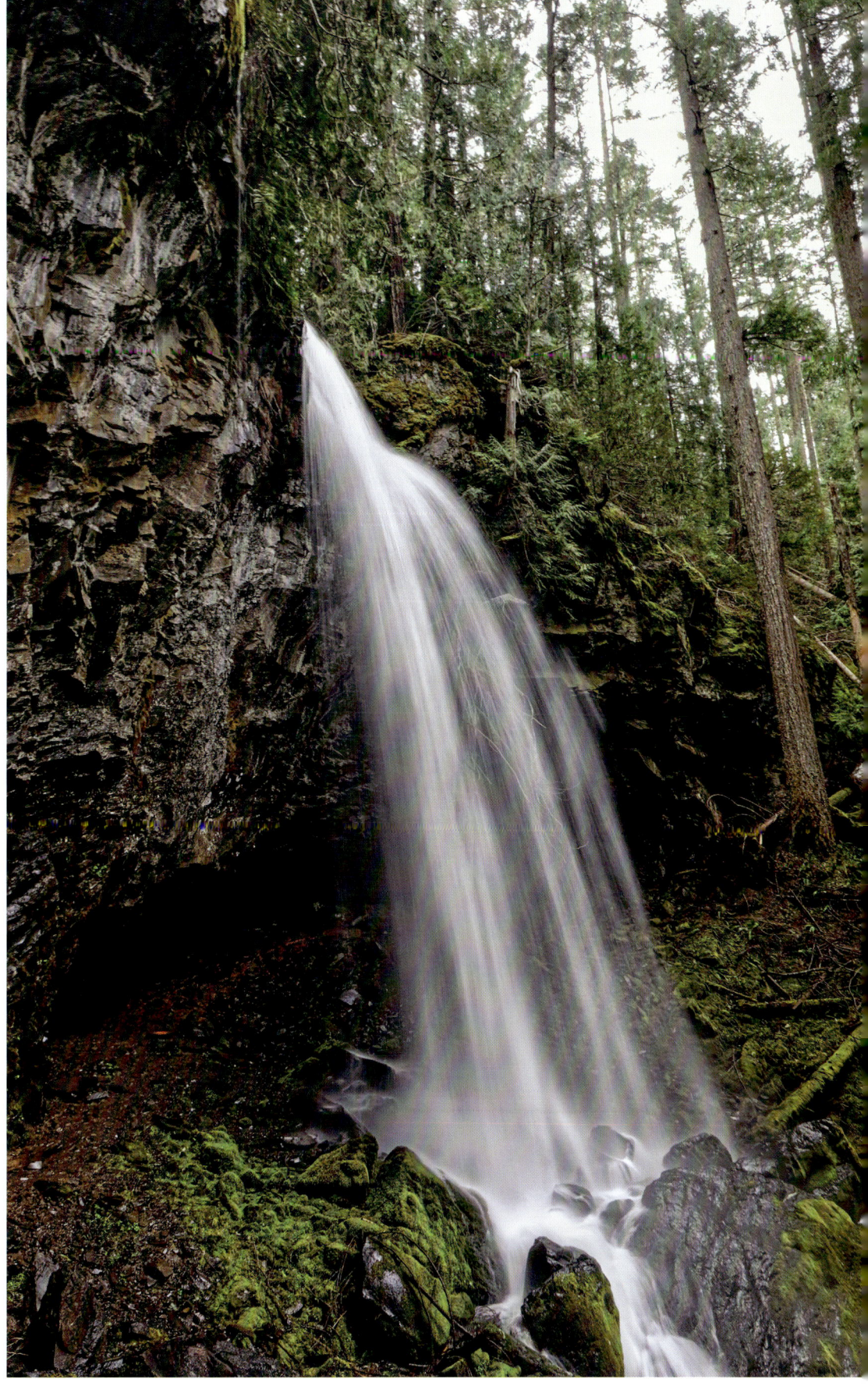

Grotto Falls. The hike to this waterfall is 2.6 miles. It's considered moderate in difficulty. It takes about two to three hours to hike to the waterfall and back. Water plunges 100 feet over a deeply cut cliff. One can walk behind the falls. *Photo by Richard Krieger*

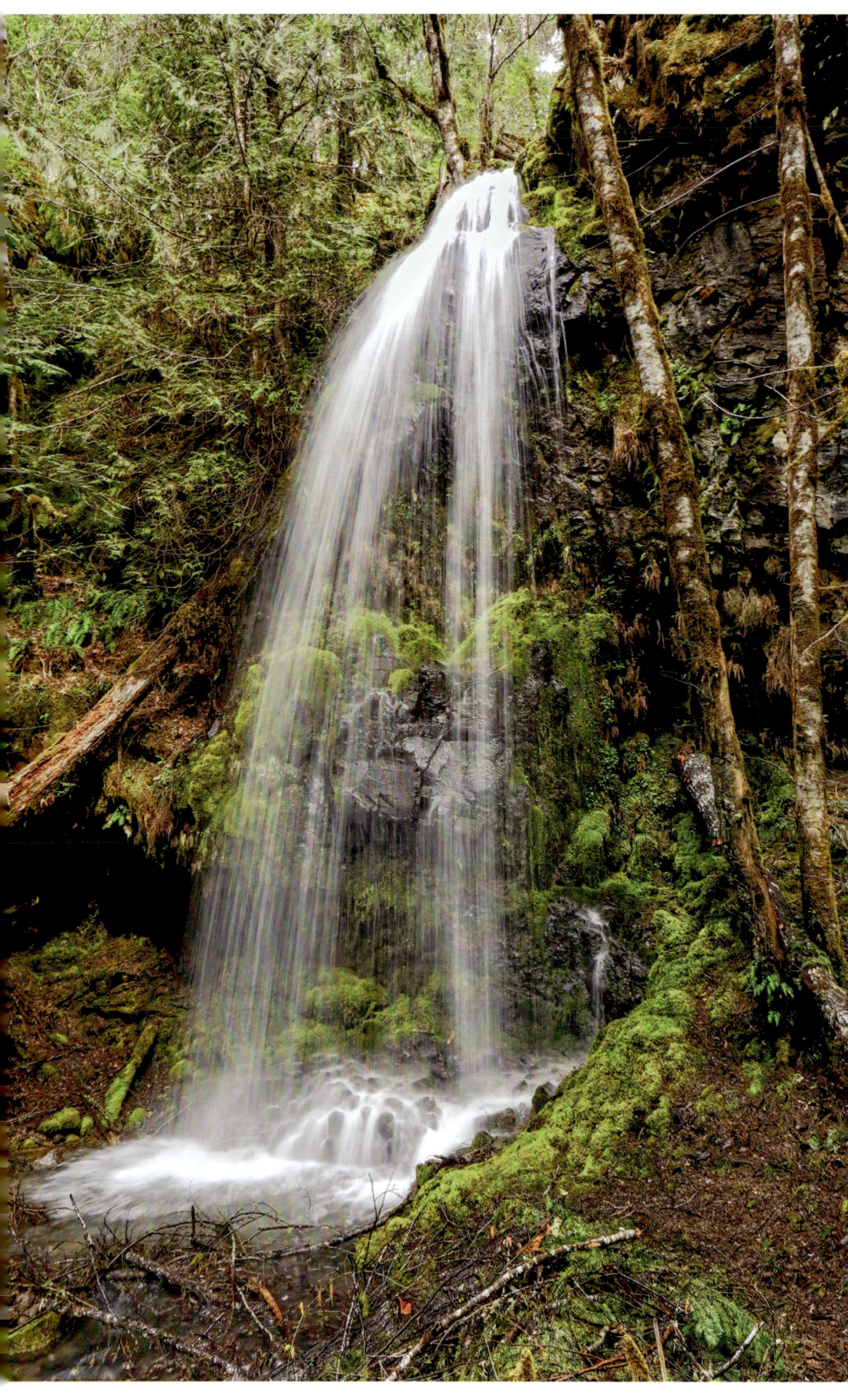

Wolf Creek Falls. This 1.2-mile trail is a fairly easy one along old-growth trees. It leads to a two-tiered waterfall that tumbles to a pool below. It's a short distance from Yakso Falls. *Photo by Richard Krieger*

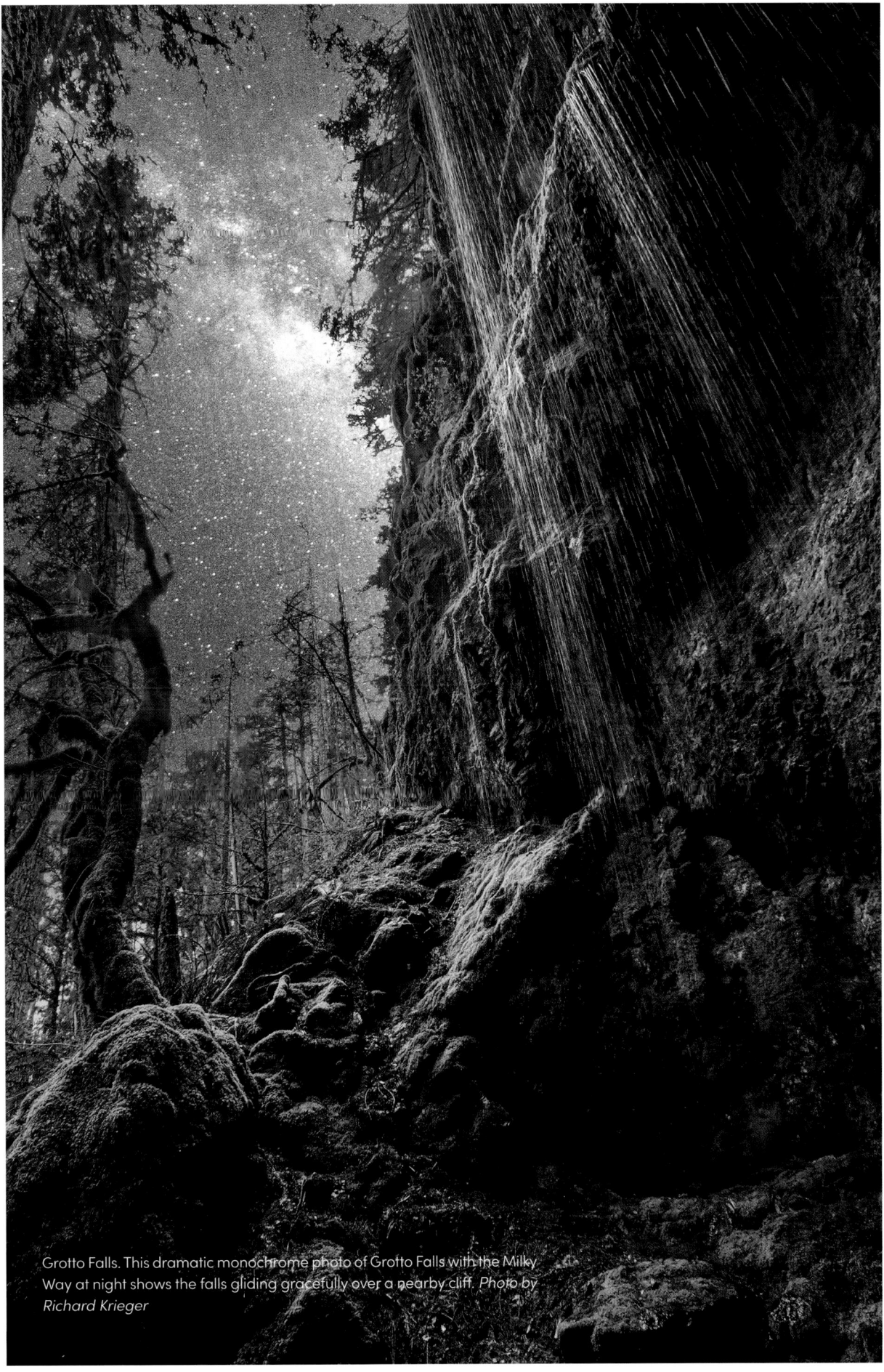

Grotto Falls. This dramatic monochrome photo of Grotto Falls with the Milky Way at night shows the falls gliding gracefully over a nearby cliff. *Photo by Richard Krieger*

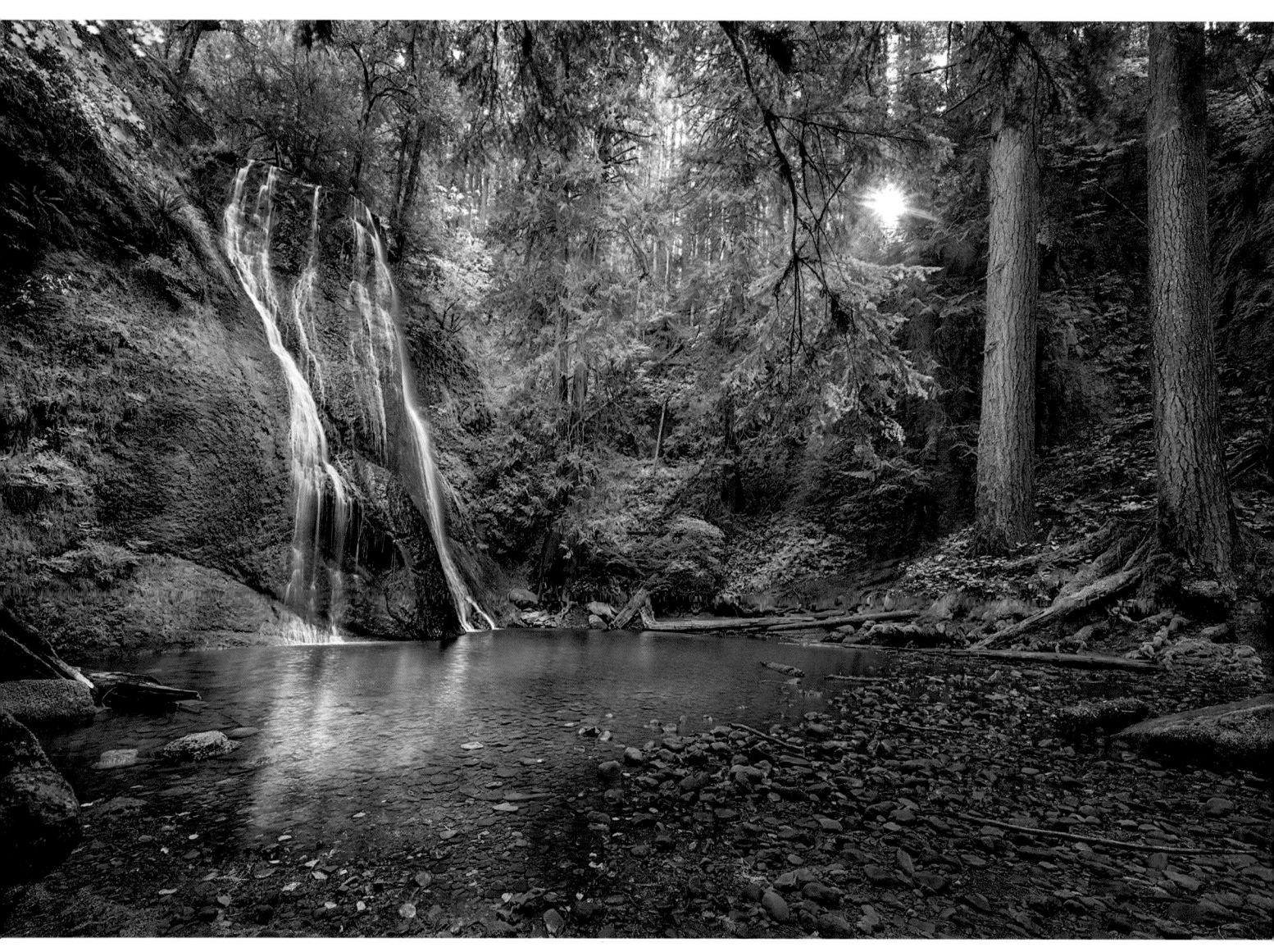

Yakso Falls. This family-friendly waterfall is not far from Wolf Creek Falls and about 27 miles from Glide, Oregon.
Photo Jim Chamberlain

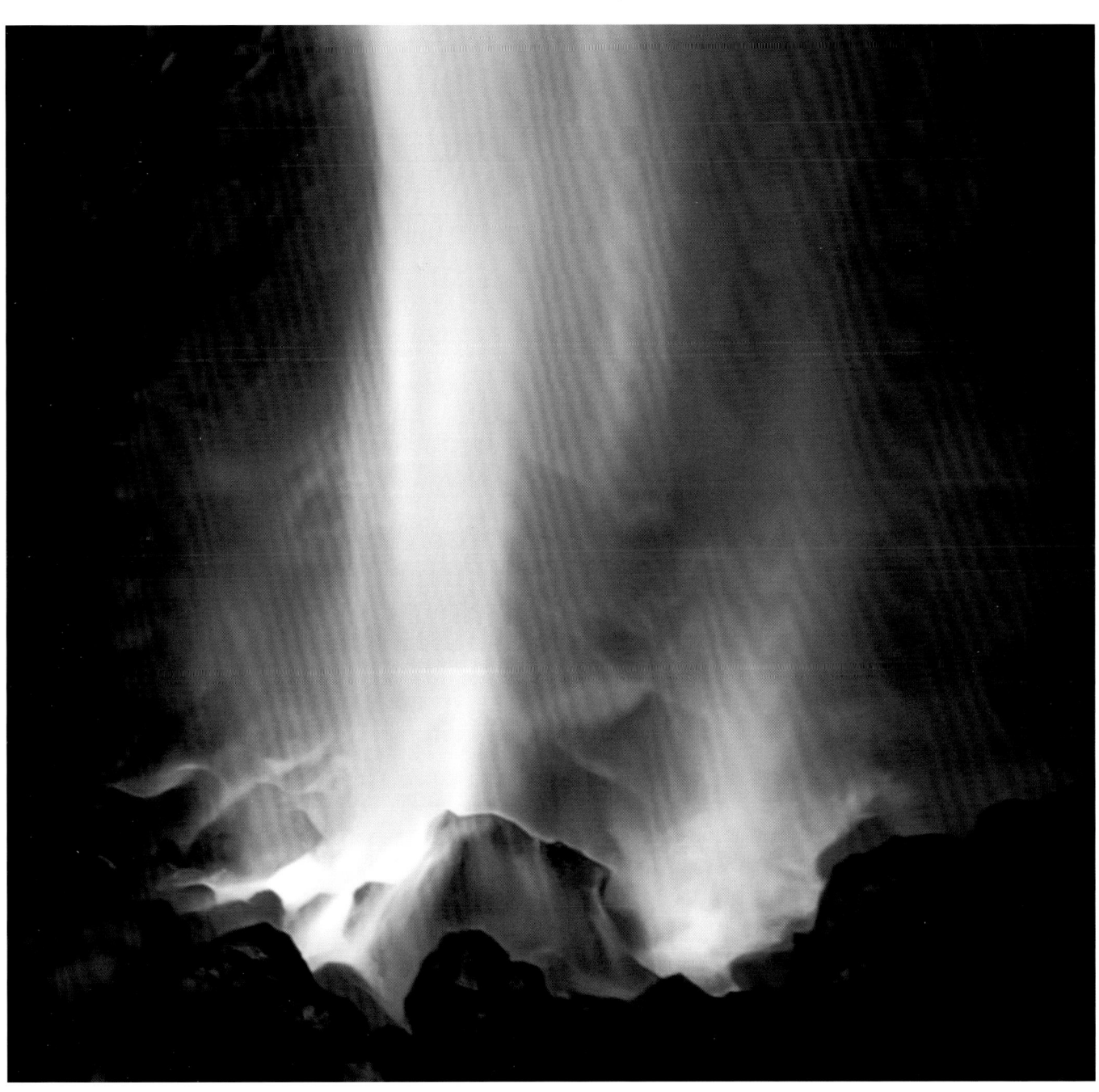

Watson Falls detail. View from the base of Watson Falls. *Photo by Sue Stendebach*

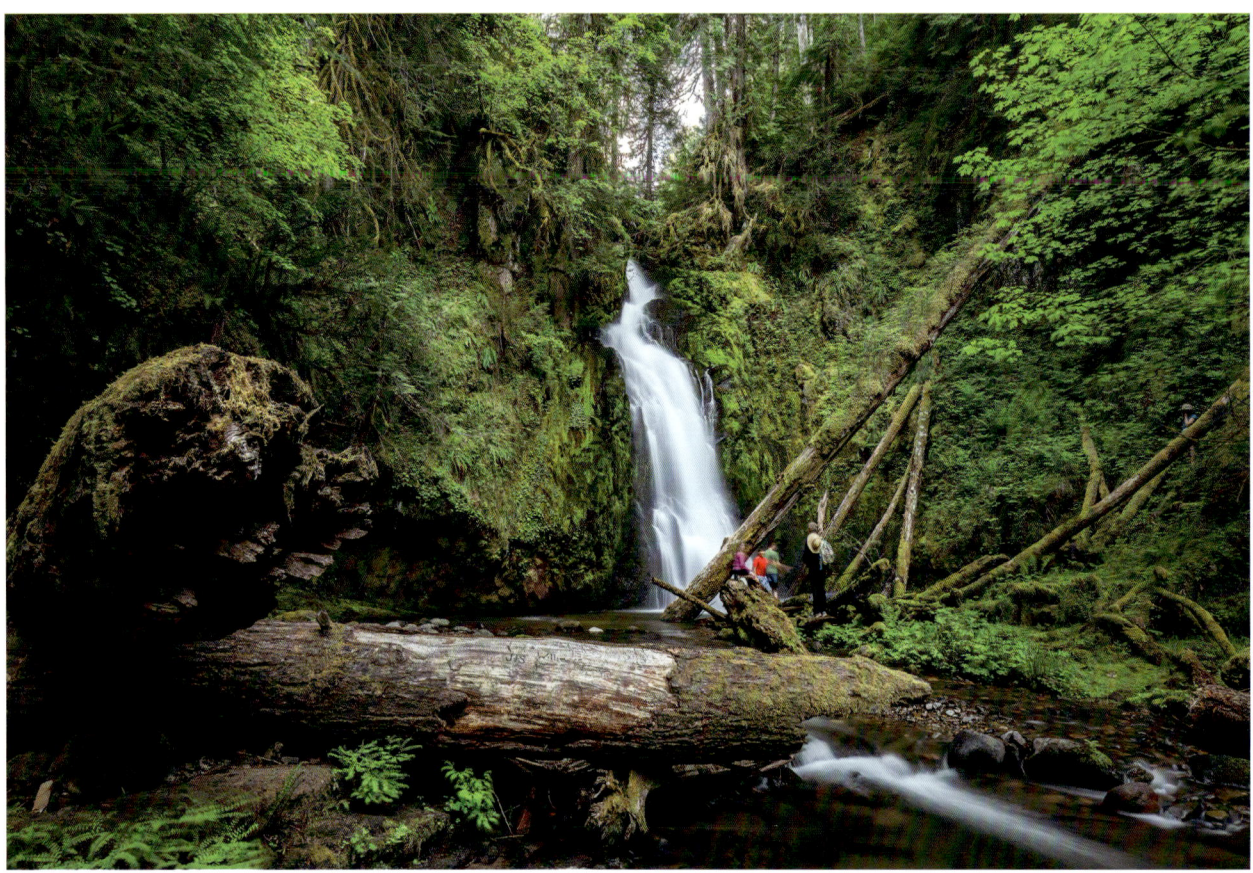

Hemlock Falls. Near Idleyld Park, this is a short, moderately challenging route that takes only about 33 minutes to complete. *Photo by Jim Chamberlain*

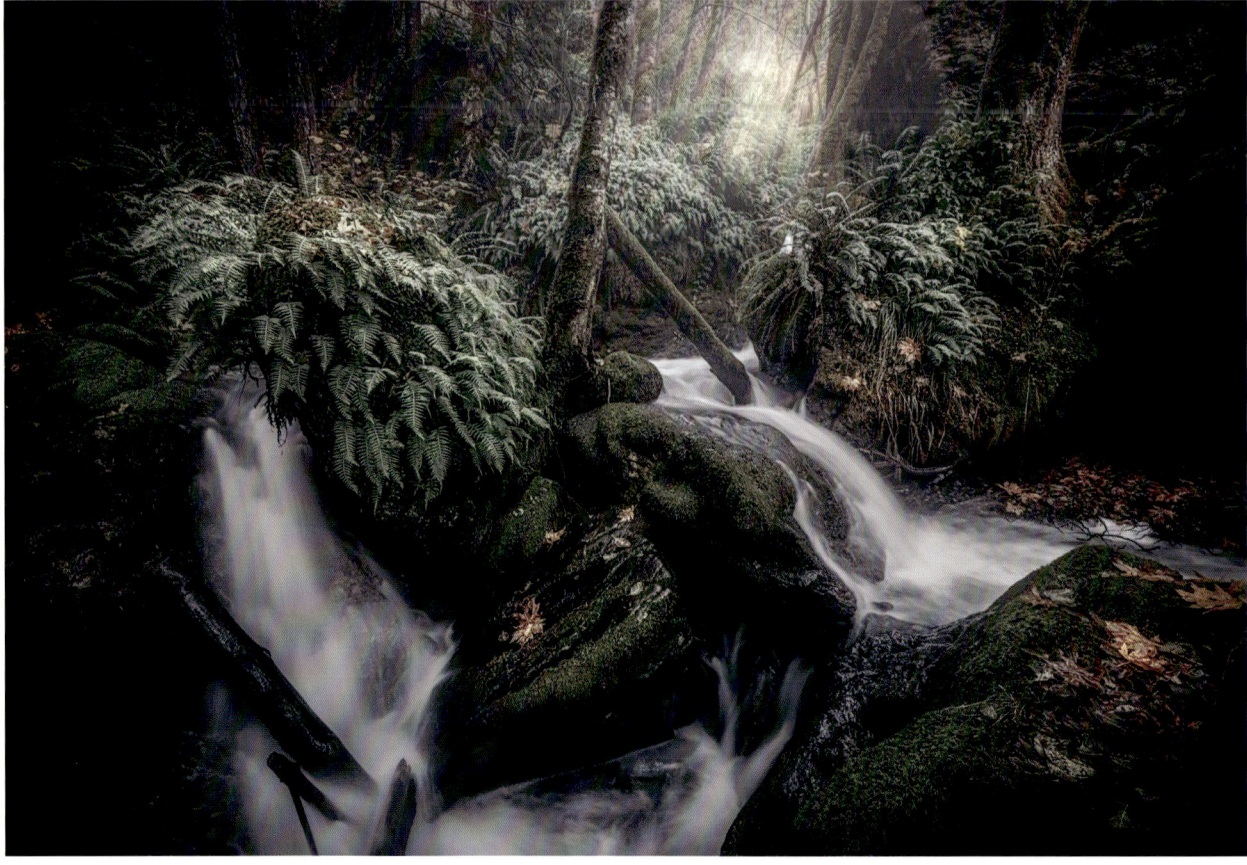

Unnamed falls Near Roseburg. Sometimes along a pleasant hike, the most unexpected waterfall will appear out of nowhere! This is one such offshoot from the Umpqua River. *Photo by Ricardo Barrera*

Steamboat Falls is a family-friendly waterfall. The reward on a hot summer day is this refreshing swimming hole. *Photo by Sue Newman*

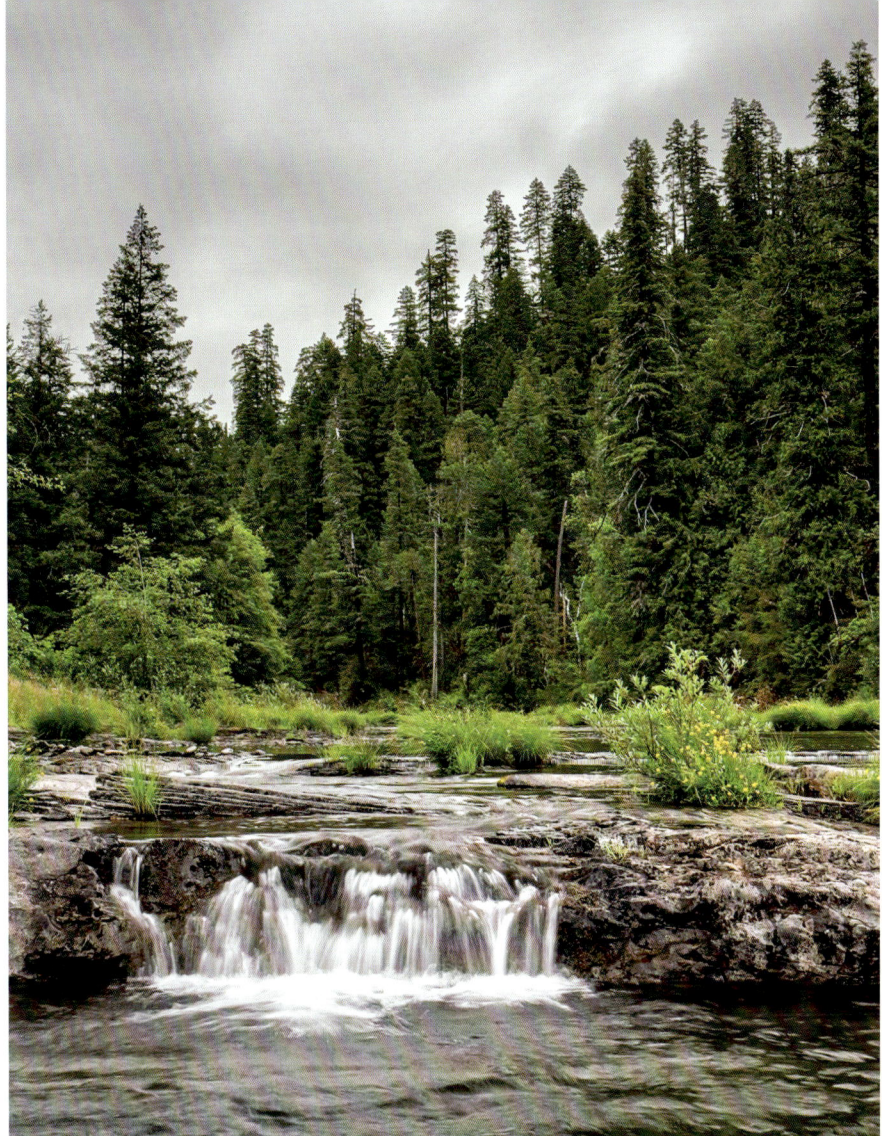

Steamboat Falls. Located off Highway 138, about three minutes from the Steamboat Falls Campground, this is a popular and easy waterfall for families to enjoy. In early summer, visitors can also see steelhead jumping the 25-foot falls next to the fish ladder. *Photo by Jay Newman*

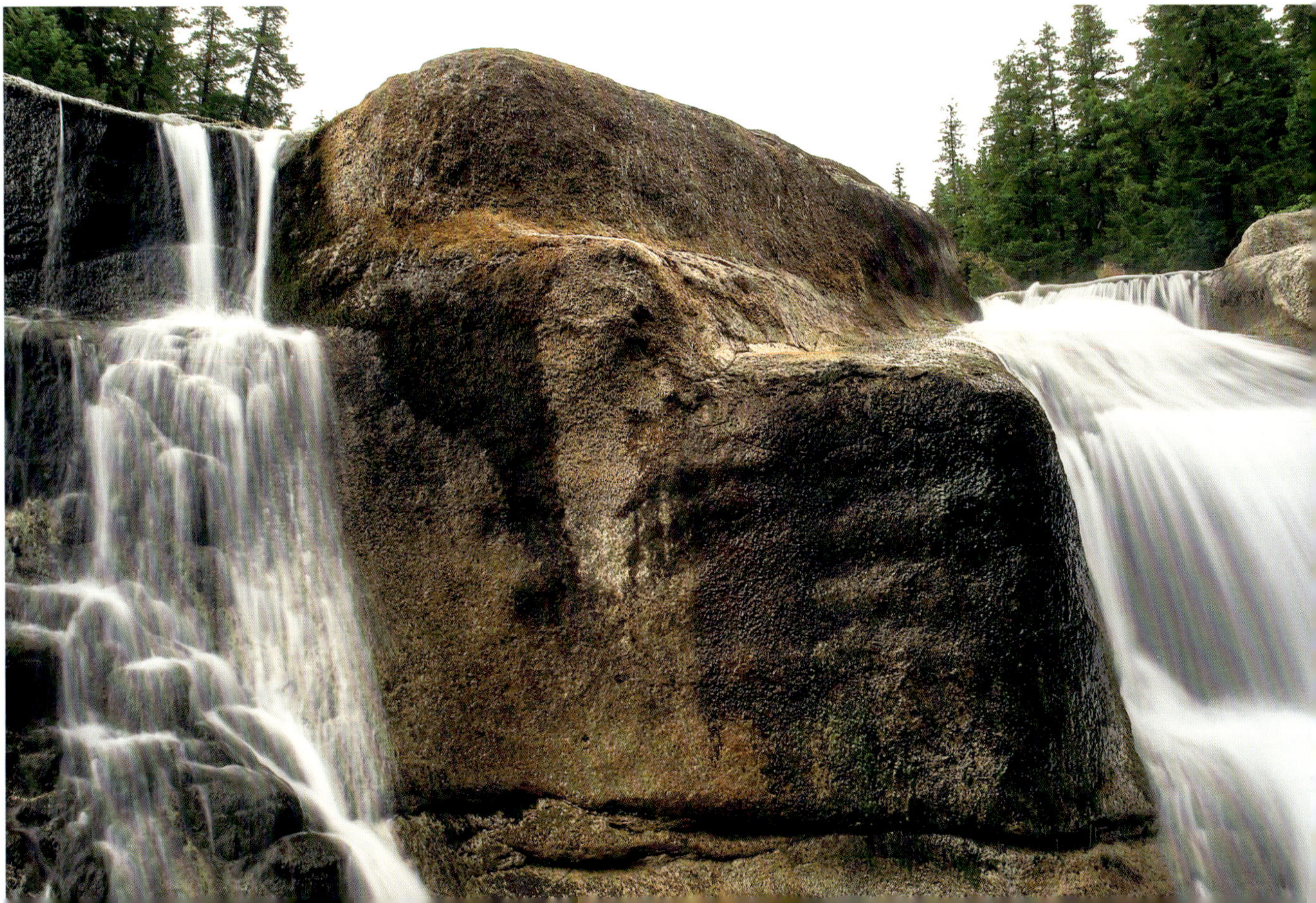

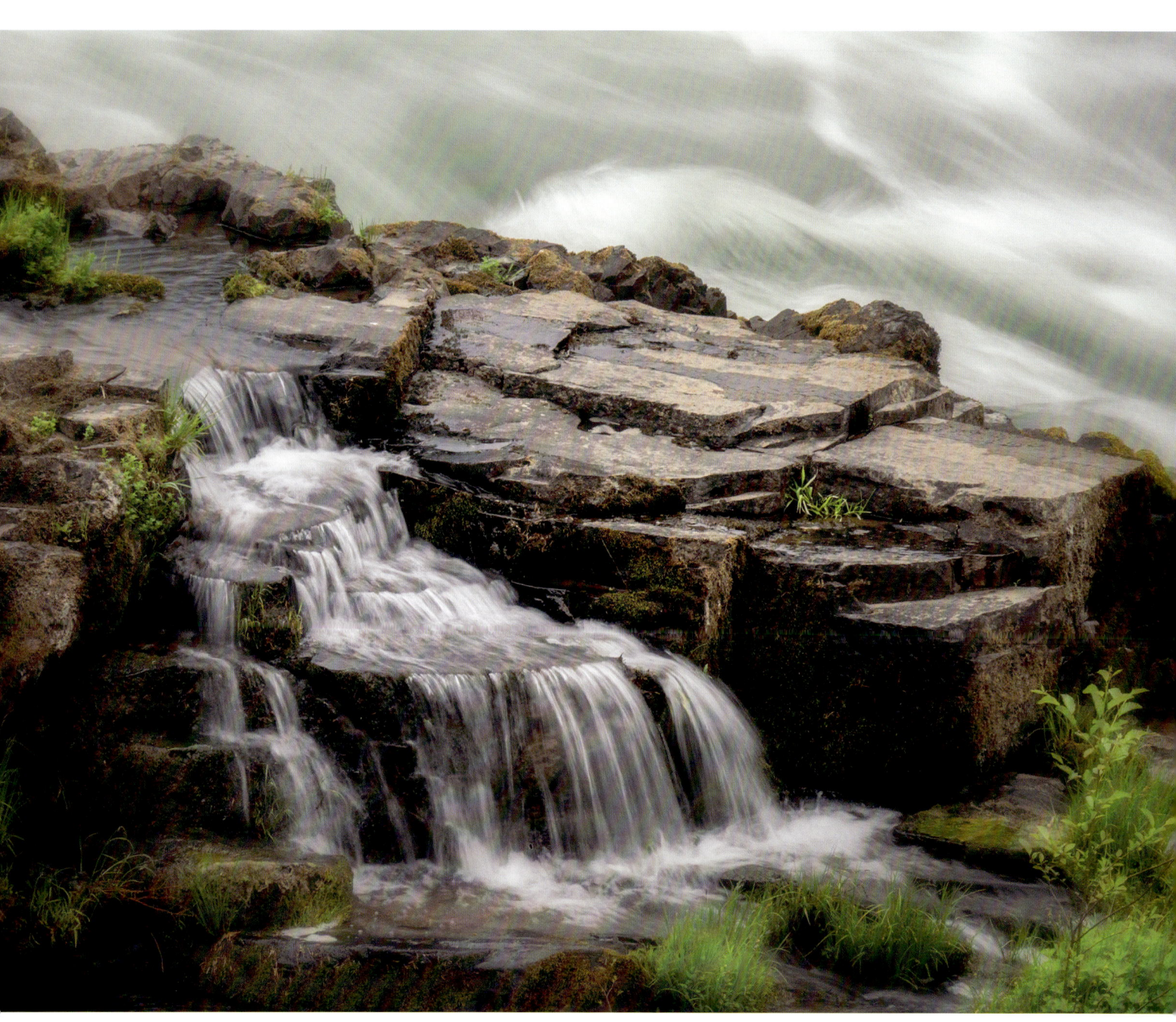

Little Creek Falls. In the middle of the Umpqua National Forest on Highway 138, just after the unincorporated town of Steamboat, is the modest "Little Creek Falls" along Steamboat Creek. It is less than a mile downstream from its big sister, "Steamboat Falls." *Photo by Fran Yates*

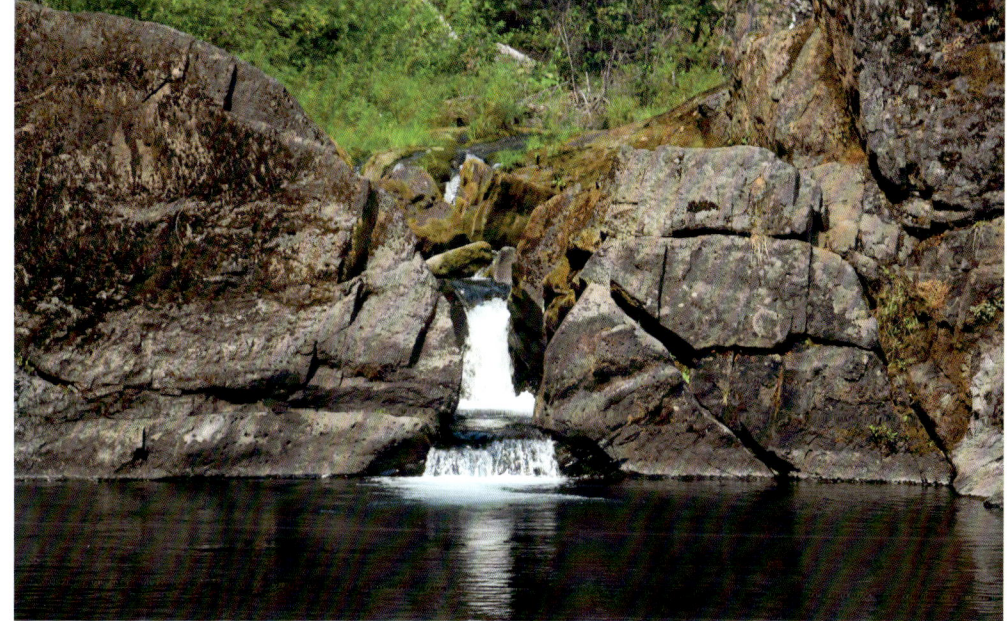

Deer Lick Falls. This small, popular swimming site in Douglas County is fed from the South Umpqua River. The waterfall flows into a deep pool in the cold, clear water of Black Rock Fork of the South Umpqua River. *Photo by Jessica King*

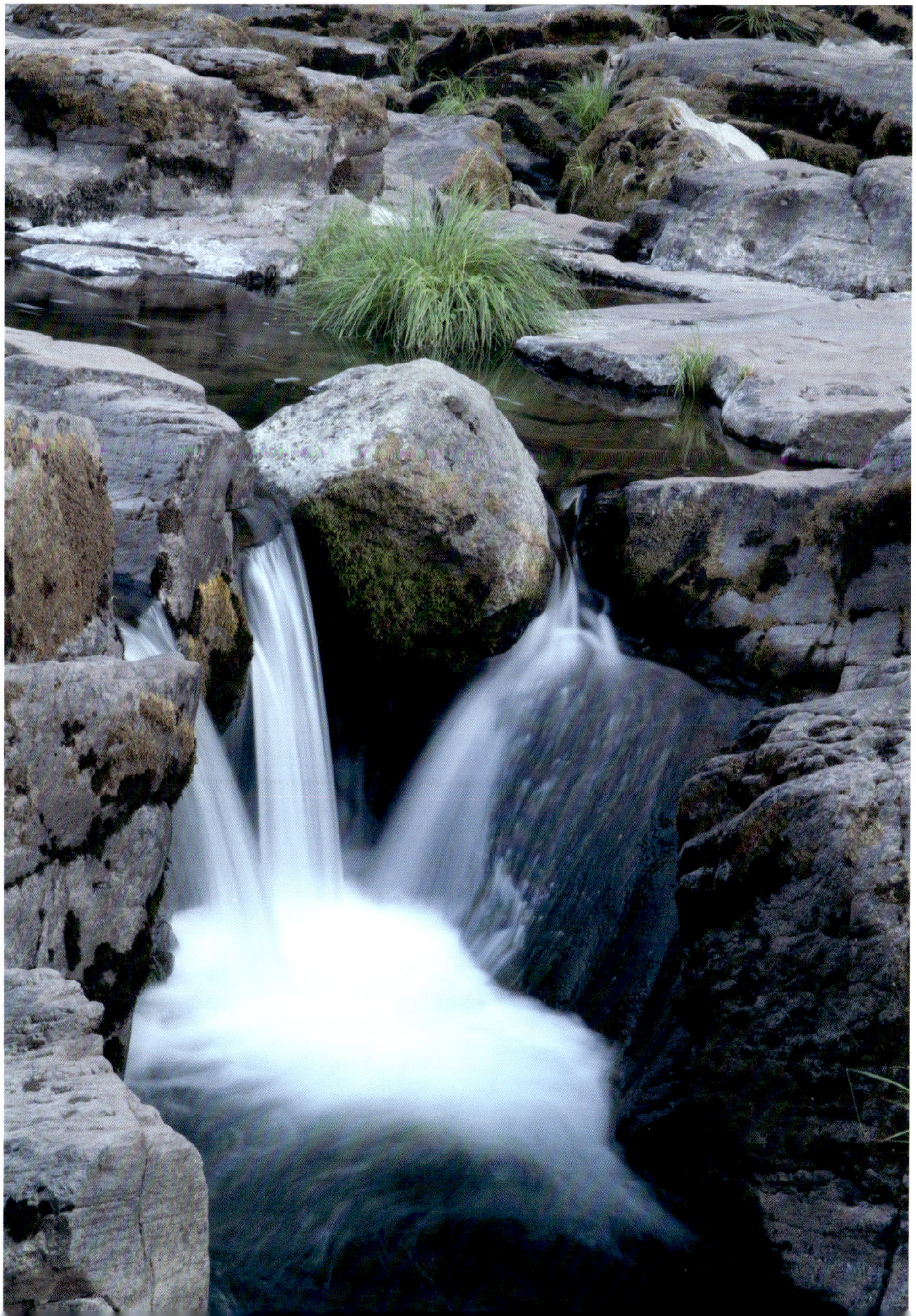

Deadline Falls. Located just a quarter mile from the trailhead, Deadline Falls is barely an official waterfall. However, salmon can often be seen swimming up the powerful falls on their way to spawn. It's one of several small cascades where the North Umpqua River rushes down the basalt riverbed. *Photo by George F. Peterson*

8

Prospect to Crater Lake
"Crater Lake Highway"

Southern Oregon's Highway 62 (Crater Lake Highway) showcases dozens of breathtaking waterfalls. When making a day trip from the Medford area to Crater Lake, it's definitely worth a few short stops to see several picturesque falls in the Prospect and Rogue River Gorge areas.

The small unincorporated town of Prospect dates back to 1870, with a current population of approximately 661. The town is surrounded by several outstanding waterfalls. Continuing the drive toward Crater Lake National Park on Highway 62, there are several great places to stretch legs. First, visit Natural Bridge in Union Creek. It's a tiny dot on the map along the quiet highway—where the Rogue National Wild and Scenic River cuts through the landscape with majestic power. Then stop for a meal, or a slice of delicious pie, at the historic Beckie's Cafe, ca. 1926 (it's also the only place to eat for miles). After Beckie's, continue just one minute (0.3 miles) to a pull-off for the Rogue River Gorge viewpoints. The raging Rogue River never disappoints! Crater Lake, Oregon's only national park, is not far from that, with several additional waterfalls to visit in and around the park.

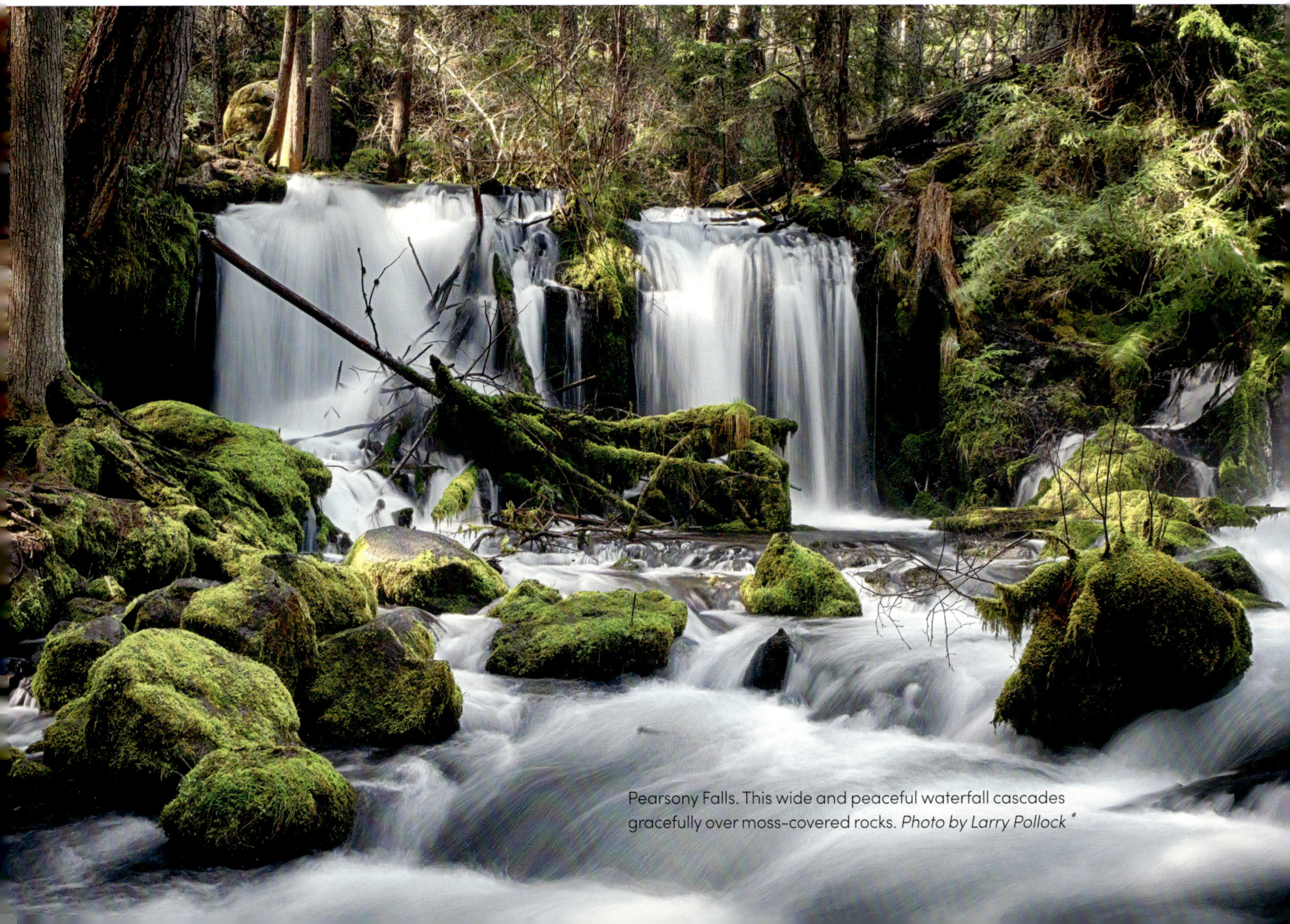

Pearsony Falls. This wide and peaceful waterfall cascades gracefully over moss-covered rocks. Photo by Larry Pollock

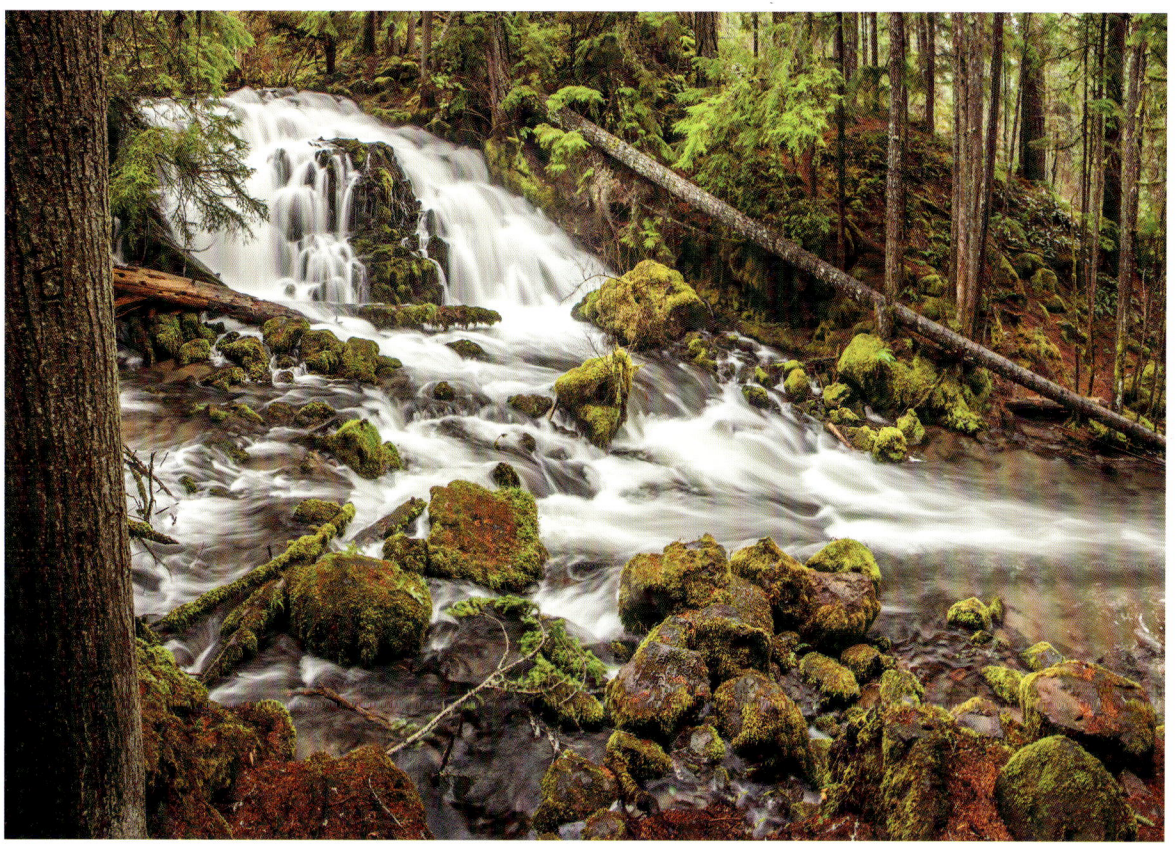

Pearsony Falls. Often considered one of the most beautiful and picturesque waterfalls in Oregon, Pearsony Falls in Prospect, Oregon, is a scenic gem. *Photo by Neal R. Thompson*

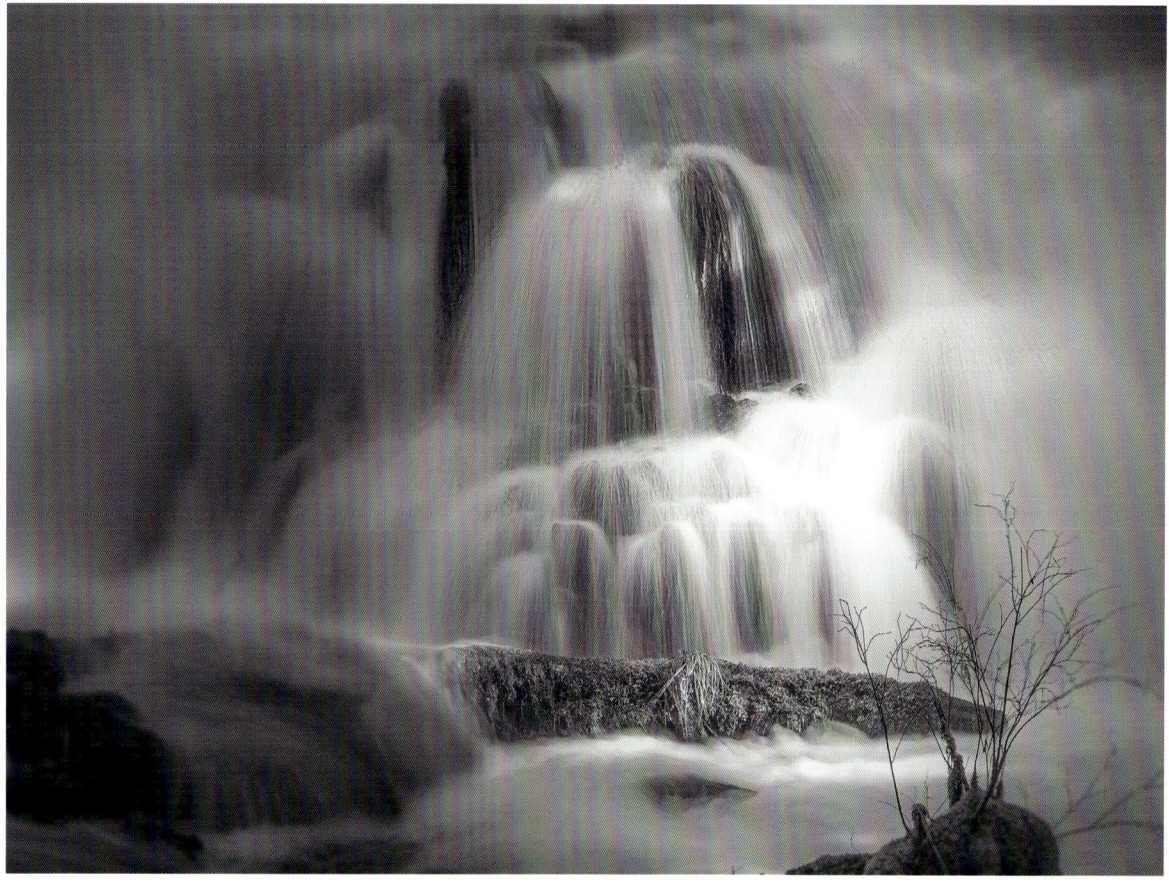

Pearsony Falls. Tucked within the Rogue River–Siskiyou National Forest, Pearsony Falls is not far from Mill Creek and Barr Creek waterfalls. It's only a 10-minute stroll from the parking lot and perfect for a short, family-friendly hike. *Photo by Tony Kilcollins*

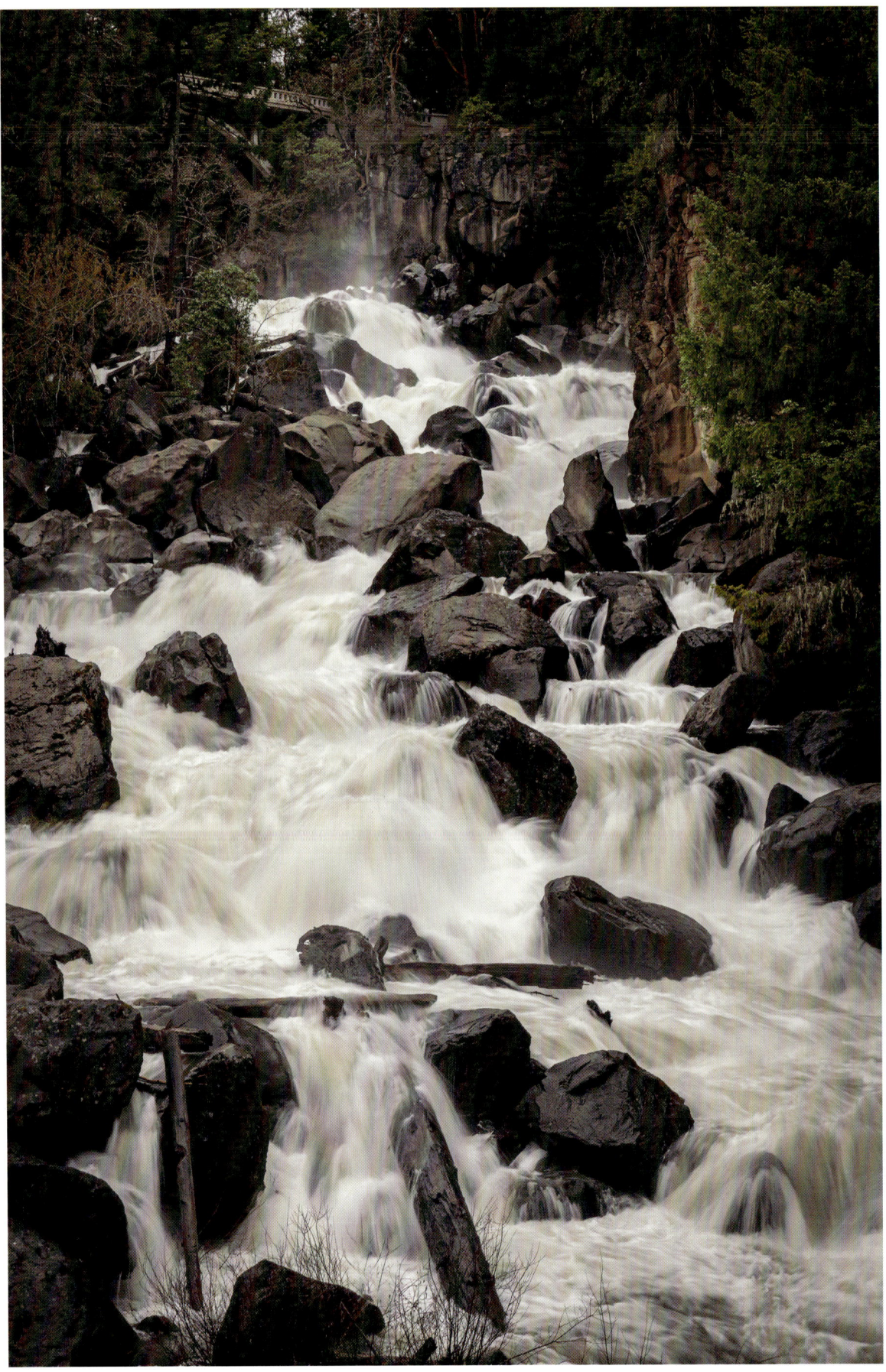

Avenue of Giant Boulders. While visiting the several Prospect, Oregon, waterfalls that also bring visitors to the Crater Lake area, be sure to check out Avenue of the Giant Boulders (sometimes called Prospect Falls). After the Mount Mazama volcanic eruption about 7,700 years ago, which formed Crater Lake, these elephant-sized boulders were flung more than 20 miles and buried. Over time, the Rogue River's flow exposed the massive rocks. *Photo by Bob Palermini*

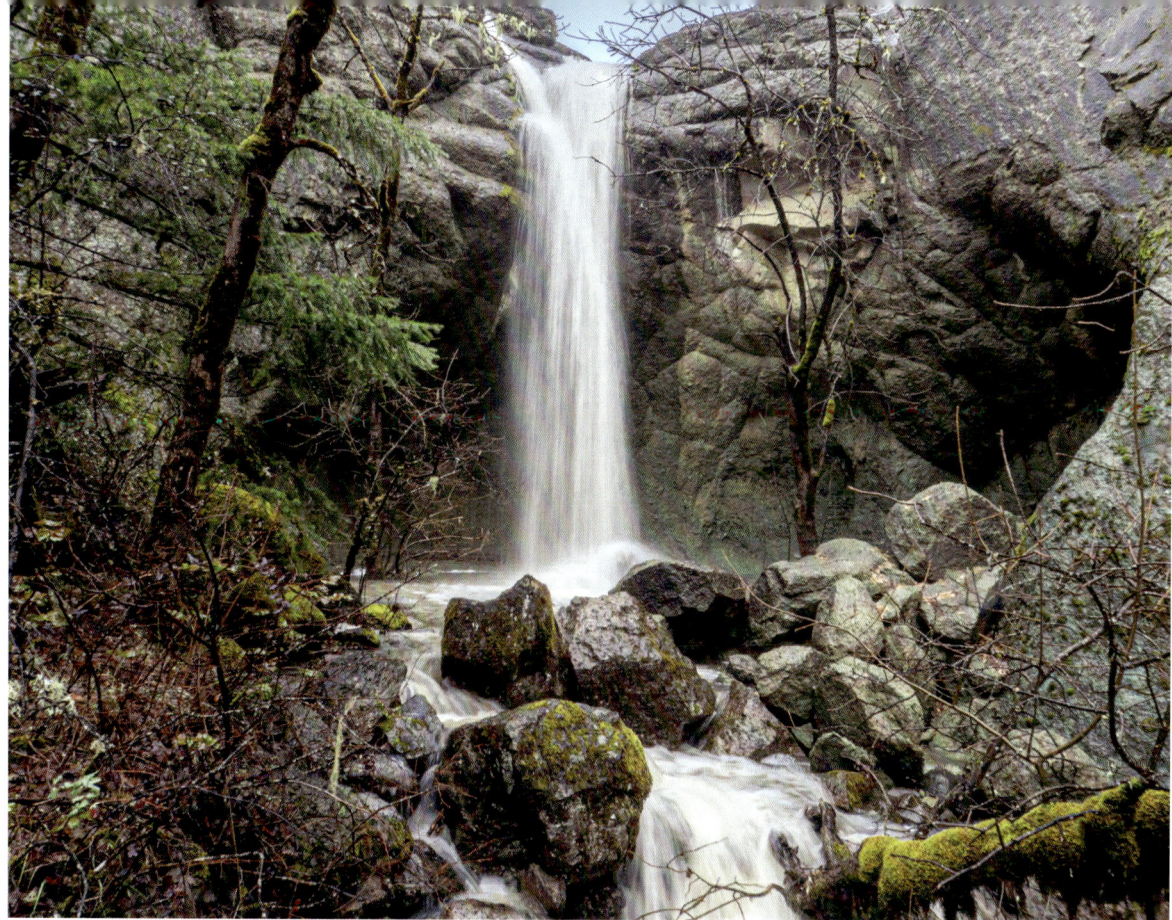

Blue Grotto Falls. This impressive falls near Lost Creek Lake was formed by ash from the eruption of Mount Mazama about 7,700 years ago. The volcano that created the caldera is now known as Crater Lake. The water falls 40 feet over a greenish rhyolite cliff. *Photo by Randy Bryan*

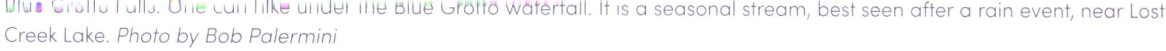

Blue Grotto Falls. One can hike under the Blue Grotto waterfall. It is a seasonal stream, best seen after a rain event, near Lost Creek Lake. *Photo by Bob Palermini*

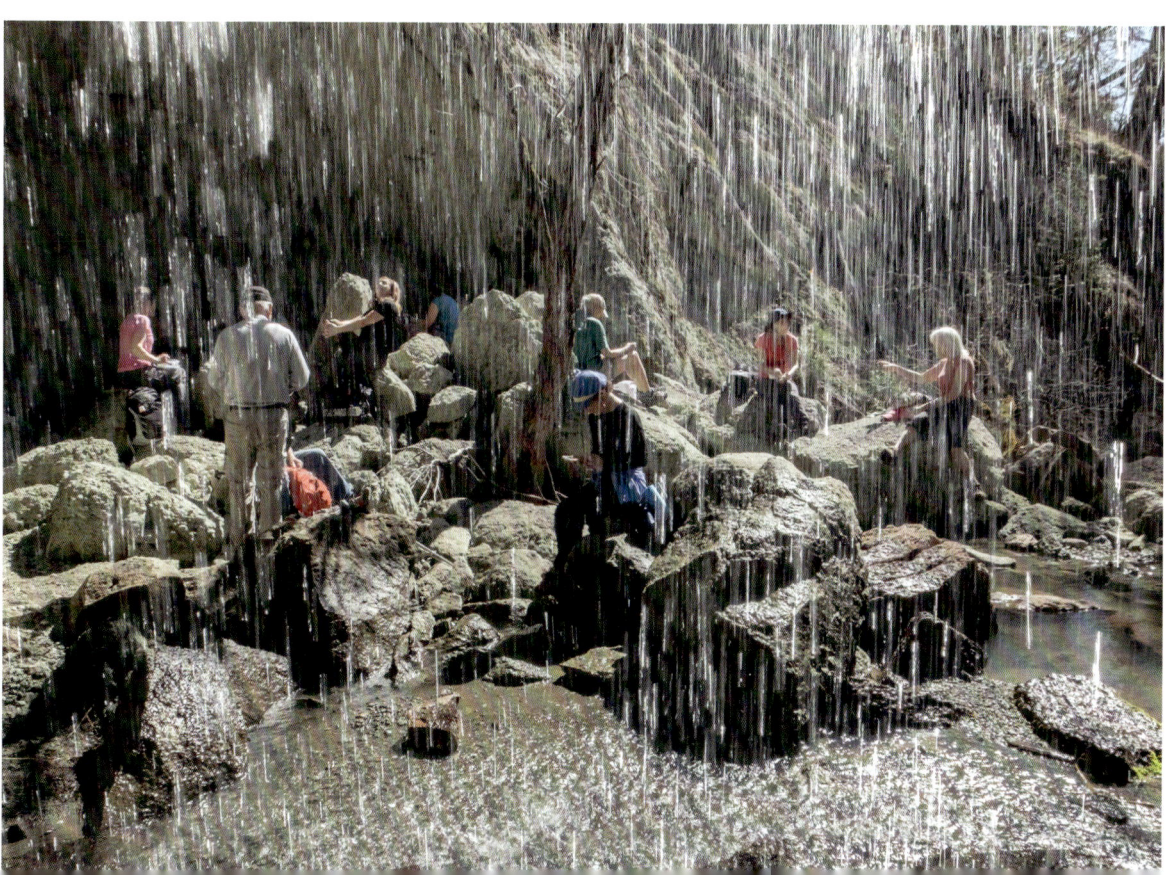

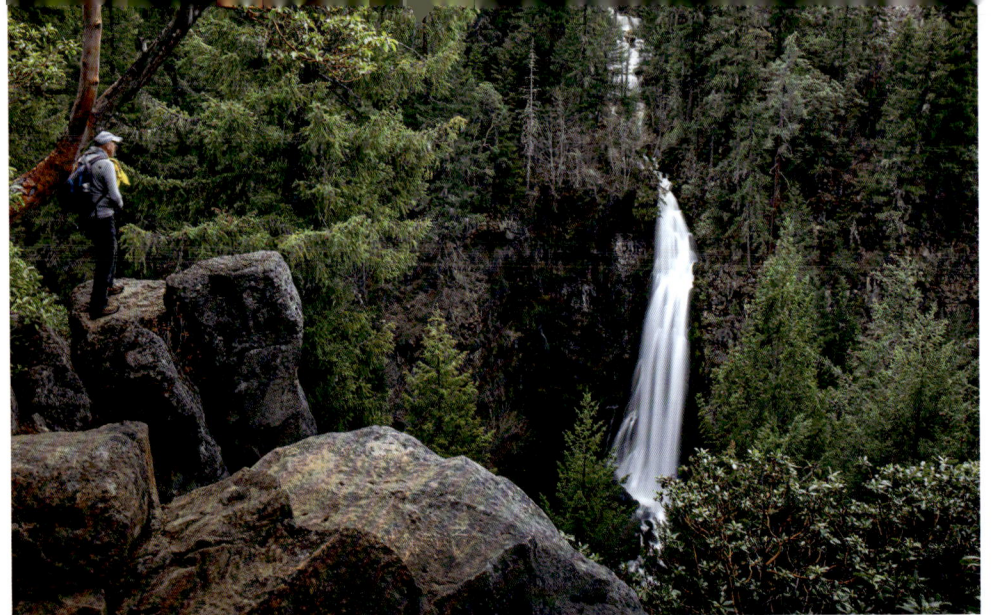

Mill Creek Falls. Located in the Rogue River Canyon, this impressive waterfall is one of the tallest in the state. The falls are surrounded by petrified volcanic ash from the eruption of Mount Mazama, which created Crater Lake. *Photo by Bob Palermini*

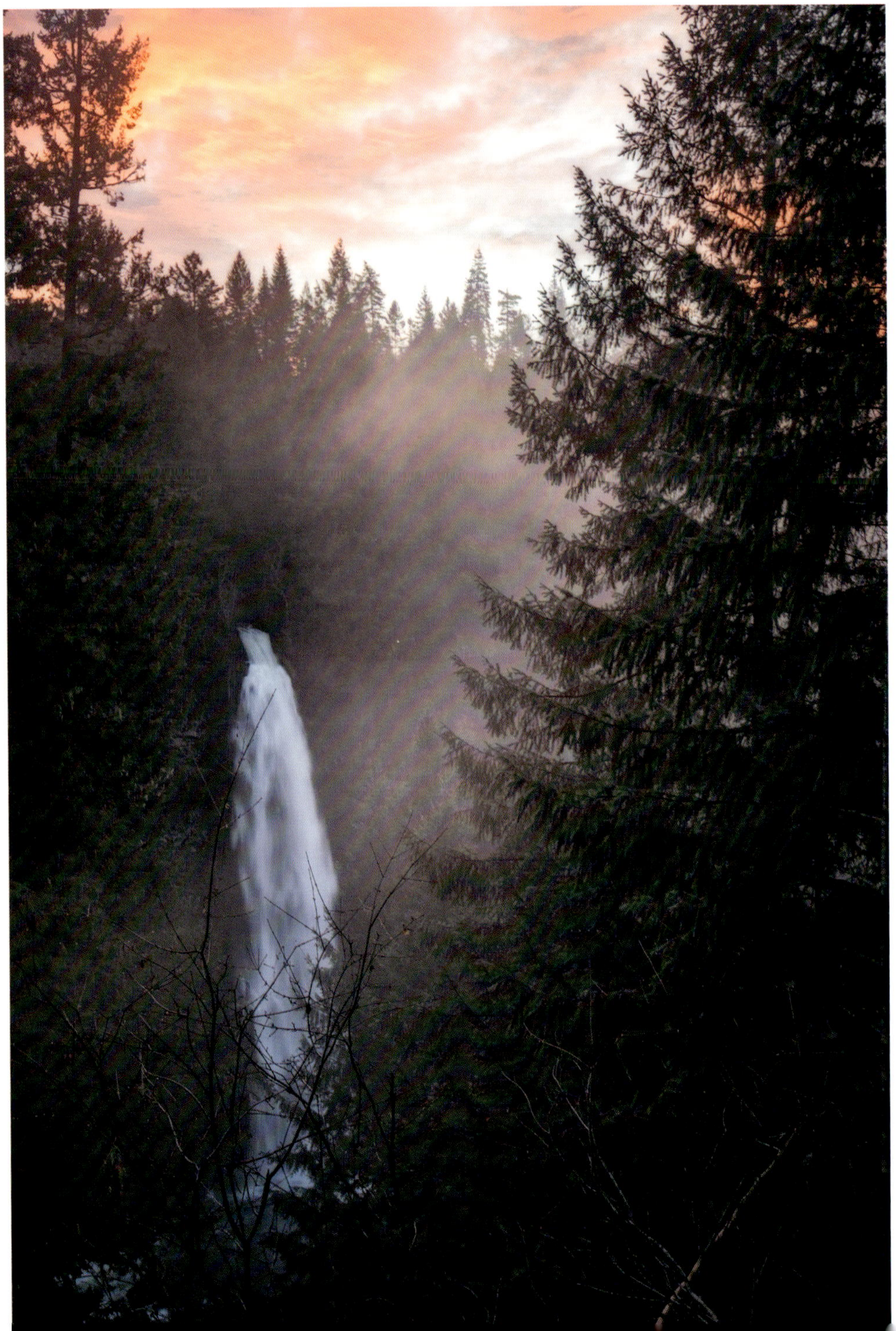

Mill Creek Falls. Mill Creek Falls is a 173-foot waterfall that plunges into the Rogue River. It is often visited with Barr Creek Falls and Avenue of the Giant Boulders in Prospect. *Photo by Earshel Hogan*

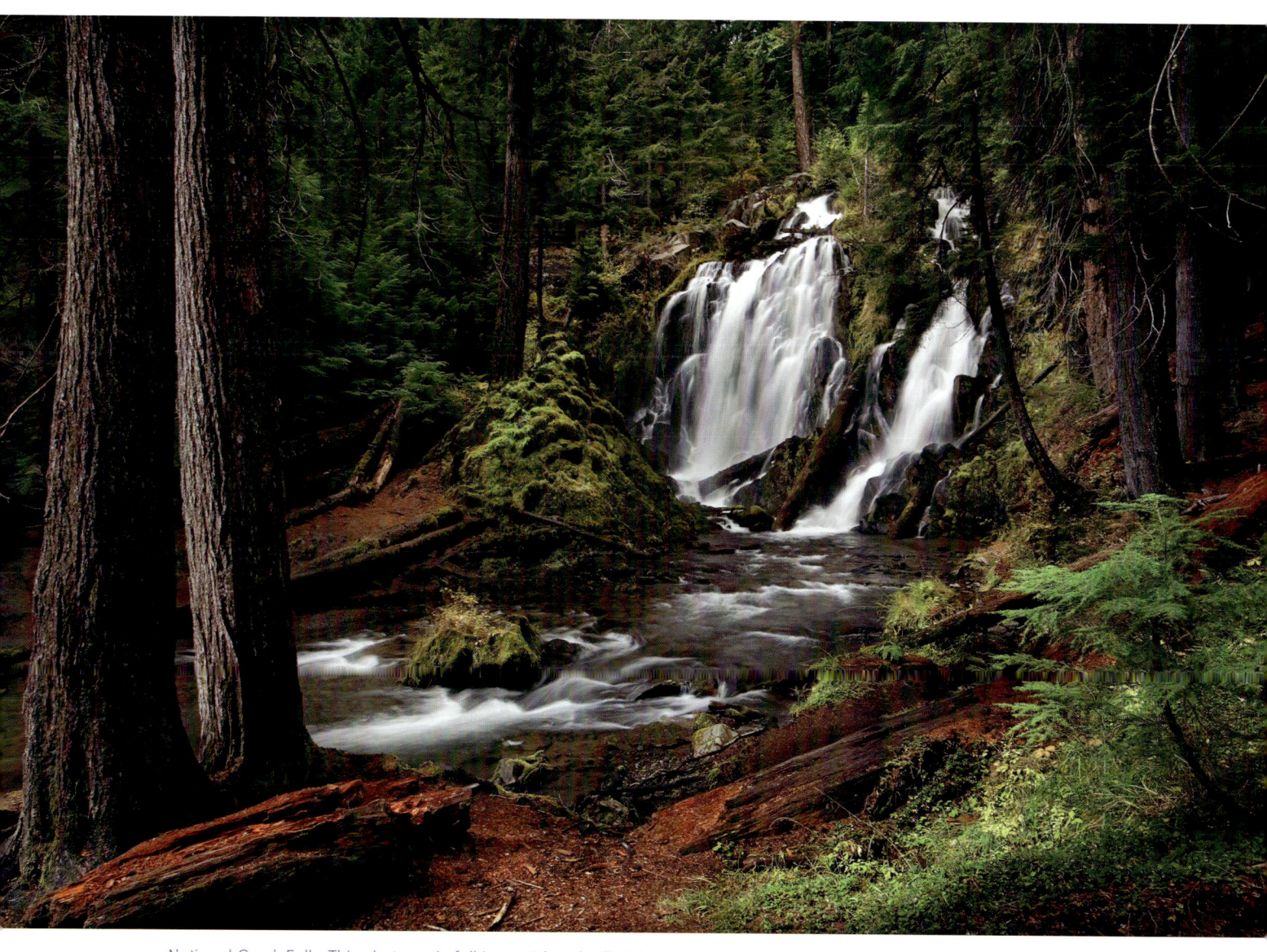

National Creek Falls. This photogenic fall is considered a "hidden gem" in the Rogue River–Siskiyou National Forest. *Photo by Sean Bagshaw*

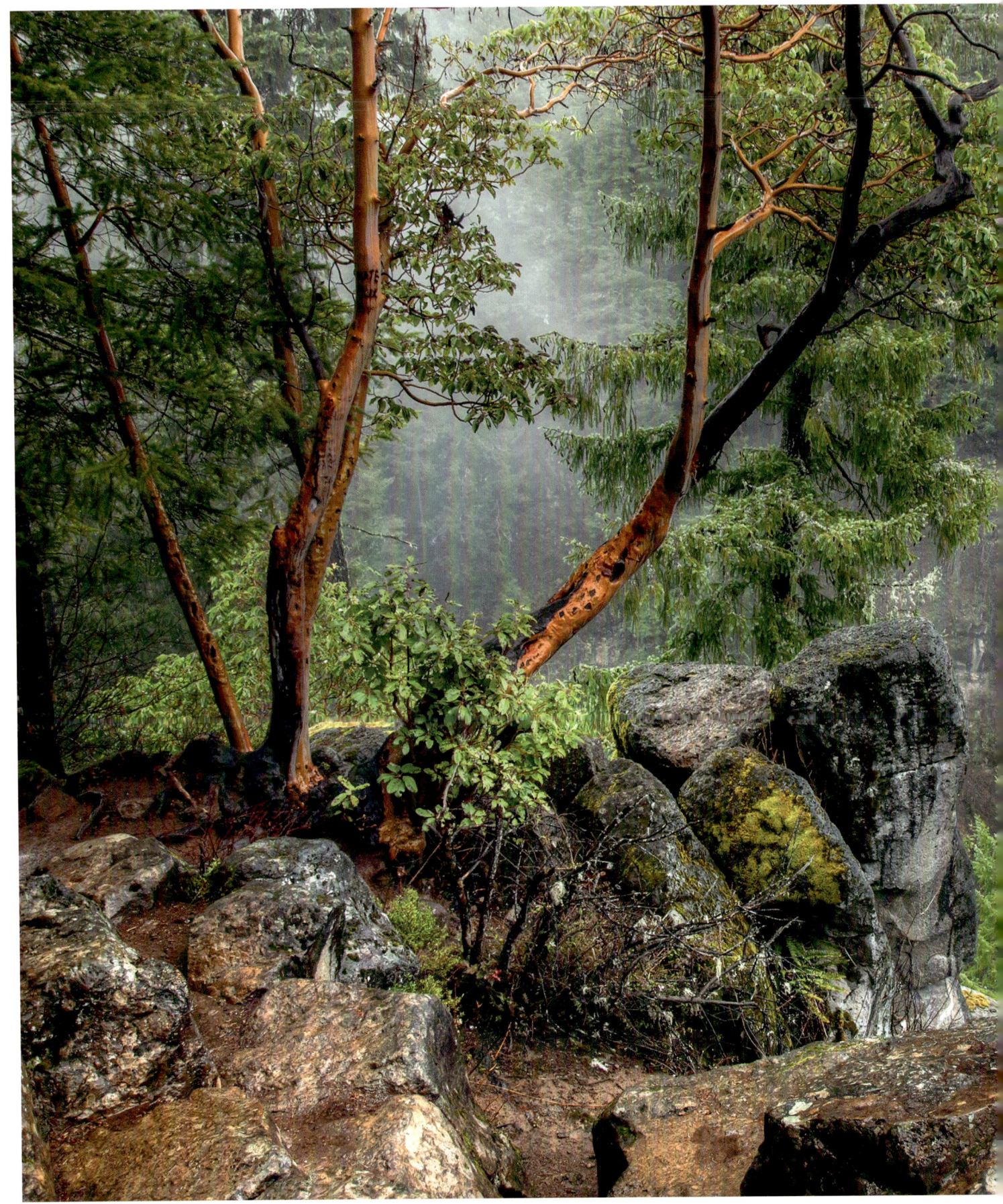

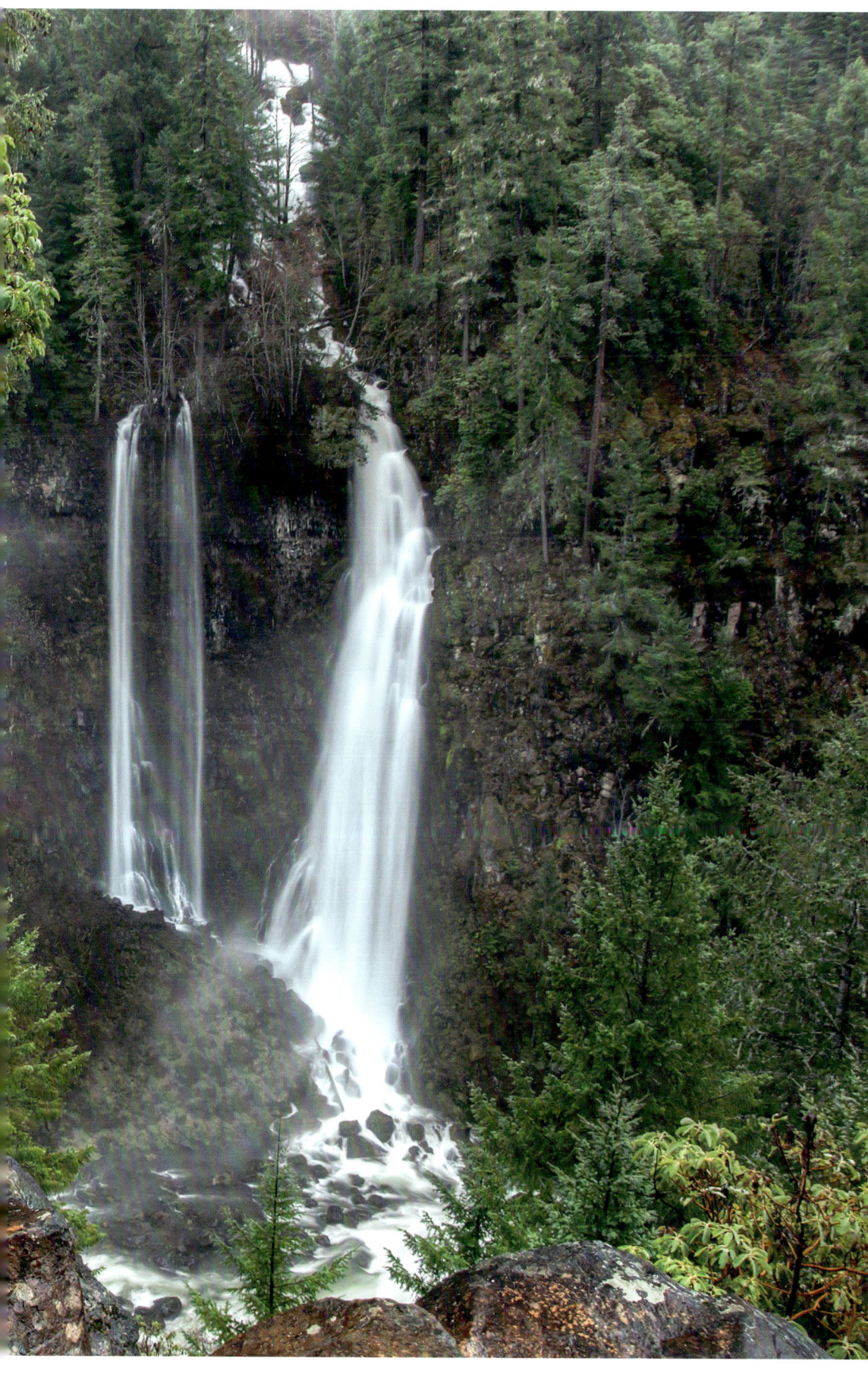

Barr Creek Falls. Along a tributary of the Rogue River in the town of Prospect is Barr Creek Falls. It is only a quarter mile from Mill Creek Falls or Avenue of the Giant Boulders, all three do-able in one visit. *Photo by Sue Newman*

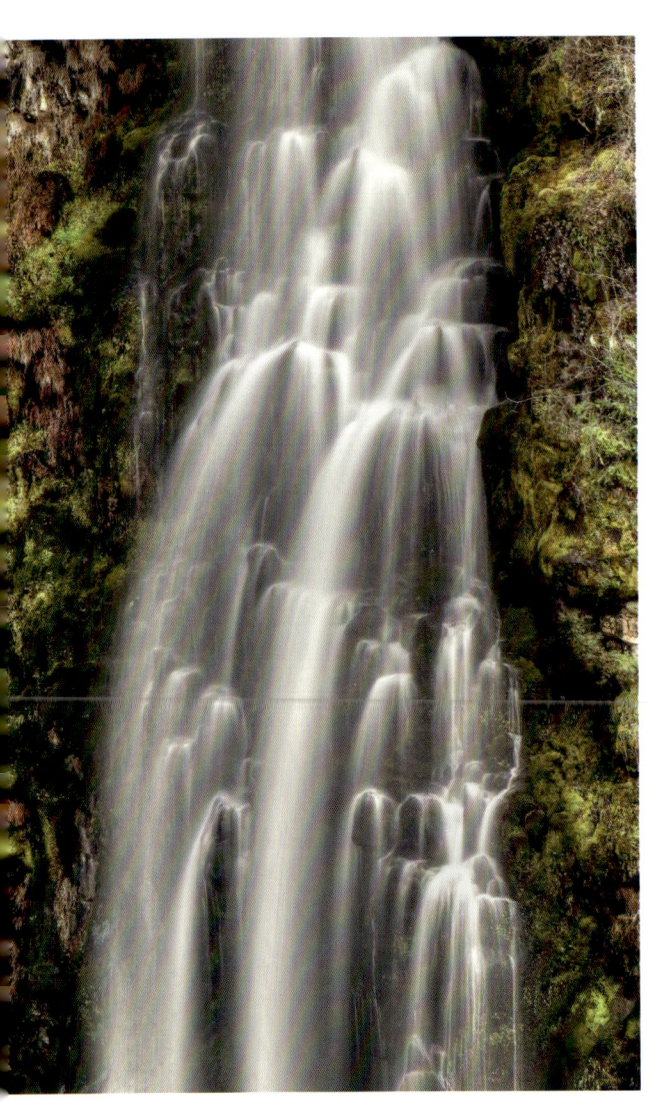

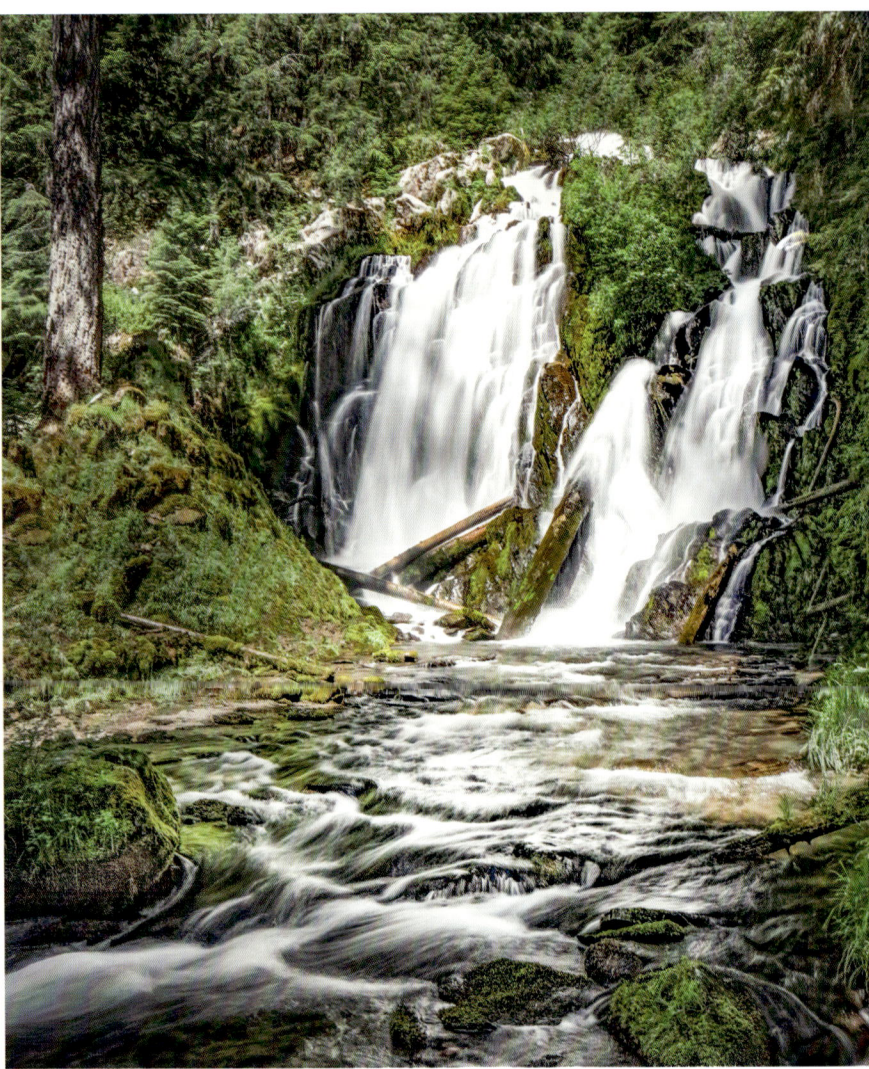

Barr Creek Falls. This graceful, veillike waterfall spills over 240 feet into the narrow gorge below. *Photo by Jay Newman*

National Creek Falls. A kid-friendly hike from Prospect, this waterfall is also a great way to cool off in the summer. *Photo by Sue Stendebach*

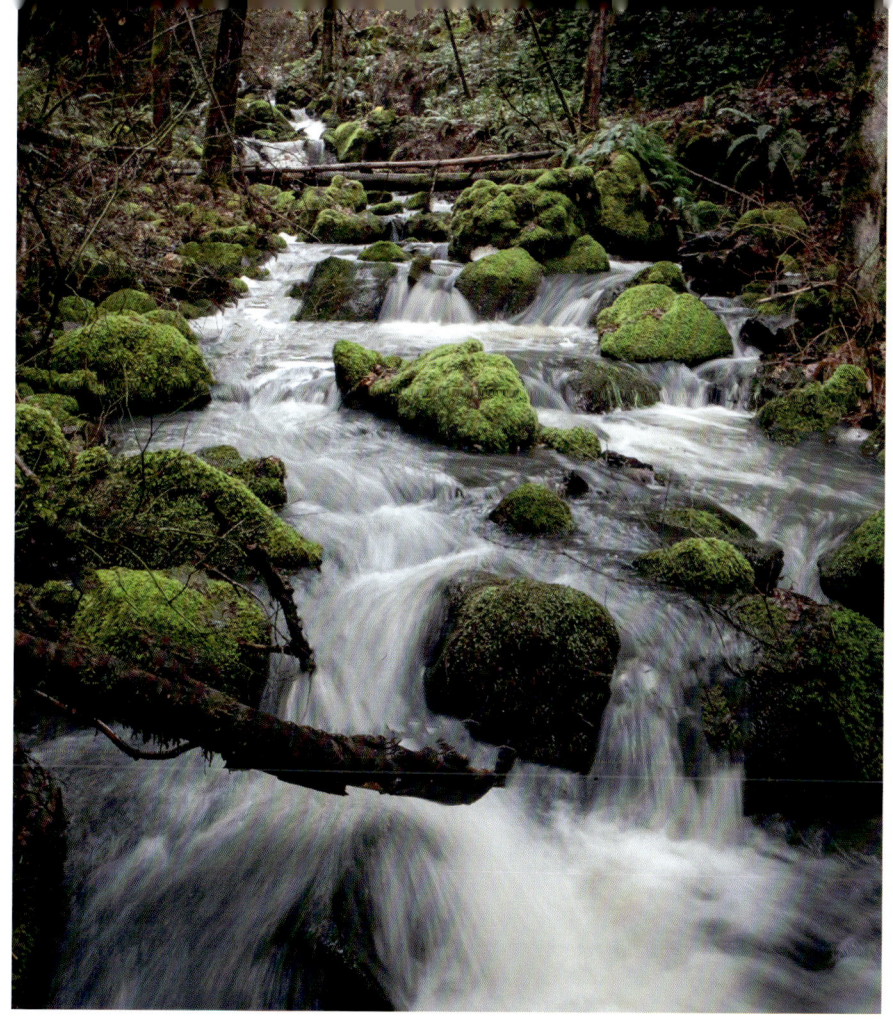

Lost Creek Lake Falls. While in Prospect, there is a 1-mile trail under the Peyton Bridge that leads to the falls, which is west of Crater Lake Highway (OR 62). Hole in the Ground Creek enters the Rogue River above Lost Creek Lake. *Photo by Bob Palermini*

Muir Creek Falls. This fairly easy, 1.1-mile-out-and-back trail is on Route 230, not far from both Crater Lake National Park and Diamond Lake. *Photo by Randy Bryan*

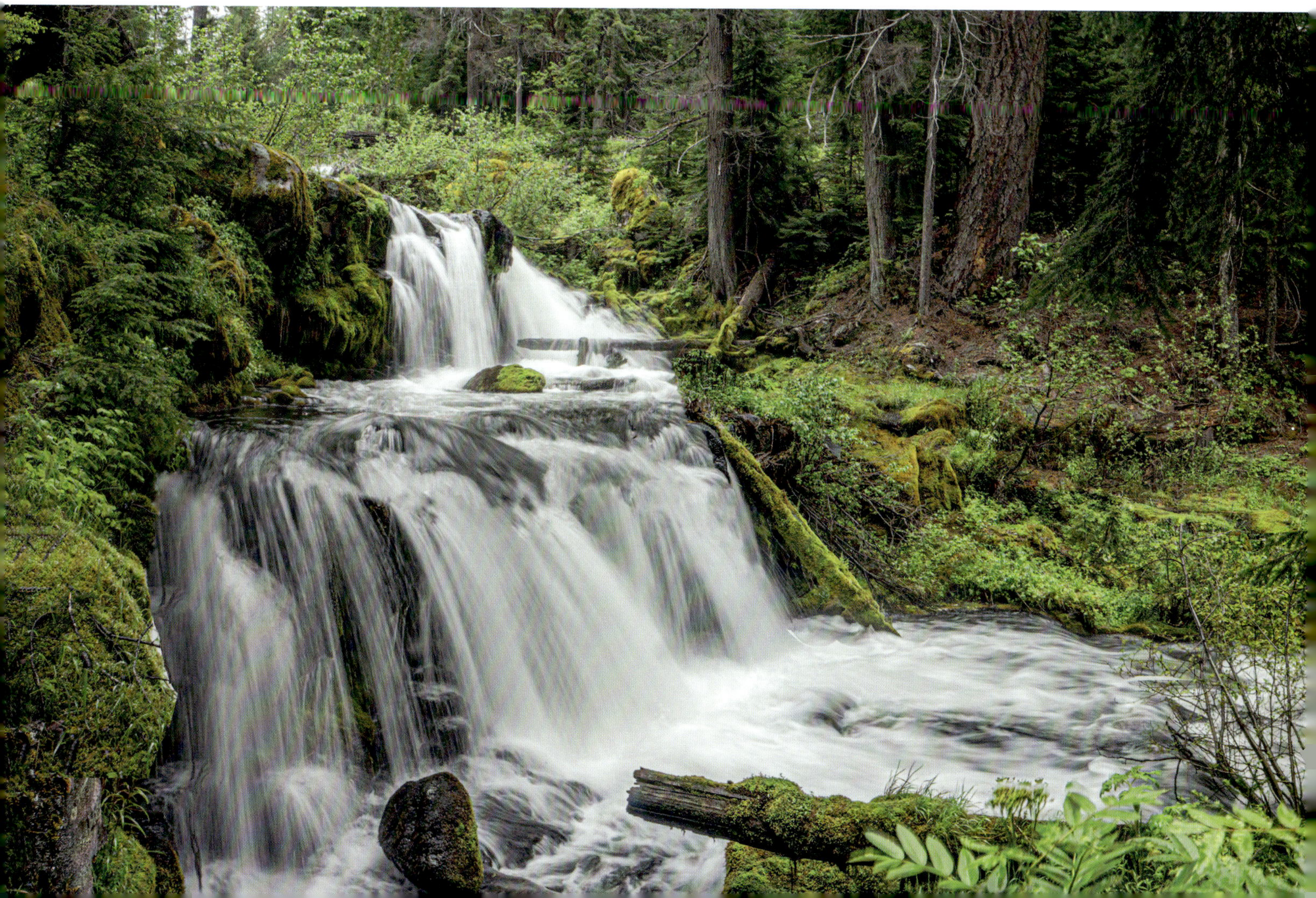

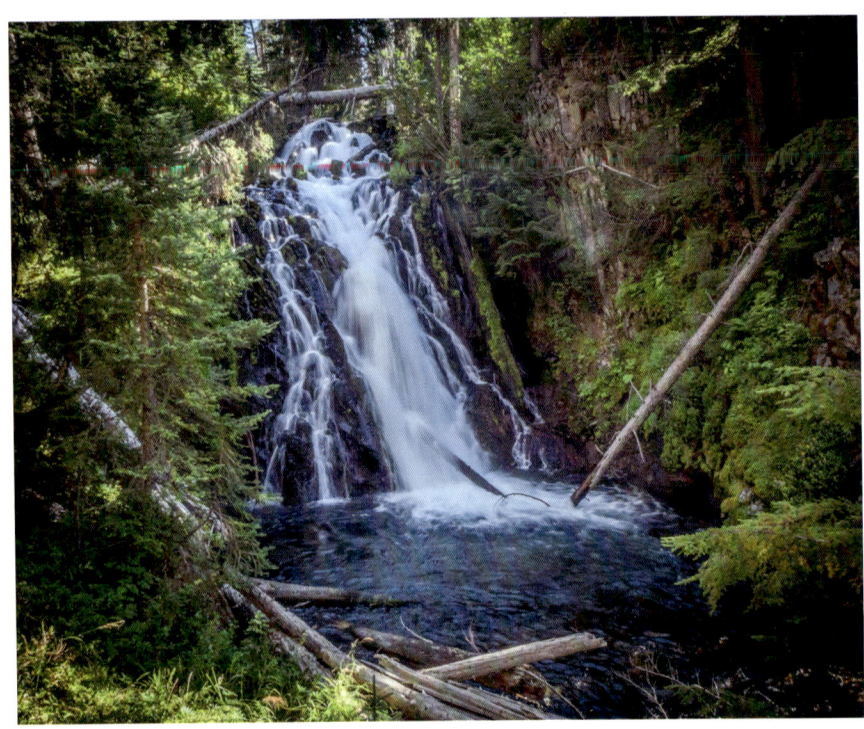

Red Blanket Falls. A moderately challenging hike near Prospect, Oregon, this sometimes-overgrown trail leads one to an impressive waterfall. It plunges 50 feet down a basalt face. The trail continues to Stuart Falls, connects to the Pacific Crest Trail, and continues past Crater Lake. *Photo by Randy Bryan*

Butte Falls. This is a wide, cascading waterfall on the Big Butte Creek outside the small town of Butte Falls, population 437, near Prospect, Oregon (not to be confused with Upper and Lower Butte Creek Falls near Portland). There is a platform for visitors to enjoy and photograph this very accessible waterfall. *Photo by Patty Albin*

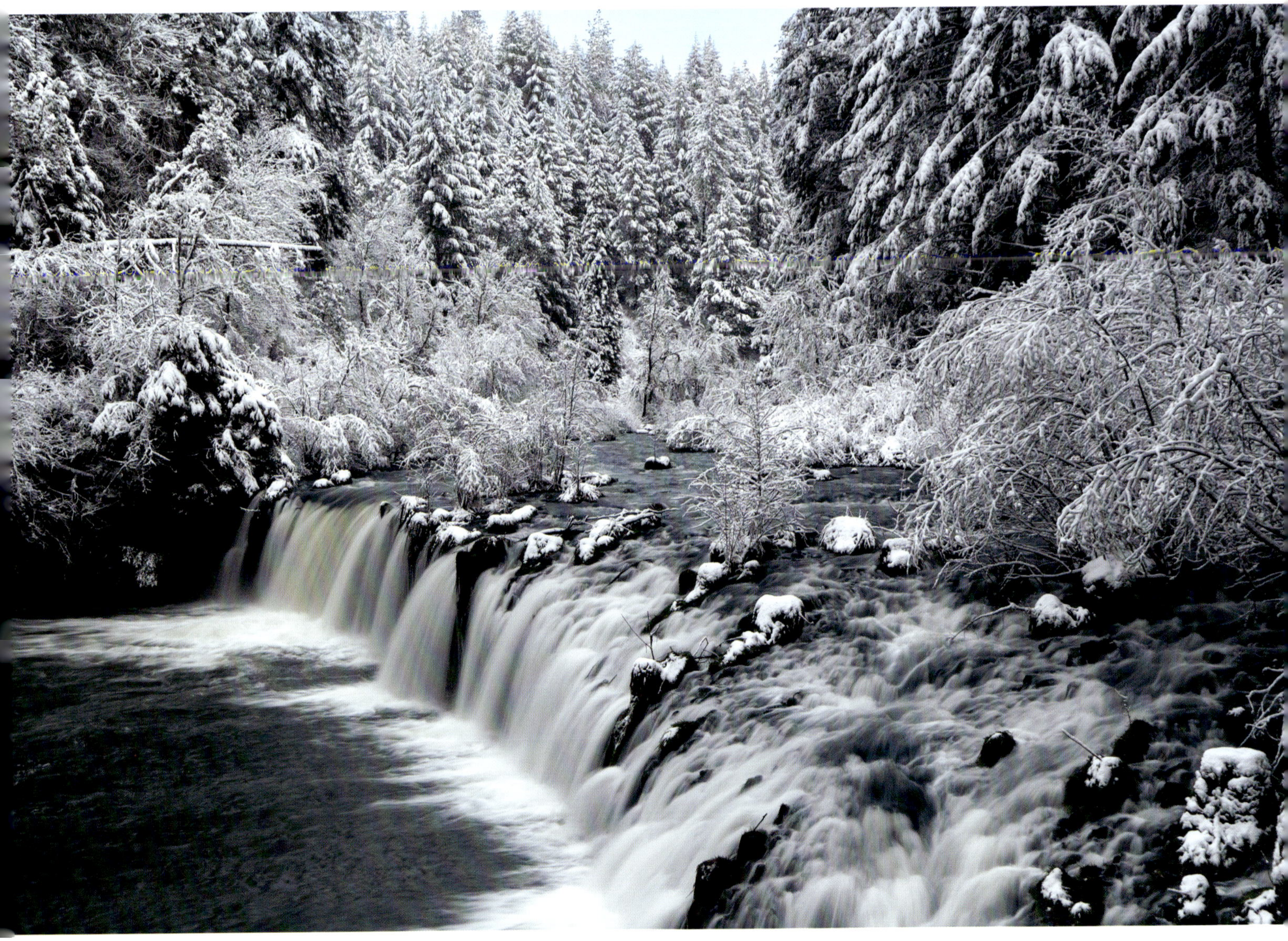

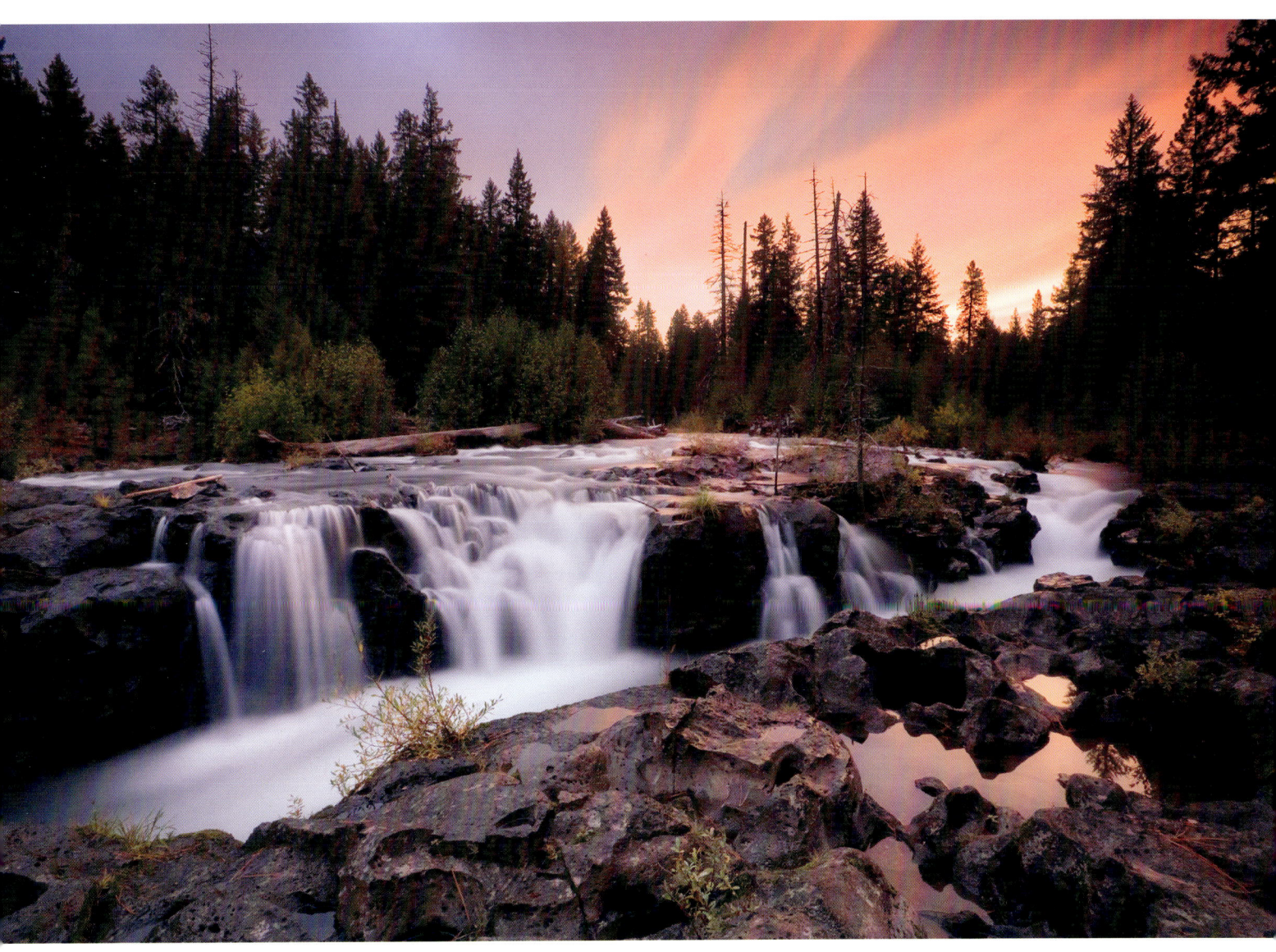

Rogue River Gorge. This is a not-to-be-missed section of the Rogue National Wild and Scenic River, just past Union Creek. After you leave Prospect, it is on the way to Crater Lake and Diamond Lake on OR 62. The whole family will enjoy watching the impressive river from tall viewpoints. *Photo by Sean Bagshaw*

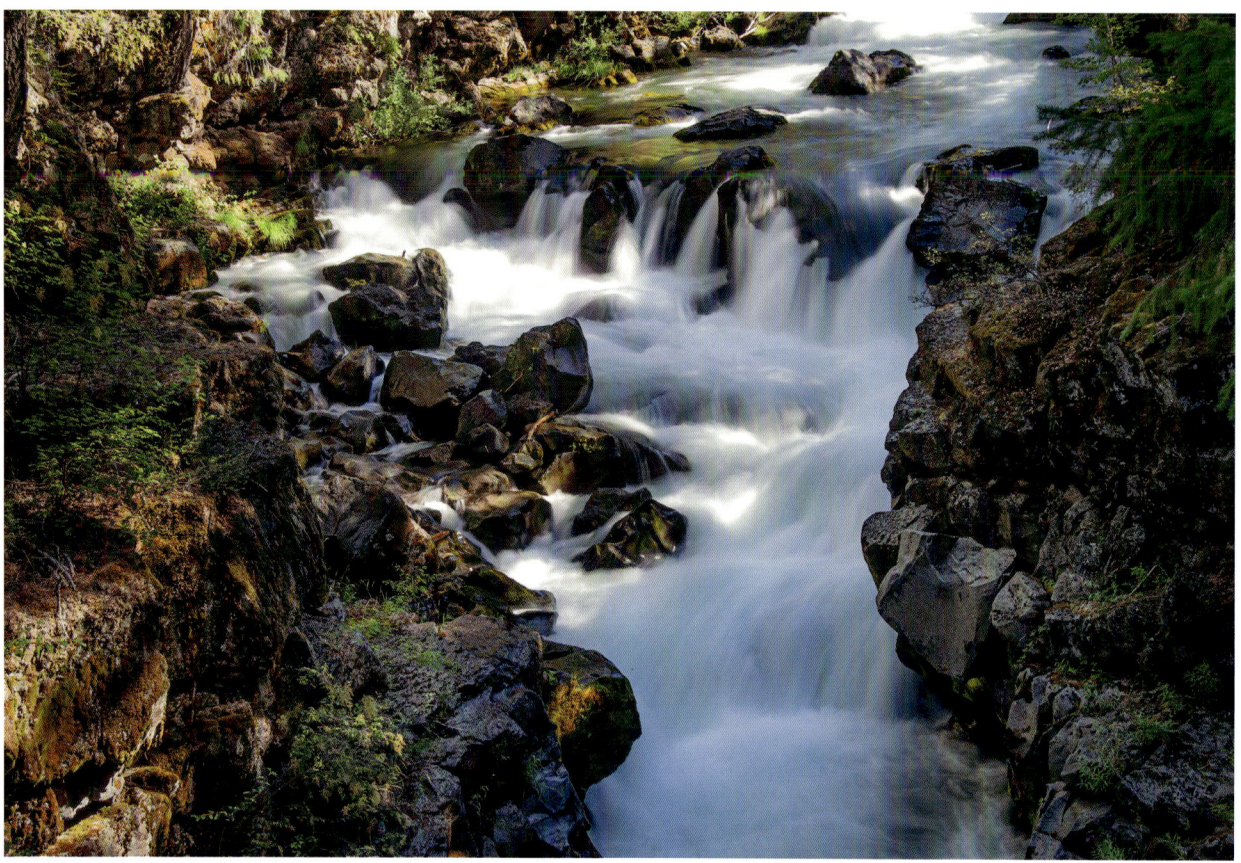

Rogue River Gorge. The Rogue River flows 215 miles from its headwaters in Crater Lake National Park to the Pacific Ocean in Gold Beach, Oregon. The river loudly tumbles over itself, forming dramatic waterfalls, while surging through canyon walls and lava tubes. *Photo by Howard Hunt*

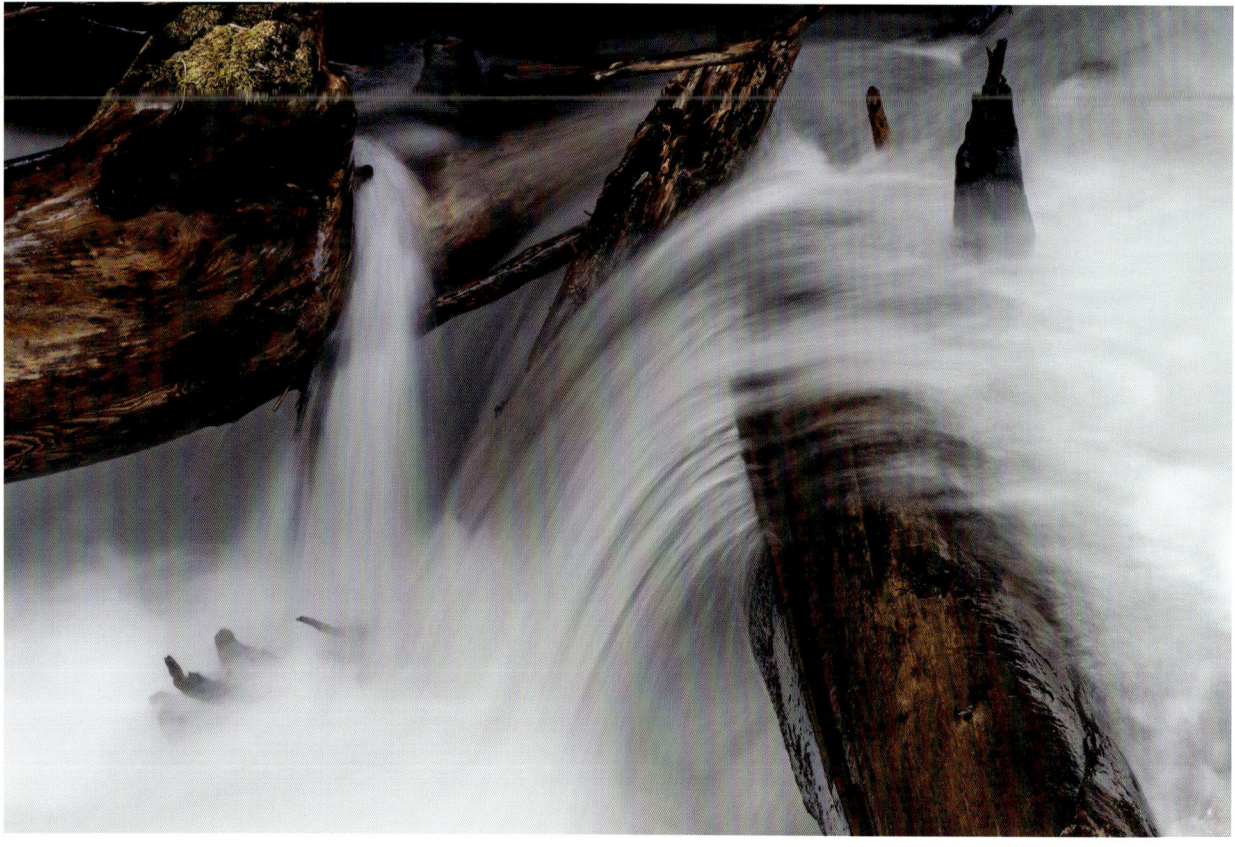

Rogue River Gorge detail. The Rogue National Wild and Scenic River rushes and cascades for miles through a constricted channel of basalt lava. *Photo by Howard Hunt*

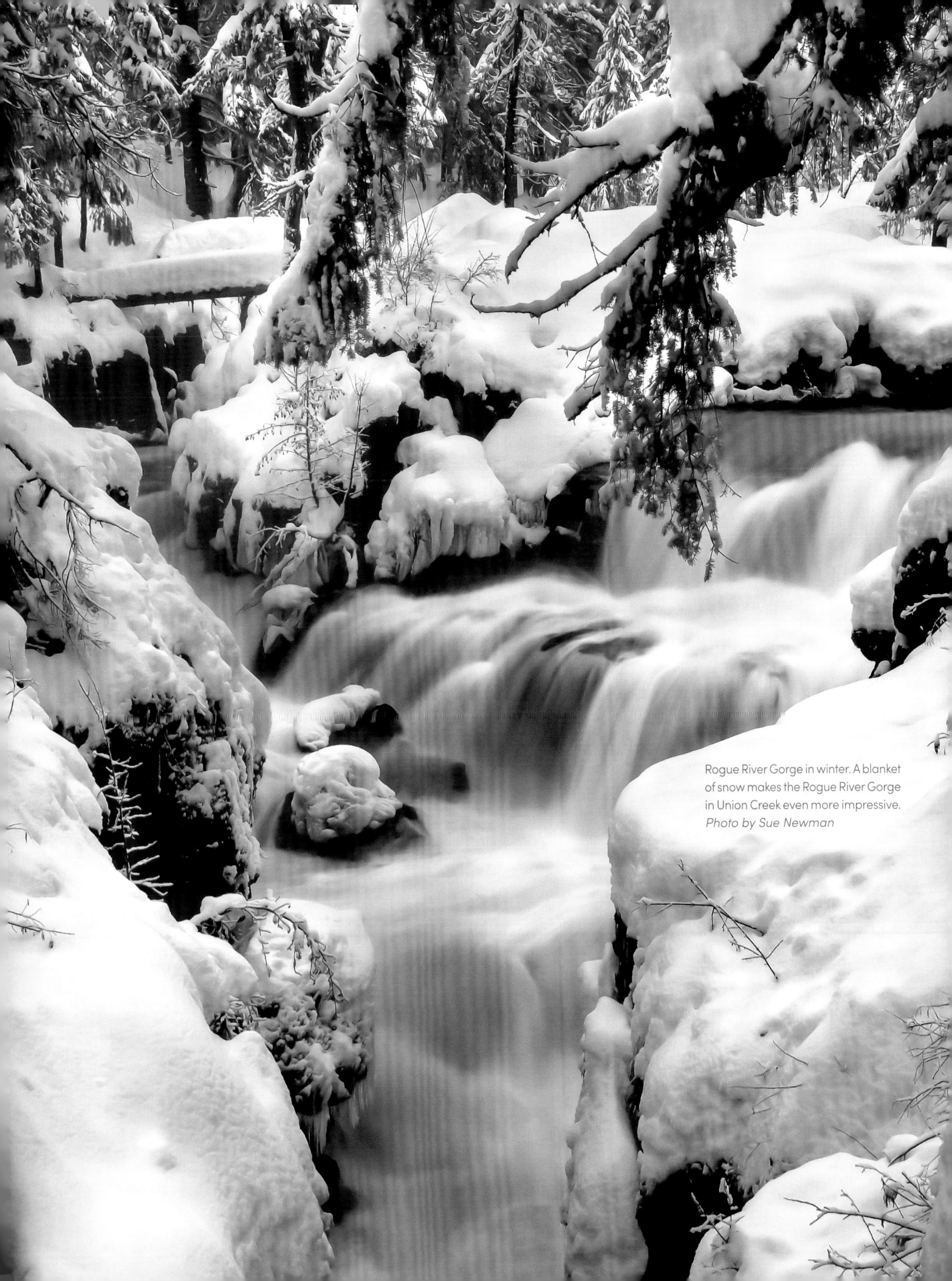

Rogue River Gorge in winter. A blanket of snow makes the Rogue River Gorge in Union Creek even more impressive. *Photo by Sue Newman*

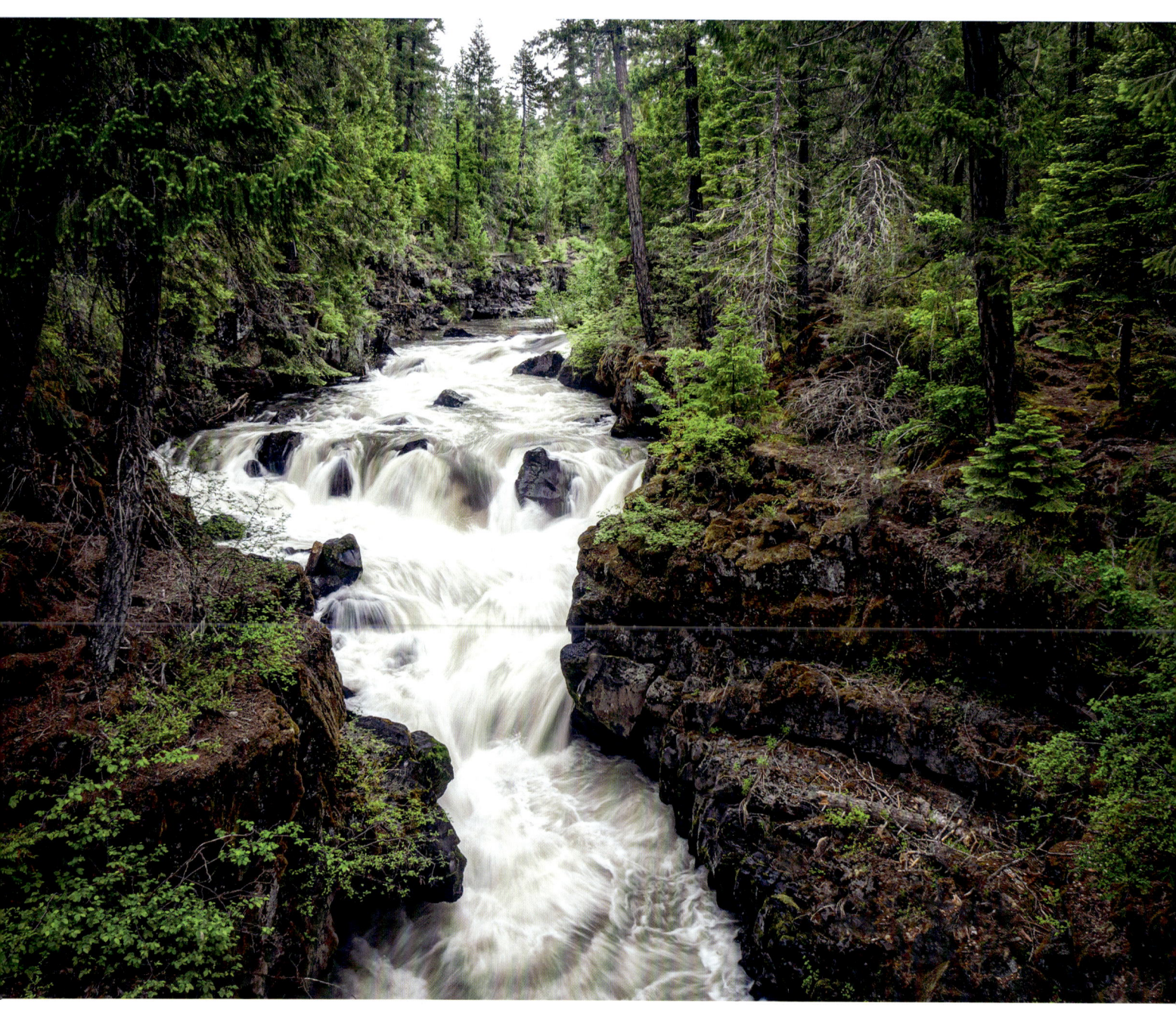

Natural Bridge. This amazing natural water feature is a popular stop along OR 62 in Union Creek, on the way to Crater Lake or Diamond Lake. Visitors can take a gentle hike along the dramatic and gushing Rogue National Wild and Scenic River, where lava tubes seem to swallow the river and then spit it out through caves and lava tubes farther downstream. This terrain creates a natural land bridge. While not an official waterfall, these gushing rapids create their own small waterfalls with deafening sounds. *Photo by Fran Yates*

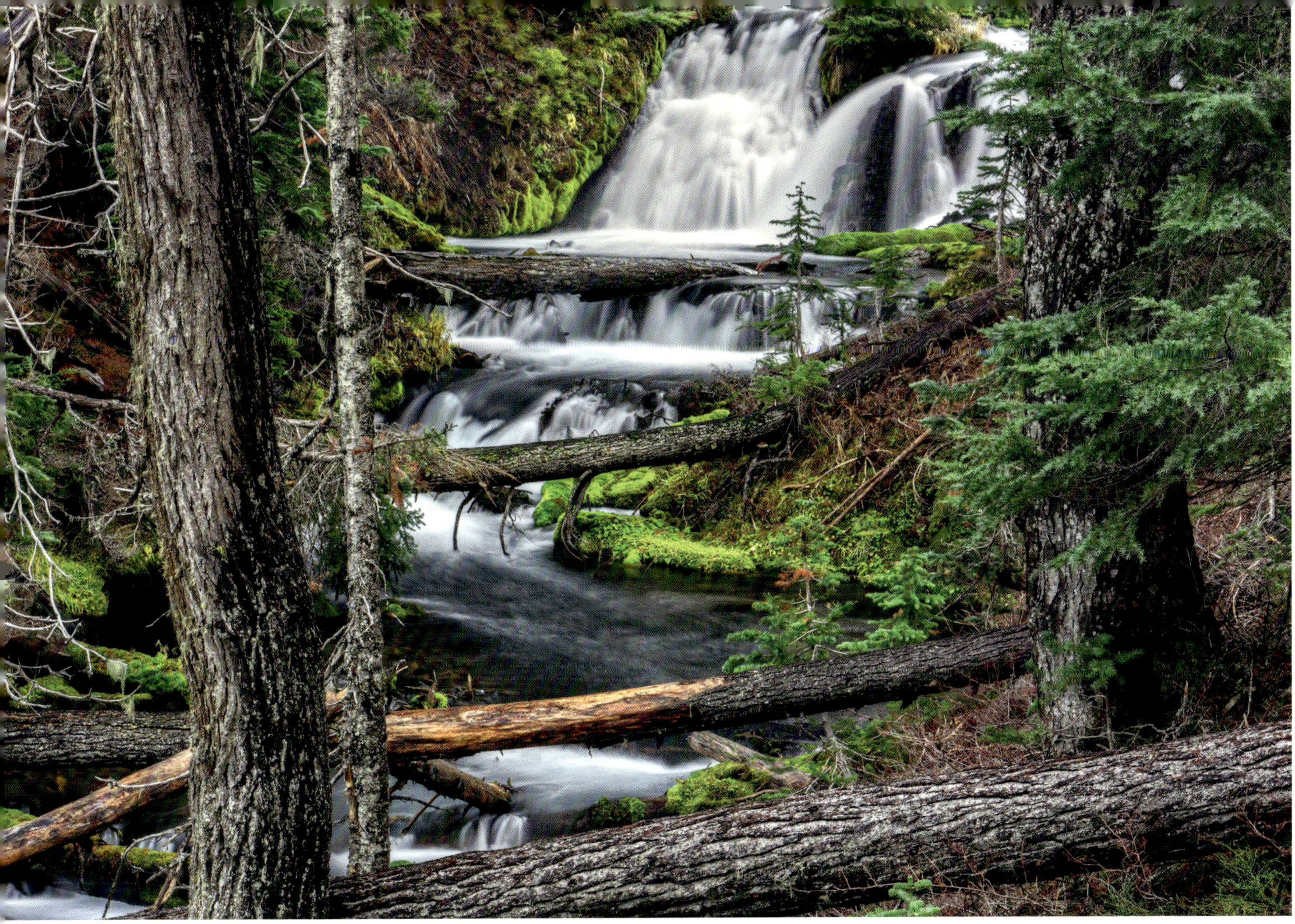

Boundary Springs. Located in Crater Lake National Park, this moderately challenging 5.2-mile-out-and-back trail leads to the headwaters of the Rogue River. The trail is not well marked, still recovering from a recent fire, and is best accessed from the northern edge of Crater Lake National Park. *Photo by Sue Newman*

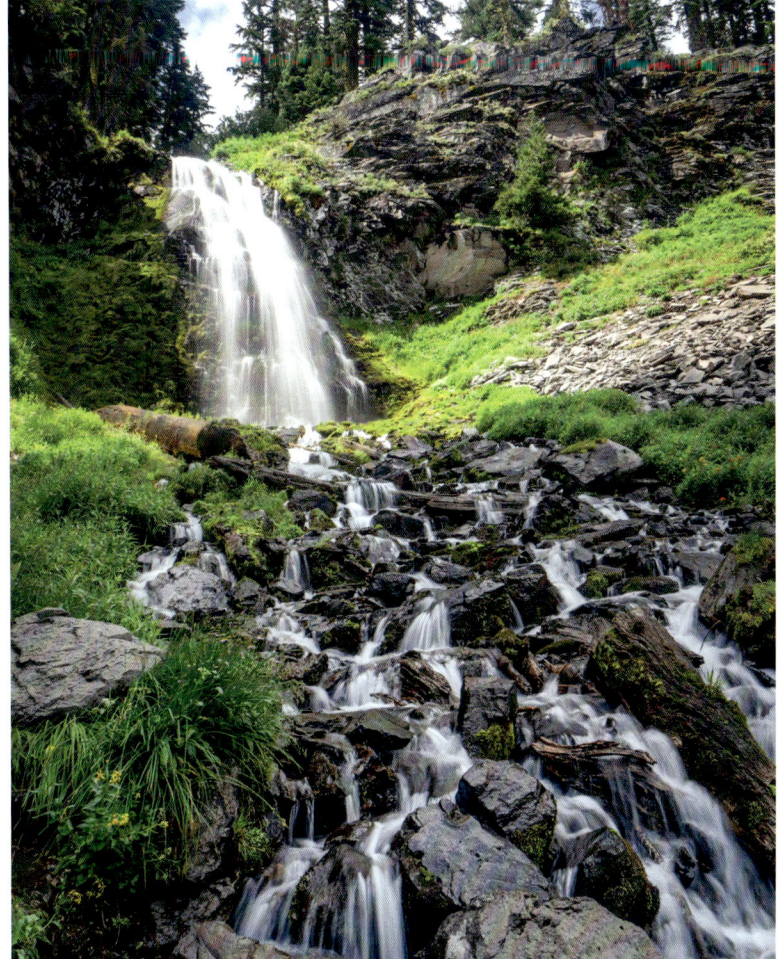

Plaikni Falls. A family-friendly waterfall inside Crater Lake National Park, this is an easy 2.0-mile-out-and-back hike. The falls can also be seen from the road along the East Rim Drive. The waterfall flows over petrified volcanic ash from the Mount Mazama eruption about 7,700 years ago. *Photo by Fran Yates*

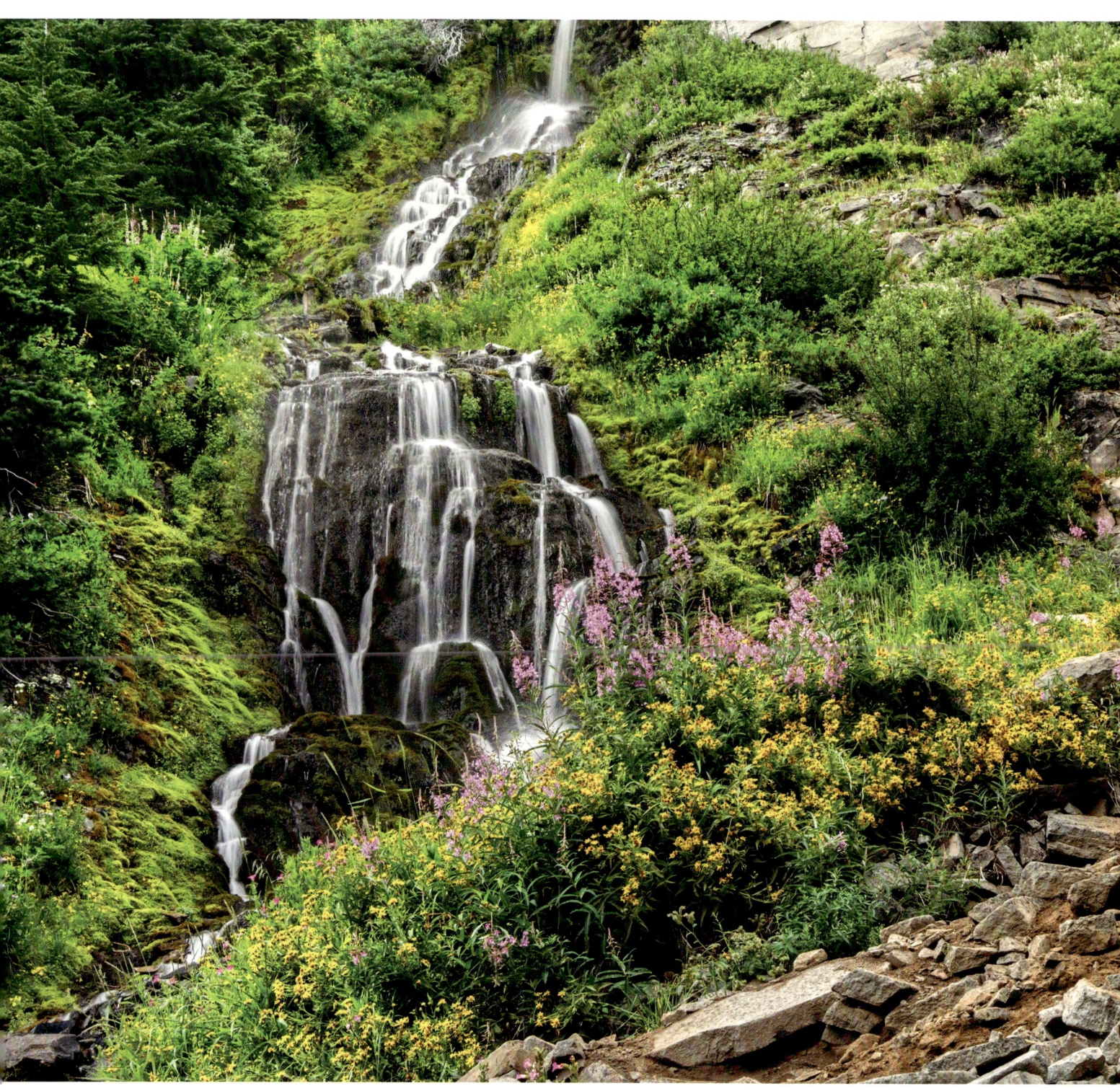

Vidae Falls. One of the best-known and most accessible waterfalls inside Crater Lake National Park, Videa Falls can be seen while driving along the Crater Lake Rim Drive. There is parking access on the road. *Photo by Sue Newman*

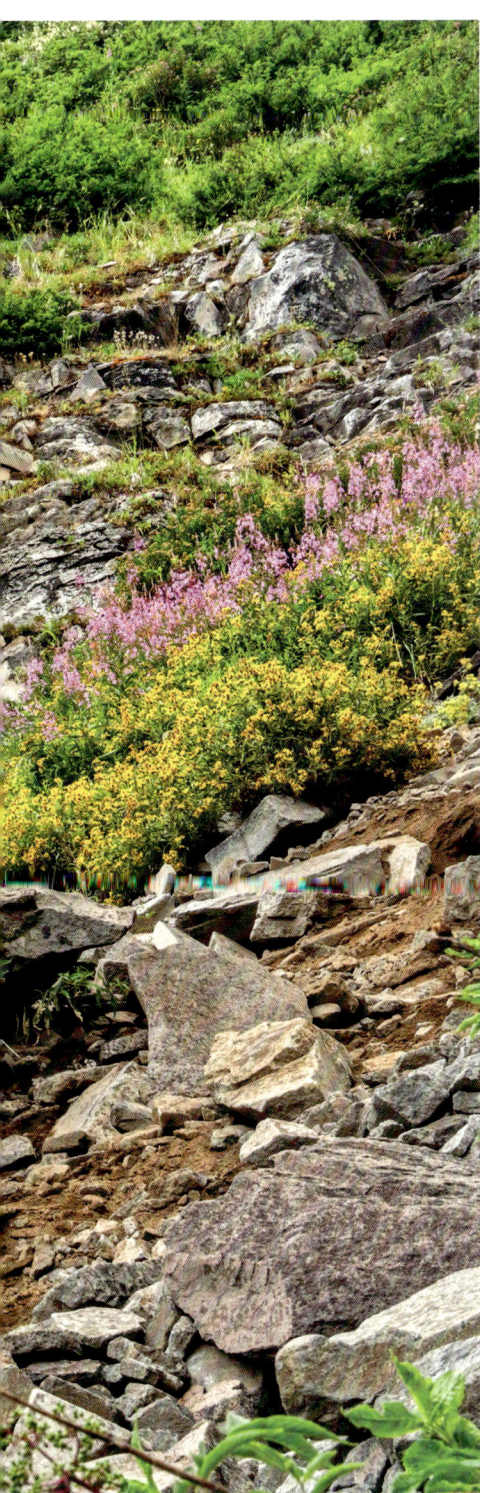

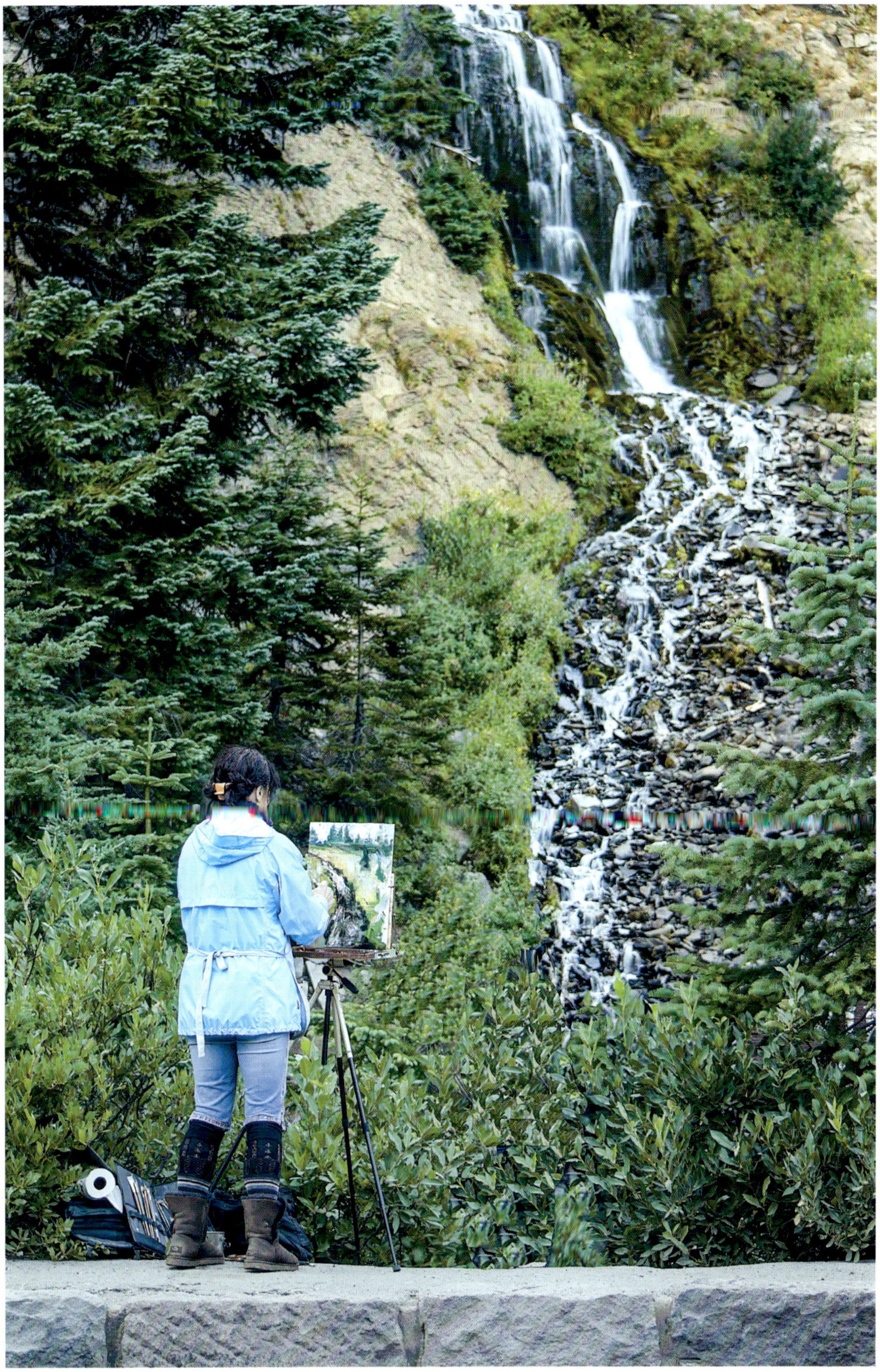

Vidae Falls. An artist re-creates this roadside waterfall inside Crater Lake National Park. It cascades from Vidae Creek. *Photo by Barbara Tricarico*

Oregon Coast and Coastal Range

Dozens of impressive waterfalls can be found within the Oregon Coast Range, an expansive area covering 17,000 square miles. A few waterfalls even empty directly onto the coastline itself. Geographically, the Oregon Coast Range sits between the Willamette Valley and the Pacific Ocean and runs south from Washington state to the California border. Many of these waterfalls can be accessed by driving west from Interstate 5 to the Oregon coast. However, be mindful, since some are located on rugged and remote mountain logging roads and may be hard to find without good maps. GPS can be spotty.

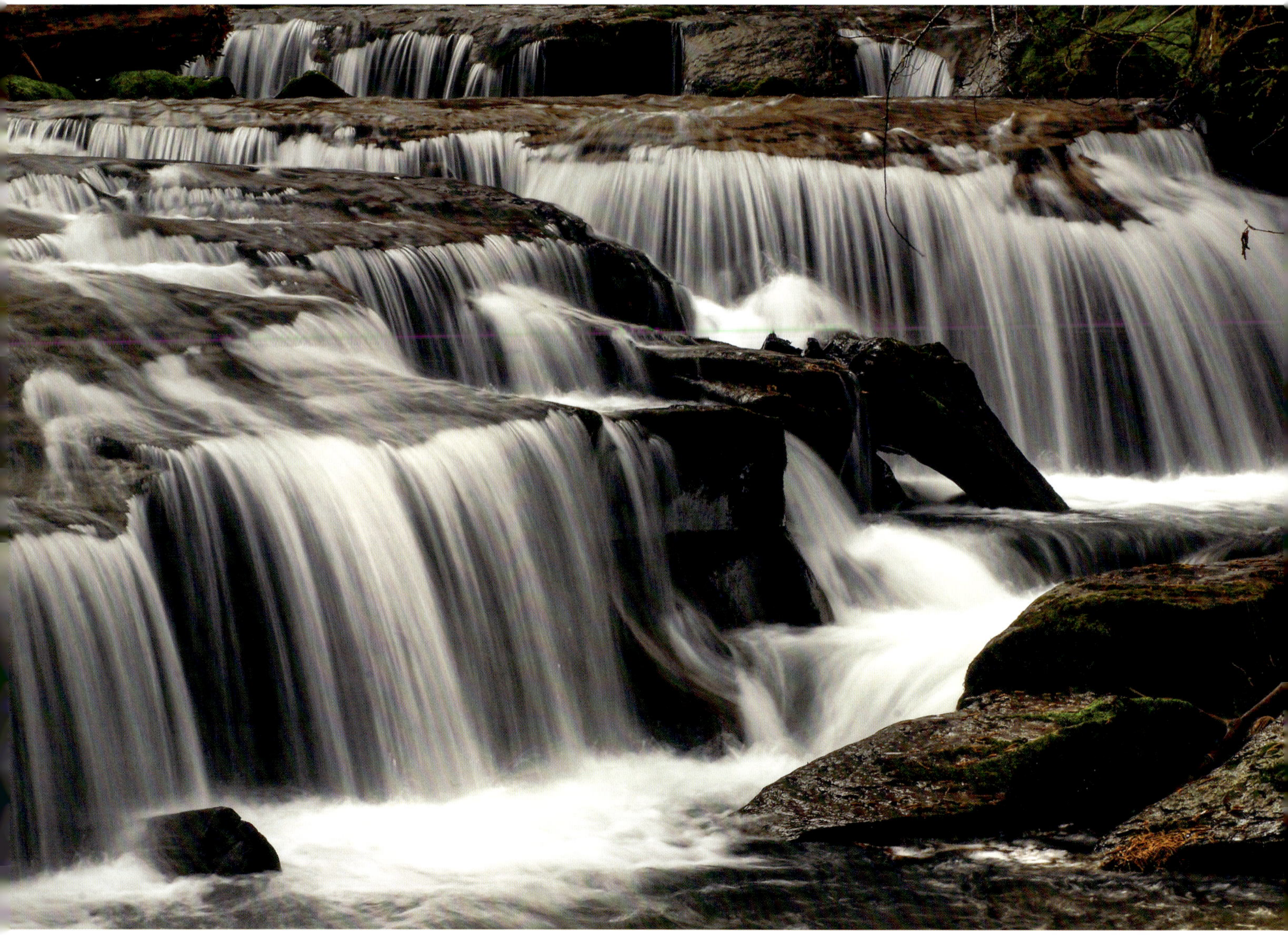

Elk Wallow Falls. This striking cascade below Sweet Creek Falls is about 30 minutes east of Florence off Route 126. The Sweet Creek Falls Trail boasts nearly a dozen technical waterfalls. The family-friendly trail is about 2.9 miles long. *Photo by Jay Newman*

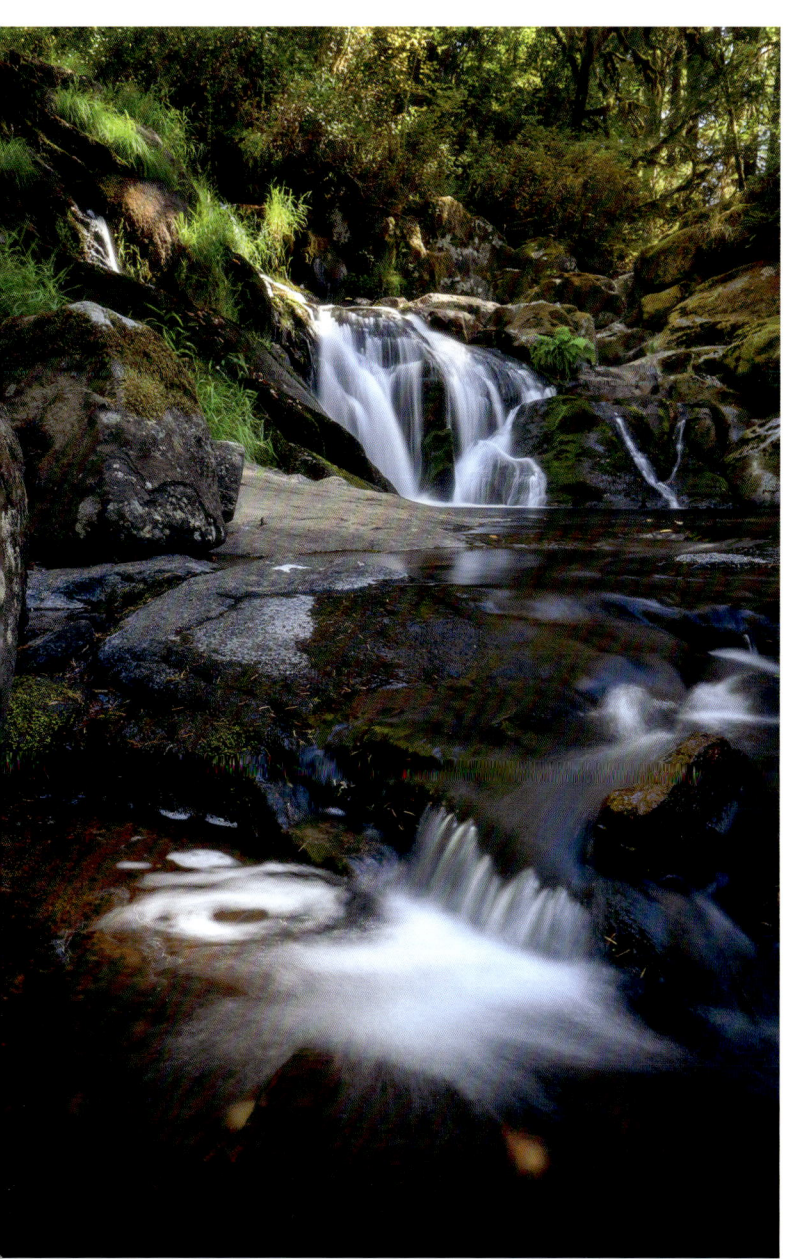

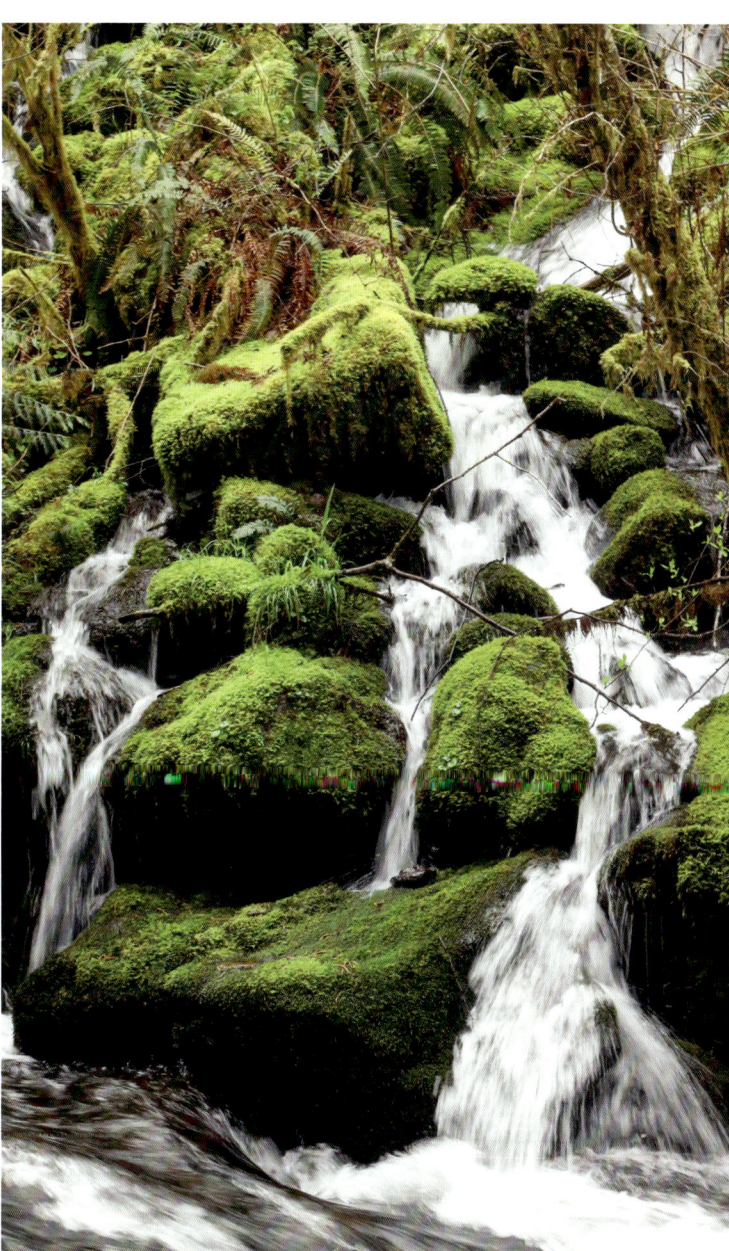

Beaver Creek Falls. Circular swirls form in a pool at the confluence of Beaver Creek and Sweet Creek. The hike is considered short and easy for families, but it can be tricky to find the trailhead. There is a cooling swimming hole in summer. *Photo by Sean Bagshaw*

Sweet Creek Falls. Located on the Sweet Creek Trail and open year-round, 11 falls can be found, including a 70-foot four-tiered waterfall. Several small ones like this flow through moss-covered rocks at its base. The falls are most abundant during the rainy spring season. *Photo by Rose Christner*

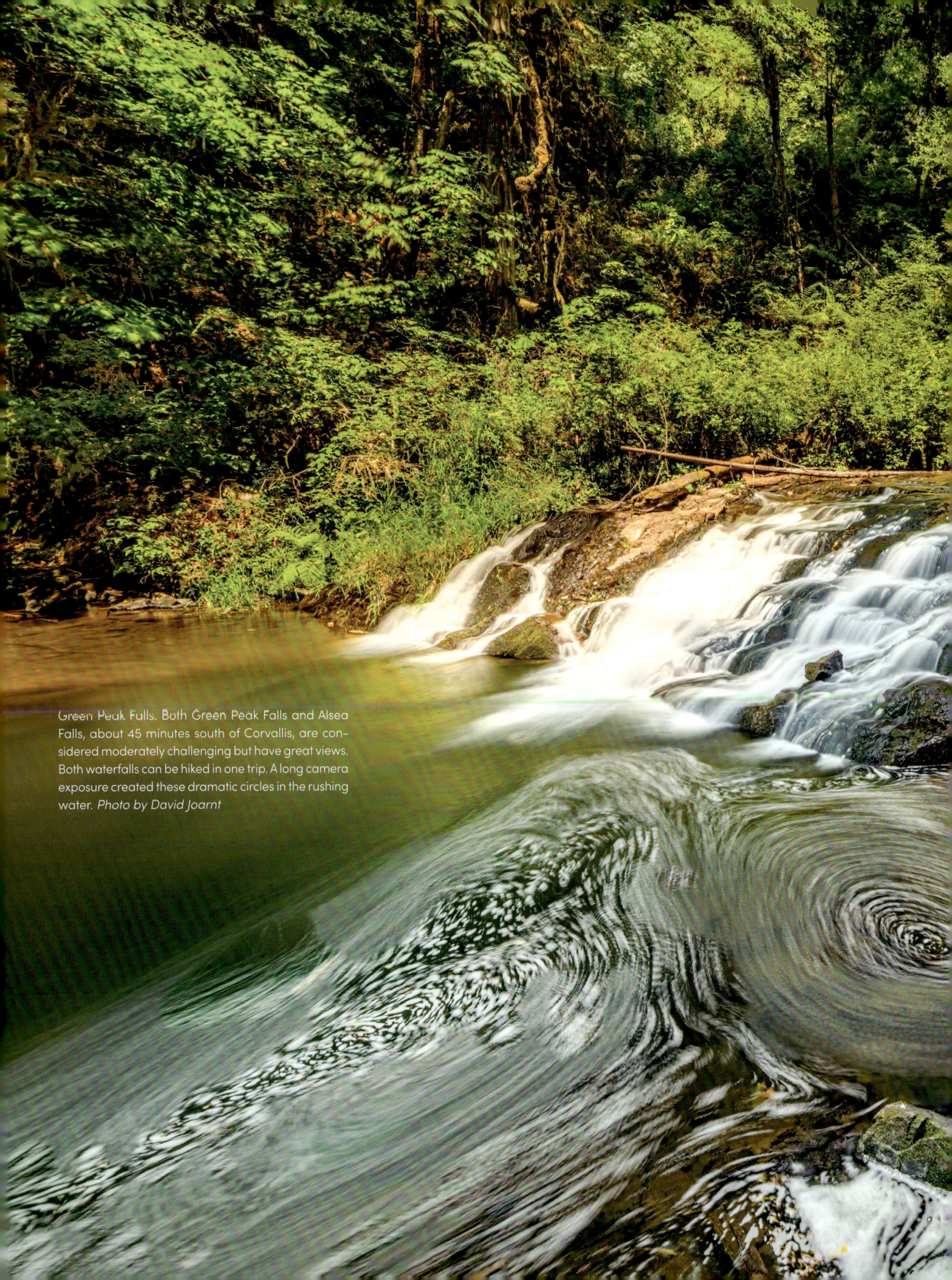

Green Peak Falls. Both Green Peak Falls and Alsea Falls, about 45 minutes south of Corvallis, are considered moderately challenging but have great views. Both waterfalls can be hiked in one trip. A long camera exposure created these dramatic circles in the rushing water. *Photo by David Joarnt*

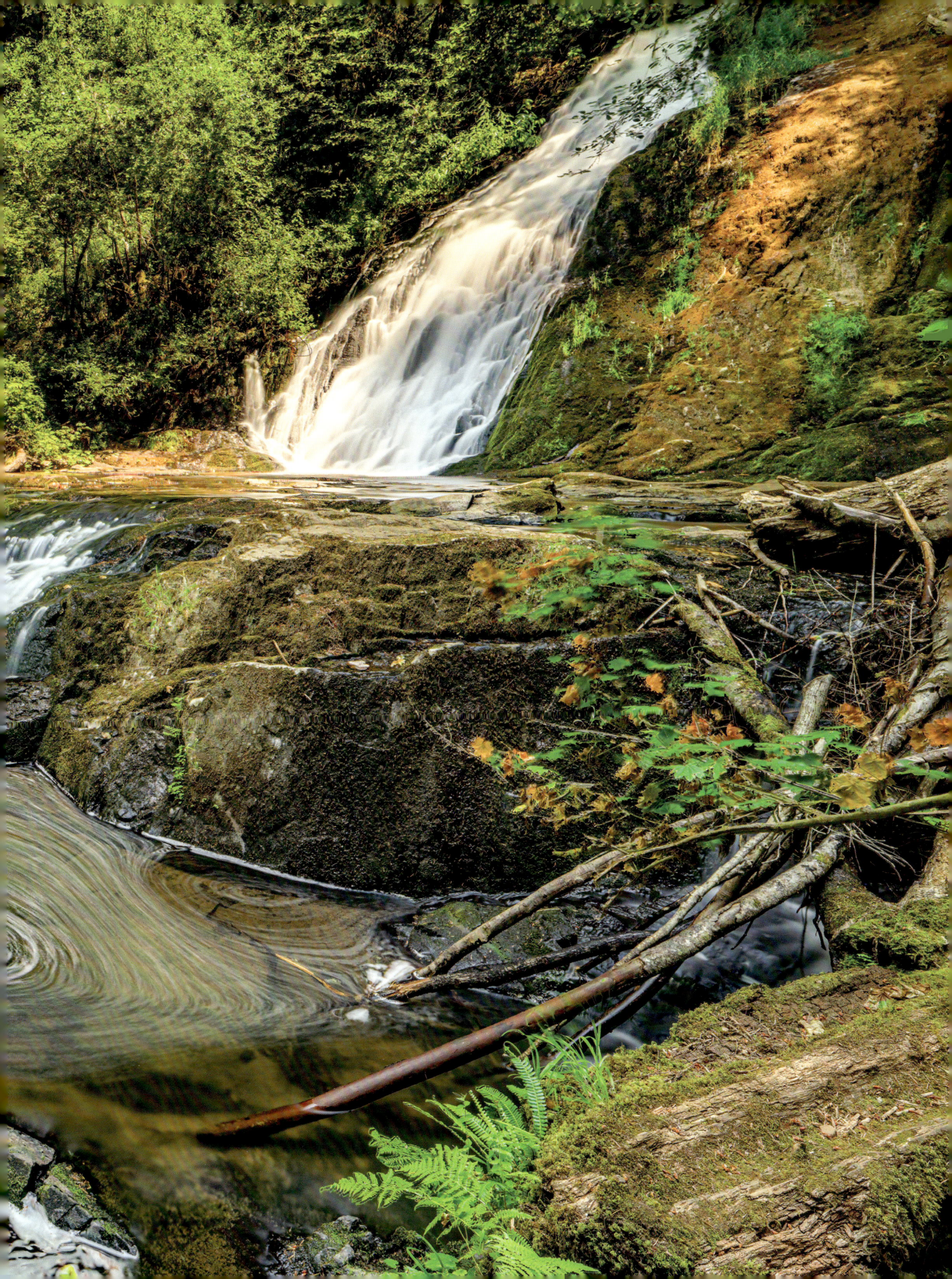

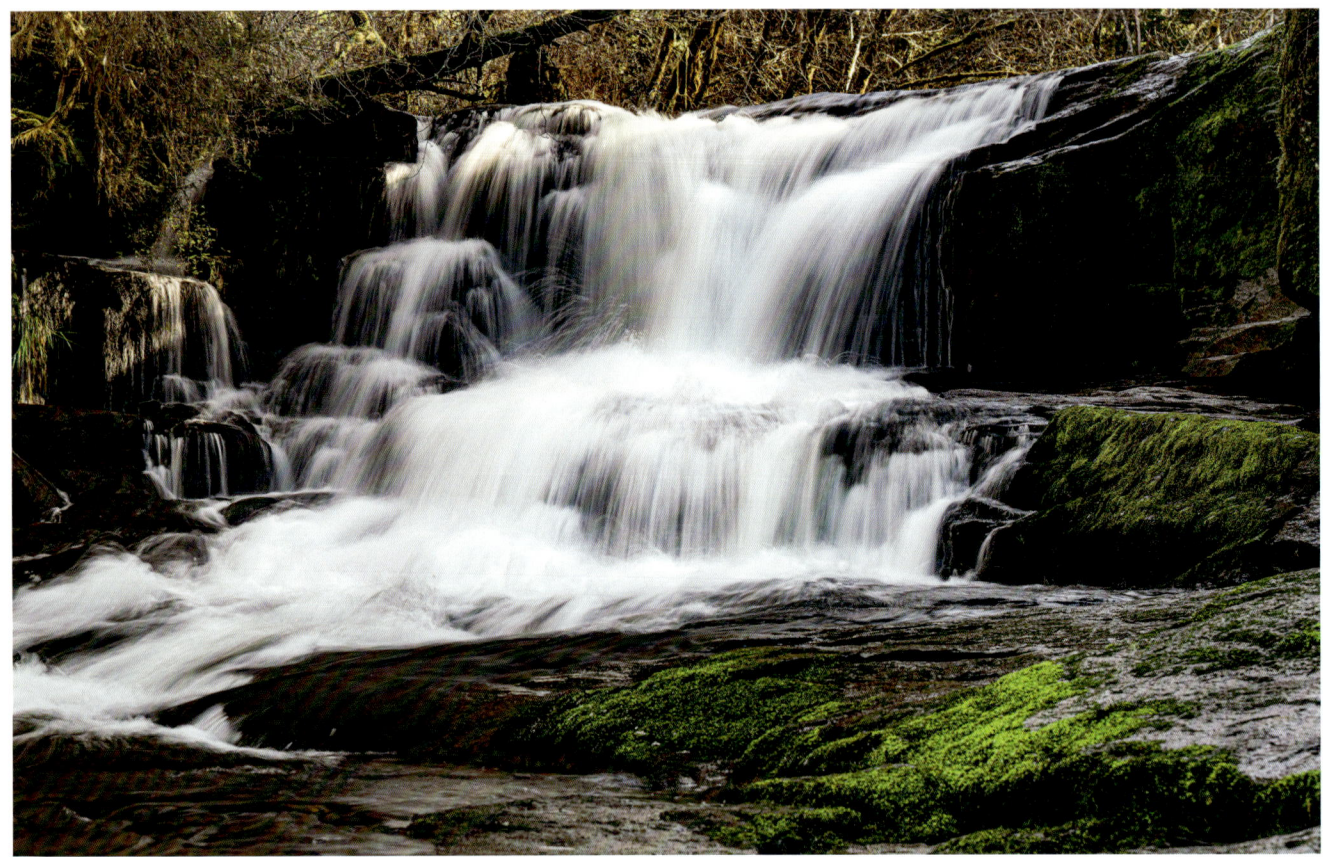

Alsea Falls. About an hour west of Salem are Alsea and Green Peak Falls. The Alsea River drops about 20-30 feet to form the falls. The site is located along a Bureau of Land Management National Back Country Byway in the Oregon Coast Range. Considered a moderately challenging route, it's about 4 miles out and back to see both falls. *Photo by Frank G. Lahman*

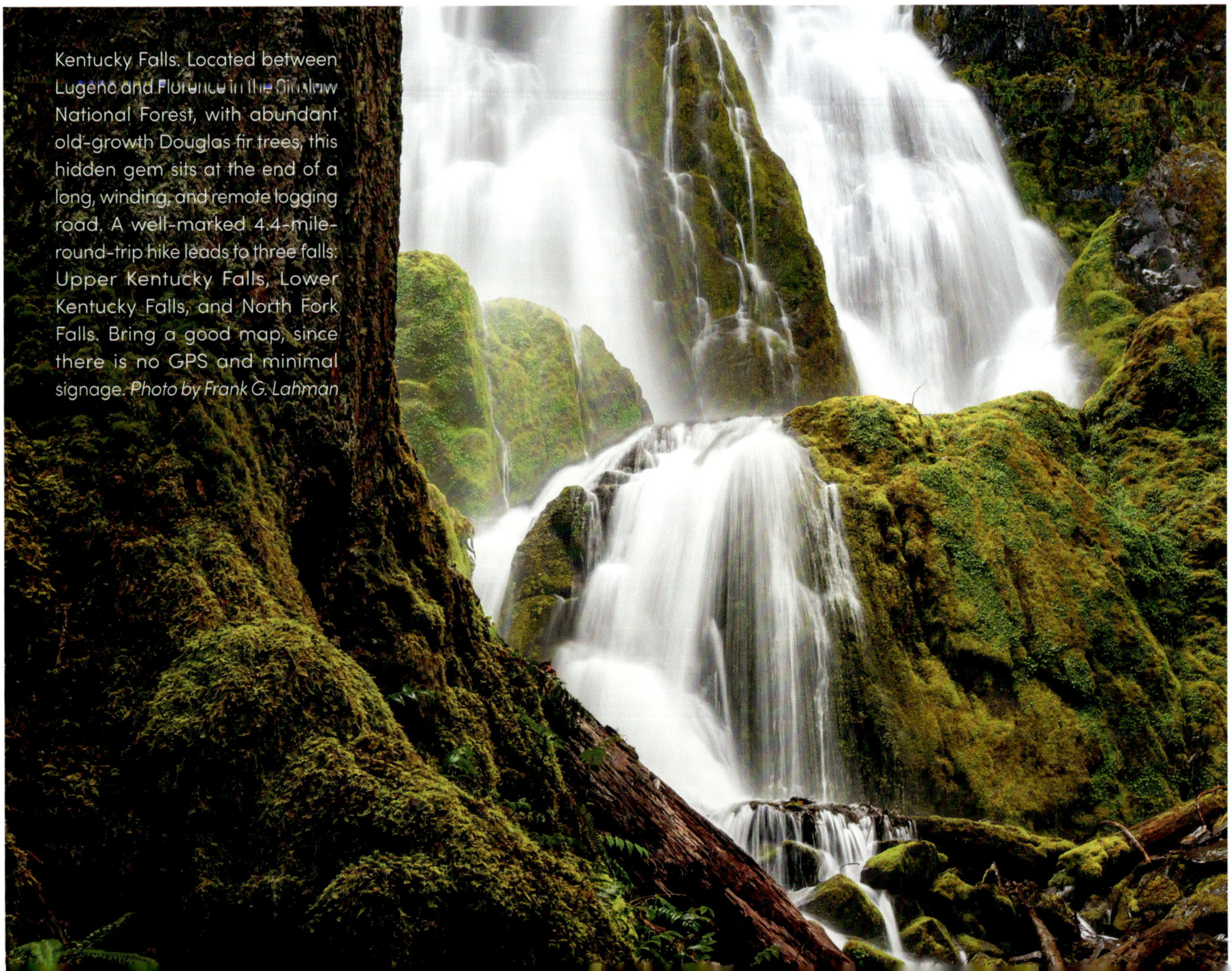

Kentucky Falls. Located between Eugene and Florence in the Siuslaw National Forest, with abundant old-growth Douglas fir trees, this hidden gem sits at the end of a long, winding, and remote logging road. A well-marked 4.4-mile-round-trip hike leads to three falls: Upper Kentucky Falls, Lower Kentucky Falls, and North Fork Falls. Bring a good map, since there is no GPS and minimal signage. *Photo by Frank G. Lahman*

Golden Falls. Located in Golden and Silver Falls State Park near Coos Bay, these two stately falls are the second- and third-tallest waterfalls in the Oregon Coast Range. A short, flat hike leads to the base of each of the two waterfalls. *Photo by Sean Bagshaw*

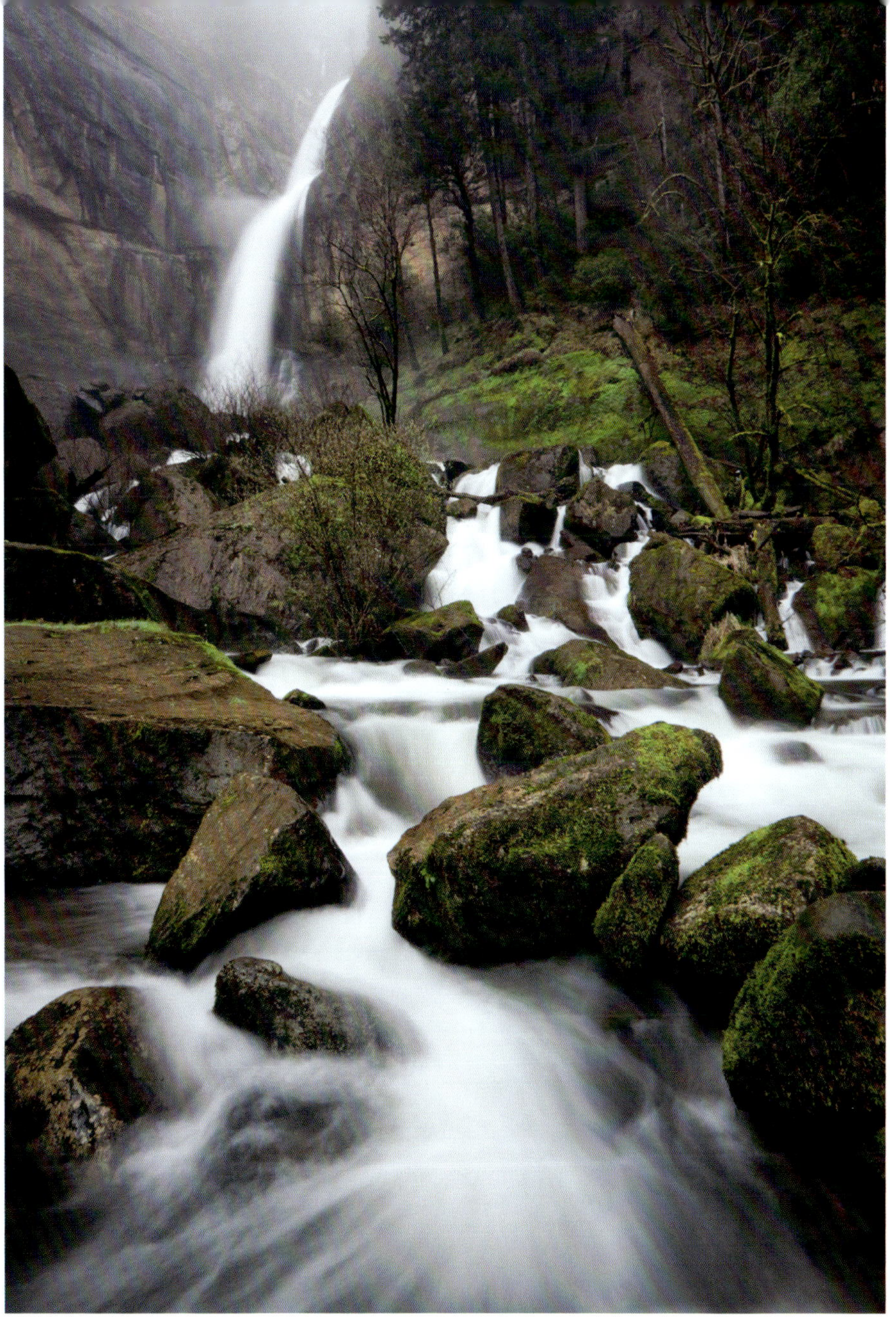

Golden Falls. A view from the top of Golden Falls, looking down. *Photo by Sue Newman*

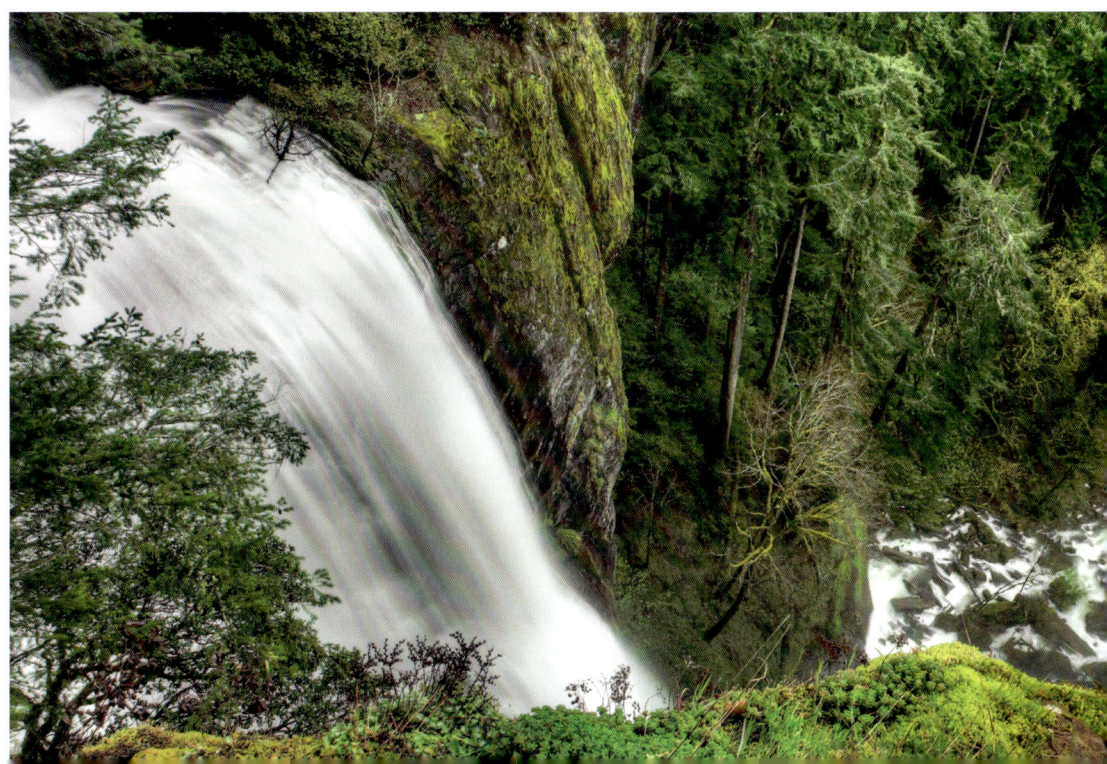

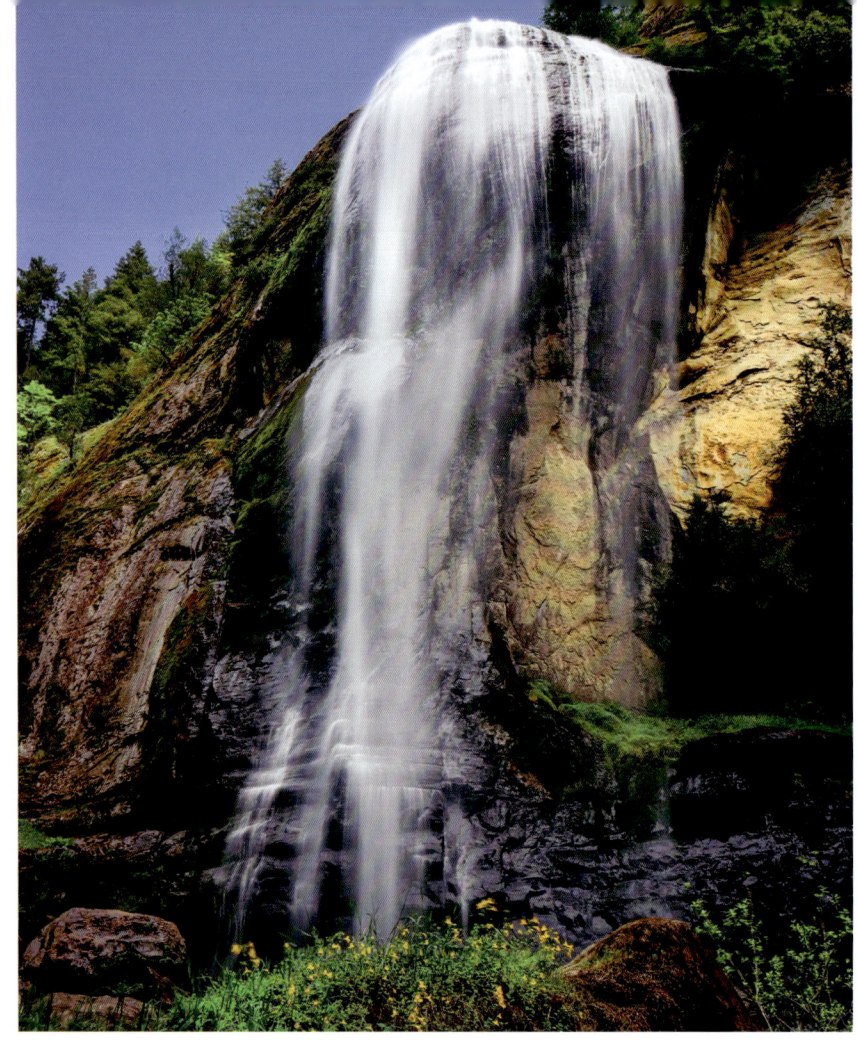

Silver Falls. Not to be confused with Silver Falls State Park in the Willamette Valley, this waterfall (named "Silver Falls") resides at Golden and Silver Falls State Park, next to its sister, Golden Falls. While the names can get confusing, this waterfall is worth a day trip if in the Coos Bay area. *Photo by Frank G. Lahman*

Silver Falls. A view from the top of Silver Falls, looking down. *Photo by Barbara Tricarico*

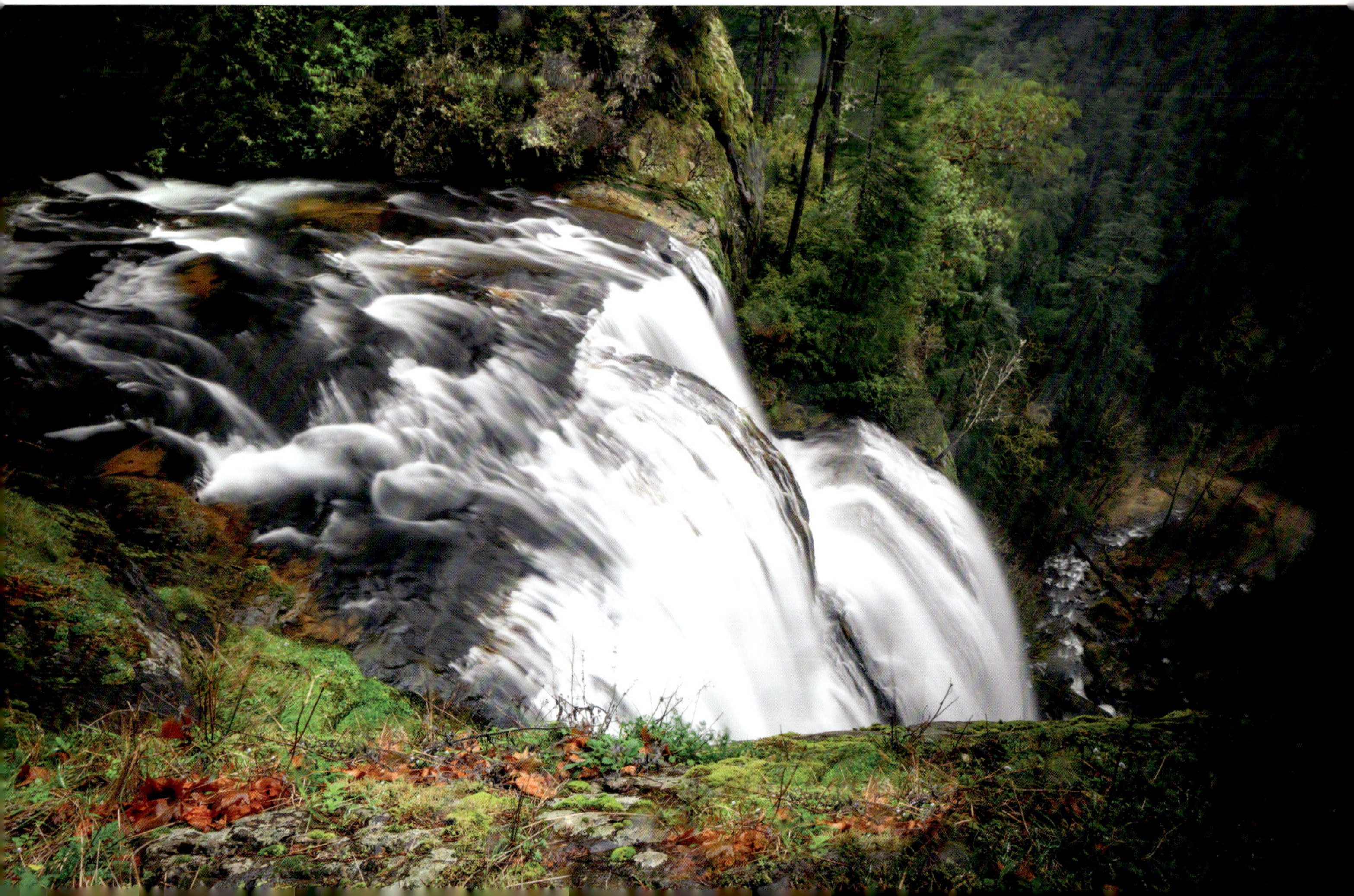

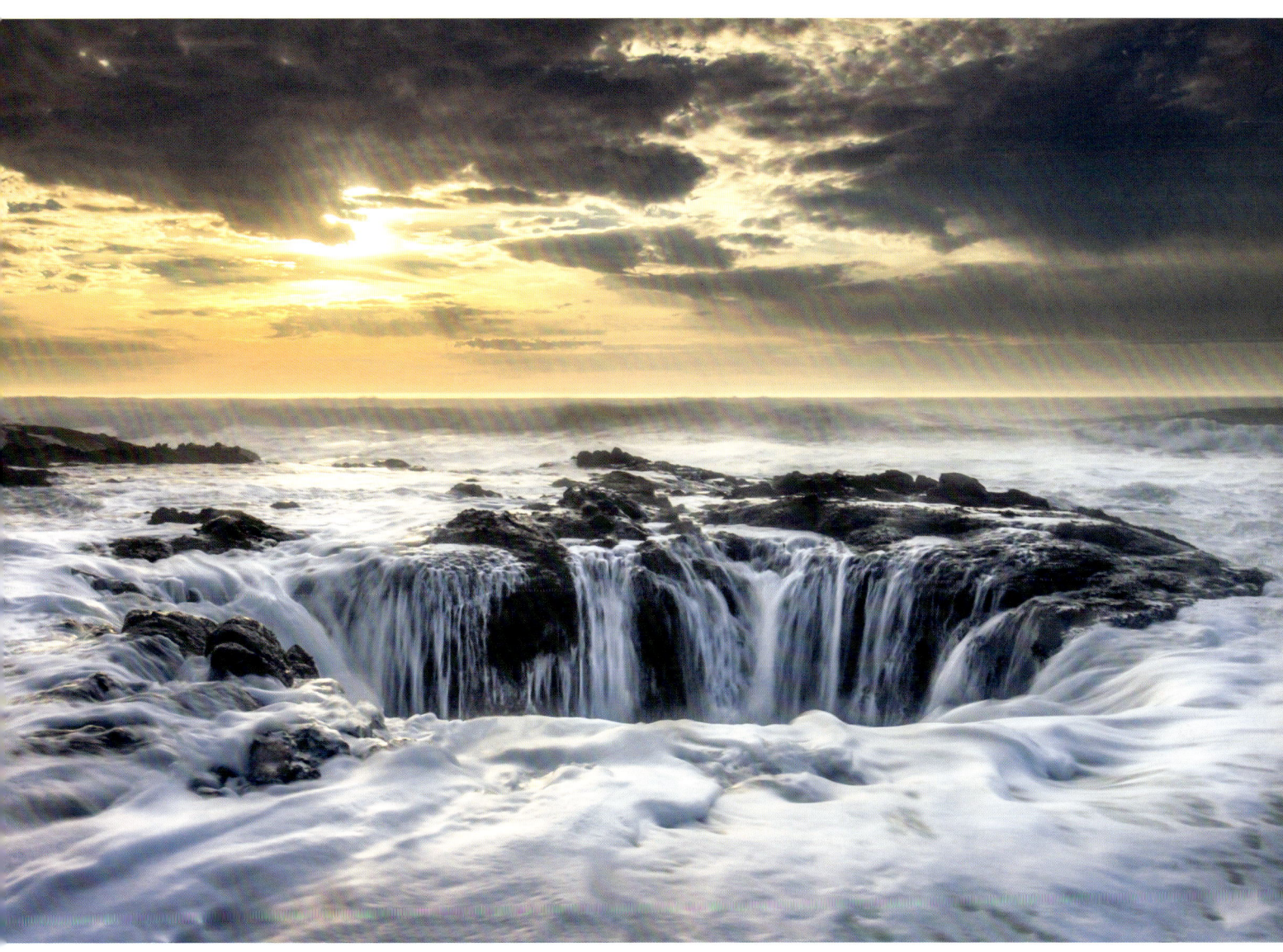

Thors Well. While not technically a waterfall, this 20-foot bowl in Yachats on the Oregon coast at times looks like one. At high tide, the well appears to be bottomless, filling and draining endlessly. If conditions are right, it can be a mesmerizing sight, especially at sunset. It was formed over thousands of years ago, probably after the roof of a volcanic rock sea cave collapsed. *Photo by Adam Marland*

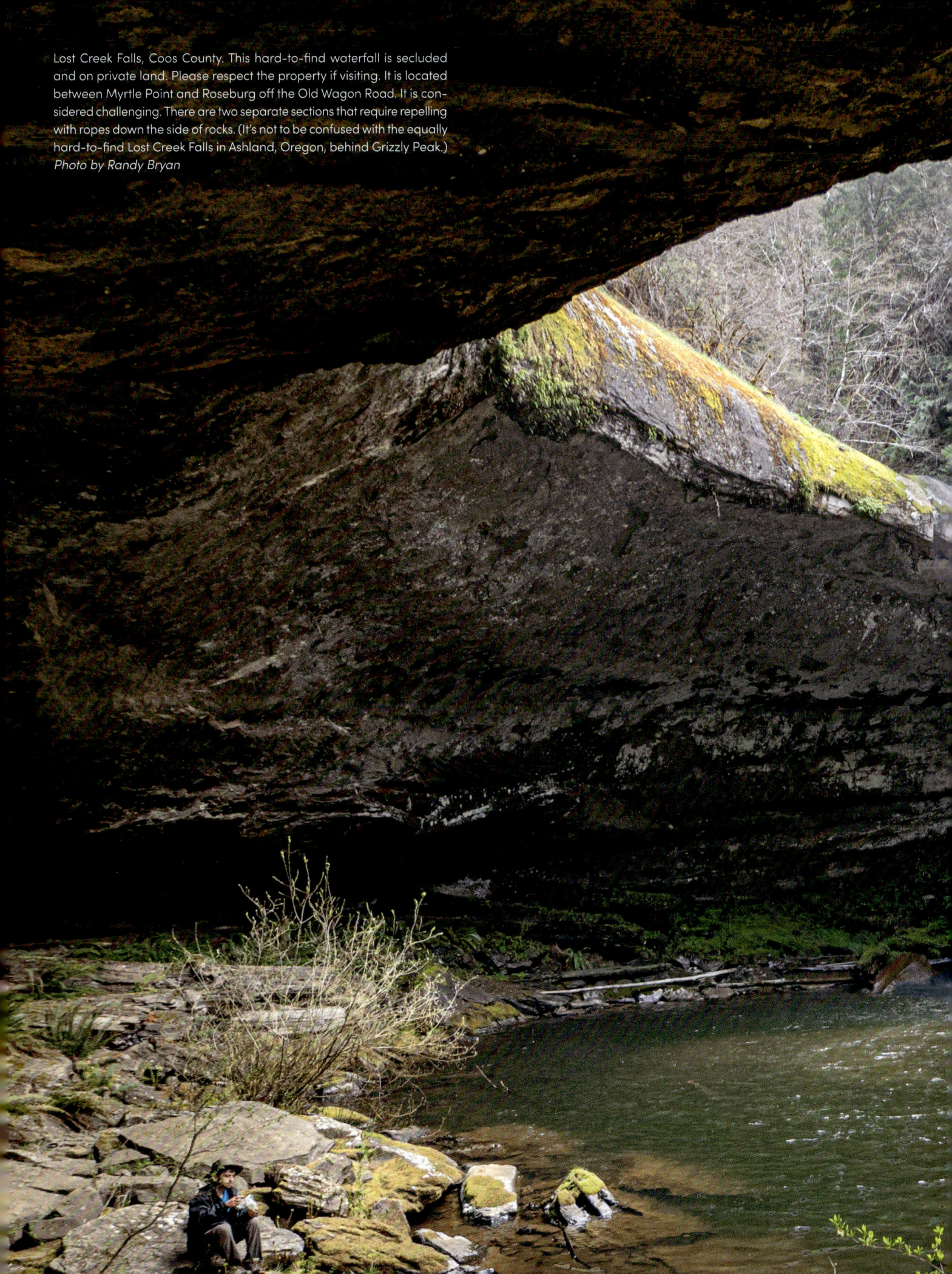

Lost Creek Falls, Coos County. This hard-to-find waterfall is secluded and on private land. Please respect the property if visiting. It is located between Myrtle Point and Roseburg off the Old Wagon Road. It is considered challenging. There are two separate sections that require repelling with ropes down the side of rocks. (It's not to be confused with the equally hard-to-find Lost Creek Falls in Ashland, Oregon, behind Grizzly Peak.)
Photo by Randy Bryan

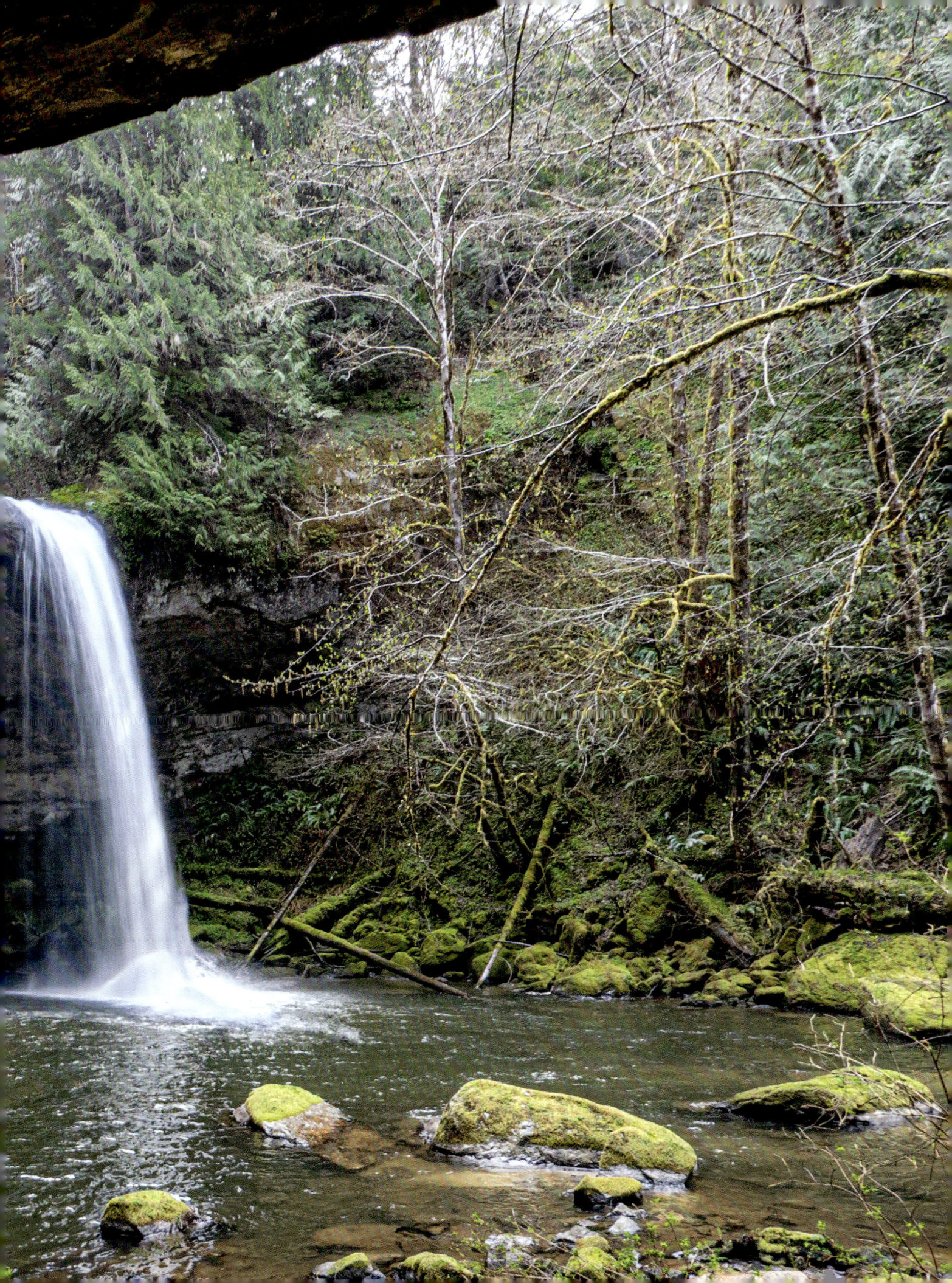

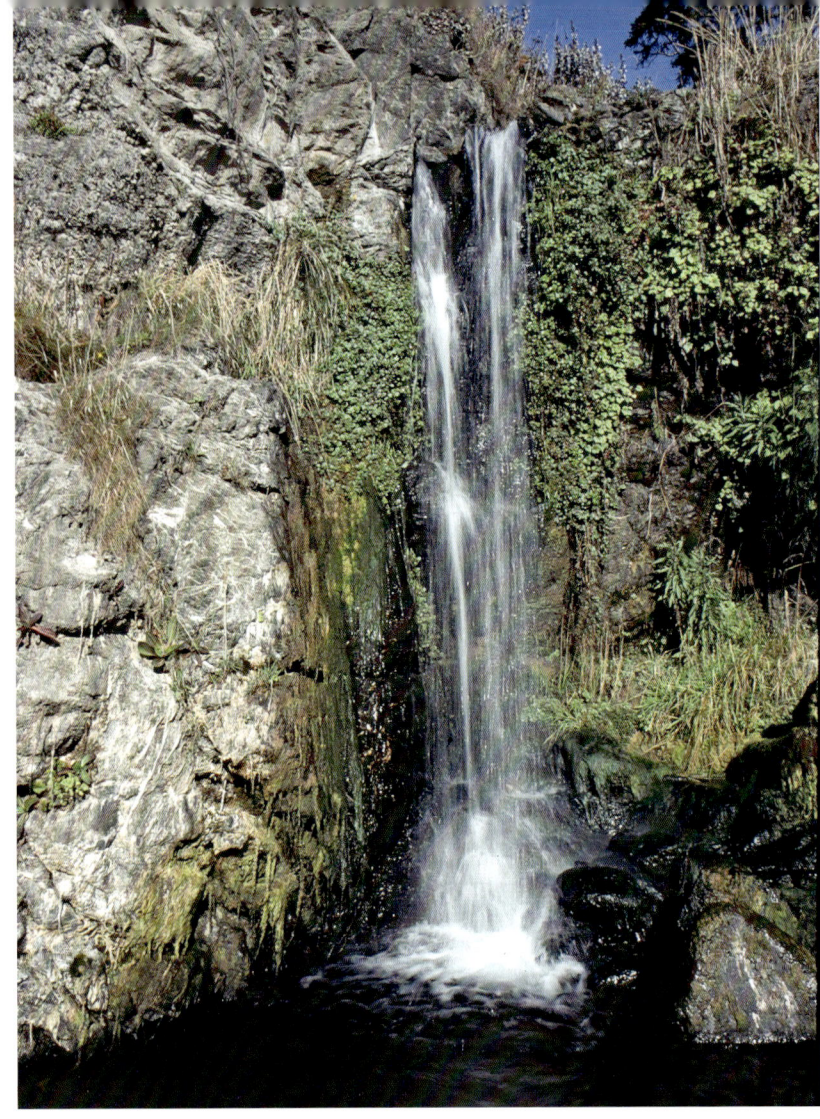

Secret Beach Waterfall. Located off Highway 101 between Brookings and Gold Beach in the Samuel H. Boardman State Scenic Corridor, this waterfall comes from Miller Creek and empties onto the beach and into the Pacific Ocean. Low tide is the best time to visit the entire Secret Beach area, including sea caves, beaches, and trails. *Photo by Mark Huddleston*

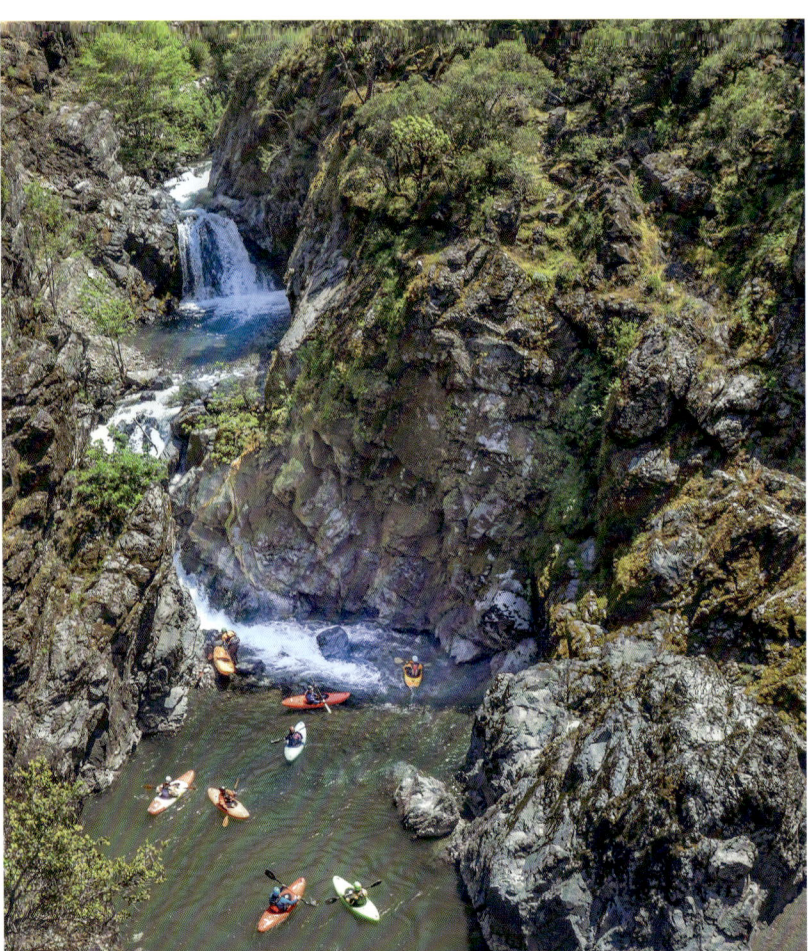

Stair Creek Falls. A unique view of Stair Creek Falls can be seen from Inspiration Point (half a mile southwest from Marial, Oregon). Often, kayakers can be seen in the Rogue River below the falls. *Photo by Tysen Mueller*

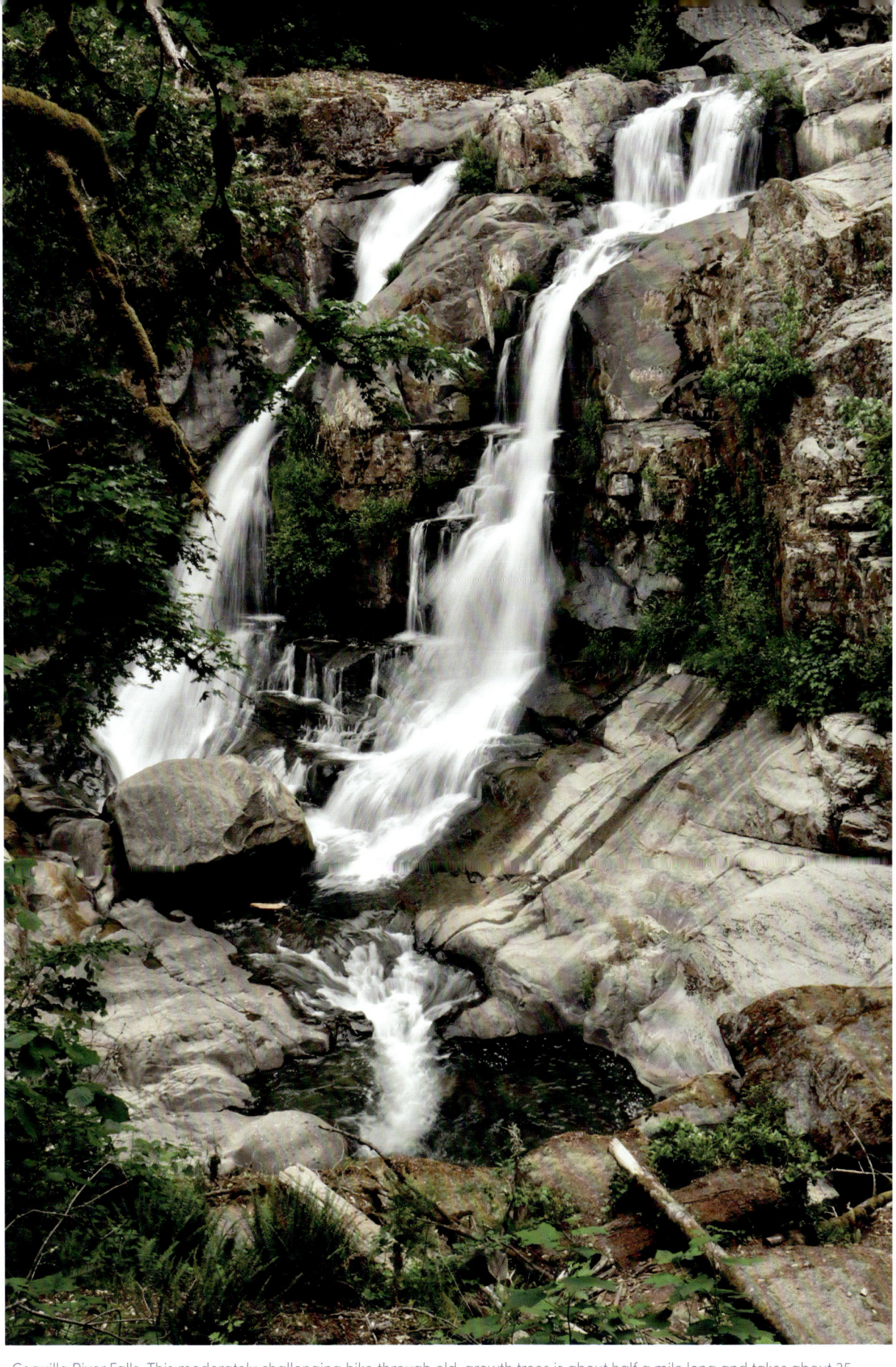

Coquille River Falls. This moderately challenging hike through old-growth trees is about half a mile long and takes about 35 minutes to complete. It's tucked into the Coastal Range near Powers, Oregon. *Photo by Richard Krieger*

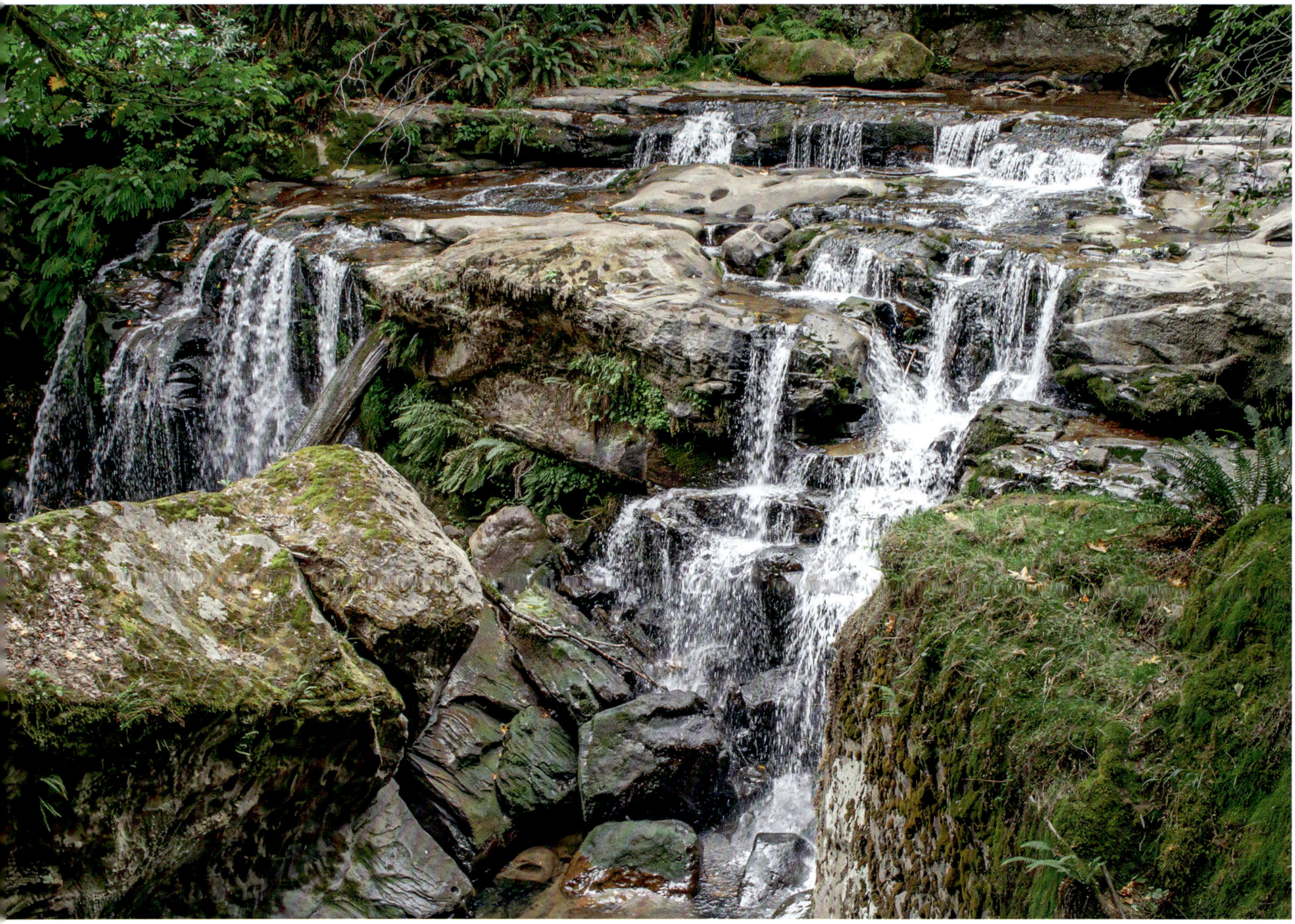

Upper East Fork Falls. This fairly low waterfall is on the East Fork of the Coquille River between Lookingglass and Coquille on the Coos Bay Wagon Road. No hiking is involved, since the falls is near the road. There are several other waterfalls in the area. *Photo by Al Ingersoll*

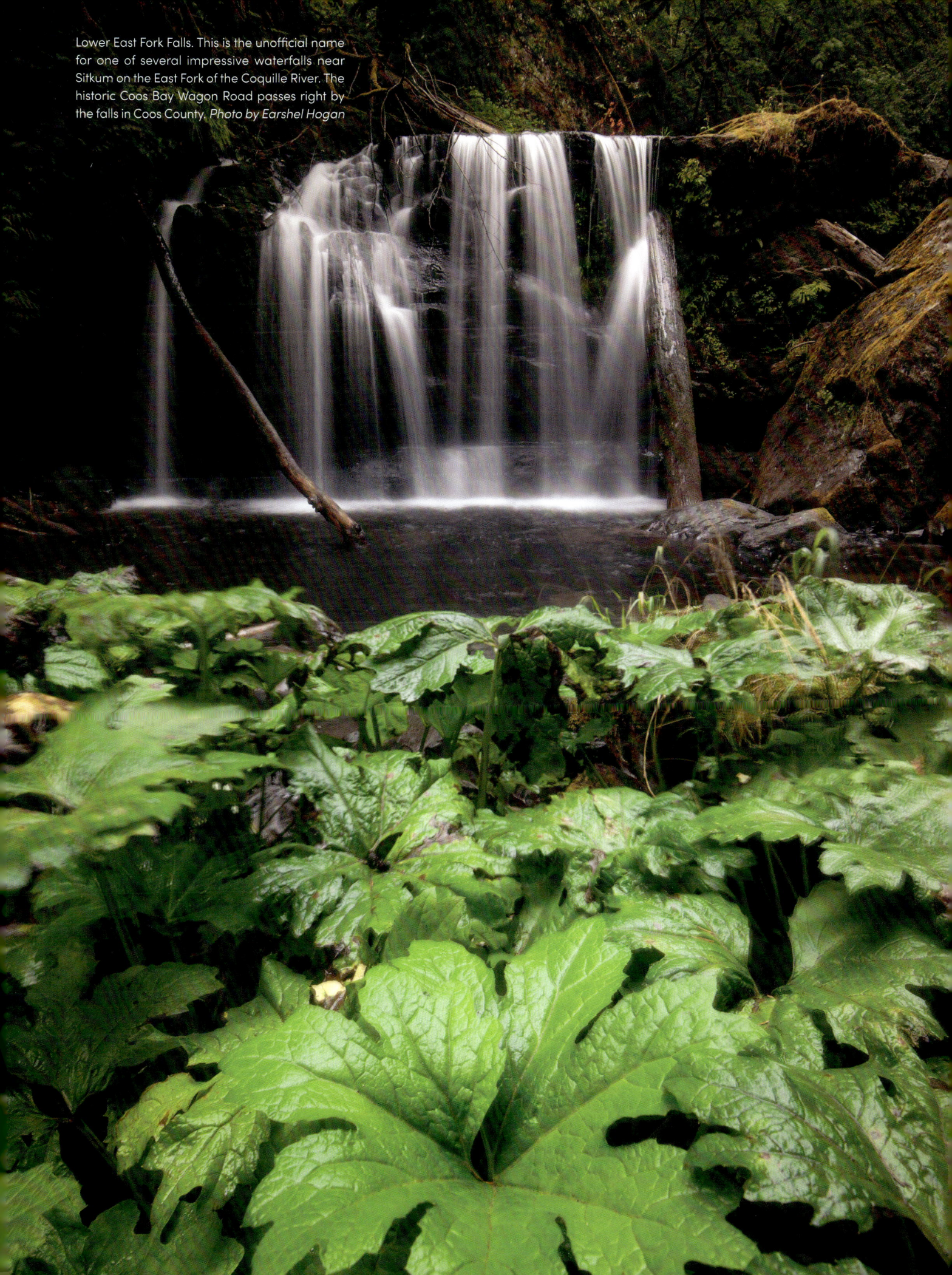

Lower East Fork Falls. This is the unofficial name for one of several impressive waterfalls near Sitkum on the East Fork of the Coquille River. The historic Coos Bay Wagon Road passes right by the falls in Coos County. *Photo by Earshel Hogan*

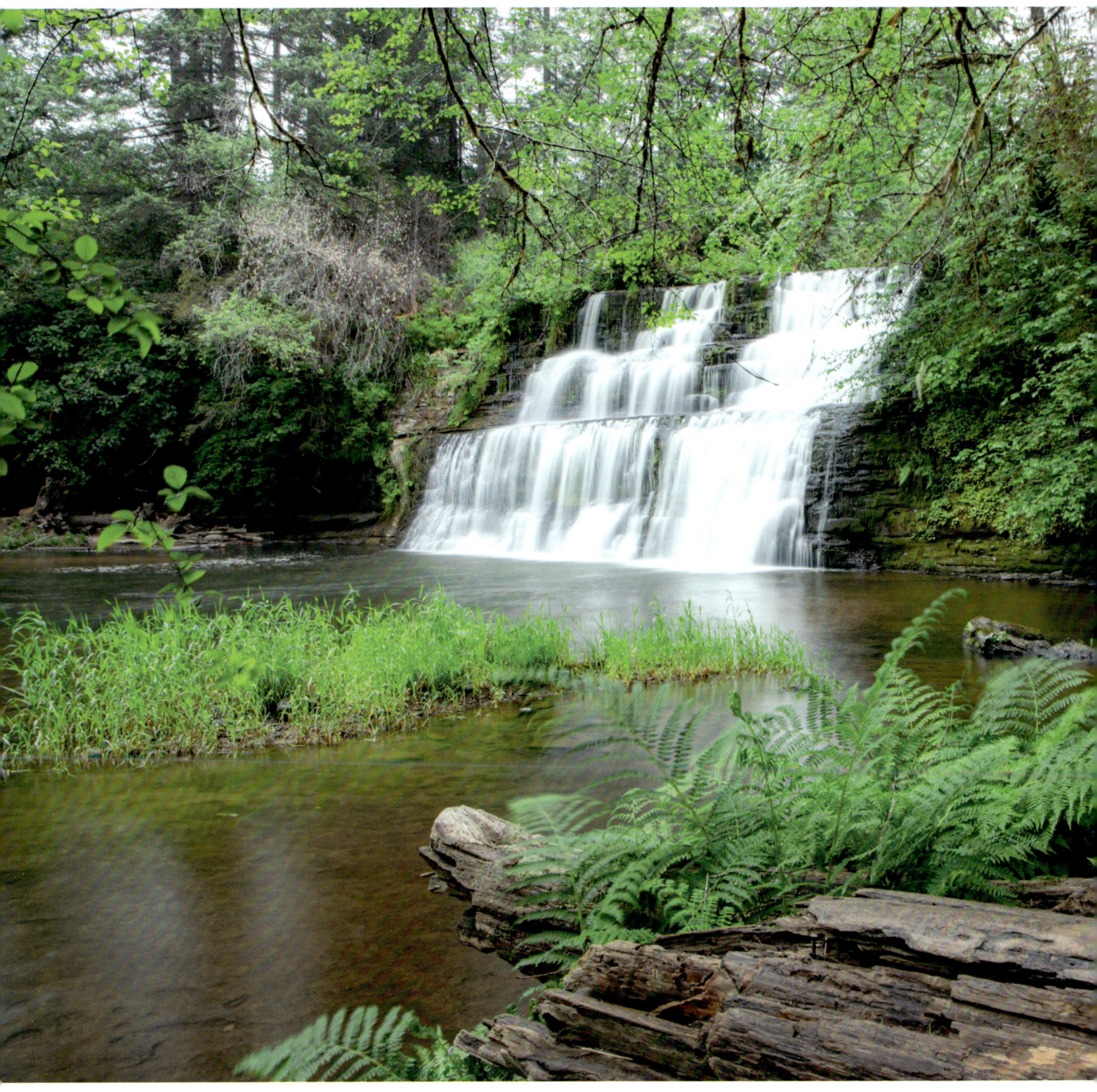

Camp Creek Falls. Between Interstate 5 and Reedsport, off the Umpqua Highway on Loon Lake Road, Camp Creek Falls drops 31 feet into a fountain-like stairstep waterfall. *Photo by Jerry Lutrell*

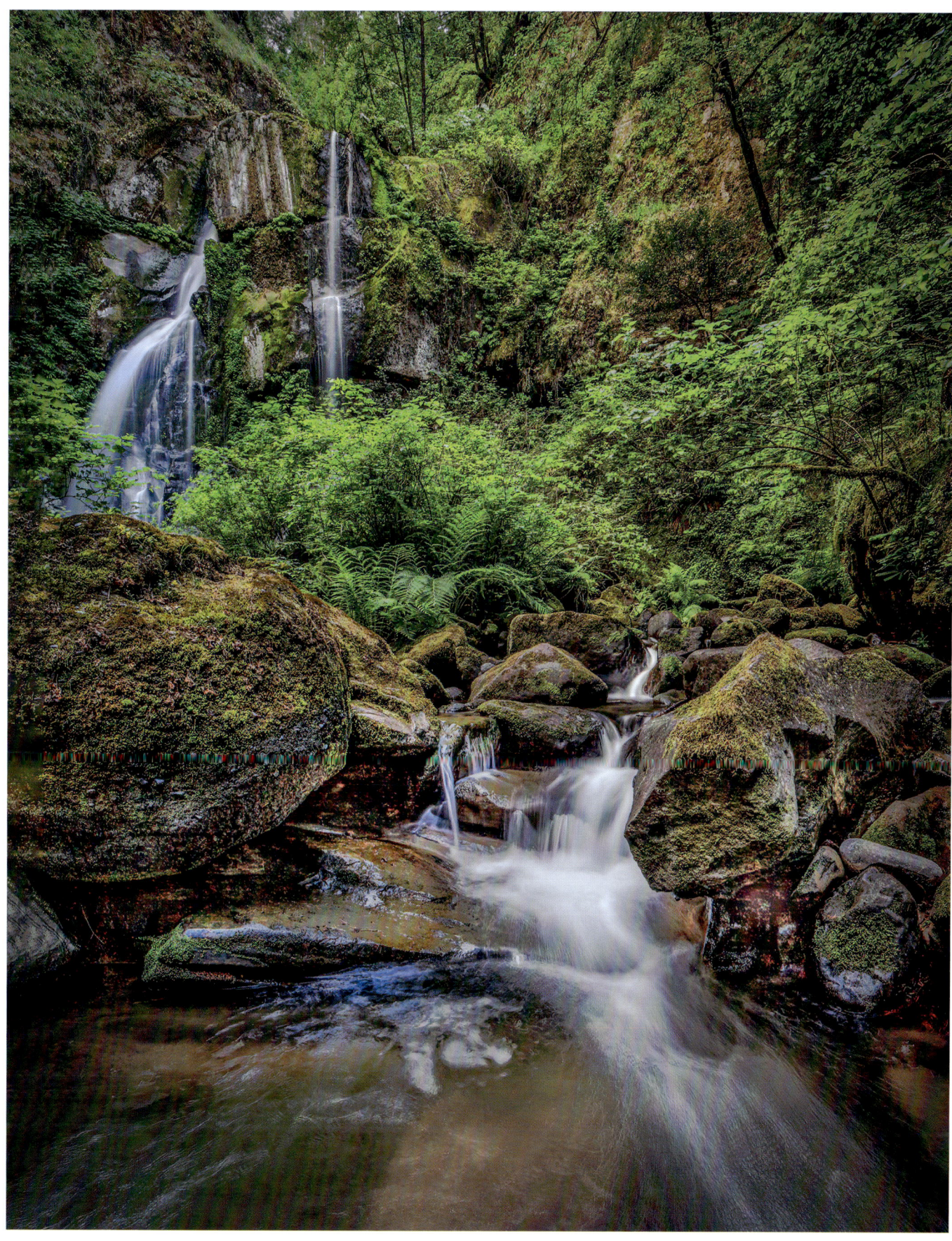

Elk Creek Falls. Located south of Powers in the Oregon Coastal Range near Coos Bay, the trail to Elk Creek Falls passes by mossy boulders and Douglas fir, alder, and myrtle trees. The waterfall spills in three tiers, totaling 191 feet. It is only a 0.4-mile-out-and-back hike and is considered a moderately challenging route. *Photo by Jim Chamberlain*

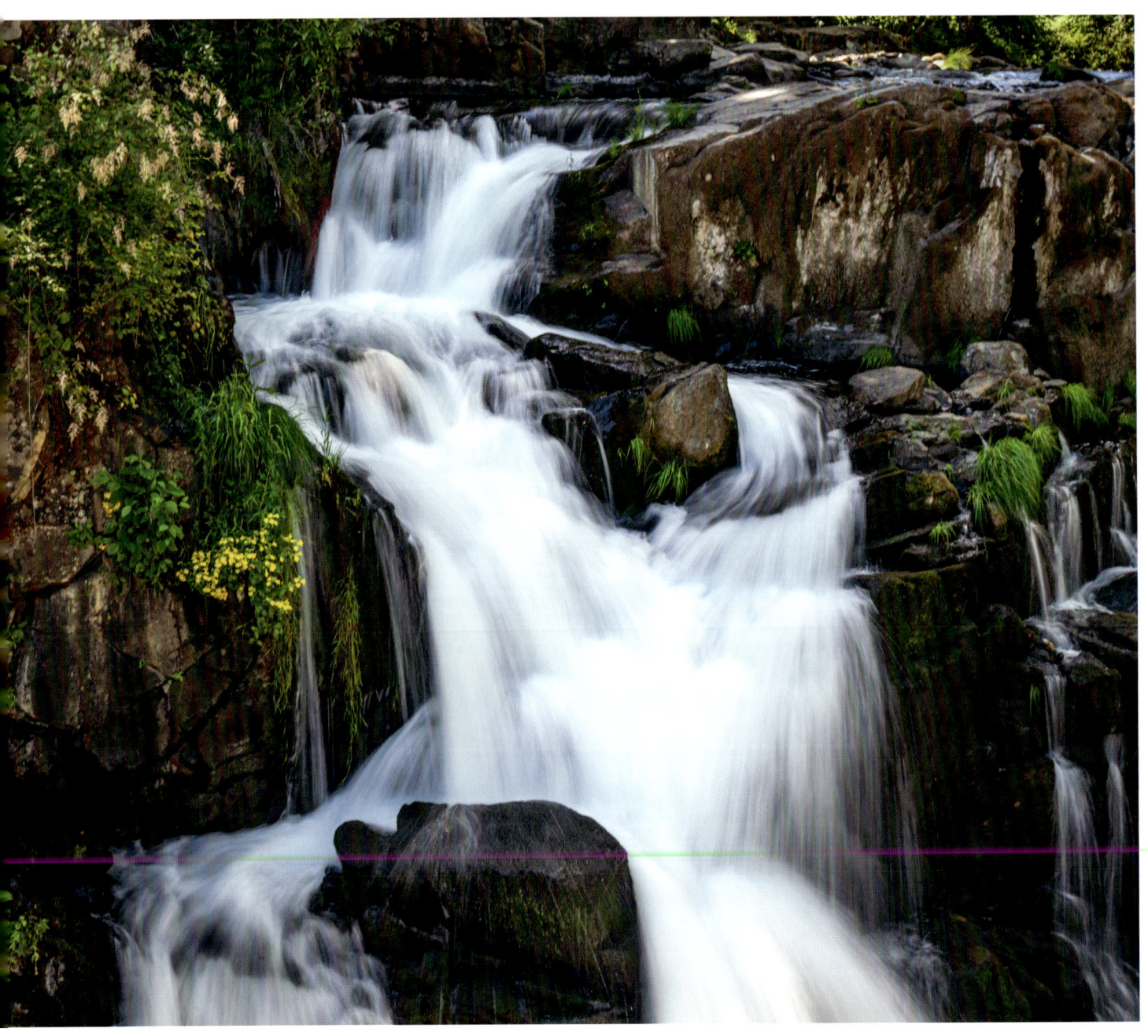

Little Luckiamute River Falls. The Luckiamute River passes right through the center of Falls City (population under 1,000). The town was named for the 25-foot waterfall, west of Salem in the Oregon Coastal Range and easy to find from a roadside hike. *Photo by Frank G. Lahman*

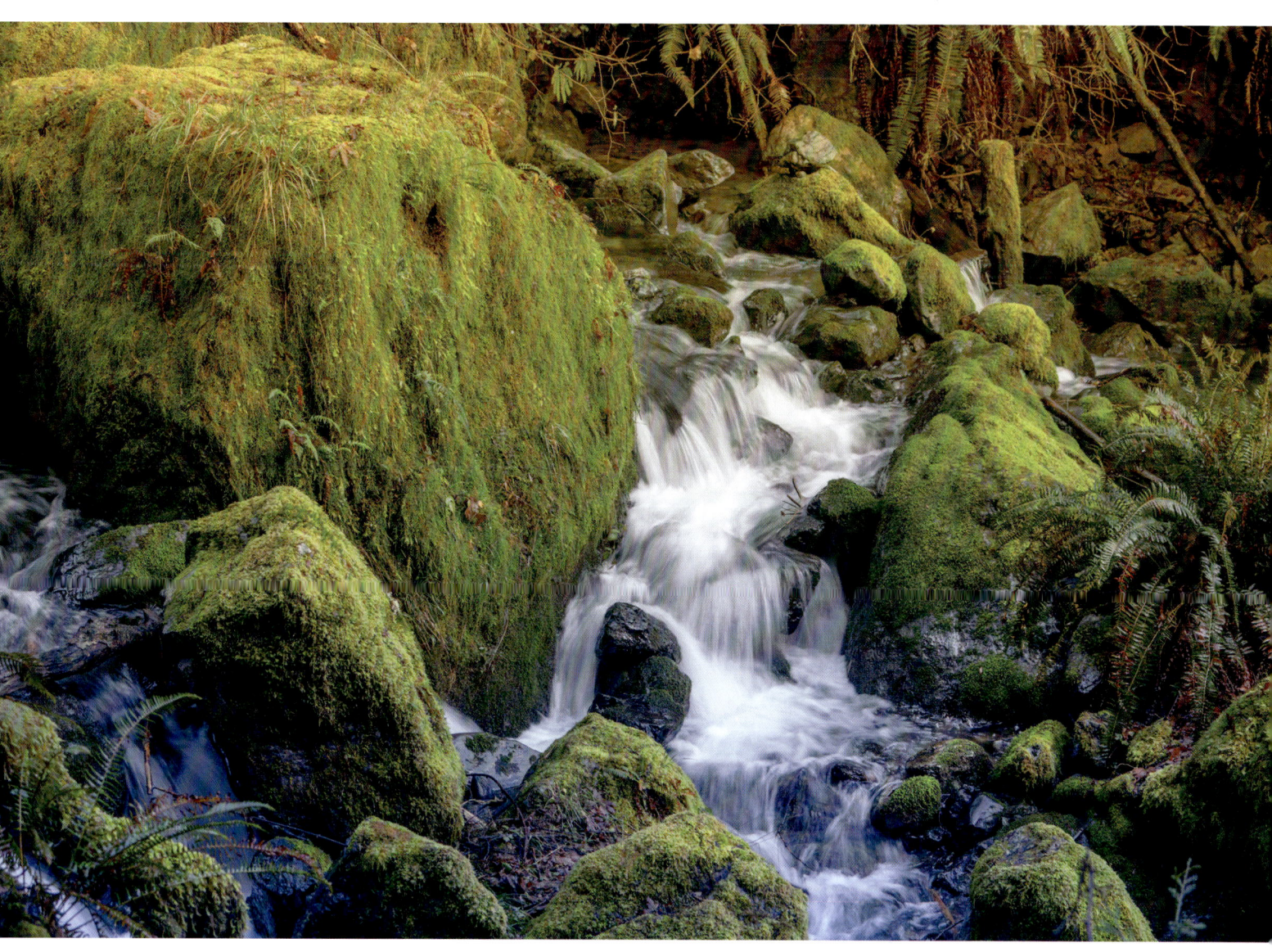

Redwood Nature Trail. Stroll through huge Oregon redwood trees and ferns to find small and unexpected waterfalls. The trail is 9 miles north of Brookings and north of Alfred A. Loeb Oregon State Park. *Photo by Jim Chamberlain*

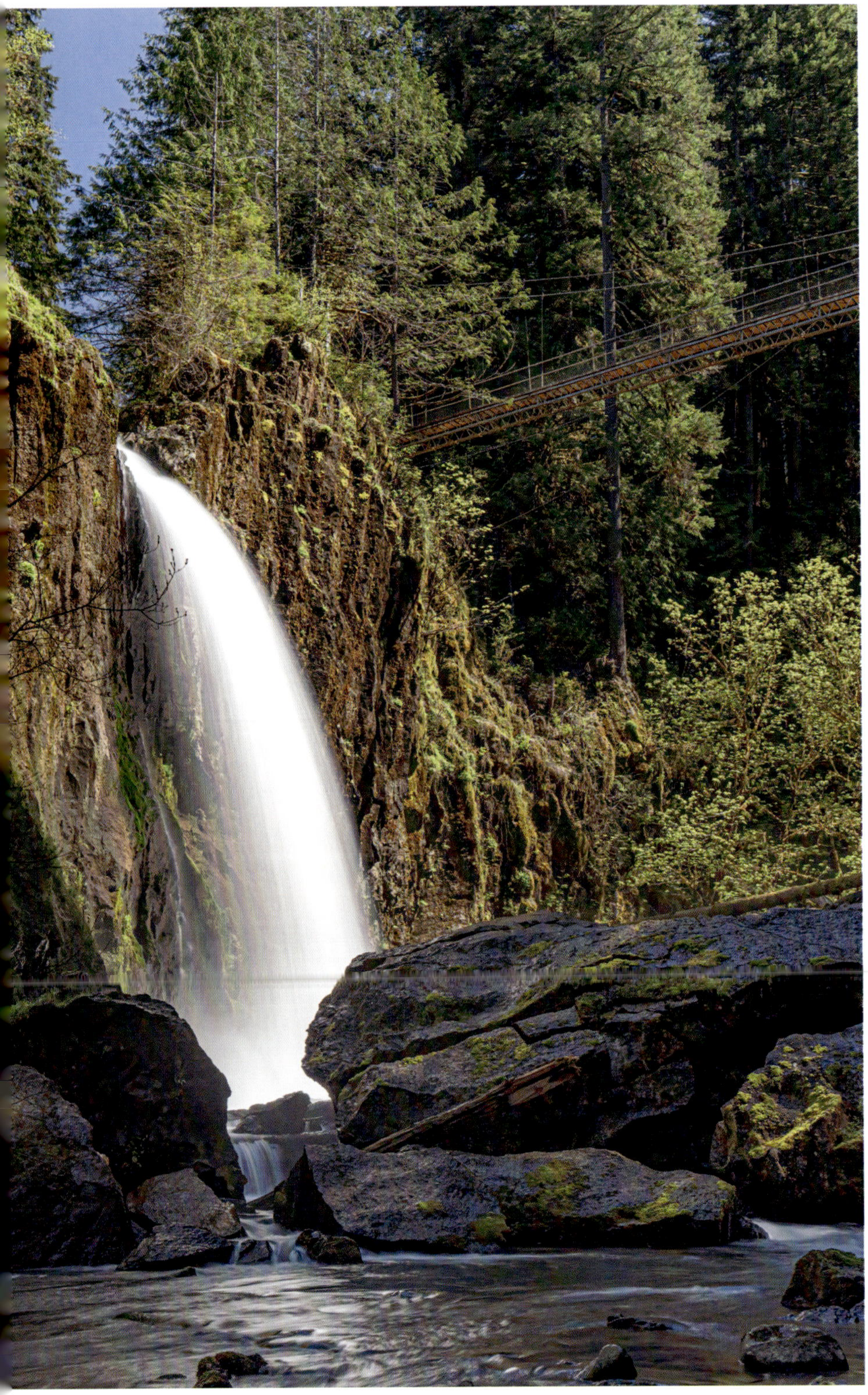

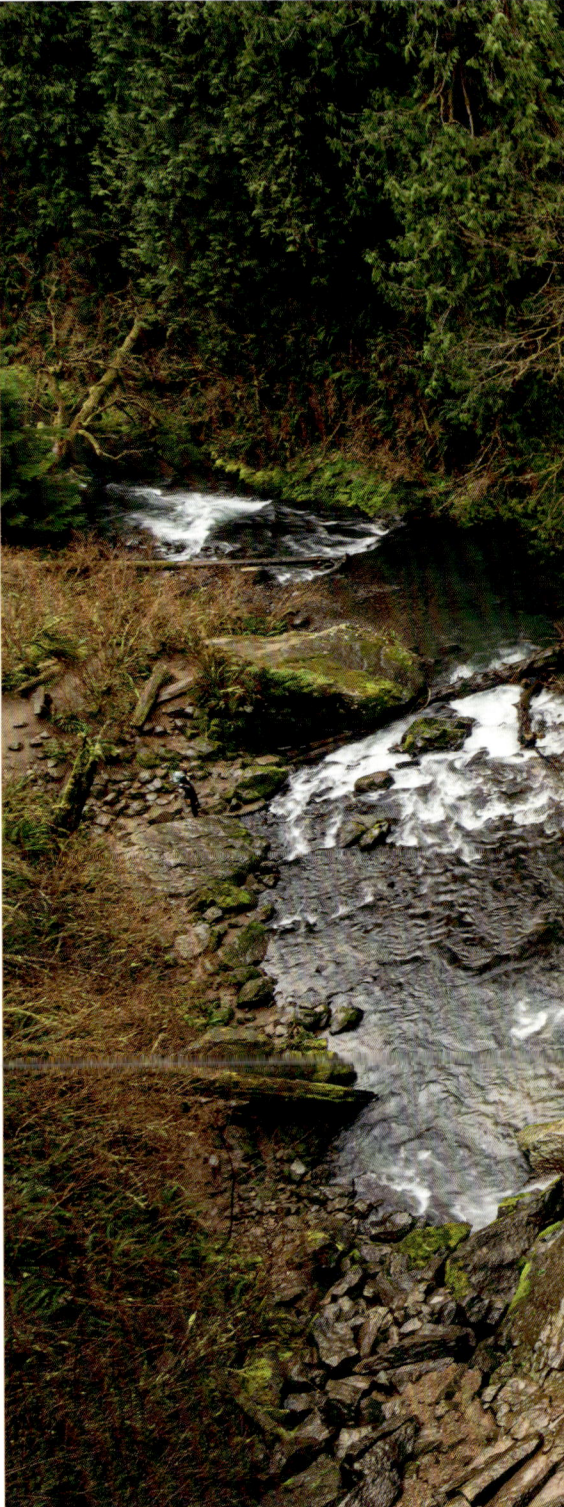

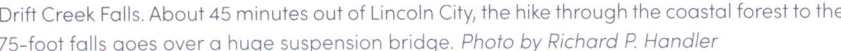
Drift Creek Falls. About 45 minutes out of Lincoln City, the hike through the coastal forest to the 75-foot falls goes over a huge suspension bridge. *Photo by Richard P. Handler*

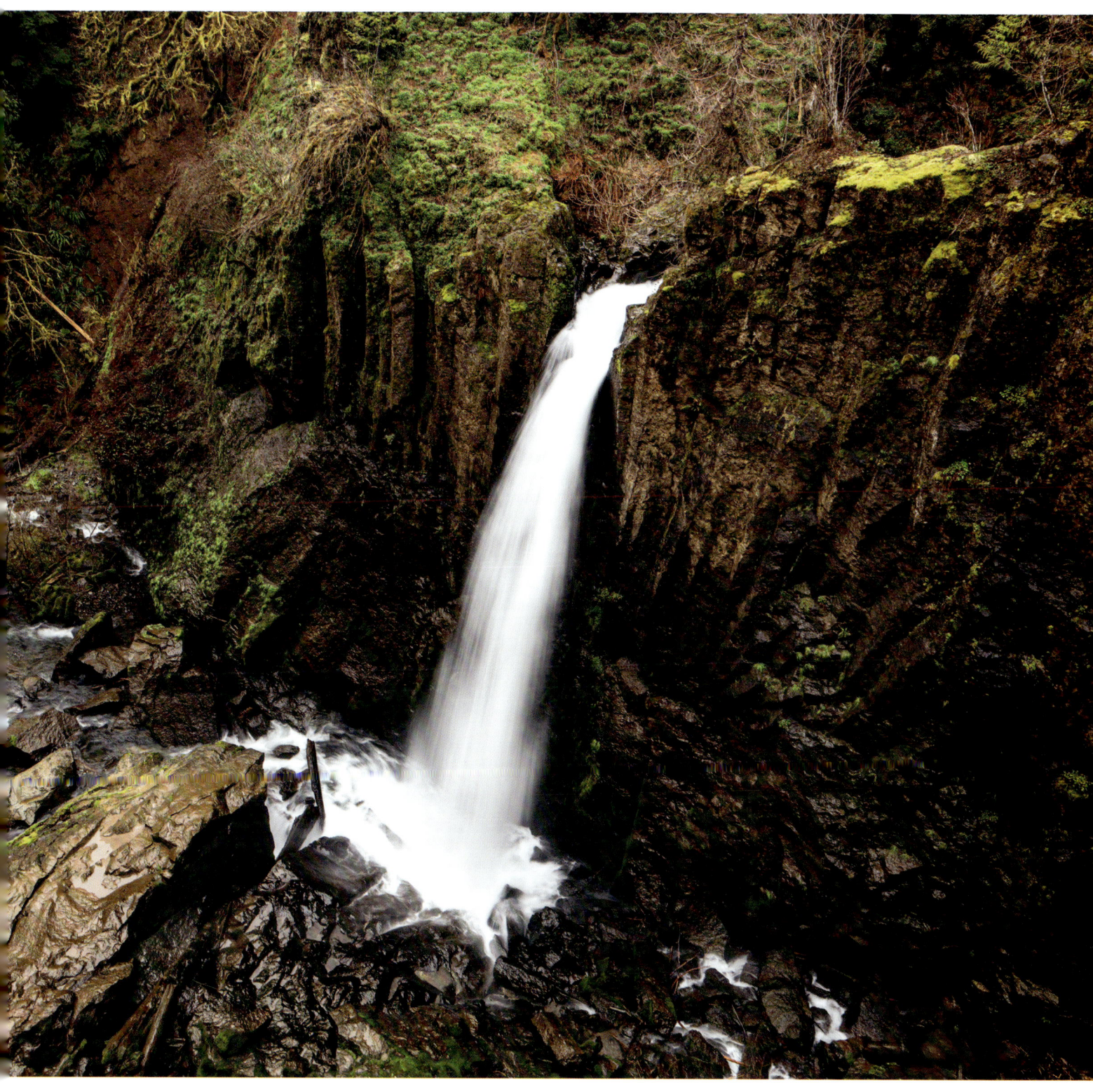

Drift Creek Falls. A dramatic view of Drift Creek Falls from the suspension bridge, 100 feet over the canyon floor.
Photo by Frank G. Lahman

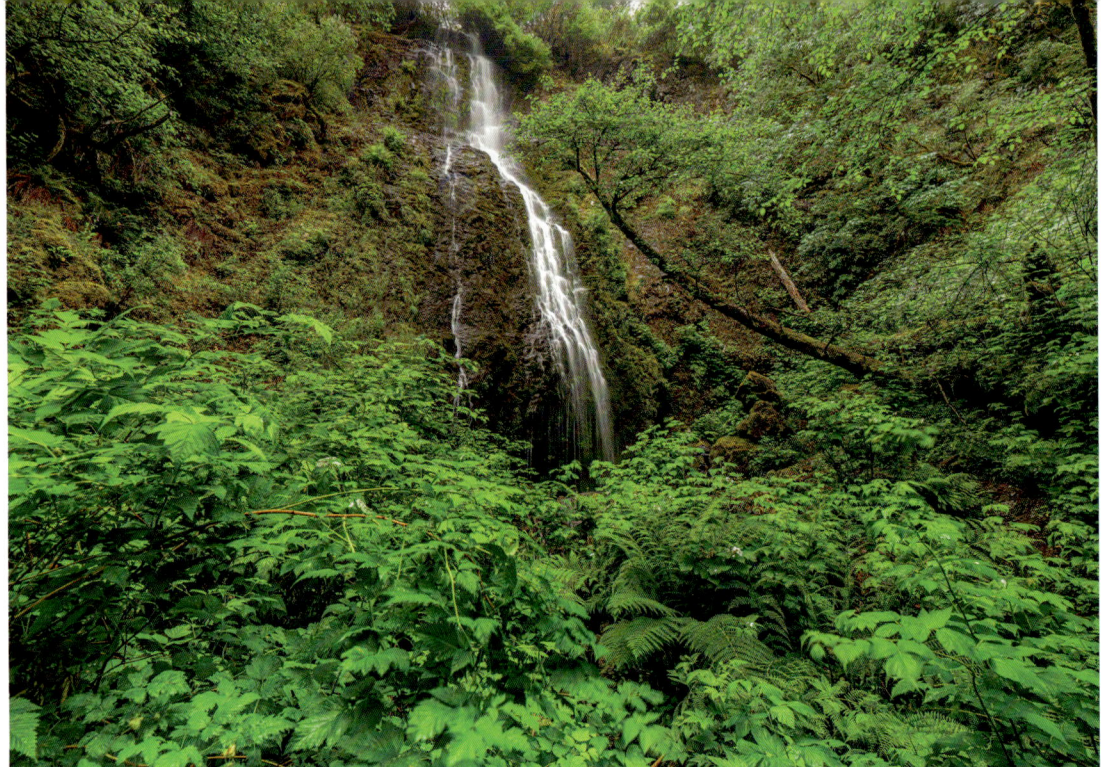

Niagara Falls. Yes, that's right. Oregon also has a Niagara Falls! Located in the Siuslaw National Forest, it is about 30 minutes from Beaver, Oregon. While not as impressive as the 190-foot Niagara Falls, this plunge-type waterfall is still awe inspiring at 107 to 122 feet (depending on the person measuring). Its sister waterfall is Pheasant Creek Falls. The hike to see both falls is about 1.5 miles out and back and is considered moderately challenging, with some steep sections. Bring good maps, since GPS may not be accurate. *Photo by David Joarnt*

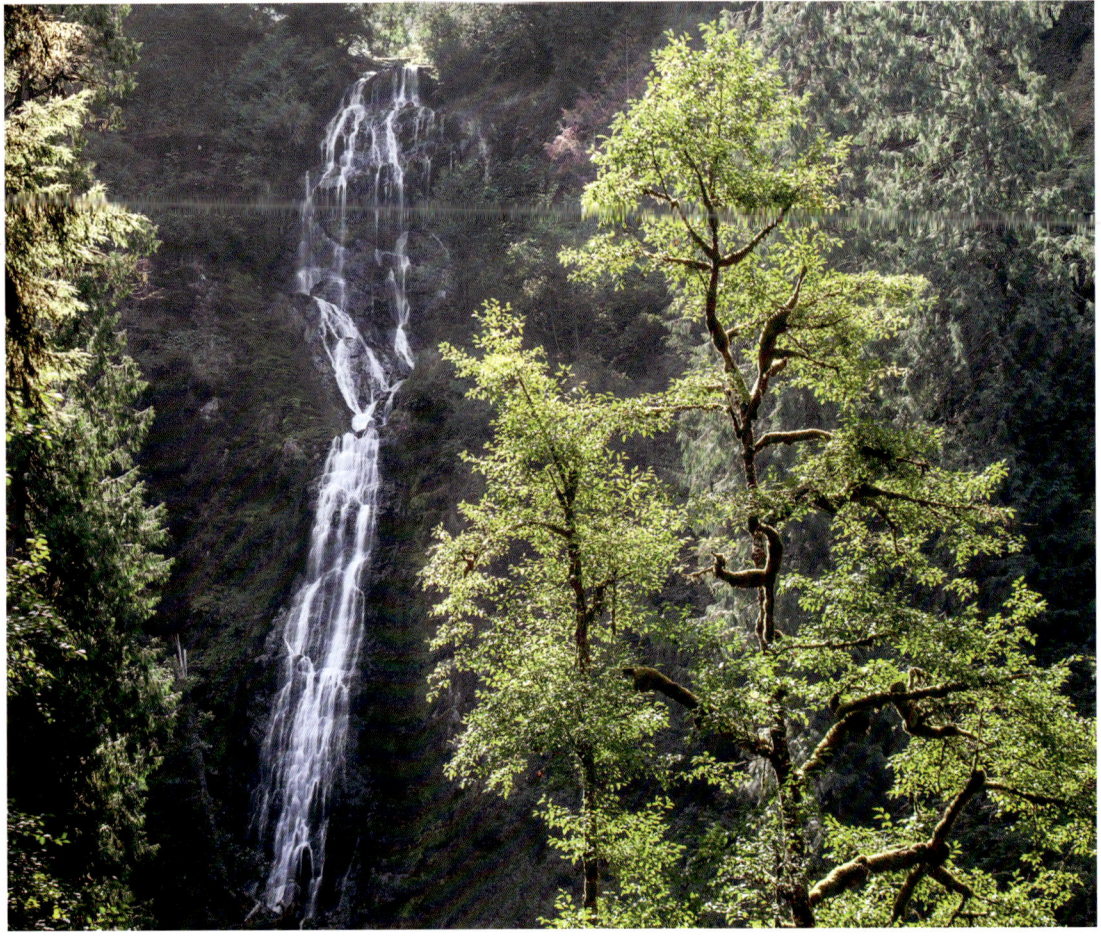

Munson Creek Falls. The tallest waterfall in Oregon's Coastal Range, at 319 feet, is Munson Creek Falls. The falls flow over several tiers and are located in Munson Creek Falls State Natural Site, about 6 miles south of Tillamook, off US Highway 101. *Photo by John Kirk*

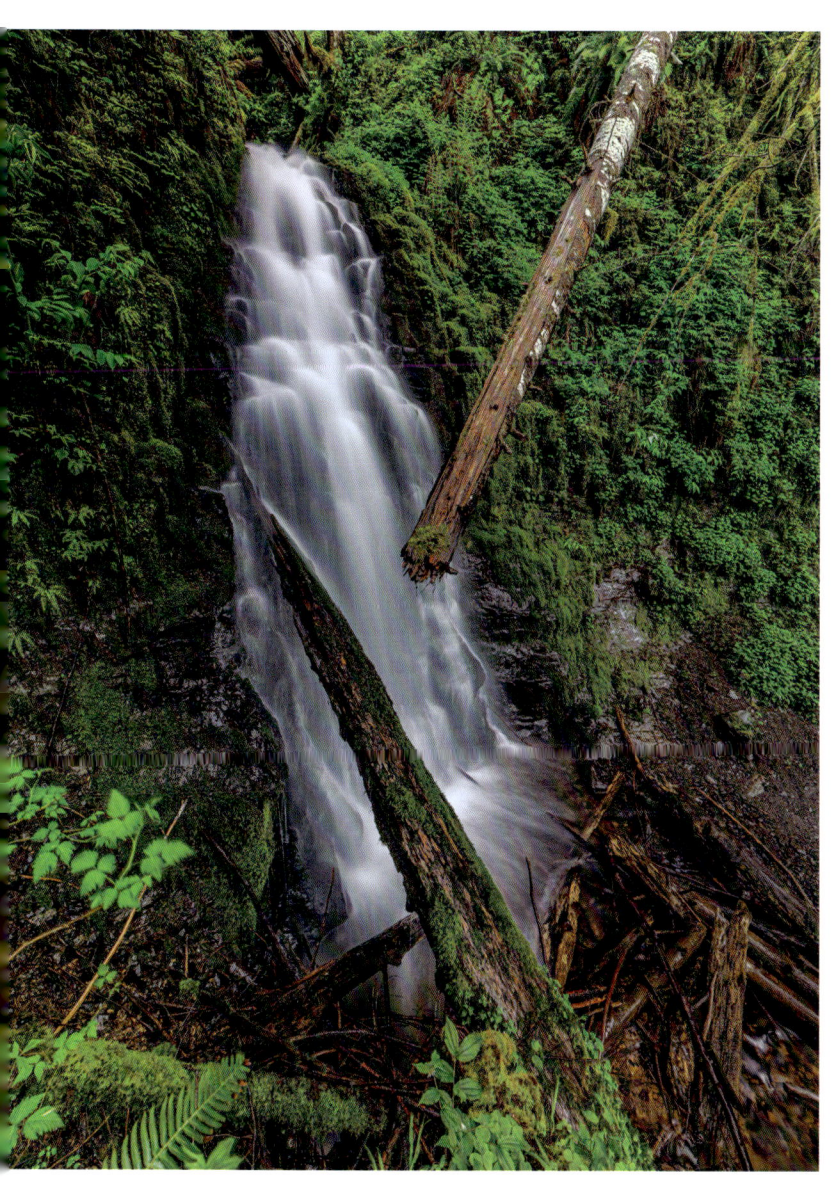

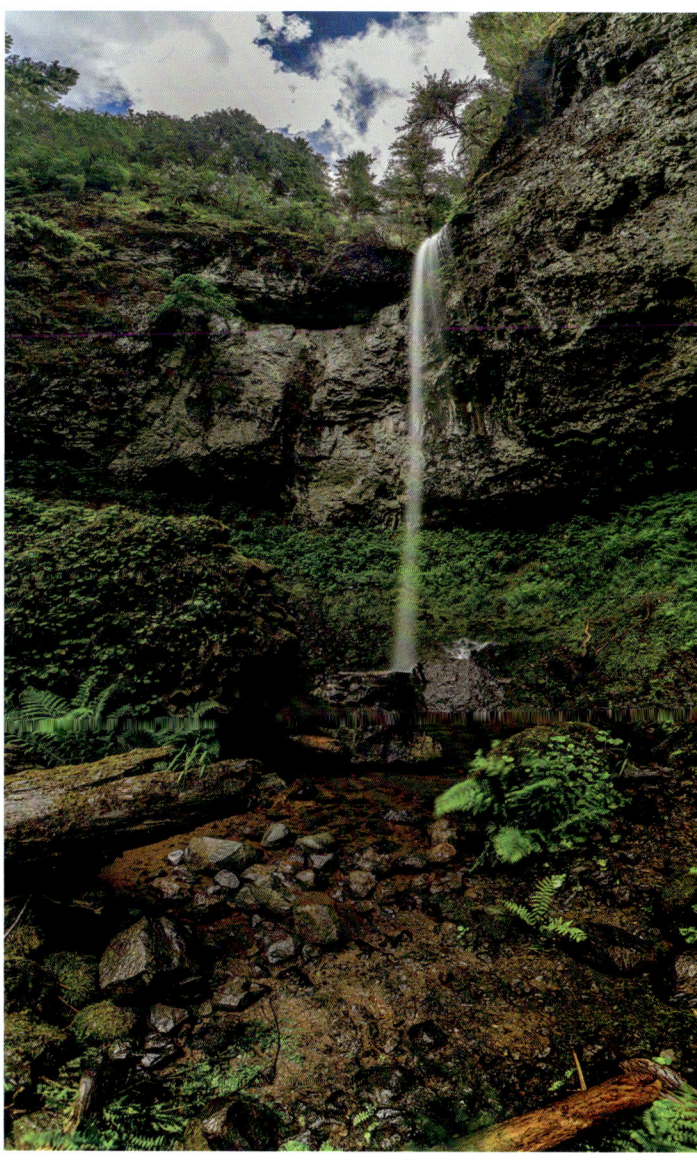

Fern Rock Falls. This roadside waterfall can be seen from Highway 6, about 30 minutes from Tillamook. After you park at the large pull-off, the trail may be hard to find. However, once found, it's only a short and easy hike to get a better view of the falls. *Photo by David Joarnt*

Pheasant Creek Falls. Situated along the trail below Niagara Falls is the segmented Pheasant Creek Falls, which is an impressive 112 feet high. During the spring, the falls are resplendent with trillium in bloom amid colorful green ferns. *Photo by David Joarnt*

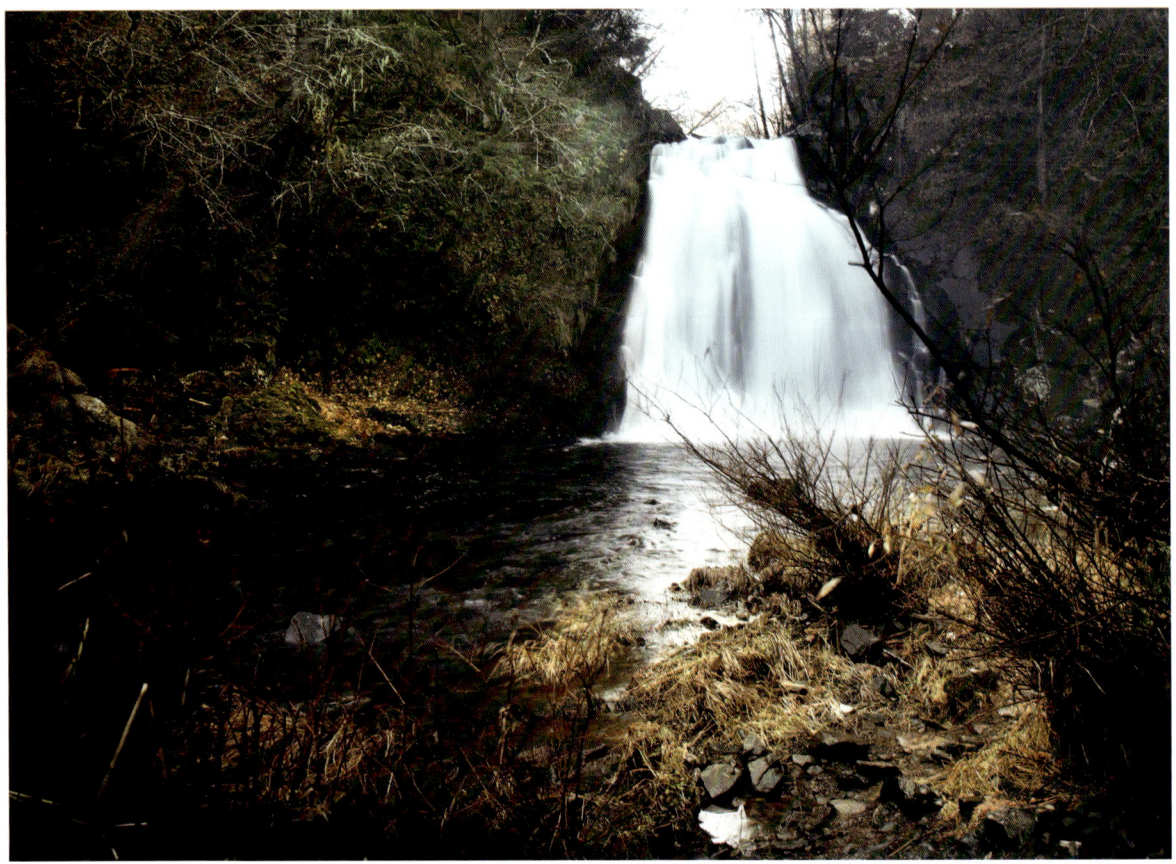

Youngs River Falls. This is located 10 miles from Astoria, and the hike to Youngs River Falls is a short, downward trail. It is a popular swimming spot due to the warm waters of the Youngs River. The falls create a lovely veil over the large rock wall, plummeting 54 feet into the pool below. The falls have been featured in several movies. *Photo by John Kirk*

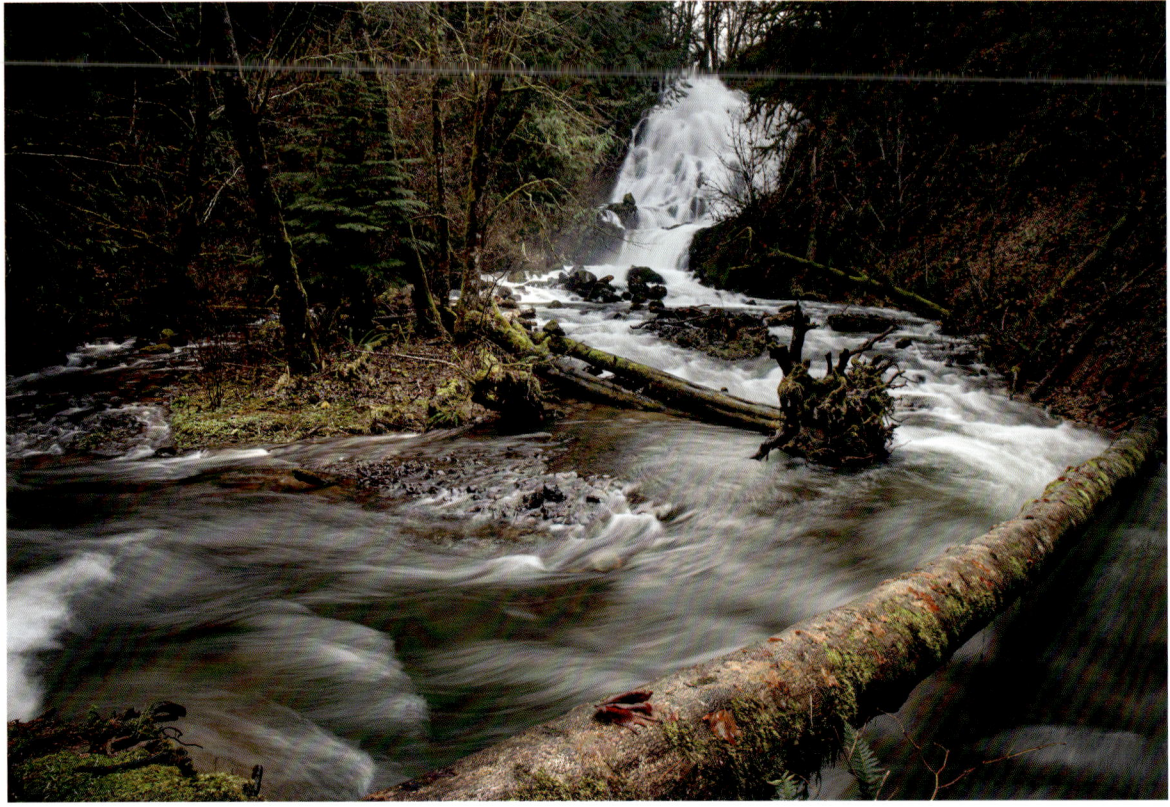

Fishhawk Falls is located 25 miles east of Astoria on Oregon Highway 202 in Lee Wooden County Park. It's a 0.5-mile-out-and-back trail and takes about 11 minutes to complete. It is often visited with Youngs River Falls. *Photo by John Kirk*

Necarney Creek Falls. This small, unofficial waterfall in Tillamook County is on an easy, half-mile loop downhill trail near Manzanita, through what feels like an old-growth forest. It's not far from Highway 101. Soothing sounds come from the creek along the hike, and the trail delivers a picturesque sheltered cove and secluded beach. *Photo by Charles Hillestad*

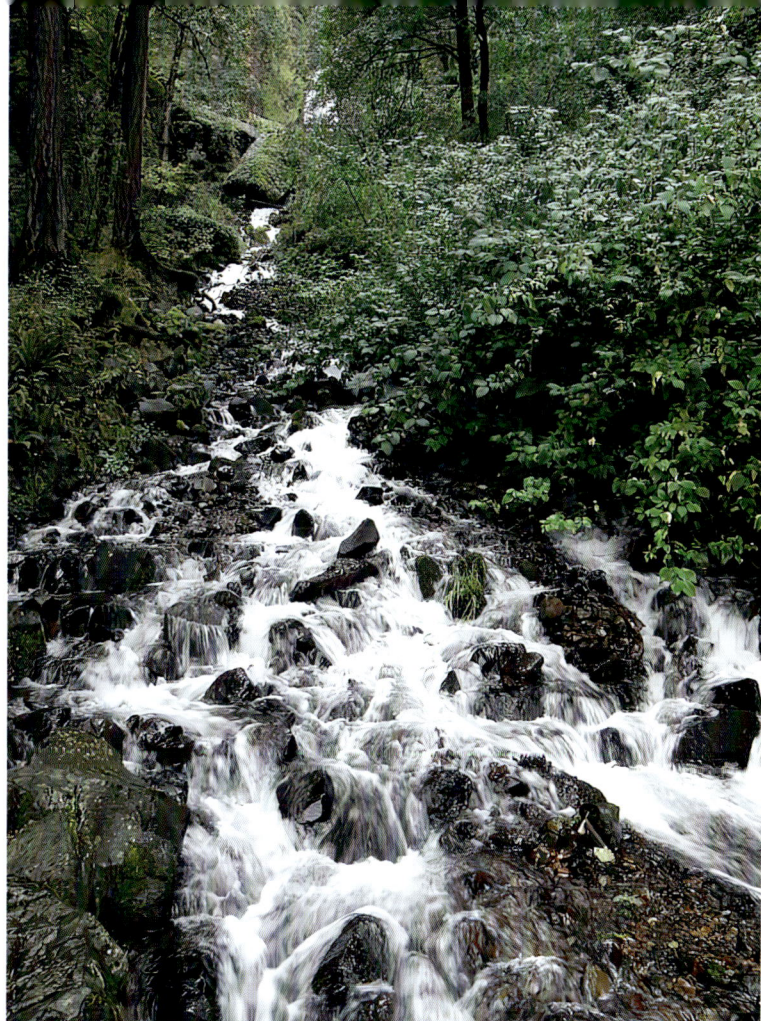

Short Sand Beach Waterfall. Mossy trees, a stream, and pretty wildflowers can often be seen on the Short Sand Beach Trail in Oswald West State Park, near Manzanita. The trail leads to this delicate waterfall, originating off the slopes of Neahkahnie Mountain. It ultimately spills directly into the ocean. It is recommended to do this hike at low tide for the best views. *Photo by Charles Hillestad*

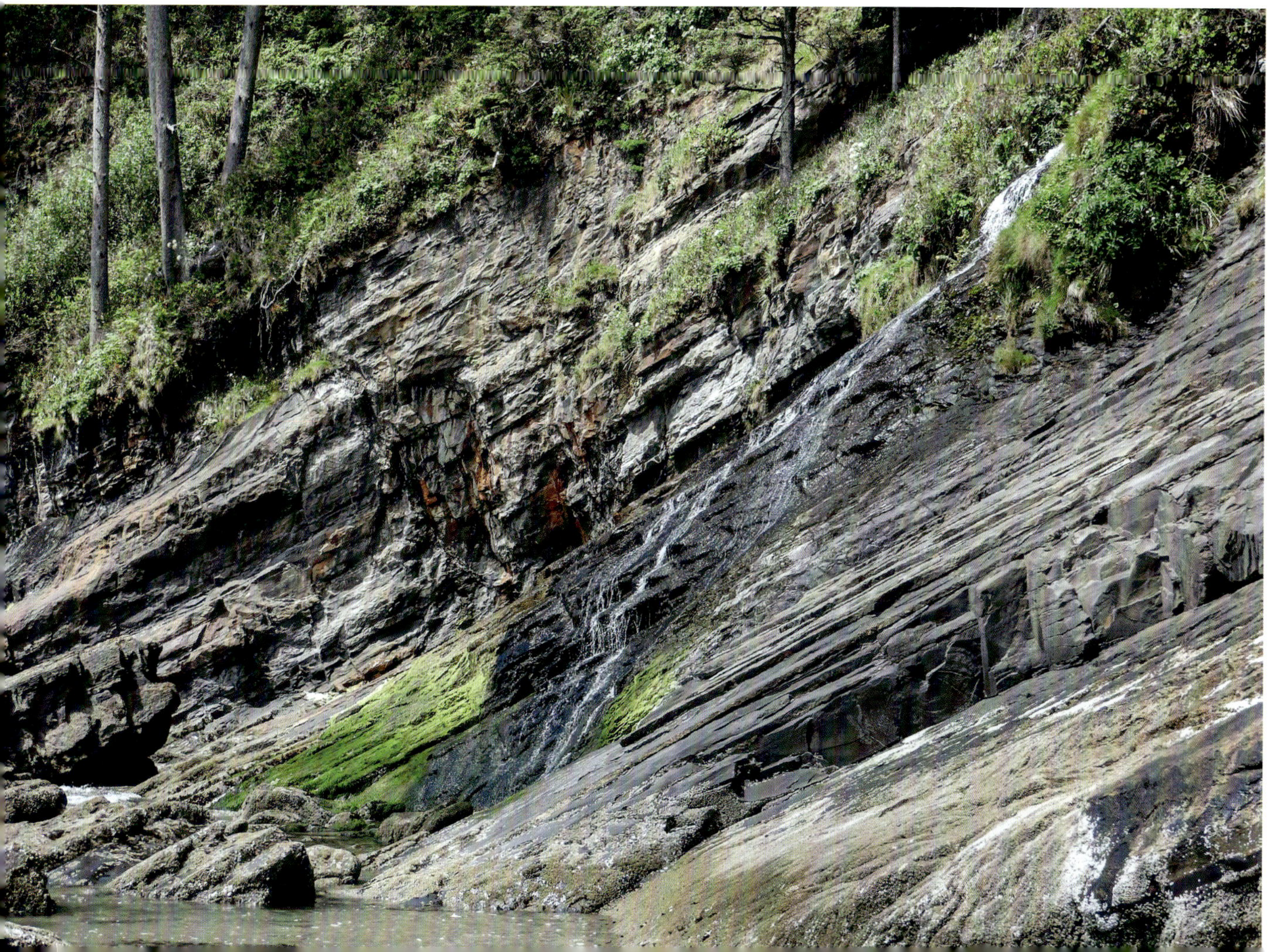

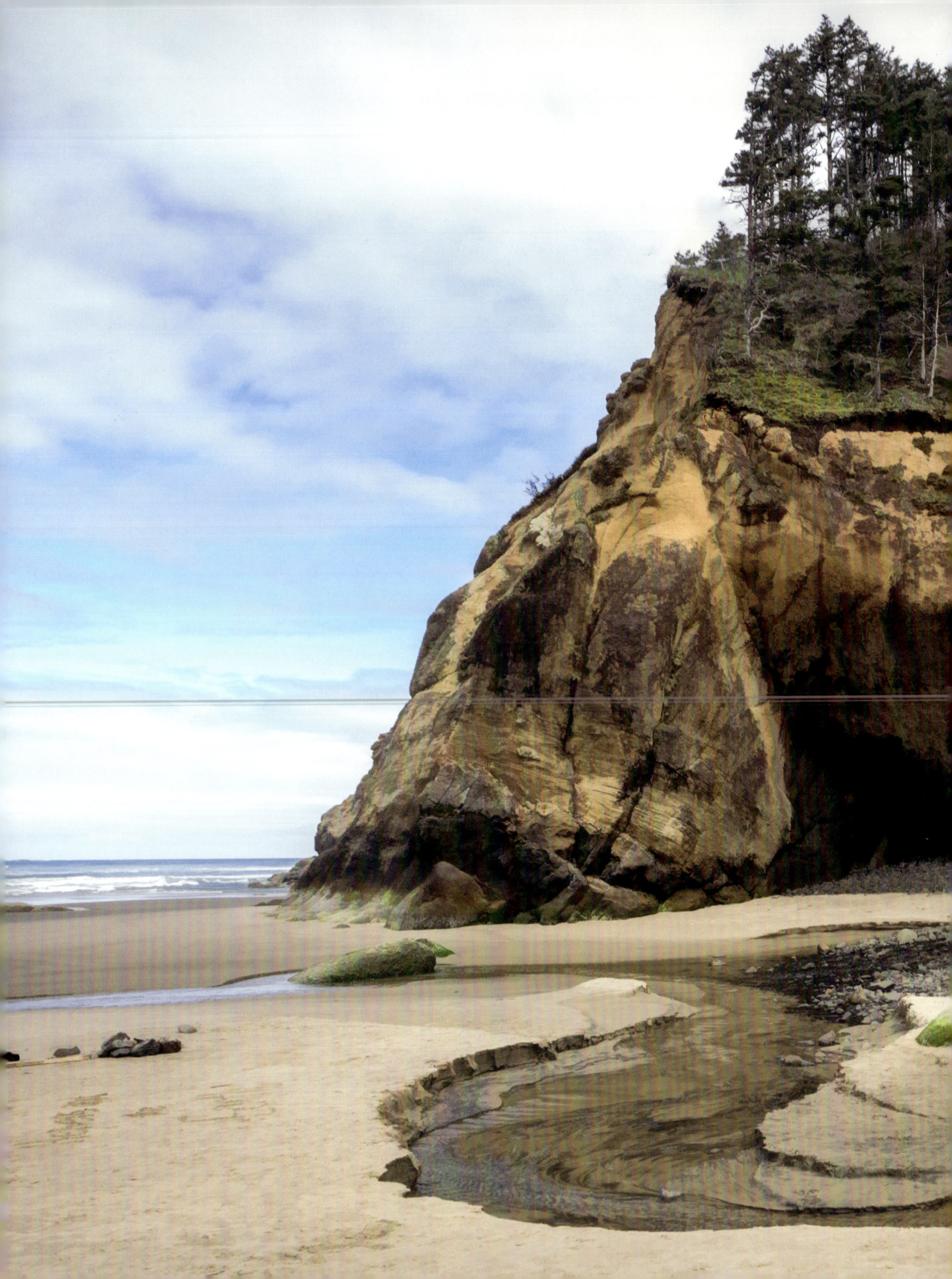

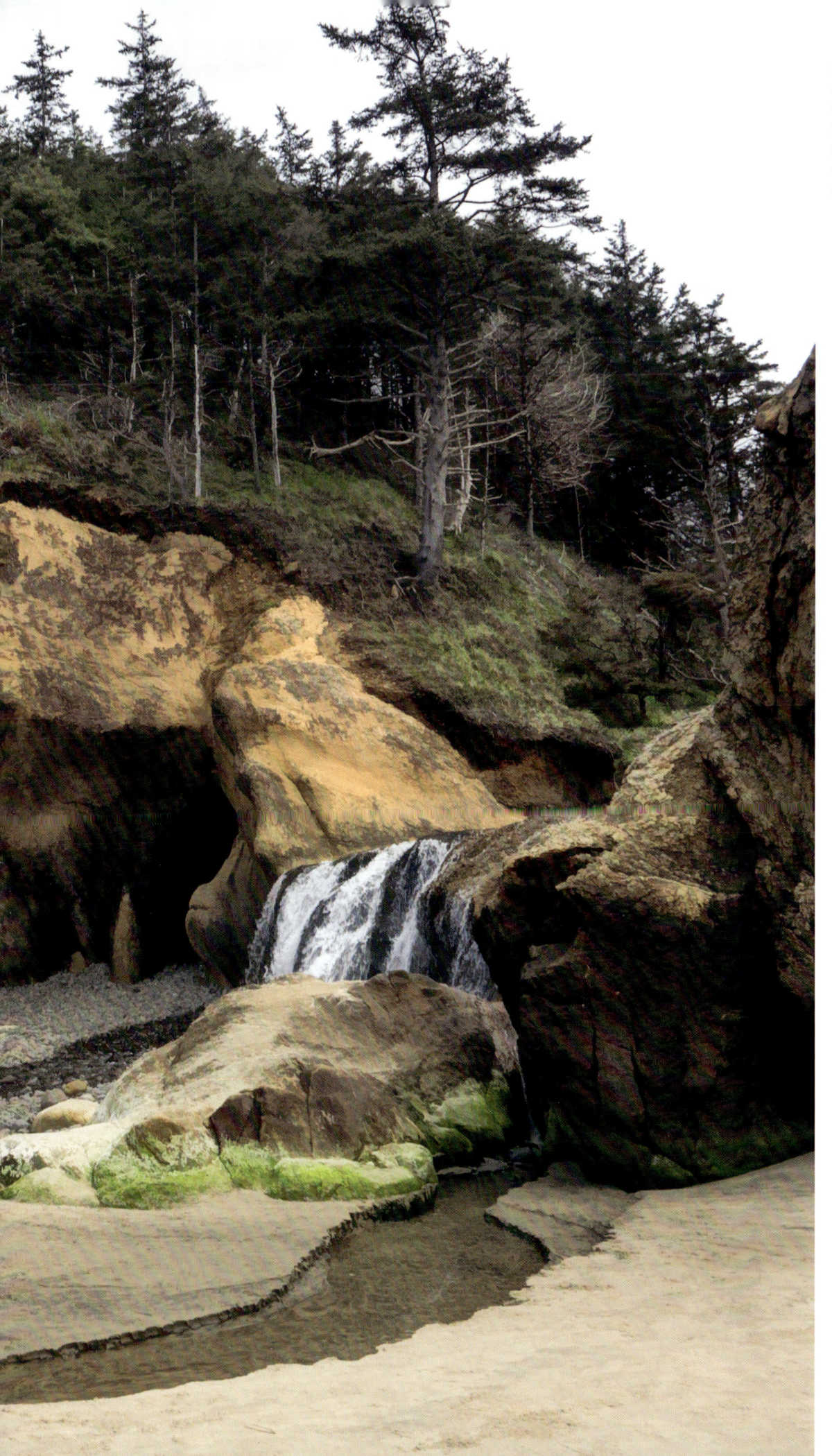

Hug Point Falls. Only a seven-minute drive south of busy Cannon Beach (at Hug Point State Recreational Site), these seasonal, peaceful falls empty directly onto the beach. *Photo by Vivian McAleavey*

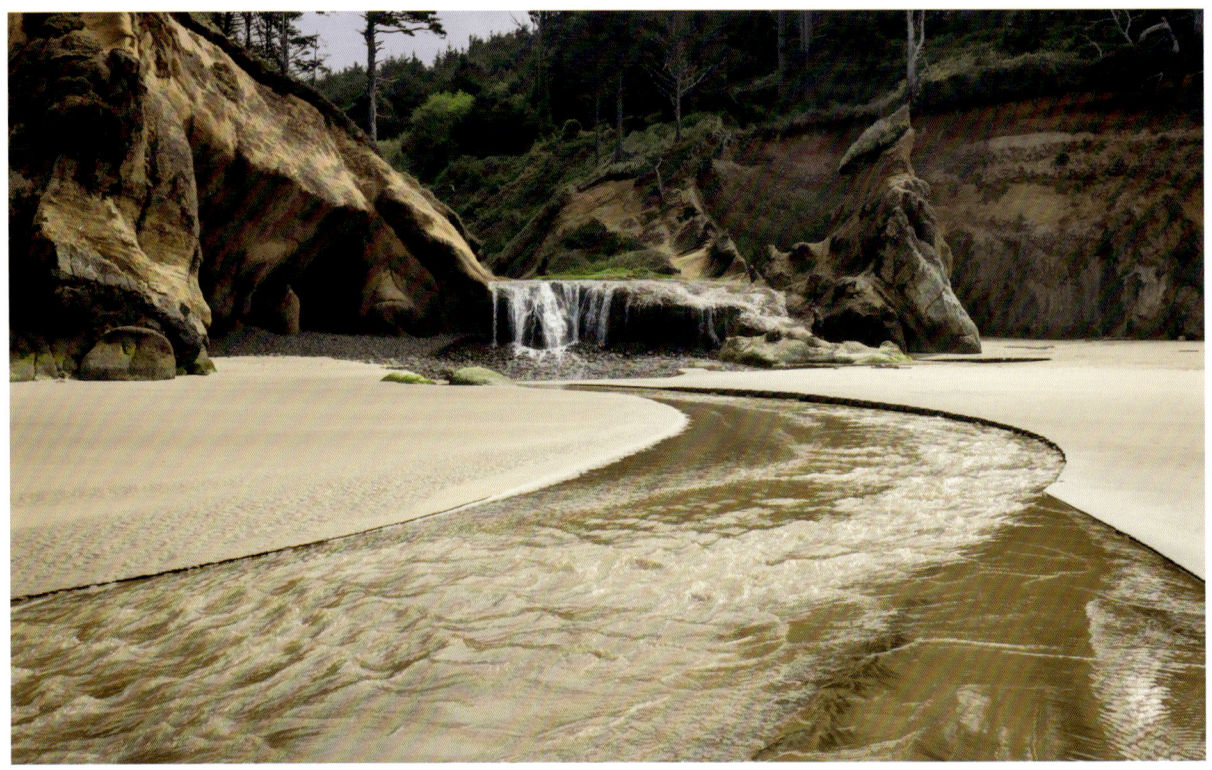
Hug Point Falls. Low tide is the safest time to explore the waterfall, caves, and tide pools on Cannon Beach. *Photo by Vivian McAleavey*

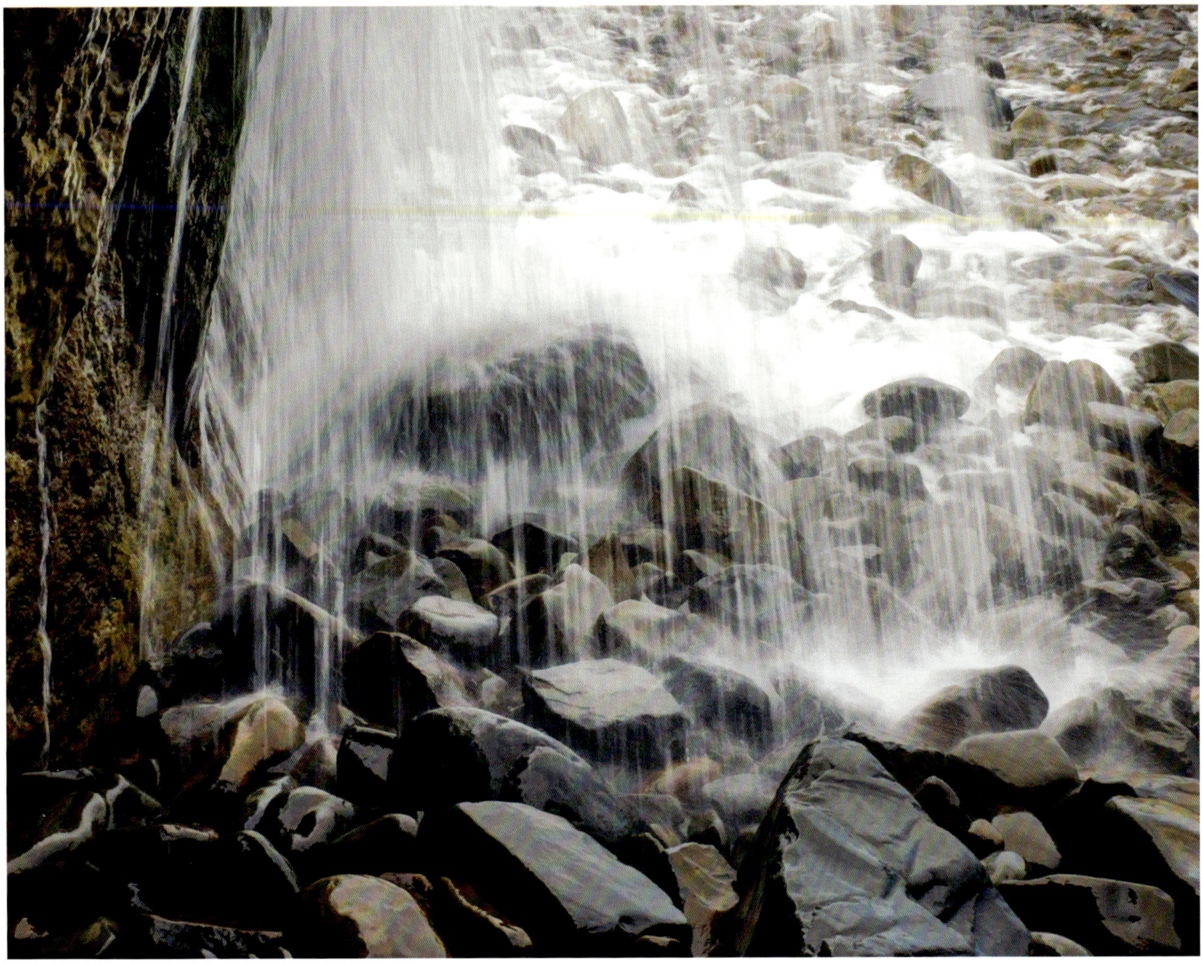

Detail of Hug Point Falls. *Photo by Vivian McAleavey*

INDEX

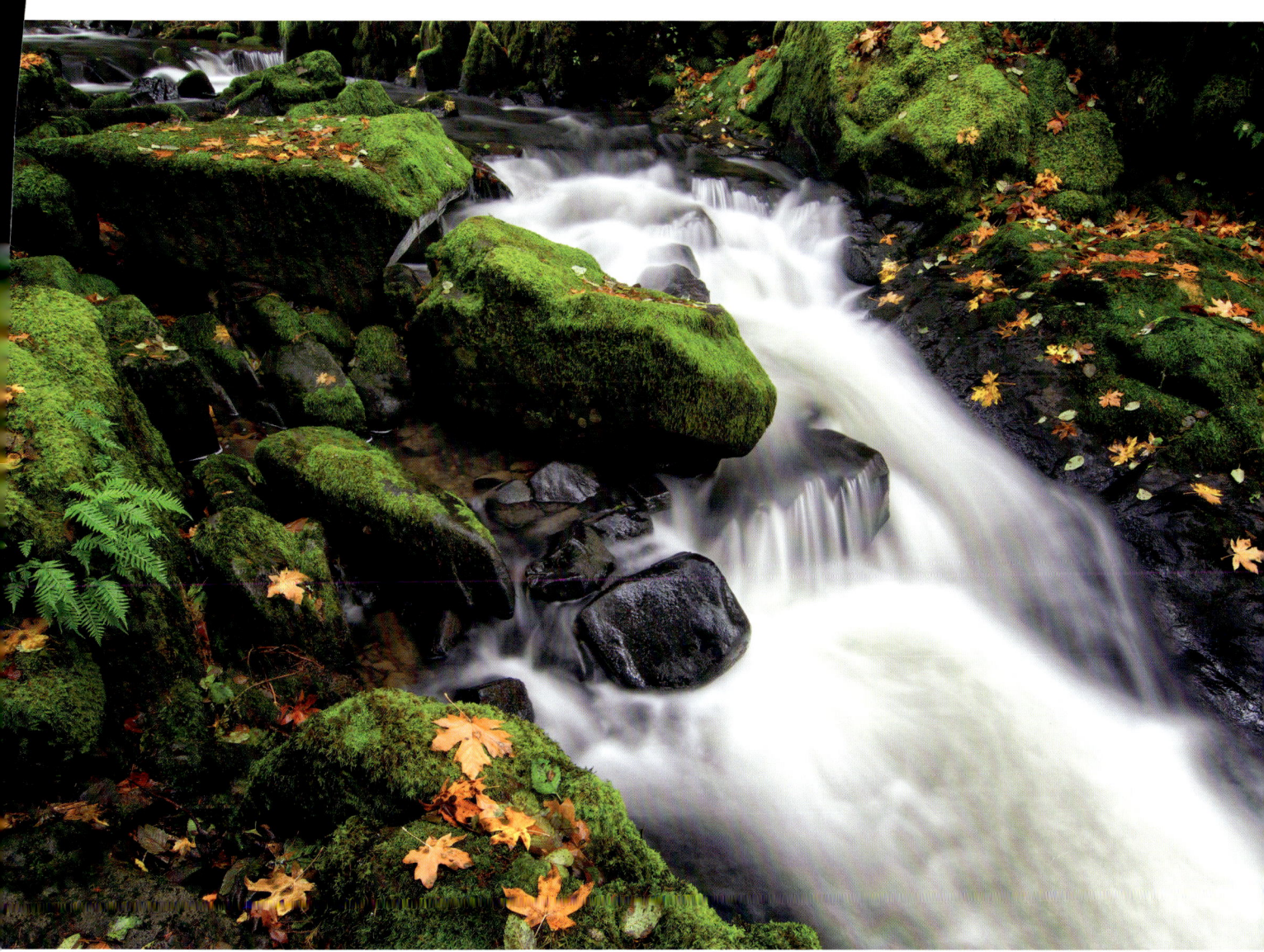

Baker Creek Falls. Located in the Willamette Valley near McMinnville. *Photo by Gary Thurman*

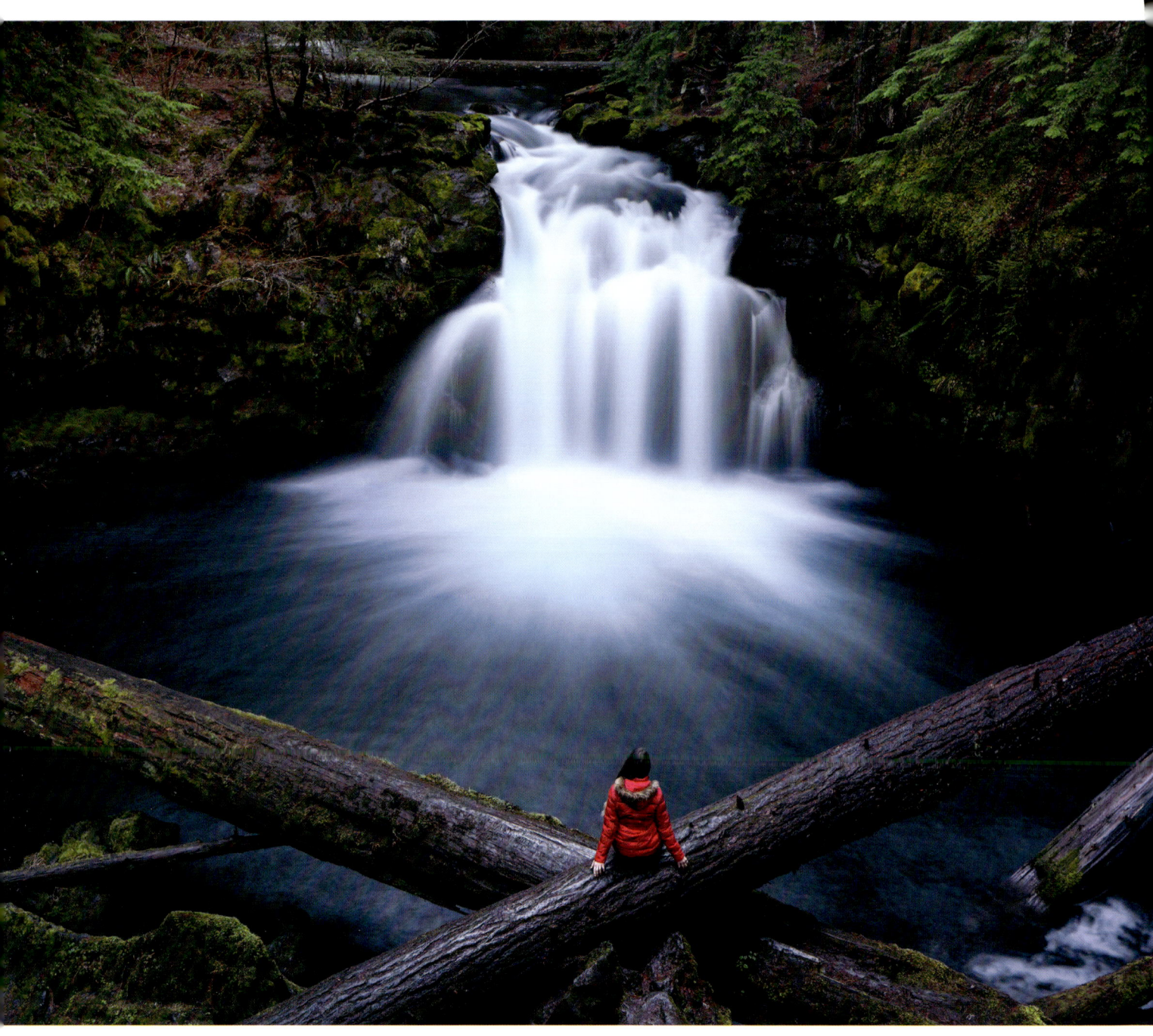

Whitehorse Falls. This is a popular Umpqua Valley waterfall. *Photo by Adam Marland*

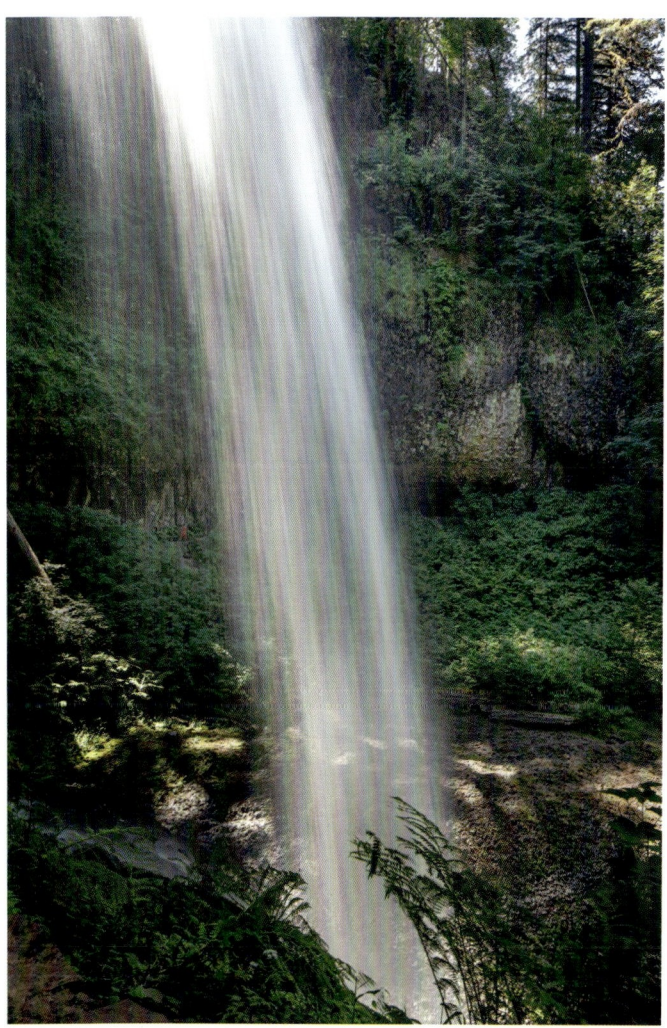

Middle North Falls. Located in Silver Falls State Park. *Photo by Bob Palermini*

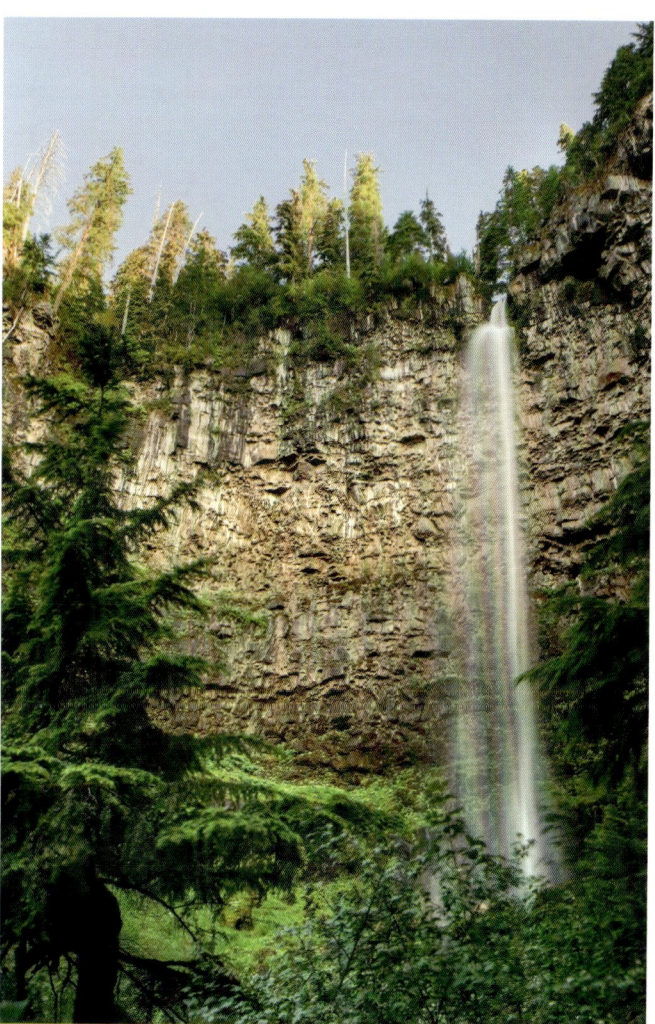

Watson Falls. This majestic waterfall in the Umpqua Valley flows 272 feet over a basalt lava cliff. It is Oregon's third-tallest waterfall. *Photo by Jay Newman*

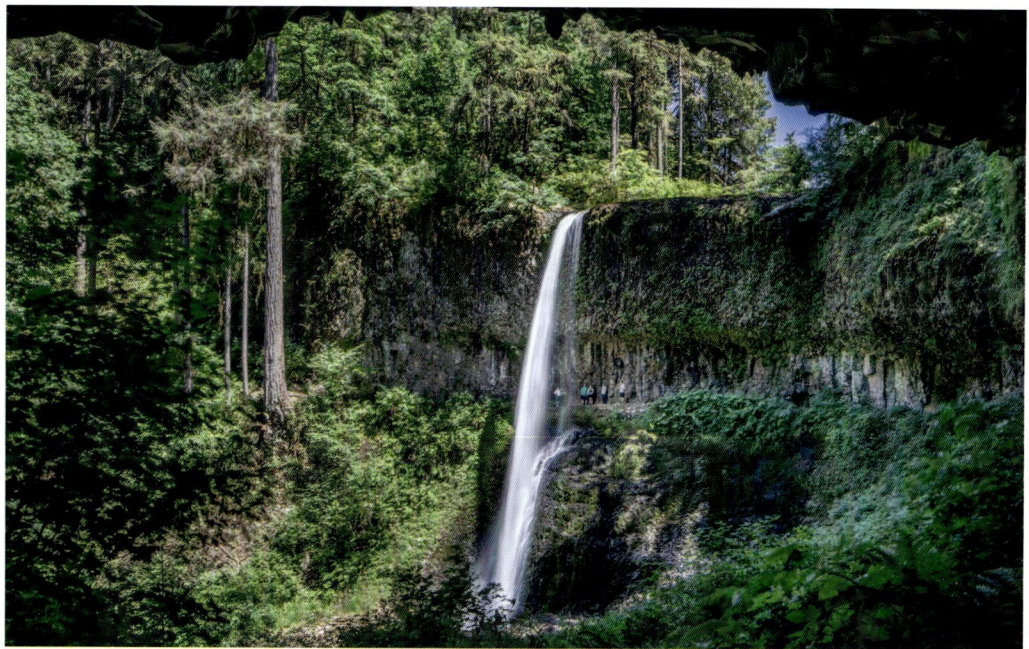

Middle North Falls. Located in Silver Falls State Park, this is one of several waterfalls that visitors can walk behind. The Civilian Conservation Corps created hiking trails throughout the entire park in the 1930s and early 1940s. *Photo by Bob Palermini*

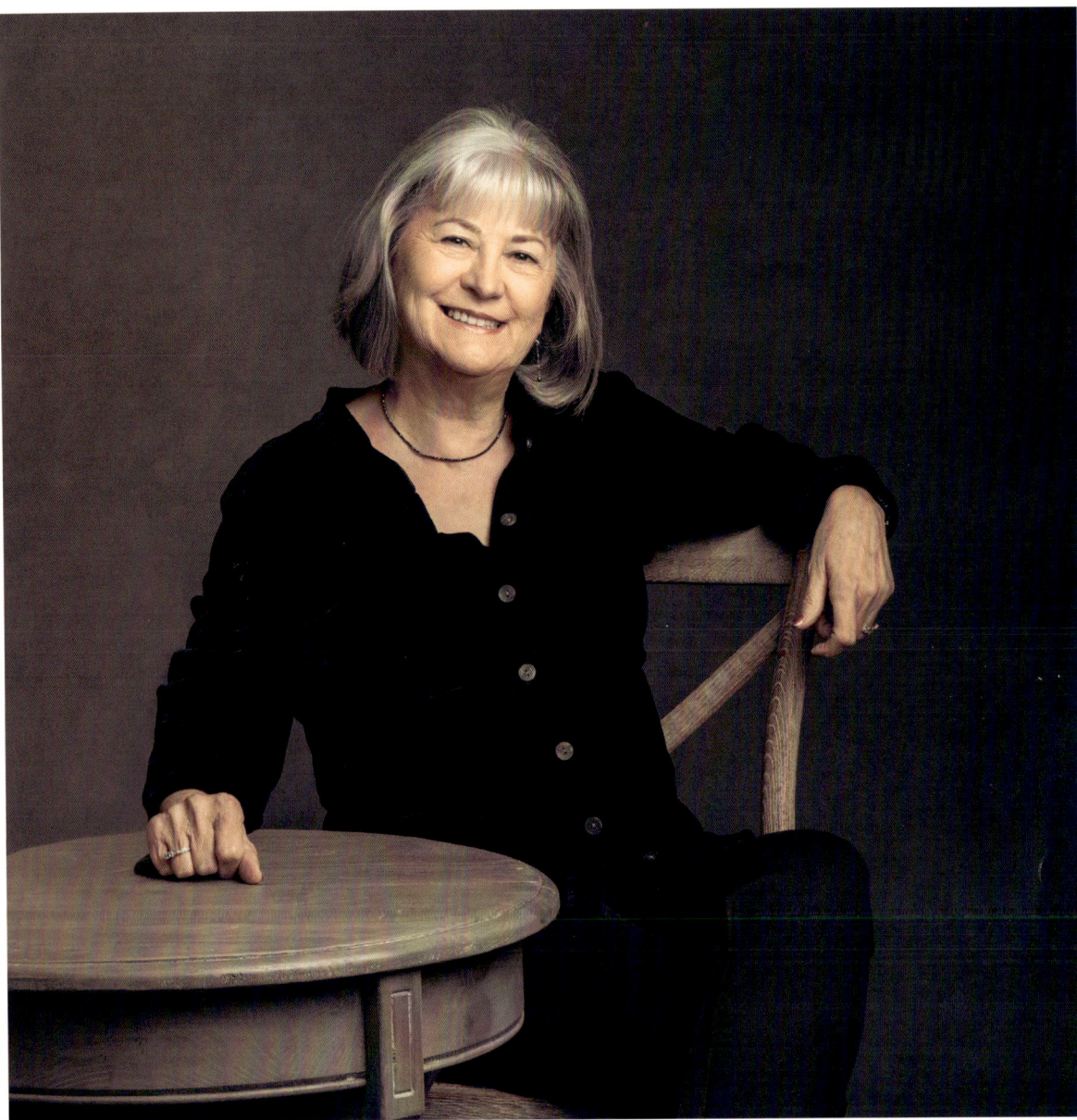

Barbara Tricarico lived and worked for decades in the northern Virginia area. She is a graduate of George Mason University (BA, English) and Gallaudet University (MA, deaf education). She worked in the Washington, DC, area as a teacher of the deaf and sign language interpreter. Barbara and her husband, Bill, retired to Ashland, Oregon in 2010, where she rekindled her love of photography. She has since compiled 10 photography books on the state of Oregon for Schiffer Publishing, including three coffee-table books titled *Oregon*, *Ashland, Oregon*, and *Ashland, Oregon Day Trips*. She also coauthored and photographed *Quilts of Virginia*. Barbara has built lasting friendships with many fellow photographers in her southern Oregon community. She is on the board of the Southern Oregon Photographic Association (SOPA), a member of the Ashland, Oregon, Chamber of Commerce, and a community volunteer. She enjoys traveling and photographing the world in her spare time and adores her four grandchildren in New York and Kentucky. She lives in Ashland, Oregon.

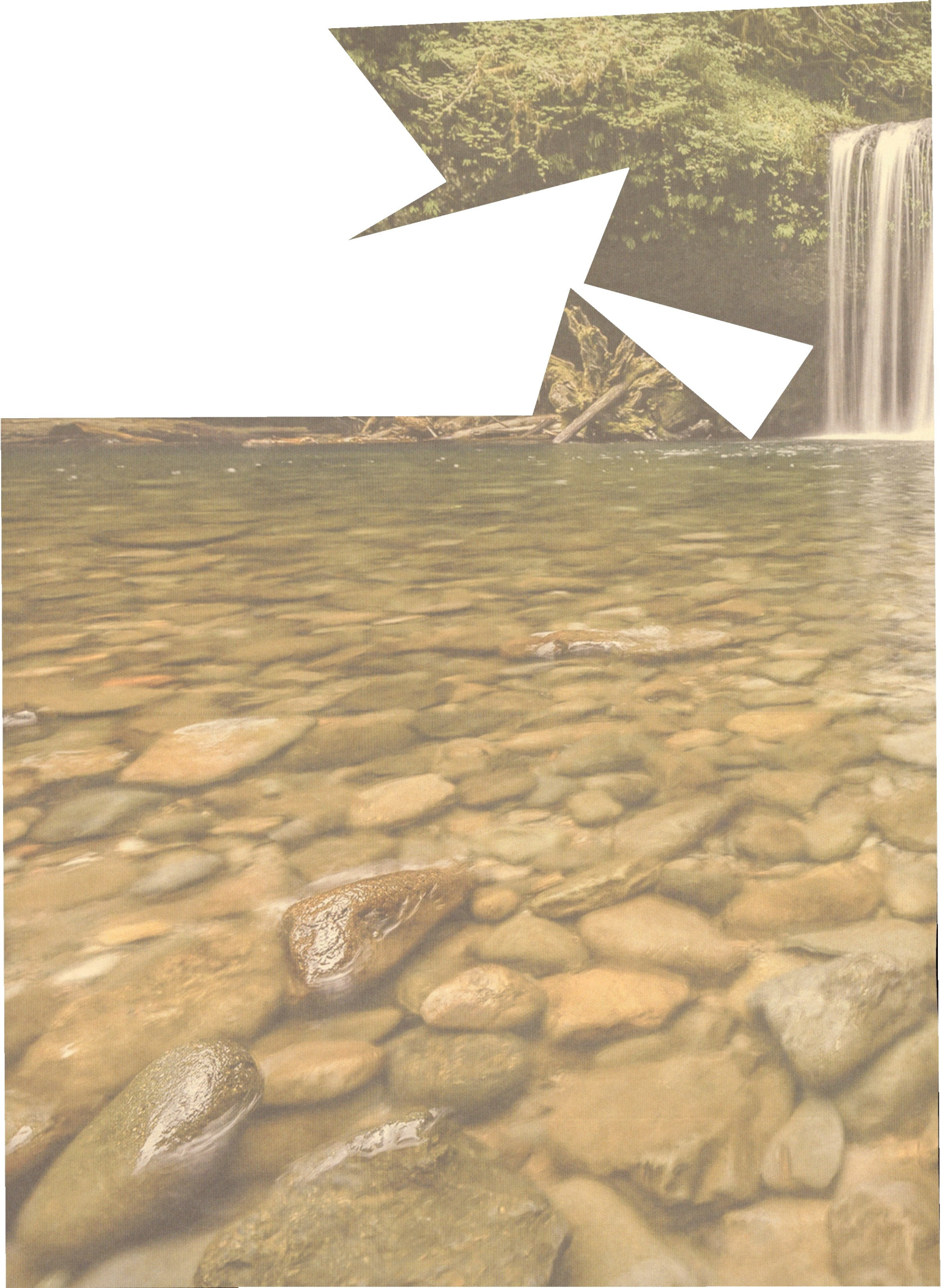